12099 REFERENCE

NA
202
.S76
1978
Vol.1

REFERENCE

Stierlin, Henri
Encyclopaedia of
world architecture

Encyclopaedia of world architecture /
Ref NA202.S76 19   27214

Stierlin, Henri,
    SOUTH PUGET SOUND COMM. COLLEG

D0820165

5601153856011538560115385601

Encyclopædia
of World Architecture

Henri Stierlin

Encyclopædia of World Architecture

1

LIBRARY
OLYMPIA TECHNICAL COMMUNITY COLLEGE
OLYMPIA, WASHINGTON

Facts On File
119 West 57th Street
New York, N.Y. 10019

Layout: Henri Stierlin
Jacket: Marcel Wyss SWB
Production: Suzanne Meister

Printing:
Imprimeries Réunies, Lausanne
Binding:
Mayer & Soutter, Renens
Photolithos (colour and jacket):
Schwitter Reproduction, Basle
Photolithos (black and white):
Aberegg-Steiner & Co AG, Berne, and
Atesa Argraf S.A., Geneva

Library of Congress Cataloging in Publication Data

Stierlin, Henri.
    Encyclopaedia of world architecture.

    English, French, and German.
    Includes index.
1. Architecture—History—Pictorial works.
I. Title.
NA202.S76   720′.9   78-26268
ISBN 0-87196-405-8

© Facts On File, Inc., New York, N.Y.

First published in English 1977
Translation © 1977 by Office du Livre

All rights reserved. No part of the contents
of this book may be reproduced without
the written permission of the publisher.

Printed in Switzerland

1   12099

Sommaire   # Inhalt   # Contents

Sommaire

Inhalt

Contents

Introduction

Einführung

Introduction

Comprendre l'architecture, c'est – à partir d'édifices existants qui dressent dans l'espace leurs formes plus ou moins complexes – essayer de se représenter l'organisation des volumes qui préside à l'élaboration du langage plastique; c'est tenter de saisir les combinaisons de structures et leurs articulations, qui conditionnent toute réalisation bâtie. Mais comprendre l'architecture, c'est surtout vouloir remonter aux sources du bâtiment, à son «idée de base», c'est-à-dire à son plan.

Car, si la visite d'un édifice dont il n'a pas vu le plan – surtout lorsque ce dernier est compliqué – peut donner à l'homme l'impression d'un fouillis, d'un chaos, d'un dédale de salles, de cours, de niveaux, etc., il recherchera tout naturellement à saisir les lois, les principes qui régissent la logique des formes. Il voudra passer de la perception générale à l'ordre conscient (ou inconscient) qui commande l'œuvre, qui l'informe. Pour cela, il n'est d'autre solution que de parcourir à rebours, en remontant vers sa source, le processus de genèse de l'œuvre. En effet, l'architecte qui a conçu un édifice aura nécessairement connu, lui aussi, le stade du plan pour passer à la réalisation. Il aura alors opéré une réduction des volumes et des espaces – que son esprit est capable de concevoir tridimensionnellement – à un système bidimensionnel, c'est-à-dire en premier lieu à une surface sur laquelle se dessinent en projection verticale les fondements de l'édifice.

En réalité, la vision du plan est le révélateur privilégié de l'architecture; certes, l'examen du plan, s'il n'est pas une condition suffisante, est essentiel à la compréhension. Car le plan exprime l'organisation fondamentale –

Architektur verstehen heißt, ausgehend von bestehenden Bauten mit ihren mehr oder weniger vielfältig aufragenden Formen sich mit der Organisation der Bauvolumen, die die plastische Gestalt bestimmt, auseinanderzusetzen. Es heißt, zu versuchen, die Verknüpfungen und die Gliederung der Strukturen – Bedingung für jeden Bau – zu erfassen, und vor allem, auf den Ursprung eines Bauwerks, seine «Grundidee», seinen Plan zurückzugehen.

In einem Bau, dessen Plan man nicht kennt, hat man oft – besonders bei einer komplizierten Anlage – den Eindruck eines Chaos, eines Labyrinths von Räumen, Höfen und verschiedenen Ebenen. Man sucht nach den Gesetzen, den Prinzipien, aus denen sich eine Logik der Formen ergibt. Man versucht, über den allgemeinen Eindruck hinaus eine bewußte – oder unbewußte –, die Gestalt des Bauwerks bestimmende Ordnung zu entdecken, die weiterhilft. Dies ist nur möglich, indem man den Entstehungsprozeß bis zum Beginn zurückverfolgt. Auch für den Architekten eines Baus lag vor der Ausführung die Planung. Er mußte dazu Körper und Räume, die er dreidimensional vor sich sah, auf ein zweidimensionales System reduzieren, also auf eine Fläche projizieren. So kam er zum Grundriß des Gebäudes.

Der Grundriß vermittelt die wesentlichsten Aufschlüsse über ein Bauwerk, und man kann lernen, ihn zu lesen. Sein Studium ist, wenn auch nicht immer allein ausreichend, so doch entscheidend für das Verständnis einer architektonischen Schöpfung; denn hier kommt die im eigentlichen Wortsinn fundamentale Ordnung zum Ausdruck. Ein Bau, der beim Durchschreiten wie ein verwir-

Understanding architecture means that, when one looks at a building, however complex it may be, one tries to visualise the relationship between the volumes that comprise it. It means seeking to grasp the way its elements are interlinked, for it is this that determines the structure of every building. Above all it means going back to its origins, to its basic concept—in a word, to its plan.

Viewing a building—particularly if it is a complicated one—without having previously seen a plan of it may well convey an impression of chaos: the place seems to be a labyrinth of halls, courtyards, different levels, and so on. One's instinct is immediately to start looking for the laws behind it, trying to isolate the principles underlying its formal organisation. One wants to get behind the overall impression to the conscious (or unconscious) order that governs and informs the whole. And the only way to do that is to trace the work back like a stream, mentally reversing the process by which it came into being. After all, the architect himself had to go through the planning stage before he could actually erect the building. What he did was to reduce the volumes and spaces that his trained mind had been able to conceive in three dimensions to a two-dimensional system; in other words, he started by taking a sheet of paper and drawing a vertical projection of the foundations.

The plan is the real 'eye-opener' when it comes to understanding architecture. With the plan one may still fail to appreciate a building to the full; without it one may never even begin to. For what the plan expresses is of course this 'fundamental' organisation that quite literally underlies everything else. A build-

dans le sens propre du terme. Un bâtiment qui n'apparaîtrait que comme un labyrinthe incompréhensible à quiconque – au sol – en parcourrait les espaces, peut devenir – vu du ciel – subitement intelligible. Les salles, les cours, les formes s'ordonnent sous les yeux de celui qui contemple d'en haut un tel édifice. Le chaos est remplacé par l'ordre.

Cette vision aérienne – qui est celle de la planche à dessin, ne l'oublions pas – appartient traditionnellement aux dieux. En effet, bien des temples (Borobudur, Angkor, pour citer les plus spectaculaires) ont été érigés pour être vus par la divinité à laquelle ils sont destinés. Et c'est par l'intelligence divine que doit être perçue l'ordonnance des bâtiments, qui, généralement, est elle-même conçue à l'image de l'ordre cosmique. C'est pourquoi le point de vue céleste reste privilégié. C'est lui qui laisse déchiffrer les intentions des bâtisseurs. C'est lui qui permet, au premier chef, de comprendre l'architecture.

Le mythe de Dédale

Cette lecture du haut des airs, n'est-ce pas le mythe de Dédale? Dédale, l'architecte du labyrinthe (ou palais) du roi Minos, fut emprisonné par le souverain. Il se dota d'ailes et parvint à s'enfuir avec son fils Icare. Echappant à sa condition, il s'envole et contemple d'en haut son œuvre qui l'avait dépassé. Il goûte alors la «vision des dieux» en leur empruntant le feu de la connaissance. Trop téméraire, Icare périt. Il monte si haut qu'il dépasse les sphères accessibles à l'homme et retombe foudroyé. Dédale, en revanche, redescend sur terre, enrichi d'une expérience unique: architecte, il a lu sur le sol le mystère de la genèse de toute œuvre. Il est l'homme qui comprend l'architecture, celle des humains comme celle de l'univers. Il sait lire et dresser un plan et enseignera son secret à toutes les nations.

Curieux destin d'ailleurs pour ce génie que d'évoquer par son nom une œuvre informe, celle d'avant la «vision»: un dédale n'est-il pas un agrégat inintelligible d'espaces juxtaposés? Et pourtant c'est à celui qui a maîtrisé l'architecture dans toute l'acception du terme que renvoie le dédale.

Dans les civilisations théocentriques, Dieu n'est-il pas l'architecte par excellence, Le Grand Architecte? Or il est dangereux de toucher au feu divin, de monter jusqu'au niveau des dieux. Et le risque couru par quiconque veut connaître le message éternel, Icare l'illustre bien, qui s'écrase au sol, victime de sa quête présomptueuse. Il a voulu aller trop loin, trop vite, trop haut. Quittant

rendes Labyrinth wirkt, schließt sich, aus der Vogelschau betrachtet, plötzlich auf: Säle, Höfe, alle Formen fügen sich zueinander. An die Stelle des Chaos tritt eine Ordnung, ein Gesetz.

Dieser Blick von oben – dem ja die Darstellung auf dem Reißbrett entspricht – war einst den Göttern vorbehalten. Zahlreiche Tempelanlagen – Borobudur, Angkor, um nur besonders eindrucksvolle zu nennen – wurden für die Augen der Gottheiten angelegt, denen sie geweiht waren. Aus göttlicher Sicht sollte die Ordnung dieser Bauten, die meist als Abbild der Weltordnung verstanden wurde, wahrgenommen werden. Darum bleibt der Blick von oben – vom Himmel – vor allen anderen ausgezeichnet; er läßt die Absichten der Baumeister am besten erkennen, vor allem durch ihn wird es möglich, Architektur zu verstehen.

Dädalus, der Baumeister

Ist dieser Blick von oben nicht auch das Grundthema der Dädalus-Sage? Dädalus, der Architekt des minoischen Labyrinths (oder Palastes), wurde von König Minos in den Kerker geworfen. Er fertigte sich Flügel an, die ihm die Flucht – zusammen mit seinem Sohn Ikarus – ermöglichten. Er erhob sich in die Lüfte und betrachtete das Werk, das er zurückließ, von oben, aus der Sicht der Götter. Ikarus stieg allzu kühn bis weit über die dem Menschen zugänglichen Sphären auf. Von der Sonne versengt, stürzte er ab und ging zugrunde. Dädalus kehrte um eine einzigartige Erfahrung reicher aus der Höhe zurück: Er, der Architekt, hatte das Geheimnis der Entstehung eines jeden Bauwerks von der Erde ablesen können. Jetzt war er der Mensch, der Architektur verstand – die der Menschen wie die des Universums –, der fähig war, einen Grundriß zu lesen und zu entwerfen. Dieses Geheimnis lehrte er alle Völker. Sein Name blieb jedoch in der Vorstellung der Welt mit dem «Labyrinth» verbunden, mit dem vor der «Vision» entstandenen Werk, jener Aneinanderreihung von Räumen, die sich dem Verständnis entzieht.

Ist in den theozentrischen Kulturen nicht Gott der Baumeister, der große Architekt? Es ist gefährlich, an das göttliche Feuer zu rühren, den Göttern gleichen zu wollen. Wer ewige Weisheit erjagen will, begibt sich wie Ikarus in Gefahr, der als Opfer seiner Anmaßung stürzte. Sein Ziel lag zu weit, zu hoch, und er wollte es zu schnell erreichen. Als er das Reich der Menschen, unsere irdische, stoffliche Welt, verließ, war er geblendet und zum Sturz verurteilt.

Und doch genügt es nicht, den Grund-

ing that one experiences as an incomprehensible maze when walking through it at ground level may suddenly become intelligible when, for example, one looks down on it from the air. From this vantage-point the halls, courtyards, etc. all fall into place; chaos gives way to order.

The aerial view—which is also that of the drawing-board—is traditionally the privilege of the gods. In fact many temples (Borobudur and Angkor, to mention only the most spectacular) were designed expressly for the visual benefit of the deity to whom they were consecrated. Their architectural organisation, usually conceived in the image of the cosmos, was intended to be perceived by the divine intelligence, and it is only from this 'god's-eye view' that the intentions of their architects become apparent. What applies to these temples applies to all building: the 'god's-eye view' of the plan is the key to understanding all architecture.

The myth of Daedalus

This, surely, is what the Daedalus myth is all about. Daedalus, the architect of the labyrinth (or palace) of King Minos, having been thrown into prison by the latter, fits himself out with a pair of wings and manages to escape with his son Icarus. It is an escape, too, from his condition, and as he soars into the sky he looks down on the work he has outgrown. For a while he enjoys the 'vision of the gods', partaking with them of the fire of knowledge.

Icarus was too bold and perished. He flew so high as to exceed the spheres accessible to man, and he was struck down. Daedalus on the other hand returned to earth the richer for a unique experience: he, the architect, had read on the ground the mystery of the genesis of all architecture. Daedalus is the man who understands architecture—that of men as well as that of the universe. He can read and draw up a plan, and he passes his secret on to all nations.

How curious that in French this genius should have given his name to a formless intricacy, as it were the state of architecture before the 'vision'. For a *dédale* in French is a maze, an unintelligible aggregate of juxtaposed interiors, yet the word is derived from the man who mastered architecture in the fullest possible sense …

In theocentric cultures, God is the architect *par excellence*, often indeed referred to as the Great Architect. It has always been a perilous undertaking, borrowing the divine fire and rising to the level of the gods, and the fate risked

le domaine des hommes, la matérialité de notre monde, il est ébloui par l'illumination et condamné à la chute.

De même, en architecture, il ne suffit pas de déchiffrer le plan pour comprendre l'œuvre. Car si le passage du chaos visuel à la lecture du plan constitue le fil d'Ariane dans le labyrinthe de la perception, l'œuvre réduite à un tracé de base, résumée à une appréhension bidimensionnelle, reste au niveau des «pures idées», des spéculations vaines. C'est une architecture «platonique», privée de toute corporalité, de toute matérialité.

Accession à la spatialité

Seules les élévations et les coupes permettent de comprendre le passage du plan au· volume et à l'espace. Cette accession à la spatialité est aussi importante que la lecture du plan; car c'est elle qui va doter l'architecture de sa spécificité; en effet, sans espace il n'est pas d'architecture. Seule la troisième dimension qualifie la réalisation. De l'élévation et de la coupe découle le matériau: bois, brique, pierre, béton, fer, etc. qu'appellent les organes architectoniques. Alors apparaissent les systèmes qui régissent à la fois l'agencement au sol et le mode de couverture: piliers, colonnes, linteaux, arcs, voûtes, coupoles. Il se forme donc, en lieu et place d'une image idéale, un langage dans toute sa matérialité, une syntaxe plastique concrète.

Les relations entre le plan et l'élévation sont d'ailleurs complexes et enchevêtrées; elles comportent toute une série d'interactions, comme celles qui existent entre les parties d'un même organisme. L'élévation, la façade, n'est-elle pas le premier aspect de l'édifice qui se révèle à la vue? Et pourtant elle n'apporte que rarement autant d'informations que le plan. A la limite, dans notre architecture moderne courante, la façade n'est-elle parfois qu'une insignifiante enveloppe qui pourra revêtir les aspects les plus divers, voire contradictoires, selon les besoins et les goûts, sans que cela doive influer sur le plan.

Ce dernier ne se livre pas de prime abord, ainsi que nous l'avons souligné. Il faut une quête difficile pour en prendre connaissance, car la vue du ciel n'est pas accessible à tout un chacun. Et pourtant, c'est à partir du plan que s'élabore un édifice. Le plan, c'est essentiellement la surface de contact de la construction avec son support naturel qu'est le sol. Le plan reflète les contingences auxquelles aucun architecte ne peut échapper dans le monde de la pesanteur et de la gravitation. C'est donc au niveau du plan que se lit le

riß zu lesen, um einen Bau zu verstehen. Wohl gibt der Schritt vom ersten chaotischen Eindruck zum Verständnis des Grundrisses eine entscheidende Hilfe, doch der auf zwei Dimensionen reduzierte Bau bleibt abstrakt, auf der Ebene der «reinen Ideen» – Architektur fern jeder Körperlichkeit und Stofflichkeit.

Die dritte Dimension – der Raum

Allein Aufriß und Schnitt führen vom zweidimensionalen Grundriß zu Körper und Raum. Dieser Schritt ist von gleicher Bedeutung wie jener zum Lesen des Grundrisses. Raum ist das wesentliche Kennzeichen der Architektur, die nur durch ihn besteht. Erst durch alle drei Dimensionen ist ein Bau bestimmt. Aus Aufriß und Schnitt wird deutlich, welche Materialien – Holz, Ziegel, Stein, Beton, Eisen usw. – die Bauelemente verlangen; das System der Pfeiler, Säulen, Balken, Bögen, Gewölbe und Kuppeln wird sichtbar, das sowohl Fundamente wie Überdachung bestimmt. An die Stelle eines Idealbildes tritt eine neue, konkrete Aussage, ein Bild des Werkes in seiner Stofflichkeit.

Die Beziehungen zwischen Grundriß und Aufriß sind komplex, verflochten und voller Wechselwirkungen wie diejenigen zwischen den Teilen eines lebenden Organismus. Wir sehen zuerst die Fassade eines Gebäudes, den Aufriß, doch nur selten sagt er uns so viel wie der Grundriß. Das kann so weit gehen, daß, wie in unserer heutigen Durchschnittsarchitektur, die Fassade nur eine nichtssagende Hülle ist, hinter der sich je nach Notwendigkeit und Geschmack die verschiedensten, selbst widersprüchlichsten Lösungen verbergen können und die keine Beziehung zum Grundriß haben muß.

Um einen Grundriß zu erfassen, ist Anstrengung nötig, denn der Blick aus der Vogelschau ist nicht jedem möglich. Doch ein Gebäude entsteht vom Grundriß her, der im wesentlichen der Berührungsebene zwischen Konstruktion und natürlichem Träger, also Erdboden, entspricht; er widerspiegelt ein Zusammentreffen, das in unserer Welt der Schwerkraft kein Architekt außer acht lassen kann. Aus dem Grundriß sind das Programm und die architektonische Grundidee am besten abzulesen.

Das Zusammenspiel, die Wechselwirkungen zwischen dem Grundriß einerseits, Schnitten und Aufrissen andererseits ergeben den sich in Länge, Breite und Höhe erstreckenden, also dreidimensionalen Baukörper. Vielerlei Beziehungen sind möglich: Ein be-

by all who seek knowledge of the eternal message is well illustrated by Icarus' crashing to the ground, a victim of his own presumptuous quest. He wanted to go too far, too fast, too high. He left the sphere of men, the materiality of our world behind him; illumination dazzled him, and he was condemned to fall.

Similarly in architecture, understanding a work involves more than just interpreting its plan. For if the passage from visual chaos to reading the plan is your Ariadne's thread in the labyrinth of perception, reduced to a two-dimensional diagram the work remains at the level of 'pure idea', of empty speculation. Architecture in two dimensions is 'Platonic' architecture; it has no body.

The third dimension

Only elevation and section can explain the passage from plan to volume and space. The step into the third dimension is as important as reading the plan, for it is this that gives a piece of architecture its identity. Indeed, without space there can be no architecture. The third dimension alone determines how an architectural idea will be carried out. Elevation and section dictate the choice of material: wood, brick, stone, concrete, iron, etc., depending on the architectural elements used. This choice in turn determines the systems governing both the layout at floor level and the type of roofing—pillars, columns, lintels, arches, vaults, domes. Gradually, in place of an ideal image, there emerges a language in all its materialism, with a tangible, flexible syntax.

The relations between plan and elevation are close and involved, comprising a whole series of interactions similar to those existing between the different parts of a living organism. Although the elevation or façade usually constitutes one's first view of a building, it rarely conveys as much information as the plan. In fact, in the normal run of modern architecture the façade is sometimes no more than an arbitrary envelope; it can present the most varied, even contradictory appearance, reflecting a variety of tastes and requirements, without this necessarily influencing the plan at all.

Unlike the elevation, the plan of a building is not something that becomes apparent at first sight. The aerial view is not available to everyone, and the only alternative is a painstaking study. Yet it is on the basis of the plan that a building takes shape. Essentially the plan represents the point of contact between the building and its natural support, the ground; it reflects the contingencies that no architect can escape

9

mieux le programme et que se perçoivent les partis architecturaux.

De la conjonction, des rapports réciproques existant entre le plan d'une part et les coupes et élévations de l'autre, naît cette incarnation de l'architecture se développant dans les six directions de l'espace (est-ouest, nord-sud, nadir-zénith), c'est-à-dire dans les trois dimensions.

Car ces relations peuvent être innombrables: un plan n'impose pas nécessairement un seul type d'élévation. Il suffit de songer aux différentes restitutions proposées par les archéologues pour certains édifices détruits dont ne subsistent que les fondations, indiquant pourtant clairement le plan ...

C'est de la cohérence entre ces deux systèmes de référence – l'horizontal et le vertical – que découlera la solution la plus harmonieuse, spatialement parlant. Car il y a une logique interne de l'espace qui résulte d'une combinatoire infiniment complexe de formules différentes. D'où les visages multiples que présente l'architecture: dans chaque civilisation, elle trouve des formes originales et caractéristiques. Comme le langage, l'architecture, au sein de chaque culture, possède sa personnalité propre. La simple lecture du plan, complétée par une coupe ou une élévation, suffit généralement à ranger une œuvre dans une famille de pensée, dans un système social, religieux ou cosmologique donné.

Réalité et photographie architecturales

Certes, toute traduction graphique en tracé bidimensionnel d'un organisme tridimensionnel, si elle constitue un moyen d'investigation utile, ne suffit pas à une totale compréhension de l'architecture. Rien ne peut suppléer la perception spatiale, globale de l'édifice réel. Elle seule permet de saisir le «climat» mental qui émane d'un bâtiment.

Seule la prise de possession physique, le parcours des espaces, permettent d'appréhender les propriétés d'une construction. Cette approche sera la clé d'une série de sensations qui varieront au gré des déplacements effectués pendant la «visite». Les espaces qui s'ouvrent, se resserrent, éclatent verticalement ou s'élargissent et se referment, la qualité de l'éclairage qui passe de la pénombre à l'aveuglement des cours à ciel ouvert, la descente dans l'obscurité des cryptes, le trajet sinueux d'un errement parmi les colonnades, le bruit des pas sur un dallage et les échos des voix sur une paroi nue, tout cela participe à une perception architectu-

stimmter Grundriß bedingt nicht notwendigerweise einen bestimmten Aufriß. Man denke nur an die verschiedenen Rekonstruktionsvorschläge der Archäologen für manche zerstörten Bauwerke, von denen nur noch die Fundamente erhalten sind, aus denen immerhin der Plan deutlich hervorgeht. Aus dem Zusammenklang der beiden Systeme, des horizontalen und des vertikalen, ergibt sich die harmonischste Lösung, denn es gibt eine innere Logik des Raums, Ergebnis der unendlich komplexen Kombinationsmöglichkeiten unterschiedlichster Formeln. Daher die vielen Gesichter der Architektur, die in jeder Kultur einen besonderen Formenschatz entwickelt hat und – wie auch jede Sprache – einen eigenen Charakter. Die bloße Kenntnis von Grundriß und Schnitt oder Aufriß genügt meist, um ein Bauwerk einer bestimmten Geisteshaltung, einem sozialen oder religiösen System, einer besonderen Weltvorstellung zuzuordnen.

Architektur und Architekturfotografie

Die zeichnerische Umsetzung eines dreidimensionalen Gebildes in einen zweidimensionalen Riß kann zwar die Auseinandersetzung mit Architektur erleichtern, reicht aber keineswegs für deren völliges Verständnis. Nichts kann das räumliche, allseitige Betrachten des ausgeführten Baues ersetzen, das allein ermöglicht, das «geistige Klima», die Ausstrahlung einer Architektur zu erfassen.

Nur durch eine «physische Besitznahme», ein Durchschreiten der Räume werden die Eigenheiten einer Konstruktion ganz begreifbar. Je nach dem Standort wandeln sich die Eindrücke: Räume öffnen und verengen sich, brechen nach oben auf, weiten sich oder werden kleiner; Licht wechselt vom sanften Dämmer zur blendenden Helle offener Höfe oder dem Dunkel tiefer Krypten; hier ein Zickzackweg zwischen Kolonnaden, dort das Hallen der Schritte auf Steinpflaster, das Echo von Stimmen an einer kahlen Wand. – All das hat teil am völligen Begreifen von Architektur. Dieses Durchwandern, das räumlich-dynamische Erfassen mit seinen Überraschungen, der Spannung, dem Erschrecken und Nachdenken führt zum Erleben der Architektur. Zu den drei Raumdimensionen kommt als vierte die Zeit hinzu, es entsteht ein Kontinuum, innerhalb dessen die architektonischen Wirkungsmöglichkeiten vollständig bewußt werden können.

Doch ohne die Hilfe der Planreduktion, die eine «grammatikalische» Analyse des Werkes erlaubt, ist die metho-

in a world of mass and gravity. So it is at the level of the plan that the architectural programme is most easily grasped and the architect's choices most clearly discerned.

These interactions, this reciprocity between the plan on the one hand and the sections and elevations on the other, constitute the framework within which a piece of architecture unfolds in the six directions of space (north-south, east-west, nadir-zenith) to achieve tangible, three-dimensional existence.

And the number of possible interactions is infinite, because a plan does not, even in ancient architecture, impose a particular type of elevation. One need only think of the different reconstructions proposed by archaeologists for buildings of which they have excavated only the foundations—which of course give a clear indication of the plan.

When these two systems of reference—the horizontal and the vertical—are brought into a coherent relationship they will produce the most harmonious solution in terms of the organisation of space. Space has a logic of its own, proceeding from an infinitely complex combination of different formulae. Hence the many faces that architecture presents. The architecture of a given civilisation, like its language, has its own personality and assumes original and characteristic forms. The information supplied by the plan of a building, supplemented by a section or elevation, is usually sufficient to place the work in a particular context, a particular social, religious, or cosmological system.

Architectural reality and the camera

Of course, no two-dimensional representation of a three-dimensional organism, however useful as an investigative aid, can furnish all the information needed for total comprehension of a work of architecture. There is no substitute for on-the-spot experience of the actual edifice. Only a visit can give one the specific mental 'climate' emanating from a building; only the act of walking round the place will enable one to appreciate its unique qualities.

Being there will trigger off a series of sensations that will vary according to the route taken by the visitor. The way the spaces expand and contract, the way they open up vertically or close in horizontally, the quality of the lighting as one passes from dim halls into the dazzle of open-air courtyards, the feeling of descending into a dark crypt or meandering through a colonnade, the sound of one's footsteps on a paved

rale complète. Ce cheminement spatio-dynamique avec ses surprises et ses attentes, ses chocs et ses méditations, telle est la compréhension vécue de l'architecture, où, aux trois dimensions spatiales, s'ajoute le paramètre du temps pour constituer le continuum dans lequel doit s'effectuer la prise de conscience totale des virtualités du bâti.

Mais sans ce guide précieux qu'est la réduction au plan, permettant l'analyse «grammaticale» de l'œuvre, il n'est pas d'approche intelligible du réel architectural.

D'ailleurs, c'est cette investigation fondée sur la lecture de l'espace et sa transcription dans un système graphique bidimensionnel qui fait le caractère fascinant de la photographie d'architecture. Car s'il est manié rationnellement, l'appareil photographique peut devenir un moyen de connaissance, un révélateur. Grâce à la vision axiale, à la prise de vue aérienne verticale ou à l'image zénithale, il est possible de reconstituer partiellement, à partir d'un donné matériel – et non plus totalement dépouillé comme l'est le plan qui recourt à un squelettique ensemble de lignes abstraites – la démarche de l'architecte: élévation, plan, système de couverture, etc. Utilisée avec la précision d'un théodolite, l'optique de la «chambre noire» permet de retrouver l'épure primitive, de prendre conscience d'une démarche intellectuelle, mais dans son «incarnation».

Familles architecturales

La concrétisation de l'architecture ne peut s'effectuer qu'au travers de certaines «mécaniques» essentielles qui régissent l'agencement des matériaux. Seules ces «mécaniques», élaborées d'abord intuitivement, puis en obéissant de plus en plus consciemment aux lois de la physique, permettent la création des espaces internes, qui sont la caractéristique fondamentale de l'architecture (opposée à la sculpture, laquelle joue avec les volumes dans la lumière, et à l'urbanisme, qui combine les masses architecturales et les «vides» en organismes cohérents).

Or ces «mécaniques» se divisent en deux grandes catégories: d'une part les systèmes «statiques», fondés sur le linteau et l'architrave (à la rigueur l'encorbellement), c'est-à-dire travaillant à la flexion, et de l'autre les systèmes «dynamiques» fondés sur l'arc, la voûte et la coupole, travaillant par poussées et contre-butées. Ces deux familles vont régir des types d'architecture distincts, mais qui peuvent coexister au sein d'une même civilisation.

dische Zugang zu einem Bau nicht möglich.

Die Architekturfotografie fasziniert, weil sie den Raum erfaßt und in ein zweidimensionales System umsetzt. Sie kann, mit Verstand eingesetzt, als wichtiges Hilfsmittel Kenntnisse und Aufschlüsse vermitteln. Mit axialen Aufnahmen, Luftaufnahmen und solchen aus der Froschperspektive läßt sich – ausgehend von den tatsächlichen Gegebenheiten und nicht von dem abstrakten Skelett eines Grundrisses – das Vorgehen des Architekten zumindest teilweise rekonstruieren: Aufriß, Plan, Systeme der Überdachung usw. Setzt man die Optik des Apparates mit der Präzision eines Theodoliten ein, hilft sie, den ursprünglichen Entwurf wiederzufinden, sich eines geistigen Prozesses in der materiellen Form bewußt zu werden.

Architektonische Gruppen

Architektur kann nur durch bestimmte elementare «Mechanismen», die den Umgang mit dem Material bestimmen, verwirklicht werden. Nur diese zunächst intuitiv entwickelten, dann immer bewußter den physikalischen Gesetzen gehorchenden «Mechanismen» ermöglichen, Innenräume zu schaffen, die ja ein wesentliches Charakteristikum der Architektur sind (im Unterschied zur Skulptur, die mit Volumen und Licht spielt, und zum Städtebau, der architektonische Massen und Leerräume zu einem harmonischen Ganzen verbindet).

Diese «Mechanismen» lassen sich in zwei Kategorien einteilen: auf der einen Seite die «statischen» Systeme mit Sturz, Architrav und – im Grenzfall – Auskragung, also mit Elementen, die auf Biegung beansprucht werden; auf der anderen die «dynamischen» Systeme mit Bogen, Gewölbe und Kuppel, bei denen dem Schub ein Widerlager entgegenwirkt. Jeder Kategorie entsprechen ganz bestimmte Architekturtypen, die jedoch innerhalb ein und desselben Kulturkreises nebeneinander bestehen können. Im allgemeinen gehen jedoch die «statischen» Systeme den «dynamischen» voraus, die bautechnisch komplexer sind.

Zu den «statischen» Systemen zählen vor allem die Bauten der Pharaonenzeit in Ägypten, der griechischen Klassik, der Achämeniden, die vorislamische Architektur Indiens ebenso wie die Holzarchitektur der Chinesen und Japaner und die präkolumbischen Bauten von Teotihuacan bis zu den Azteken (die Maya bilden eine Ausnahme).

Zur zweiten Gruppe gehören die Bauten der hellenistisch-römischen Welt. Auf sie gehen die meisten der durch Bo-

floor, the echo of voices off a bare wall—they are all part of it. It is this spatio-dynamic experience with its surprises and anticipations, its shocks and its moments of contemplation that ultimately holds the key to understanding architecture. To the three dimensions of space is added the parameter of time, the continuum within which one 'takes in' the totality of what a building is about.

But again, without that invaluable guide, the plan, and the 'grammatical' analysis it provides, there is no way one can make sense of the reality of a work of architecture.

Incidentally, it is this type of investigation, based on a reading of space and a translation of it into two-dimensional graphic terms, that makes architectural photography so fascinating. Properly handled, with the aid of axial and zenithal shots, the camera can to some extent reveal, on the basis of material data—rather than an abstract skeleton of lines on paper—the way in which the architect proceeded: plan, elevation, roofing system, and so on. Used with the precision of a theodolite, the camera can lead us from the 'embodiment', back through intellectual process to the original conception.

Architectural families

Architecture achieves embodiment through the medium of certain essential 'mechanisms' which govern the working of the materials. Only by means of these 'mechanisms', worked out at first intuitively, then in more and more conscious obedience to the laws of physics, is it possible to create internal spaces, the essential feature of architecture (as opposed to sculpture, which plays with volumes in light, and town-planning, which combines in a coherent form architectural masses and voids).

These techniques fall into two broad categories: on the one hand there are the static systems based on lintel, architrave and corbelling, and using the principle of flexion; on the other hand there are the dynamic systems based on arch, vault and dome, and using thrust and counterthrust. These two families constitute quite distinct types of architecture that may nevertheless coexist within a single civilisation. The 'statics' do tend to precede the 'dynamics', however, by reason of their relative architectural simplicity.

Among the former one thinks primarily of the monuments of Pharaonic Egypt, classical Greece and Achaemenid Persia; other examples are India before the Moslem conquest, the wooden architecture of China and Japan, and pre-

Les statiques, toutefois, précèdent généralement les dynamiques, en raison de la plus grande complexité de ces derniers, du point de vue architectonique.

Parmi les premières, on citera en particulier les réalisations de l'Egypte pharaonique, de la Grèce classique et des Achéménides, comme celles de l'Inde avant l'invasion islamique, ainsi que les architectures de bois chinoise et japonaise, les édifices précolombiens, de Teotihuacan aux Aztèques (exception faite des Mayas, qui connaissent un destin particulier sur lequel nous reviendrons).

Parmi les secondes, on mentionnera essentiellement le monde hellénistico-romain, dont vont dériver la grande majorité des architectures fondées sur l'arc, la voûte et la coupole, que ce soient celles des paléochrétiens, des Byzantins, du Roman et du Gothique, de la Renaissance et du Baroque, mais aussi celles de l'Islam cordoban, seldjoukide, ottoman et même moghol.

Entre ces deux entités, qui peuvent ici et là s'interpénétrer, on trouve un monde intermédiaire, groupant des cultures fort diverses, qui met pourtant uniformément en œuvre la fausse voûte ou voûte en encorbellement. Sa technique appartient incontestablement au premier groupe, alors que ses formes s'apparentent au second. La voûte en encorbellement refuse le jeu des poussées et des contre-butements, pour n'accepter de l'arc que l'apparence; car elle ne recourt qu'à un empilement de matériaux obéissant à un pur équilibre statique des masses. Ce stade technologique, qui apparaît aussi bien dès les couloirs des grandes pyramides égyptiennes que dans les tholoï mycéniennes, trouve sa pleine expression avec l'architecture des Mayas, celle des Khmers d'Angkor, ou dans certains sanctuaires de l'Inde médiévale.

Paradoxalement d'ailleurs, c'est à cette technique des assemblages à joints horizontaux et des blocs en avancée les uns par rapport aux autres et disposés en anneaux concentriques superposés en encorbellement que recourent les Romains pour les parties supérieures de la plus fantastique des coupoles qu'ils érigent: celle du Panthéon, d'un diamètre intérieur de 43,30 m. Ils prouvent par là même que la formule de la voûte en encorbellement recèle des possibilités considérables qui n'ont pas été suffisamment exploitées par les peuples qui y ont systématiquement recouru. (Notons que lorsqu'elle est utilisée par les Romains qui connaissent la vraie coupole, cette formule, qui présente des joints rayonnants dans le seul plan horizontal et non dans le plan vertical des assises, recourt consciemment à des jeux de forces annulaires qui revêtent

gen, Gewölbe und Kuppeln bestimmten Architekturstile der Folgezeit zurück: frühchristliche und byzantinische, romanische und gotische Architektur, die Werke der Renaissance und des Barock, aber ebenso auch die islamische Architektur von Córdoba, die der Seldschuken, Osmanen und Moguln.

Zwischen diesen beiden Gruppen, die sich hier und da überschneiden können, steht eine dritte, der ganz verschiedene Kulturen angehören, die alle das «falsche Gewölbe», das heißt das Kraggewölbe benutzen. Diese Form gehört technisch eindeutig zur ersten Gruppe, formal ist sie jedoch der zweiten Gruppe verwandt. Beim Kraggewölbe spielen Schub und Widerlager keine Rolle, es übernimmt vom Gewölbe nur die äußere Erscheinung. Das Material ist bei dieser Bauform so in horizontalen Schichten übereinandergelegt, daß jede Schicht über die vorige etwas auskragt und die Massen sich im Gleichgewicht befinden. Auf dieser Stufe der Technik stehen sowohl die Gänge in den großen ägyptischen Pyramiden als auch die mykenischen Tholoi; in der Architektur der Maya, den Bauten der Khmer in Angkor und bei manchen mittelalterlichen Heiligtümern Indiens fand diese Form ihre reifste Ausprägung.

Erstaunlicherweise haben die Römer diese Technik der horizontal versetzten, nach innen vorkragenden Ringe, die konzentrische Kreise bilden, für die großartigste Kuppel, die sie je gebaut haben, übernommen: Die Pantheonkuppel mit einer Spannweite von 43,30 Metern ist auch in ihren oberen Teilen in dieser Art ausgeführt. Damit wird deutlich, daß das Kraggewölbe Möglichkeiten birgt, die von den Völkern, die es ständig benutzten, nie voll ausgeschöpft wurden. Die Stabilität der Kragkuppel, bei der die Fugen jedes einzelnen Ringes radial auf den Kreismittelpunkt gerichtet sind, nicht aber die gesamten Fugen auf den Kugelmittelpunkt, beruht auf der Verspannung der Ringe.

Kehren wir zu den beiden genannten Grundtypen, dem «statischen» und dem «dynamischen», zurück. Wir dürfen nicht vergessen, daß sich die Eigenschaften der verfügbaren Materialien stark auf die Verbreitung der beiden Konstruktionsarten ausgewirkt haben. In waldreichen Gebieten wurde häufiger mit Sturz und Architrav gebaut – selbst in der Steinarchitektur, als das Holz knapp wurde oder weil man dem Werk Dauer sichern wollte. Gebiete mit wenig Wald und ohne einen Stein, der sich zu großen Blöcken zuhauen läßt und auf Biegung beansprucht werden kann – Mesopotamien, das Indus-Gebiet – entwickelten Wölbungsformen aus kleinem Bruchsteinmauerwerk oder Ziegeln (der Iglu ist sogar aus Eis).

Columbian architecture from Teotihuacan to the Aztecs (but not including the Mayas who, as we shall see, went their own way).

Among the latter it is essentially the Hellenistic and Roman worlds that spring to mind, the cradle of the vast majority of architectural traditions based on the arch, the vault and the dome, which includes Early Christian, Byzantine, Romanesque, Gothic, Renaissance and Baroque, as well as those of the Islamic world—Cordoban, Seljuk, Ottoman, and even Mogul.

Between these two categories, which may overlap here and there, we find an intermediate group of widely divergent civilisations that nevertheless all make use of the false or corbelled vault. While there is no doubt that in terms of technique this belongs in the first family, the shapes it employs relate it to the second. Repudiating the play of thrust and counterthrust, the corbelled vault borrows no more than the outward appearance of the arch. It relies on piling up material in obedience to a purely static equilibrium of masses. The technology of corbelling, which dates back to the corridors of the great Egyptian pyramids and the *tholoi* or domed tombs of Mycenae, really comes into its own in Mayan architecture, in the architecture of the Khmers of Angkor, and in certain Indian sanctuaries of the medieval period.

Paradoxically it was this technique of using horizontally-jointed blocks in concentric rings, each one a little smaller than the one below so as to project slightly beyond it, that the Romans chose for the upper part of the most fantastic dome they ever built—that of the Pantheon, which has an internal diameter of 43.3 m. In fact in doing so they demonstrated that the corbelled vault has possibilities far exceeding those exploited by the peoples who made systematic use of it. It is interesting that when the Romans, who knew the true vault, used this formula of radial joints (all in the horizontal plane rather than in the vertical plane of the courses) they deliberately had recourse to ring forces of curvature which acted as a restraint and ensured the cohesion of the whole.

But to get back to our two 'families', the static and the dynamic, a point to be borne in mind is of course that the method of construction adopted by a particular civilisation will be influenced by the properties of the materials at its disposal. Countries with plenty of timber will more often be found using lintel and architrave systems—and may even cling to those systems long after exhaustion of their timber supplies, or a concern for greater permanence, has prompted them to build with stone in-

un caractère de contention et assurent la cohésion de l'ensemble.)

Mais revenons aux deux types que nous avons indiqués: le statique et le dynamique. On se gardera d'oublier que les propriétés des matériaux dont disposent les sociétés influent grandement sur l'aire de chacun de ces deux modes de construction. Les pays riches en bois connaîtront plus fréquemment les formules fondées sur le linteau et l'architrave (même s'il s'agit de survivances, d'architectures «pétrifiées», lorsque l'approvisionnement en bois se fait plus difficile, ou lorsqu'une recherche de pérennité des œuvres humaines a conduit à recourir à la pierre). Les terres pauvres en forêts ou même en grandes pierres de taille capables de travailler à la flexion (Mésopotamie, Indus) verront se développer une architecture de voûtes en brique ou en petit appareil maçonné (ou même en glace, comme l'igloo!).

Mais ne tombons pas dans un déterminisme fonctionnaliste: les connaissances ou les lacunes technologiques ne sont pas la seule clé des formes architecturales. Certaines civilisations sont comme «allergiques» à des solutions qu'elles n'ignorent pourtant pas à proprement parler, mais dont elles refusent l'application généralisée. Des réflexes traditionnalistes peuvent jouer. Ainsi toute l'époque ptolémaïque, qui s'étend sur plus d'un demi-millénaire, reste fidèle aux solutions statiques de l'architrave de grès pesante et dispendieuse, bien que les cultures hellénistique puis romaine eussent submergé l'Egypte, important les formules de l'arc, de la voûte et de la coupole. D'ailleurs, dans cette Egypte pharaonique, la voûte en brique fut très tôt connue (les magasins du Rammesséum en témoignent), mais elle ne parvint jamais à s'imposer dans les temples, où même les salles voûtées restent couvertes en blocs appareillés en encorbellement, c'est-à-dire en fausse voûte (tel le sanctuaire du temple funéraire de la reine Hatshepsout à Deir el Bahari).

Enfin les usages locaux ont pu jouer un rôle considérable dans l'adoption de certaines techniques de couverture. Et si le monde romain a généralement recouru à la *coupole sur pendentifs*, qu'il léguera à Byzance, adversaire acharné des Sassanides de Perse, ces derniers en revanche, comme leurs successeurs musulmans en Iran, utiliseront le plus souvent la *coupole sur trompes*.

Ces deux formules – le pendentif et la trompe – représentent donc le signe d'un clivage culturel profond entre deux aires de civilisations bien délimitées, malgré les emprunts réciproques qu'elles connaissent. Cette prédilection de l'Iran pour la trompe découle des techniques

Aber hüten wir uns vor einem funktionalistischen Determinismus: Architektonische Formen lassen sich nicht ausschließlich mit dem Vorhandensein oder Fehlen technischer Kenntnisse erklären. Manche Kulturen scheinen gegen gewisse Lösungen «allergisch» zu sein, sie kennen sie zwar, lehnen aber generell ihre Anwendung ab. Dabei kann die Tradition eine Rolle spielen: Während der Ptolemäer-Zeit blieb man den schweren, teuren Sandsteinarchitraven treu, obwohl durch das Eindringen des Hellenismus und durch die Römer Bogen, Gewölbe und Kuppel in Ägypten bekannt geworden waren. Übrigens war in der Pharaonenzeit das Ziegelgewölbe schon früh bekannt, wie die Magazine des Ramesseums beweisen. Es hat sich im Tempelbau aber niemals durchsetzen können; dort blieb man beim Kraggewölbe (Totentempel der Königin Hatschepsut, Deir-el-Bahari).

Schließlich spielten auch lokale Gewohnheiten bei der Übernahme bestimmter Wölbungstechniken eine große Rolle. Im römischen Reich baute man im allgemeinen Pendentif kuppeln, diese Form übernahm Byzanz. Nun waren die Byzantiner die erbittertsten Feinde der Sassaniden, die ihrerseits, wie auch ihre muselmanischen Nachfolger in Persien, hauptsächlich Trompenkuppeln benutzten.

Pendentif und Trompe sind hier also sichtbare Zeichen einer tiefen Kluft zwischen zwei klar abgegrenzten Kulturen, die jedoch sonst manches voneinander übernehmen. Die Vorliebe des Iran für die Trompe erklärt sich aus der dortigen Ziegelbauweise, bei der der Übergang vom quadratischen Grundriß zum Rund der Kuppel durch ein rudimentäres Halbkuppelsystem bewerkstelligt wurde. Wir kennen den Übergang vom Quadrat zum Kreis durch Einschaltung der Trompe von den Feueraltären des Zoroasterkults, ebenso auch bei den Bauten der Sassaniden, Seldschuken, Timuriden und Safawiden. In der safawidischen Spätzeit taucht auch in Persien das Pendentif auf, vielleicht durch Vermittlung der benachbarten Osmanen, die als direkte Erben von Rom und Byzanz dieser Form für die Wölbung ihrer großen Säle stets treu blieben. Hier spielten der Einfluß der frühchristlichen anatolischen Bauten und – nach der Eroberung Konstantinopels – der starke Eindruck der Hagia Sophia eine Rolle.

Der Gegensatz zwischen den beiden Architekturkategorien verwischte sich erst durch die modernen Werkstoffe (Eisen und Stahlbeton). Bei der monolithisch wirkenden Stahlbetonwölbung ist die Frage, ob Biegungsbeanspruchung oder Schub-Widerlager-System, nicht mehr zu beantworten.

stead. Countries with few forests, and no stone that can be dressed in large enough blocks to operate on the flexion principle (e.g. Mesopotamia and the Indus valley), will tend, on the other hand, to evolve vault systems using brick or small-scale masonry (or even ice, like the igloo!).

Not that we should let ourselves fall into the trap of functional determinism: technological skills and blind spots are not the only key to architectural forms. Some civilisations are, as it were, 'allergic' to certain forms; while not unaware of them entirely, they refuse to adopt them in any systematic way. Traditionalist reflexes may play a part here. Throughout the Ptolemaic period, for example, Egypt remained faithful to the static form of the heavy—and expensive—stone architrave, although during that half-millennium the country was swamped by the Hellenistic and then Roman civilisations with their arches, vaults and domes. This was so despite the fact that the brick vault had been discovered under the early Pharaohs, as witness the store-rooms at the Ramesseum; for it was never adopted for temples, where even the vaulted halls are 'false vaults' of corbelled masonry (e.g. the sanctuary of the funerary temple of Queen Hatshepsut at Deir al-Bahri).

Finally, local usage may have had a lot to do with the adoption of a particular roofing technique. Whereas the Roman world mostly used the dome on pendentives, handing this practice on to the Byzantines, Byzantium's bitterest enemy the Sassanids, like their Moslem successors in Persia, usually stuck to the dome on squinches.

These two forms—pendentive and squinch—represent a deep cultural gulf between two clearly defined cultural areas, a gulf that is not belied by the extensive borrowing that went on in both directions across it. The Persians' preference for the squinch stemmed from the techniques of their popular brick architecture, in which only a rudimentary *cul-de-four* system is used to effect the transition between the square of the ground plan and the circular base of the dome. This passage from square to circle by means of squinches characterises the sun-worship altars of Zoroastrianism and, later, the great monuments of the Sassanid, Seljuk, Timurid and Safavid dynasties. Right at the end of this last Persian dynasty, however, the pendentive did make an appearance, possibly as a result of contact with Persia's Ottoman neighbours. For the Ottomans, direct heirs of the Roman and Byzantine worlds, remained consistently faithful to the pendentive for their enormous vaulted halls, influenced

propres à l'architecture populaire de brique, où seul un rudimentaire système en cul-de-four est pratiqué pour opérer la liaison entre le plan quadrangulaire et la coupole circulaire. Ce passage du carré au cercle par l'entremise de la trompe régit les autels zoroastriens destinés au culte du feu, puis les grandes réalisations sassanides, seldjoukides, timourides et safavides. Tout à la fin de cette dernière dynastie persane, le pendentif fait pourtant son apparition, au contact peut-être des Ottomans voisins. Car, héritiers directs du monde romain et des Byzantins, les Ottomans restent toujours fidèles au pendentif pour leurs vastes salles voûtées, influencés qu'ils sont tant par les bâtiments paléochrétiens d'Anatolie que par l'éblouissement éprouvé face à Sainte-Sophie, après la conquête de Constantinople.

Ce ne sera qu'avec l'avènement des matériaux modernes (métal et béton armé) que cette opposition entre familles architecturales s'estompera. L'aspect quasiment «monolithique» d'un voile de béton armé, par exemple, récuse la distinction entre travail à la flexion et système de poussée et de contre-butement proprement dit.

Variété de plans

Mais qu'apporte la lecture du plan à laquelle est confronté celui qui veut comprendre l'architecture? Elle montre des visages fort divers selon le type d'organisation adopté, dont dépend directement le degré de rigueur du système. Le plan peut être totalement libre ou simplement régi par une formule répétitive. Mais il peut se conformer aussi à un système axial qui impose à toute la composition un ordre symétrique. Son organisation s'apparente alors à celle d'un organisme vivant supérieur.

Le plan peut revêtir également une double symétrie axiale qui aboutit à une formule centrée. Le plan centré sera quadrangulaire, hexagonal, octogonal ou circulaire, revêtant des symbolismes divers et des fonctions idéologiques complexes. Enfin, à partir des solutions ortho-, hexa-, ou octogonales se développent des trames régulières, comme celle du damier hippodamien, par exemple, sans toutefois qu'il en découle forcément une symétrie. Ces trames régulières connaissent également un mode de croissance capable de se ramifier à l'infini, à partir d'un réseau fondé sur divers types d'angles (90°, 60° ou 45°). Chacun de ces systèmes est applicable tant à une échelle globale – celle de l'urbanisme – qu'à un édifice donné, voire à l'un des organes d'un bâtiment.

Vielfalt der Grundrisse

Was erfährt nun derjenige, der lernen will, Architektur zu verstehen, aus Grundrissen, mit denen er konfrontiert wird? Er lernt zunächst vor allem die verschiedenen «Gesichter» der Pläne kennen, die sich aus der jeweils für einen Bau gewählten Organisationsform ergeben, von der das System direkt abhängt. Ein Grundriß kann völlig frei von einem sichtbaren System, aber ebenso durch eine mehrfach wiederholte Formulierung bestimmt sein; er kann axial, also symmetrisch angelegt und damit der Organisation eines höheren Lebewesens vergleichbar sein. Hat ein Grundriß zwei oder mehr Symmetrieachsen, so ergibt sich eine zentrierte Form mit einem Mittelpunkt. Ein solcher Grundriß kann quadratisch, vieleckig oder rund sein, Symbolwert haben oder geistige Zusammenhänge widerspiegeln. Aus vier-, sechs- oder achteckigen Einheiten können regelmäßige, schachbrettartige oder ähnliche Raster gebildet werden, doch muß sich daraus nicht unbedingt Symmetrie ergeben. Diese regelmäßigen Raster können sich, auf bestimmten Winkelgrößen (90°, 60°, 45°) aufgebaut, ins Unendliche ausdehnen. Jedes dieser Systeme läßt sich sowohl in großem Maßstab – beim Städtebau – als auch bei einem einzelnen Bau oder nur einem Teil einer Anlage anwenden.

So sind aus Grundrissen alle Möglichkeiten, von der rein zufälligen Form über die organisch gewachsene einer natürlichen, volksnahen, traditionellen oder auch spontanen Architektur bis zur strengen, orthogonalen oder zentralen Ordnung abzulesen.

Schlußfolgerung

In den Grund- und Aufrissen eines Bauwerks werden also dessen innerer Aufbau, die bestimmenden Kraftlinien und seine allgemeine Gliederung sichtbar, ähnlich wie Röntgenstrahlen Skelett und Organe des Menschen erkennen lassen.

Aber der Plan vermittelt nicht nur ein Verständnis der jeweiligen Architektur selbst, auch Architekturgeschichte wird mit ihm faßbar. Vergleicht man Pläne einander entsprechender, chronologisch aufeinander folgender Bauten, zeichnen sich die großen Linien von Entwicklungstendenzen einer Kultur deutlich ab, die bei der Begegnung mit dem errichteten Bauwerk leicht verborgen bleiben.

Ist ein solcher Vergleich zwischen frühen und späten Bauten schon innerhalb einer einzelnen Kultur fruchtbar, wieviel mehr ist es dann ein Studium der

by the Early Christian buildings of Anatolia as well as by the wonder that Hagia Sophia inspired in the conquerors of Constantinople.

It was only with the advent of modern materials (metal and reinforced concrete) that this gulf between the two architectural families gradually disappeared. The monolithic aspect of a reinforced concrete skin renders irrelevant the distinction between flexion and thrust-and-counterthrust systems.

The variety of plans

Anyone wishing to understand a work or architecture, then, must learn to decipher and read the plan, but what does this give him?

It may reveal a wide variety of aspects depending on the type of organisation adopted, which in turn dictates how strict the system will be. The plan may be entirely free, or it may be governed by a simple repetitive formula. Alternatively it may follow an axial system which imposes symmetry on the whole composition.

Equally, the plan may be characterised by double axial symmetry, producing a centralised formula. Such a plan may be square, hexagonal, octagonal or round, embodying various types of symbolism as well as complex ideological functions. Rectangular, hexagonal and octagonal shapes can also be developed into regular patterns—the Hippodamian grid, for example—that need not be symmetrical. These patterns are capable of being extended indefinitely in the form of a web made up of ninety-, sixty-, or forty-five-degree angles. Finally, each of these systems is as applicable on the scale of town-planning as on that of an individual building or even a particular organ of a building.

So from the completely random approach to the strictest kind of rectangular or centralised organisation, including between those extremes the organic forms that spring from natural, popular, folk, or spontaneous architecture, all types of composition can be traced through the medium of the plan, which reveals the deliberate intentions or subconscious motivations of the architect or builder.

Conclusion

Reading the plans of a monument makes it possible to discern the 'bones' of the building, its lines of force and overall articulation, rather as an X-ray photograph shows up the skeleton and organs of the human body.

But if plans help one to understand

14

Ainsi donc, de l'aléatoire complet à la stricte organisation orthogonale ou centrée, en passant par les formes organiques nées d'une architecture naturelle, populaire, folklorique ou spontanée, tous les degrés de composition sont perceptibles au travers du plan, qui révèle les intentions volontaires ou les motivations subconscientes des bâtisseurs.

Conclusion

Grâce à la lecture des plans d'un monument, il devient donc possible de percevoir l'ossature de l'édifice, ses lignes de force et son articulation générale, à la manière dont les rayons X nous révèlent le squelette et les organes humains.

Mais le plan, s'il nous aide à comprendre l'architecture, est aussi le moyen d'en saisir l'histoire: c'est par la comparaison entre des plans successifs d'édifices analogues que se dessinent les grands traits d'une évolution vers laquelle tend – presque inconsciemment – une civilisation. Ce que ne peut exprimer clairement une perception vécue des édifices, la lecture des plans permet de le rendre évident.

Si une telle comparaison entre avant et après est fructueuse à l'intérieur de chaque culture, combien l'étude des similitudes ou des analogies l'est-elle plus encore, lorsque l'on dispose d'un instrument qui offre un résumé analytique de toutes les grandes périodes de l'activité architecturale sur la planète. La réduction à une même méthode d'approche pour les œuvres caractéristiques de tous les peuples bâtisseurs, le traitement de tous les types d'édifices selon les mêmes normes graphiques, la possibilité de comparer les créations de civilisations souvent fort éloignées dans le temps ou l'espace, ou évoquées par des auteurs qui s'ignorent les uns les autres, telles sont les ressources qu'apporte cette publication globale destinée à nous mieux faire «comprendre l'architecture».

Ähnlichkeiten und Übereinstimmungen zwischen allen großen Epochen der Architektur unseres Planeten – anhand eines Mittels, das uns erlaubt, zu vergleichen und mit einem Blick Ergebnisse zu gewinnen.

In der hier vorgelegten umfassenden Veröffentlichung sind charakteristische Werke aller Völker, die Architektur geschaffen haben, in der gleichen Weise dargestellt; Bauten aller Art – reduziert auf den zweidimensionalen Plan – sind nach übereinstimmenden graphischen Normen wiedergegeben. Damit wird die Möglichkeit geboten, Schöpfungen aus räumlich und zeitlich weit auseinanderliegenden Kulturen oder von Architekten, die nichts voneinander wußten, miteinander zu vergleichen. Im Studium des Gemeinsamen und des Spezifischen erschließt sich die Welt der Architektur.

architecture, they also help one to grasp its history. By comparing the plans of a succession of similar buildings one can isolate the broad features of the evolution of a civilisation, which cannot easily be achieved by simply viewing the buildings.

And if this kind of before-and-after comparison is fruitful within a given civilisation, how much more fruitful is the study of analogies between all the major periods of architectural activity in man's history by means of an analytical summary of those periods. In adopting a uniform approach to the most characteristic works of all architectural cultures, treating all types of building in accordance with the same graphic norms, and making it possible to compare the architectural creations of civilisations often far removed from one another in time and space, and usually dealt with by separate authors, this book hopes to provide a comprehensive as well as comprehensible guide to world architecture.

Egypte   Ägypten   Egypt

L'architecture de la vie quotidienne en Egypte est construite en brique crue, en palmes et en bois: maisons d'habitation, fermes et magasins, palais et forteresses eux-mêmes sont donc bâtis en matériaux périssables. Seule l'architecture religieuse est en dur, qu'il s'agisse des sanctuaires ou des édifices funéraires. C'est donc elle qui nous est le mieux connue.

Aux origines, aux époques prédynastique et thinite (3100 à 2700), des similitudes apparaissent avec la Mésopotamie: murs à redents qui animent les façades. Le besoin de pérennité, correspondant à l'éternité des dieux, conduit les bâtisseurs à rechercher dans la pierre un matériau impérissable pour les constructions du culte des dieux et des défunts. L'ensemble du pharaon Djéser (IIIe dynastie) marque la naissance, 2700 ans avant notre ère, de la première grande architecture de pierre. Une aire entourée d'un mur d'enceinte de 556 × 278 m, haut de 10 m, en calcaire finement appareillé et redenté, enferme une pyramide à six degrés qui mesure 109 × 121 m à la base, pour une hauteur de 60 m.

A l'Ancien Empire (2700 à 2200) s'ouvre une période de gigantisme, avec les grandes pyramides de Dachour et de Giza, comportant un temple de la vallée et un temple haut réunis par une chaussée. Dès cette époque tout le vocabulaire architectural et décoratif du «style» pharaonique existe. Du Moyen Empire (2050 à 1800), peu d'œuvres ont échappé à la destruction. A Deir el Bahari, le temple funéraire de Mentouhotep annonce celui de la reine Hatshepsout (1500), alors qu'à Karnak fut retrouvée, démontée, la Chapelle Blanche de Sésostris Ier (vers 2000 av. J.-C.).

Die ägyptischen Profanbauten – Wohnhäuser, Bauernhöfe, Lagerhäuser, Paläste und Festungen – wurden aus ungebrannten Ziegeln, Schilf und Holz errichtet, nur für die Sakralarchitektur – Tempel und Grabbauten – verwendete man Stein; deshalb wissen wir auch über sie am besten Bescheid.

In den Anfängen, der vordynastischen und der Thinitenzeit (ca. 3100–2700), bestehen Ähnlichkeiten mit mesopotamischen Bauten, so die Mauergliederung durch Vor- und Rücksprünge. Die Notwendigkeit, den ewigen Göttern unvergängliche Werke zu errichten, führte dazu, für den Götter- und Totenkult den dauerhaften Stein zu verwenden. Mit dem um 2700 v. Chr. errichteten Grabbezirk des Pharao Djoser (3. Dynastie) in Saqqara beginnt die monumentale Steinarchitektur. Eine 10 m hohe, durch Vor- und Rücksprünge gegliederte Mauer aus sorgfältig gefügten Kalksteinquadern umschließt einen Bezirk von 278 × 556 m, in dem sich auf einer Basis von 121 × 109 m eine 60 m hohe Pyramide erhebt.

Mit den großen Pyramiden von Dahschur und Gise, zu denen jeweils ein Taltempel und ein höher liegender, mit diesem durch einen Weg verbundener Totentempel gehören, schuf das Alte Reich (ca. 2700–2200 v. Chr.) gigantische Werke. Von dieser Epoche an ist das gesamte architektonische und dekorative Vokabular des «Pharaonenstils» ausgebildet.

Aus dem Mittleren Reich (ca. 2050 bis 1800) sind nur wenige Bauten erhalten: Der Totentempel Mentuhoteps (11. Dynastie) bereitet den Totentempel der Königin Hatschepsut (18. Dynastie) vor; in Karnak wurde ein Pavillon Sesostris' I. (um 2000 v. Chr.) – in einen

The everyday architecture of ancient Egypt employed perishable materials; dwellings, farms, shops, even palaces and fortresses, were all built of unfired brick, papyrus and wood. The Egyptians used stone only for their religious architecture, their shrines and funerary monuments. Consequently it is this we know most about.

At the beginning, in the pre-dynastic and Thinite periods (3100–2700 B.C.), there were similarities with Mesopotamian architecture; redans were used, for example, to animate façade walls. The need for a durability in keeping with the eternity of the gods prompted architects to seek an imperishable material for buildings associated with divine worship or with the cult of the dead. The complex of Pharaoh Djoser (Third Dynasty) marks the emergence, around 2700 B.C., of the earliest significant architecture in stone. In an enclosure measuring 556 m. by 278 m., surrounded by a 10 m. high redan wall of delicately jointed limestone blocks, a six-stepped pyramid (base 109 m. by 121 m.) rises to a height of 60 m.

The Old Kingdom (2700–2200 B.C.) ushered in a period of architectural grandeur with the great pyramids of Dahshur and Giza, the latter including a valley temple and a raised temple linked by a causeway. By this period the entire architectural and decorative vocabulary of the Pharaonic 'style' was fully developed. Few works of the Middle Kingdom (2050–1800 B.C.) have survived: the funerary temple of Mentuhotep at Deir al-Bahri anticipated that of Queen Hatshepsut. At Karnak archaeologists found traces of the 'White Shrine' of Sesostris I (c. 2000 B.C.).

The New Kingdom (1580–1085 B.C.)

LIBRARY
OLYMPIA TECHNICAL COMMUNITY COLLEGE
OLYMPIA, WASHINGTON

Au Nouvel Empire (1580 à 1085) débute une période d'intense construction sous les Aménophis, Thoutmosis et surtout Ramsès. D'innombrables et vastes sanctuaires avec leurs pylônes et leurs salles hypostyles jonchent le pays. Ces temples obéissent à la double loi de l'espace décroissant et de la lumière s'amenuisant plus on pénètre vers le saint des saints. De sa grande cour à ciel ouvert jusqu'au naos plongé dans les ténèbres, l'édifice, avec ses enceintes successives, présente partout les mêmes traits: fruit des murs, tores d'angle, corniche égyptienne, colonnes palmiformes. Ce style trouvera son épanouissement aux époques ptolémaïque et romaine (237 av. à 250 apr. J.-C.) dans des œuvres remarquablement conservées: Edfou, Dendéra, Philae.

späteren Pylon verbaut – wiederentdeckt und wiederaufgebaut.

Das neue Reich (ca. 1580–1085) zeichnet sich durch eine intensive Bautätigkeit unter den Königen Amenophis, Thutmosis und Ramses aus. Zahllose Heiligtümer mit Pylonen und Säulensälen sind über das ganze Land verstreut. Bei allen diesen Tempeln verengt sich der Raum, je mehr man sich dem Allerheiligsten nähert, und das Licht nimmt ab. Vom großen offenen Hof bis zu dem in Dunkel getauchten Naos zeigt die Anlage mit ihren mehrfachen Mauergürteln überall die gleichen Merkmale: geneigte Mauern, Rundstäbe an den Gebäudeecken, Hohlkehlengesimse, Säulen mit Palmenkapitell. Dieser Stil erlebte seine Blüte in der Ptolemaier- und der Römerzeit, aus denen gut erhaltene Werke erhalten sind: Edfu, Dendera, Philae.

saw the beginning of a period of intensive building under the Amenhoteps, the Thutmoses, and above all the Ramses. Countless huge sanctuaries with pylons and hypostyle halls sprang up all over the country. They conformed to a double law of decreasing space and diminishing light the closer one approached to the holy of holies. From their enormous open-air courtyards to the darkness of the *naos*, these temples with their successions of precincts all presented the same features: battered walls (i.e. tapering toward the top), torus quoins, Egyptian cornices and papyrus columns. The style reached its peak during the Ptolemaic and Roman periods (237 B.C–A.D. 250) in such remarkably well-preserved works as Edfu, Dendera and Philae.

1 Pyramide à degrés du pharaon Djéser à Saqqara. A gauche, l'une des chapelles reconstituées (IIIe dynastie, vers 2700 av. J.-C.).
2 La «Chapelle Blanche» ou kiosque de Sésostris Ier, à Karnak, datant du Moyen Empire (1950 av. J.-C.).
3 Le temple funéraire de la reine Hatshepsout, à Deir el Bahari (vers 1500 av. J.-C.).
4 Portique de la cour du grand temple d'Horus à Edfou, datant de la période ptolémaïque (IIe s. av. J.-C.).

1 Saqqara, Stufenpyramide des Pharao Djoser; links eine der rekonstruierten Kapellen (3. Dynastie, um 2700 v. Chr.)
2 Karnak, Pavillon Sesostris' I. (Mittleres Reich, 1950 v. Chr.)
3 Deir-el-Bahari, Totentempel der Königin Hatschepsut (um 1500 v. Chr.)
4 Edfu, Portikus im Hof des Großen Horus-Tempels (Ptolemaier-Zeit, 2. Jh. v. Chr.)

1 Stepped pyramid of Pharaoh Djoser, Saqqara. Left, one of the reconstructed chapels (Third Dynasty, *c*.2700 B.C.).
2 Kiosk of Sesostris I, known as the 'White Shrine', Karnak (Middle Kingdom, 1950 B.C.).
3 Funerary temple of Queen Hatshepsut, Deir al-Bahri (*c*.1500 B.C.).
4 Portico in the courtyard of the great temple of Horus, Edfu (Ptolemaic period, second century B.C.).

1

2

3

4

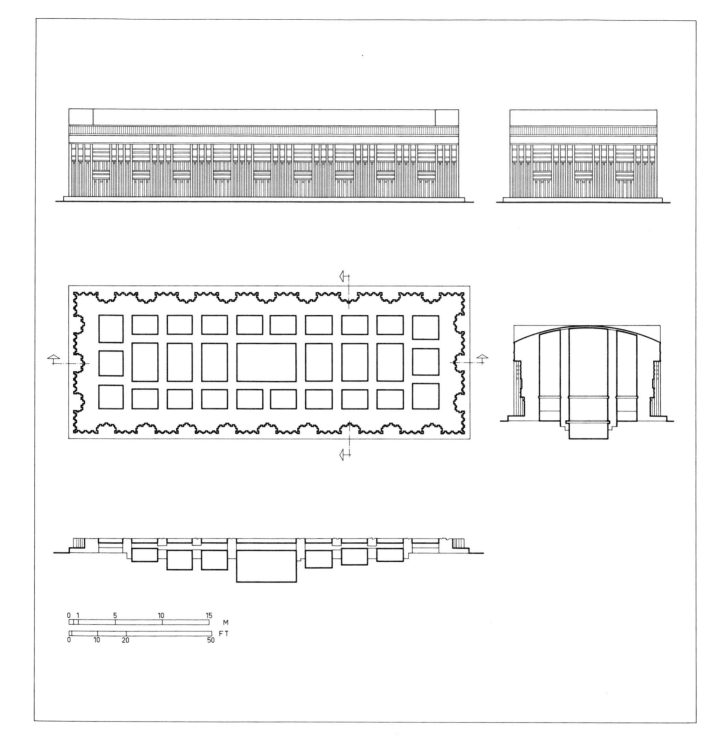

| 0 | 1 | 5 | 10 | 15 | | M |
| 0 | 10 | 20 | | 50 | | F T |

Tombe royale de la Iʳᵉ dynastie à Saqqara, datant de 3100 à 3000 avant notre ère. Elévations des façades reconstituées, plan, coupe transversale reconstituée et coupe longitudinale des chambres souterraines 1:400. Longue de plus de 40 m et large de 15 m, cette construction en brique crue présente un décor à redents qui s'apparente aux édifices contemporains de Mésopotamie.

Saqqara, Königsgrab der 1. Dynastie, 3100–3000 v.Chr. Die Umfassungsmauer des über 40 m langen und 15 m breiten Bauwerks aus ungebrannten Ziegeln ist durch Vor- und Rücksprünge gegliedert ähnlich gleichzeitigen mesopotamischen Bauten. Fassaden (Rekonstruktion), Grundriß, Querschnitt (Rekonstruktion), Längsschnitt durch die unterirdischen Kammern 1:400.

Royal tomb of the 1st Dynasty, Saqqara, 3100–3000 B.C. Elevations of the reconstructed façades, plan, reconstructed cross section and longitudinal section of the underground chambers 1:400. Measuring more than 40 m. in length and 15 m. in width, this unfired brick building is decorated with ribs in a manner recalling Mesopotamian buildings of the same period.

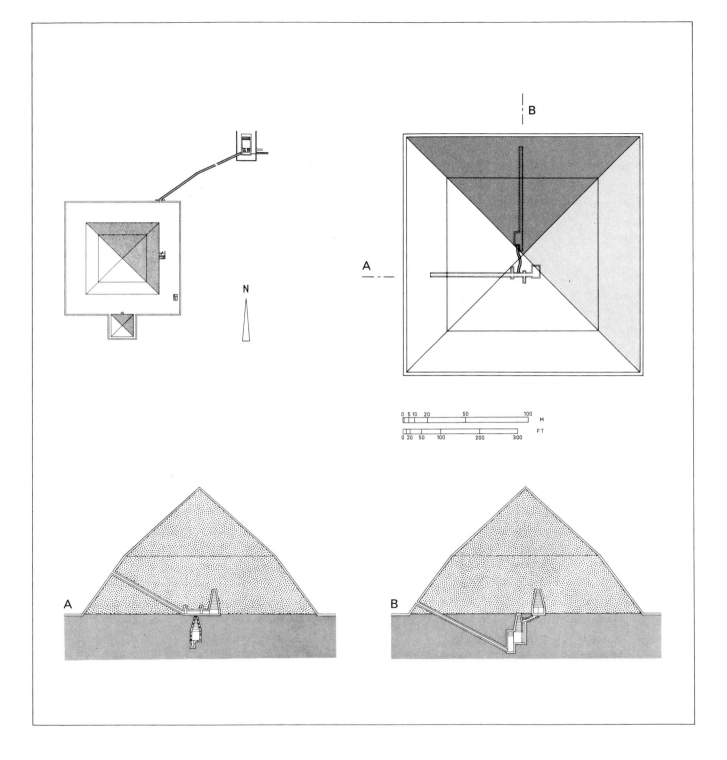

Pyramide sud, ou rhomboïdale, de Da-chour, construite par Snéfrou vers 2625 avant notre ère. Situation avec temple bas 1:10000, plan et coupes 1:3000. L'édifice funéraire doit son nom à la modification de la pente de ses faces, la partie inférieure étant inclinée à 54° et la partie supérieure à 43°. Longueur de la base carrée: 188,5 m; hauteur: 97 m. Le parement est en partie conservé.

Dahschur, Knickpyramide des Snofru, um 2625 v. Chr. Die Pyramide verdankt ihren Namen dem geknickten Umriß, der sich durch den Wechsel des Böschungs-winkels – unten 54°, oben 43° – ergibt. Sie hat eine Höhe von 97 m über einer quadratischen Basis von 188,5 m Sei-tenlänge. Die Verkleidung ist teilweise erhalten. Lageplan mit Taltempel 1:10000; Grundriß und Schnitte 1:3000.

South or rhomboid pyramid, Dahshur, built by Snefru *c*.2625 B.C. Site plan: 1:10,000, with lower temple; plan and sections 1:3000. The tomb owes its name to the double slope of its sides, the lower parts being at an angle of 54° and the upper parts at 43°. Base 188.5 m. square, height 97 m. Part of the facing is still intact.

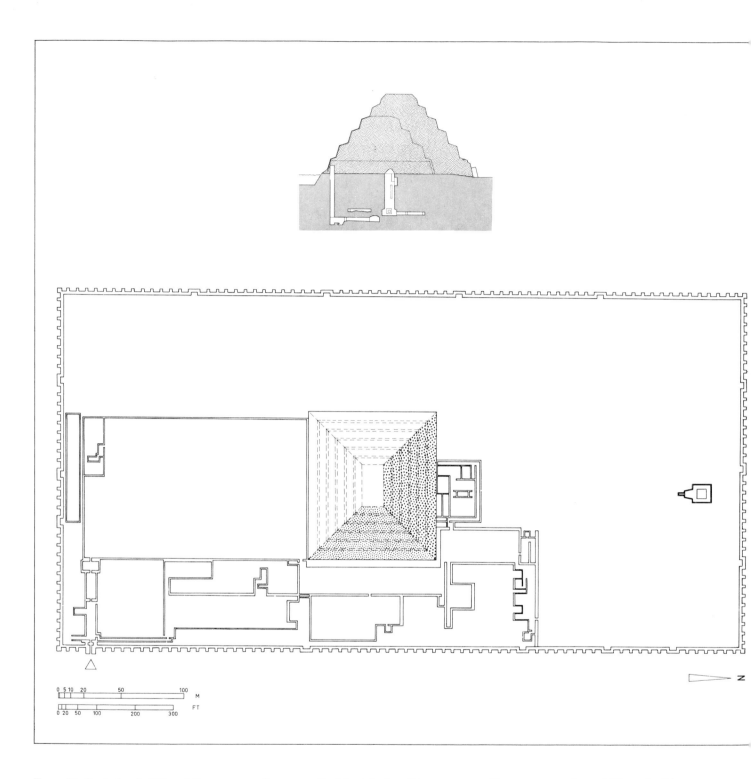

Ensemble funéraire de Djéser à Saqqara, construit vers 2700 avant notre ère. Dans une enceinte rectangulaire de 555 m × 278 m, formée de murs de calcaire à redents finement appareillés et hauts de 10 m, s'élève la première pyramide de l'histoire pharaonique. Plan d'ensemble et coupe de la pyramide à degrés 1:3000. La pyramide a été édifiée en trois étapes distinctes.

Saqqara, Grabbezirk des Djoser, um 2700 v. Chr. Innerhalb einer 10 m hohen Umfassungsmauer aus sorgfältig gefügten Kalksteinquadern erhebt sich die erste Pyramide der Pharaonenzeit, die ihre heutige Gestalt in drei deutlich unterscheidbaren Bauphasen erhielt. Plan und Schnitt durch die Pyramide 1:3000.

Funerary complex of Pharaoh Djoser, Saqqara, built c. 2700 B.C. A 10 m. high limestone wall, carefully jointed and decorated with ribs, surrounds a precinct measuring 555 m. by 278 m. and containing the first pyramid of the Pharaonic period. Overall plan and section of the stepped pyramid 1:3000. The pyramid was erected in three separate stages.

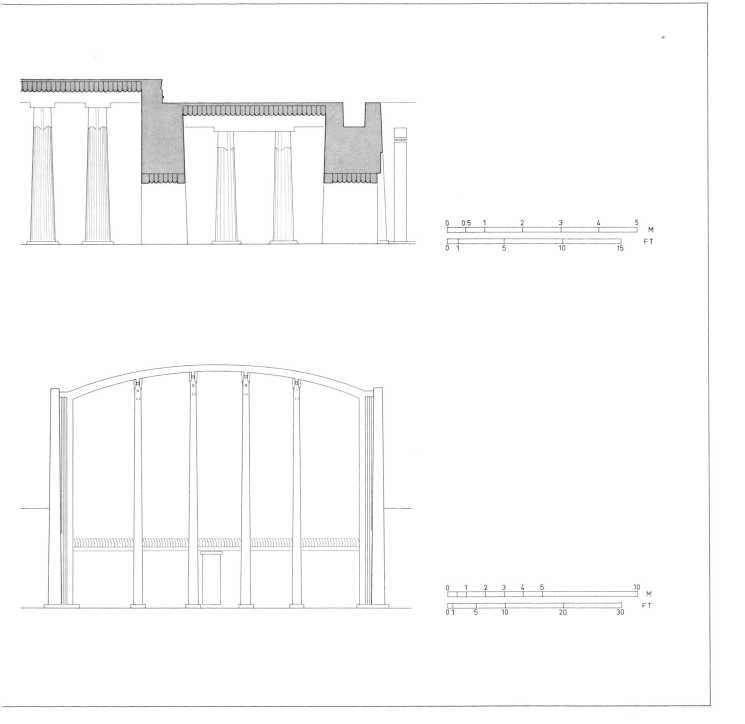

0 0.5 1   2   3   4   5
                                              M
                                              FT
0 1   5   10   15

0 1 2 3 4 5   10
                                              M
                                              FT
0 1   5   10   20   30

L'ensemble funéraire du pharaon Djéser est l'œuvre du «divin» Imhotep, premier architecte dont le nom nous soit parvenu, qui réalisa la première grande architecture de pierre de l'humanité. Coupe longitudinale de la colonnade d'entrée 1:100. Façade reconstituée par Philippe Lauer de la «Maison du Sud» 1:200. La toiture cintrée reproduit l'habitat traditionnel du Delta.

Saqqara, Grabbezirk des Djoser. Die Anlage ist das Werk des später vergöttlichten Imhotep, des ersten Architekten, dessen Namen wir kennen. Das gerundete Dach des Süd-Palastes ist von dem traditionellen Wohnhaustyp des Nildeltas übernommen. Längsschnitt der Eingangshalle zum Grabbezirk 1:100; Fassade des Süd-Palastes (Rekonstruktion Philippe Lauer) 1:200.

Funerary complex of Pharaoh Djoser, the work of the 'divine' Imhotep, the earliest architect whose name has survived and the man responsible for the first major stone architecture in the history of mankind. Longitudinal section of the entrance colonnade 1:100; Philippe Lauer's reconstruction of the façade of the 'South Building' 1:200. The tunnel roof was that of the traditional Delta dwelling-house.

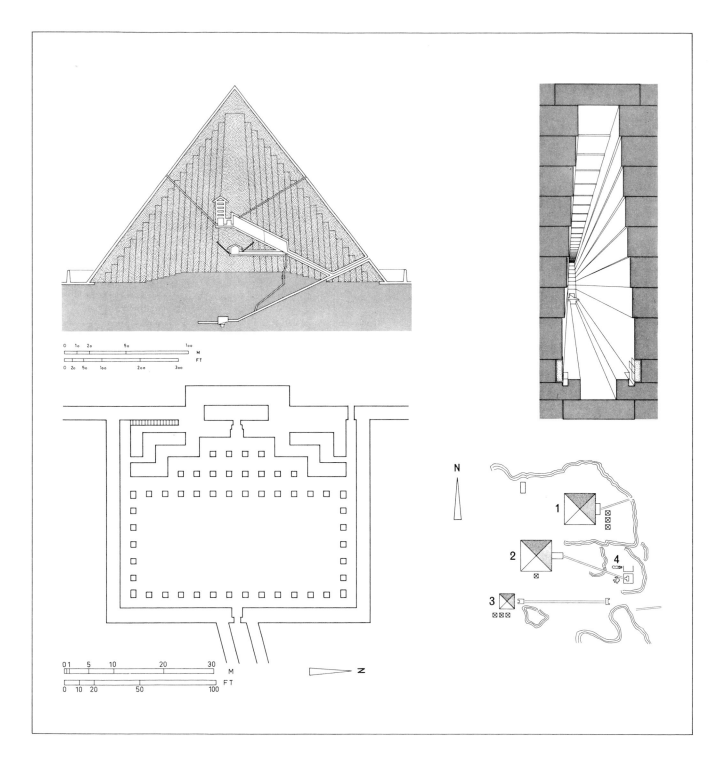

Pyramide de Chéops à Giza, édifiée vers 2600 avant notre ère. Haute de 146,5 m pour une base carrée de 230 m de côté, cette construction, la plus énorme de l'histoire, dépasse 2,5 millions de m³. Coupe 1:3000, plan du temple haut 1:750, coupe axonométrique de la grande galerie en encorbellement et plan masse du site de Giza 1:30000. 1) Chéops, 2) Chéphren, 3) Mykérinos, 4) Sphinx.

Gise, Cheops-Pyramide, um 2600 v. Chr. Dieses gewaltigste Bauwerk der Geschichte hat bei einer Höhe von 146,5 m über einer quadratischen Basis von 230 m Seitenlänge einen Rauminhalt von über 2,5 Millionen Kubikmeter. Schnitt 1:3000; Grundriß des Totentempels 1:750; axonometrischer Schnitt durch die große Galerie mit Kraggewölbe; Lageplan von Gise 1:30000: 1) Cheops, 2) Chefren, 3) Mykerinos, 4) Sphinx.

Cheops pyramid, Giza, built *c.* 2600 B.C. Rising to a height of 146.5 m. on a base measuring 230 m. square, this building, the largest in history, occupies more than 2.5 million m³. Section 1:3000; plan of the raised temple 1:750; axonometric section of the great corbelled gallery and plan of the Giza site 1:30,000. 1) Cheops, 2) Chephren, 3) Mycerinus, 4) Sphinx.

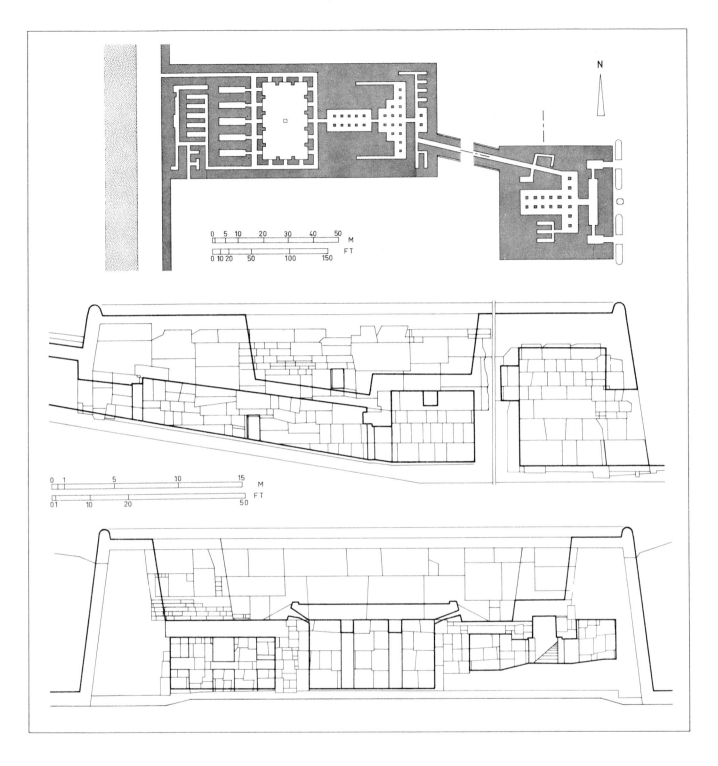

Temple haut (à gauche) et Temple bas (à droite) de Chéphren à Giza, construits vers 2550 avant notre ère. Plan 1:1500. Le temple bas est le mieux conservé de l'Ancien Empire et présente, à l'intérieur, ses mur et supports de granit rose traité en appareil colossal. Coupe longitudinale, montrant la liaison avec la chaussée couverte longue de 400 m, et coupe transversale 1:300.

Gise, Totentempel (links) und Taltempel (rechts) des Chefren, um 2550 v. Chr. Der Taltempel ist der besterhaltene des Alten Reiches; Mauern und Pfeiler des Innern sind aus gewaltigen Rosengranitquadern. Grundriß 1:1500; Längsschnitt mit dem Zugang zum 400 m langen, überdachten Verbindungsweg und Querschnitt des Taltempels 1:300.

Upper (left) and lower (right) temples of Chephren, Giza, built c. 2550 B.C. Plan 1:1500. The lower temple is the best preserved of the Old Kingdom. The walls and supports of the interior use pink granite masonry on a colossal scale. Longitudinal section, showing the transition to the 400 m. long covered causeway, and cross section 1:300.

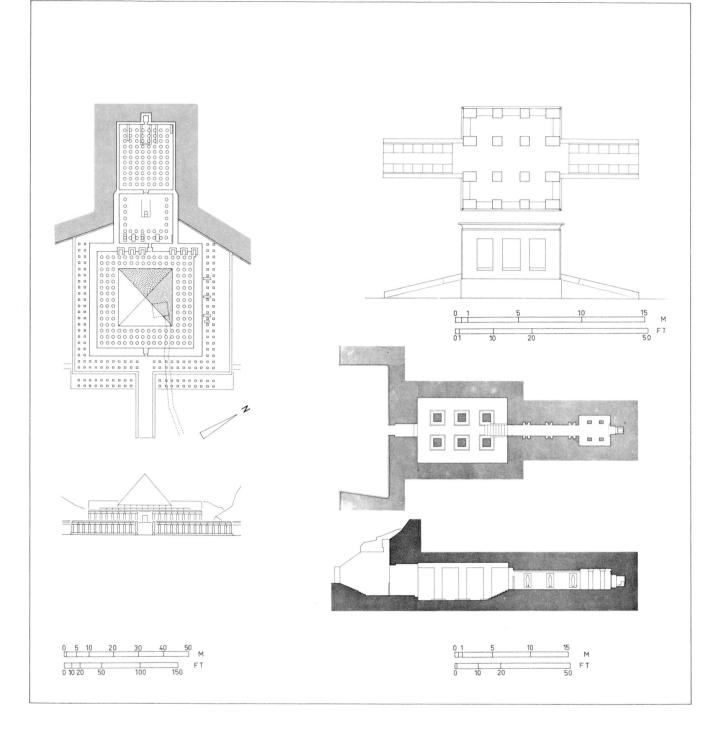

A gauche, **Temple funéraire de Mentou-hotep à Deir el Bahari,** construit vers 2050 au pied de la falaise libyque en face de Karnak. Cette œuvre du Moyen Empire combine la pyramide et la salle hypostyle. Plan et élévation 1:1500. A droite, en haut, **Kiosque de Sésostris Ier à Karnak** (1950 av. J.-C.), plan et profil 1:300. En bas, **Hypogée de Sarenpout II à Assouan** (vers 1900 av. J.-C.), coupe et plan 1:500.

Links: **Deir-el-Bahari, Totentempel Men-tuhoteps II.,** um 2050 v. Chr. Dieses Bauwerk des Mittleren Reiches, gegen-über von Karnak, ist eine Verbindung von Pyramide und Pfeilerhalle. Grund- und Aufriß 1:1500. Rechts oben: **Kar-nak, Pavillon Sesostris I.,** 1950 v. Chr. Grundriß und Aufriß einer Seite 1:300. Unten: **Assuan, Grab des Fürsten Sarenput II.,** um 1900 v. Chr. Grundriß und Schnitt 1:500.

Top left, **Funerary temple of Mentuho-tep, Deir al-Bahri,** built *c.*2050 at the foor of the Libyan cliff opposite Kar-nak. This Middle Kingdom monument combines both pyramid and hypostyle hall. Plan and elevation 1:1500. Top right, **Kiosk of Sesostris I, Karnak** (1950 B.C.), plan and profile 1:300. Below, **Hypogeum of Sarenput II, Aswan** (*c.*1900 B.C.), section and plan 1:500.

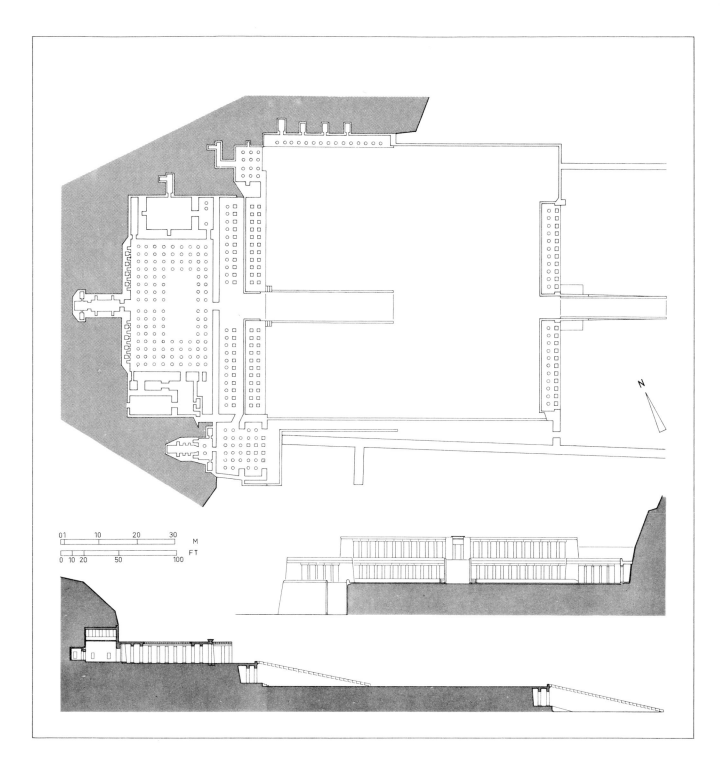

Temple funéraire de la reine Hatshepsout
édifié vers 1500 av. J.-C. à Deir el Bahari au pied de la falaise libyque, au nord de celui de Mentouhotep. Cette œuvre de l'architecte Sénenmout, avec ses terrasses bordées de colonnades et ses plans inclinés, est d'une grande originalité, tout en puisant aux traditions du Moyen Empire. Plan, élévation des portiques et coupe longitudinale 1:1000.

Deir-el-Bahari, Totentempel der Königin Hatschepsut am Fuß des Steilrandes der Libyschen Wüste nördlich des Totentempels Mentuhoteps II., um 1500 v. Chr. Dieses Werk des Baumeisters Senmut mit den von Pfeilerhallen gesäumten Terrassen und mit Rampen beruht zwar auf der Tradition des Mittleren Reiches, ist aber von ausgeprägter Eigenart. Grundriß, Aufriß der Pfeilerhallen und Längsschnitt 1:1000.

Funerary temple of Queen Hatshepsut, Deir al-Bahri, built *c.*1500 B.C. at the foot of the Libyan cliff to the north of the temple of Mentuhotep. The architect was Senenmut. Terraces bordered with colonnades and inclined planes make this a work of great originality that still owes much to Middle Kingdom tradition. Plan, elevation of the porticoes, and longitudinal section 1:1000.

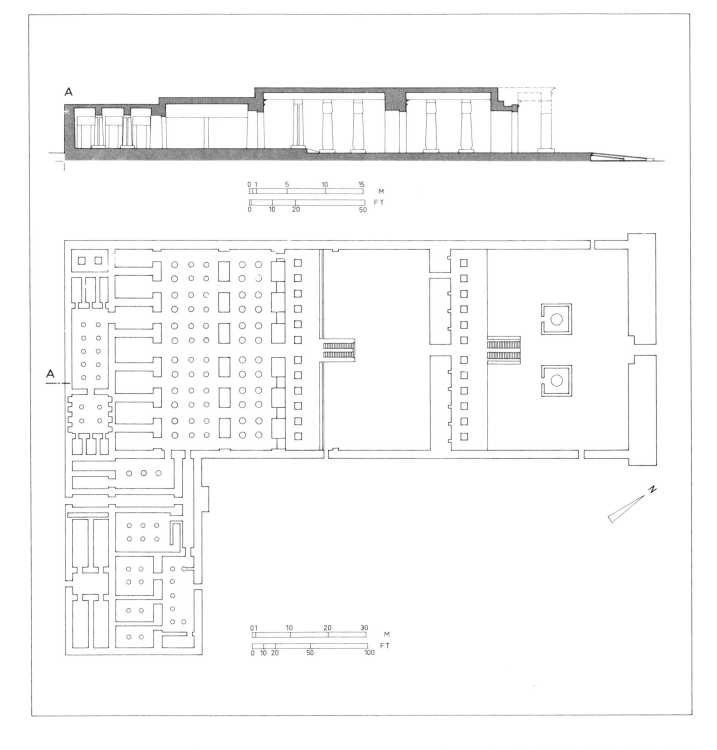

Temple de Séthi Ier à Abydos, édifié vers 1300 avant notre ère. Les deux pylônes précédant les deux cours de la partie antérieure du temple sont aujourd'hui détruits. Les hypostyles et les sept chapelles dédiées à sept grands dieux sont remarquablement conservées pour un temple du Nouvel Empire. Plan 1:1000. Coupe longitudinale de la partie couverte 1:500.

Abydos, Tempel Sethos I., um 1300 v. Chr. Die jedem der beiden Höfe vorgelagerten Pylonen sind heute zerstört. Vor dem Tempelinnern liegen die Hypostyle, die ebenso wie die sieben Hauptgöttern geweihten sieben Kapellen für einen Tempel des Neuen Reiches bemerkenswert gut erhalten sind. Grundriß 1:1000; Längsschnitt des überdachten Teils 1:500.

Temple of Seti I, Abydos, built *c.*1300 B.C. The two pylons in front of the two courtyards of the fore-part of the temple are no longer standing. The hypostyles and the seven shrines dedicated to seven major gods are remarkably well preserved for a New Kingdom temple. Plan 1:1000. Longitudinal section of the covered part 1:500.

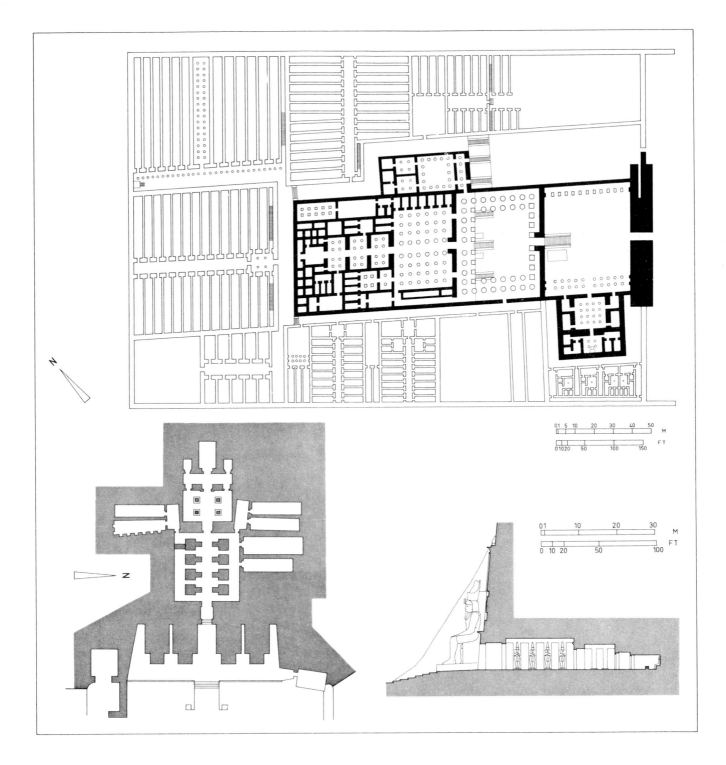

En haut: **Temple funéraire de Ramsès II, dit Ramesséum, à Thèbes,** construit vers 1250 av. J.-C. Autour du temple que précèdent un pylône (détruit) et deux cours, les magasins remplissent l'espace entouré d'une enceinte. Ces constructions de brique crue sont un des rares exemples d'architecture civile. Plan 1:2000. En bas: **Grand Spéos d'Abou Simbel,** par Ramsès II. Plan et coupe longitudinale 1:1000.

Oben: **Theben, Ramesseum,** um 1250 v. Chr. Um den Totentempel Ramses' II. mit zwei Höfen und einem jetzt zerstörten Pylon liegen Magazine. Diese aus ungebrannten Ziegeln errichteten Bauten gehören heute zu den seltenen Beispielen ägyptischer Profanarchitektur. Grundriß 1:2000. Unten: **Abu Simbel, Großer Felsentempel Ramses' II.** Grundriß und Längsschnitt 1:1000.

Above, **Funerary temple of Ramses II (the 'Ramesseum'), Thebes,** built *c.* 1250 B.C. In front of the temple are a pylon (now destroyed) and two courtyards, and the space between it and the surrounding wall is filled with storehouses. These buildings of unfired brick are among the rare surviving examples of Egyptian secular architecture. Plan 1:2000. Below, the **Great Speos, Abu Simbel,** by Ramses II. Plan and longitudinal section 1:1000.

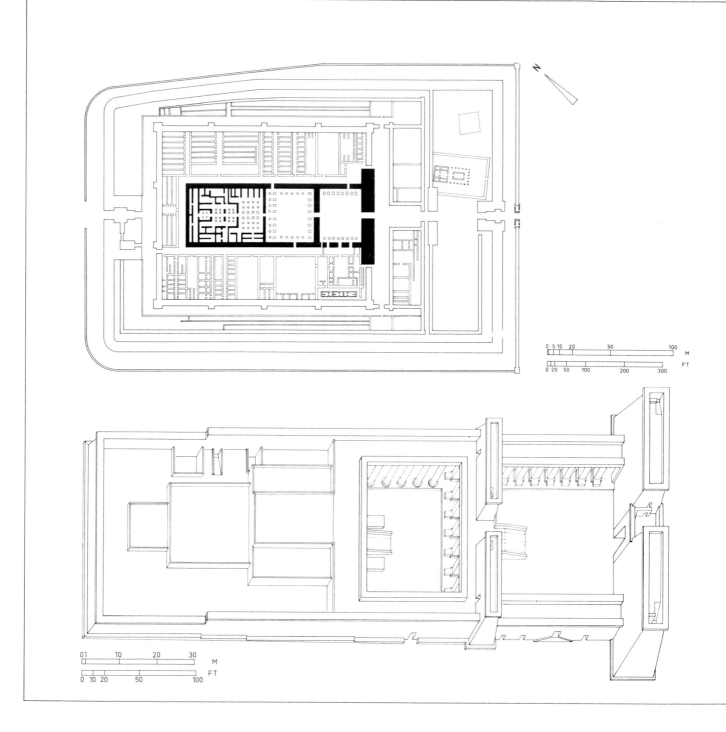

Temple funéraire de Ramsès III à Medinet Habou (Thèbes), construit vers 1175 avant notre ère. L'enceinte est doublée par un système de fortifications composé d'un premier mur bas, précédant une énorme muraille de brique épaisse de 10 m et haute de 18 m s'ouvrant à l'est et à l'ouest par des tours de pierre. Situation 1:3000 et isométrie du temple 1:1000.

Medinet Habu (Theben), Totentempel Ramses' III., um 1175 v.Chr. Der Tempelbezirk ist von einer doppelten Befestigung aus einer niedrigen Außenmauer und einer gewaltigen, 10 m starken und 18 m hohen Ziegelmauer mit Torbauten im Osten und Westen umgeben. Lageplan 1:3000; isometrische Ansicht des Tempels 1:1000.

Funerary temple of Ramses III, Medinet Habu (Thebes), built c.1175 B.C. The precinct is surrounded by a system of fortifications, comprising one low wall and a second, massive brick wall 10 m. thick and 18 m. high with stone tower openings to east and west. Situation 1:3000 and isometric projection of the temple 1:1000.

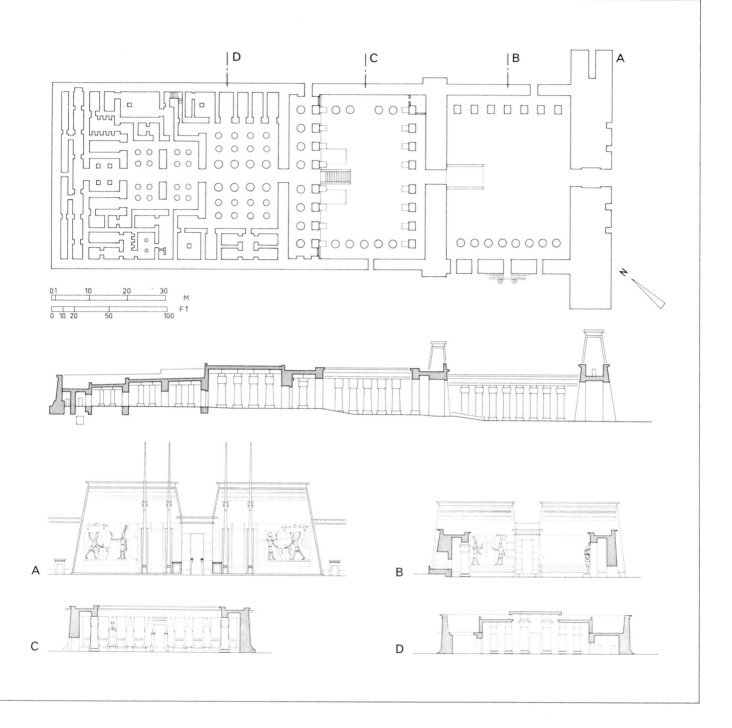

01   10   20   30   M

0 10 20   50   100   FT

N

A

B

C

D

Le Temple de Medinet Habou, précédé de son grand pylône, large de 70 m et haut de 24 m, s'ouvre sur une première cour. Un second pylône donne accès à la seconde cour, puis viennent les hypostyles entourées de chapelles. Plan, coupe longitudinale, élévation du premier pylône (A), coupe transversale de la cour (côté pylône) (B), coupe de la deuxième cour (C) et de l'hypostyle (D) 1:1000.

Medinet Habu, Totentempel Ramses' III. Durch einen 70 m breiten und 24 m hohen Pylon gelangt man in den ersten Hof, durch einen zweiten in den nächsten, dann folgen die von Kapellen umgebenen Hypostyle. Grundriß, Längsschnitt, Aufriß des ersten Pylons (A), Querschnitt des ersten (B) und zweiten (C) Hofes und der Säulenhalle (D) 1:1000.

Temple of Medinet Habu. It has in front of it a great pylon measuring 70 m. in width and 24 m. in height and opens on to a courtyard. A second pylon leads to a second courtyard, after which come the hypostyles surrounded by shrines. Plan longitudinal section, elevation of the first pylon (A), cross section of the courtyard (B), section of the second courtyard (C) and the hypostyle (D) 1:1000.

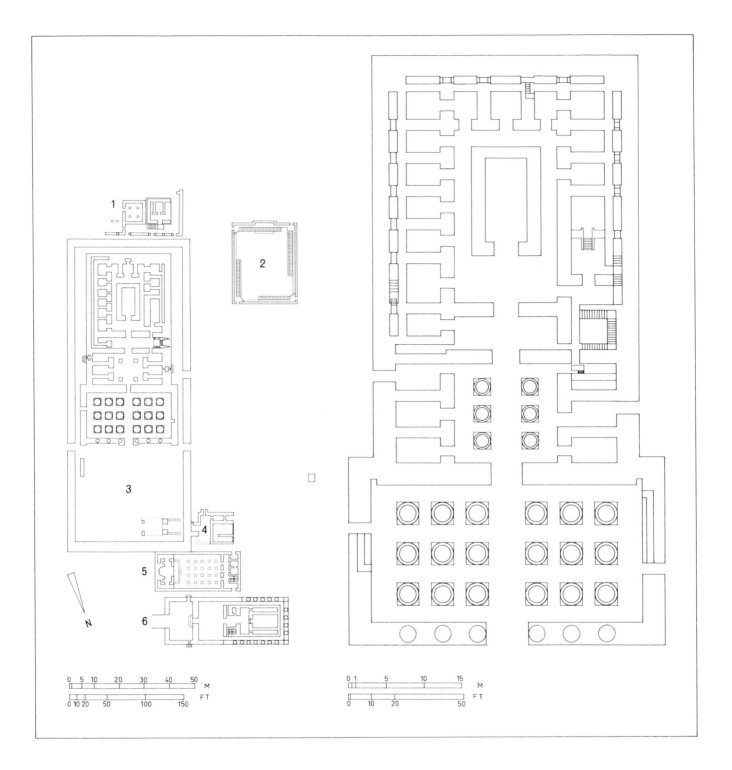

Grand Temple de Dendéra, dédié à la déesse Hathor, datant de 80 av. à 50 apr. J.-C. Œuvre de la période ptolémaïque et romaine, cet édifice grandiose s'apparente au temple d'Edfou. Plan de situation avec les édifices environnants: 1) Temple d'Isis, 2) Lac sacré, 3) Temple d'Hathor, 4) Mammisi de Nectanébo, 5) Eglise copte, 6) Mammisi d'Auguste 1:1500, et plan 1:500.

Dendera, Großer Hathor-Tempel, 80 v. Chr.–50 n.Chr. Dieser großartige Bau der Ptolemaier- und Römerzeit ist dem Tempel von Edfu ähnlich. Lageplan 1:1500: 1) Isistempel, 2) heiliger See, 3) Hathor-Tempel, 4) Mammisi des Nektanebos, 5) koptische Kirche, 6) Mammisi des Augustus; Grundriß des Hathor-Tempels 1:500.

Great Temple, Dendera, built between 80 B.C. and A.D. 50 and dedicated to the goddess Hathor. A work of the Ptolemaic and Roman period, this imposing edifice is not unlike the Edfu temple. Site plan showing the neighbouring buildings: 1) temple of Isis, 2) sacred lake, 3) temple of Hathor, 4) mammisi of Nectanebo, 5) Coptic church, 6) mammisi of Augustus 1:1500; plan 1:500.

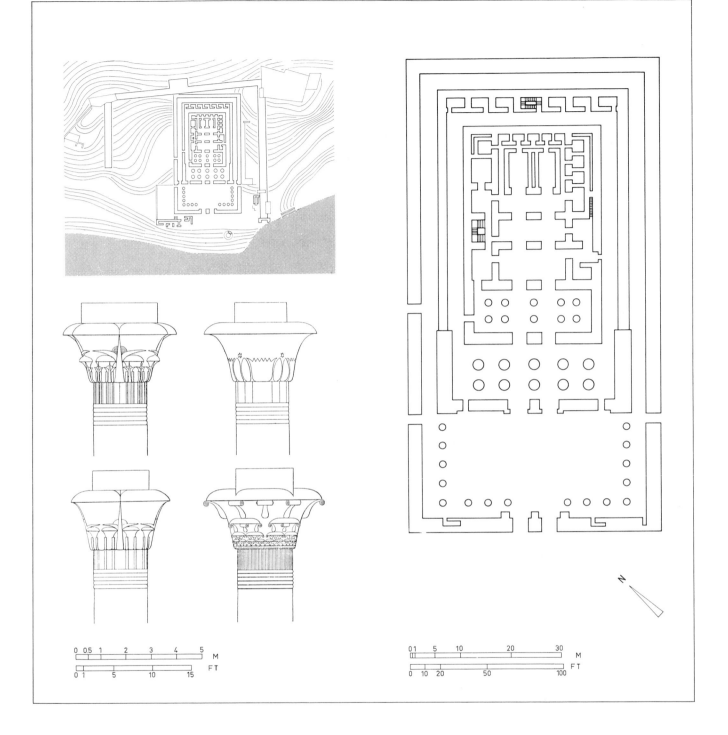

Temple de Kom Ombo, construit entre 181 av. et 30 apr. J.-C. Œuvre ptolémaïque, ce sanctuaire double, dédié à Horus l'Ancien et à Sobek, se dresse sur un éperon dominant le cours du Nil. La décoration se poursuit jusqu'à Macrin au IIIe siècle. Situation 1:3000, plan 1:750 et détails des chapiteaux 1:150.

Kom Ombo, Tempel, zwischen 181 v. Chr. und 30 n.Chr. Der den Gottheiten Suchos und Haroëris geweihte Doppeltempel der Ptolemaierzeit erhebt sich auf einem Gebirgsvorsprung über dem Nil. An der Ausschmückung wurde noch im 3.Jh. unter Macrinus gearbeitet. Lageplan 1:3000; Grundriß 1:750; Kapitelle 1:150.

Temple of Kom Ombo, built between 181 B.C. and A.D. 30. Another Ptolemaic work, this double shrine, dedicated to Horus the Ancient and Sobek, stands on a spur overlooking the Nile. Decoration continued into the reign of Macrinus (third century A.D.). Site plan 1:3000; plan 1:750; details of the capitals 1:150.

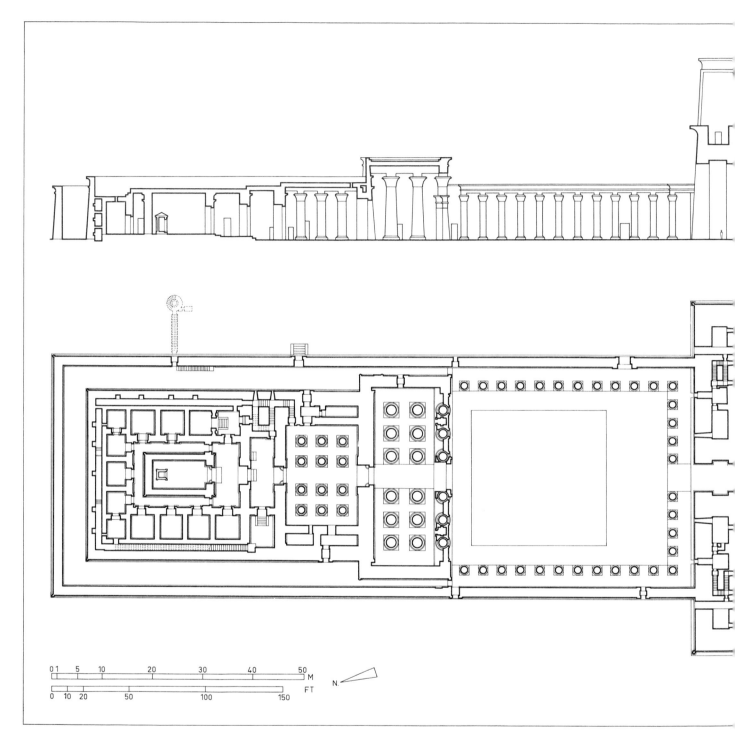

0 1 5 10 20 30 40 50 M
0 10 20 50 100 150 FT

N.

Grand Temple d'Edfou, dédié au dieu Horus, construit entre 237 et 57 av. J.-C., long de 140 m et dominé par un pylône haut de 36 m. Après la cour du sanctuaire, jusqu'à la deuxième hypostyle, dont l'édification dura 95 ans, vinrent la grande hypostyle (de 140 à 124), le mur d'enceinte, la cour et le pylône (en 116). Plan et coupe longitudinale 1:750.

Edfu, Großer Horus-Tempel, 237–57 v. Chr., 140 m lang, überragt von einem 36 m hohen Pylon. Zuerst wurde der Hof bis zur zweiten Säulenhalle, deren Bauzeit 95 Jahre betrug, errichtet, dann der große Säulensaal (140–124 v. Chr.), die Umfassungsmauer, Vorhof und Pylon (116 v. Chr.). Längsschnitt und Grundriß 1:750.

Great Temple of Edfu, built 237–57 B.C. and dedicated to the god Horus, is 140 m. long and is dominated by a 36 m. pylon. After the courtyard of the shrine and the second hypostyle, which took 95 years to build, came the main hypostyle (140–124 B.C.), surrounding wall, courtyard and pylon (in 116 B.C.). Plan and longitudinal section 1:750.

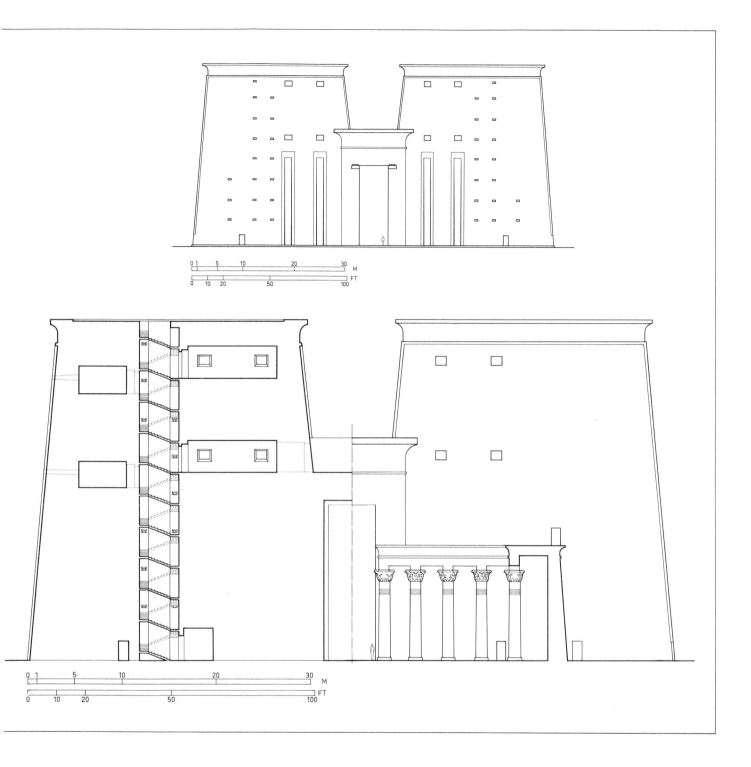

Bien que ne datant que du IIe siècle avant notre ère, **le grand pylône du Temple d'Horus à Edfou** est l'une des plus grandioses réalisations de l'Egypte pharaonique. Ses 36 m de haut se divisent en 10 étages et donnent accès à des chambres. Coupe et élévation côté cour 1:400. Elévation extérieure, avec les rainures destinées aux quatre mâts portant les oriflammes 1:750.

Edfu, Großer Pylon des Horus-Tempels, 2.Jh. v.Chr. Der Bau gehört zu den großartigsten Schöpfungen der Pharaonenzeit. Er ist 36 m hoch und in 10 Stockwerke mit Kammern unterteilt. Fassade mit den Rillen für die vier Fahnenmasten 1:750; Schnitt und Aufriß der Hofseite 1:400.

Great Pylon of the temple of Horus, Edfu. Although dating only from the second century B.C., this is one of the most imposing achievements of Pharaonic architecture. It is 36 m. high, comprises ten storeys, and has rooms inside. Section and elevation (courtyard side) 1:400. Outside elevation, showing the grooves designed to take four flagpoles, 1:750.

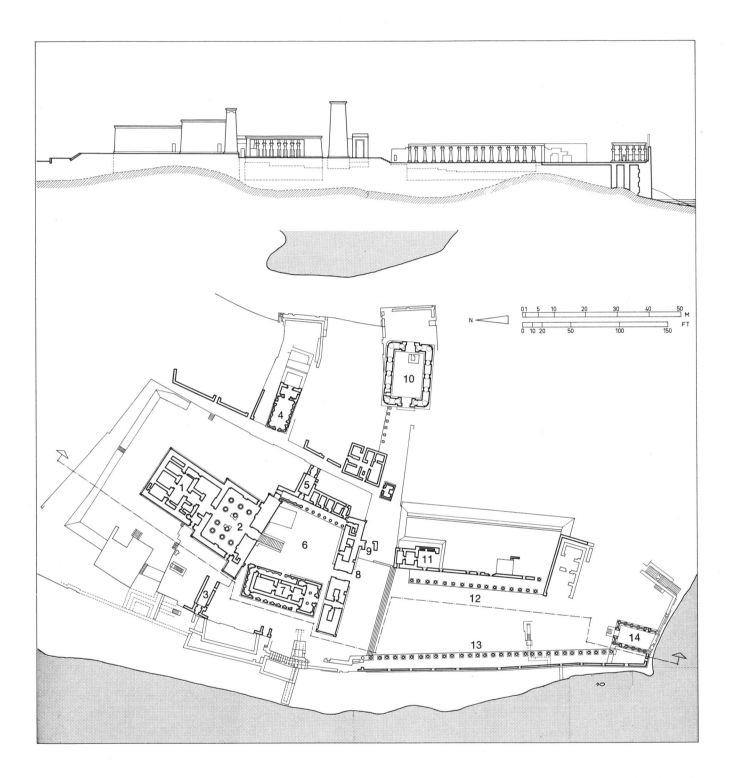

Temple de Philae, dédié à la déesse Isis, datant de la période ptolémaïque, et construit entre le IVᵉ s. avant et le IVᵉ s. apr. J.-C. Elévation latérale et plan 1:1200. 1) Temple d'Isis, 2) Salle hypostyle, 3) Chapelle d'Osiris, 4) Temple d'Hathor, 5) Passage, 6) Cour, 7) Mammisi, 8) Pylône de Nectanébo, 9) Porte de Philadelphe, 10) Kiosque de Trajan, 11) Temple d'Imhotep, 12–13) Portiques, 14) Kiosque.

Philae, Isis-Heiligtum, Ptolemaierzeit (das Heiligtum wurde im 4. Jh. v. Chr. begonnen, die letzten Bauten im 4. Jh. n. Chr. vollendet). Aufriß der Westseite, Lageplan 1:1200: 1) Isis-Tempel, 2) Hypostyl, 3) Osiris-Kapelle, 4) Hathor-Tempel, 5) Durchgang, 6) Hof, 7) Mammisi, 8) Pylon des Nektanebos, 9) Philadelphos-Tor, 10) Trajans-Kiosk, 11) Imhotep-Tempel, 12) u. 13) Säulengänge, 14) Kiosk.

Temple of Philae, dedicated to the goddess Isis, dating from the Ptolemaic period, built between the fourth century B.C. and the fourth century A.D. Side elevation and plan 1:1200. 1) temple of Isis, 2) hypostyle hall, 3) shrine of Osiris, 4) temple of Hathor, 5) passage, 6) courtyard, 7) mammisi, 8) pylon of Nectanebo, 9) Philadelphos gate, 10) kiosk of Trajan, 11) temple of Imhotep, 12–13) porticoes, 14) kiosk.

Du Moyen-Orient aux Mégalithes

Mittlerer Osten und Megalithbauwerke

From Middle East to megaliths

En même temps que l'Egypte, une foule de civilisations, au Moyen-Orient, élaborent des architectures très diverses, les unes fondées sur la brique, les autres sur la pierre de taille. La Mésopotamie, dès l'an 3000 avant notre ère, édifie des temples aux murs redentés, entièrement construits en brique et couverts de toitures plates. Par leur système décoratif, ces sanctuaires s'apparentent aux tombes thinites sur les rives du Nil. C'est au sommet de véritables montagnes artificielles, dominant la cité établie dans la plaine fertile, qu'ils vont bientôt se dresser pour former les ziggourats. Sur son gigantesque soubassement, le temple haut, auquel conduisent des volées d'escaliers ou des rampes hélicoïdales, distingue nettement la ziggourat de la pyramide égyptienne. Cités, fortifications et enceintes sont entièrement bâties en brique crue, avec parfois un revêtement en briques cuites, par endroits vernissées et polychromes.

Parallèlement à l'architecture de limon propre aux plaines alluvionnaires – tant du Tigre et de l'Euphrate que de l'Indus – une architecture mégalithique va progressivement recouvrir toute l'Europe préhistorique, à la fin de l'époque néolithique et à l'âge du bronze. Des réalisations colossales, caractérisées par le recours à d'énormes rochers, à peine dégrossis mais soigneusement appareillés, apparaissent tant à Malte et dans le sud de l'Espagne qu'en Bretagne, en Angleterre et au Danemark au IIIᵉ millénaire. Menhirs, dolmens, alignements, dont le nombre dut avoisiner 50000 en Occident, témoignent de l'existence d'un système religieux commun et de modes de sépulture identiques. Le plus extraordinaire monument de cette époque est l'ensemble circulaire de

Zur gleichen Zeit wie Ägypten bildeten zahlreiche Kulturen des Nahen und Mittleren Ostens eine eigene Architektur aus; einige Völker benutzten dabei die Ziegelbauweise, andere den Steinbau. In Mesopotamien errichtete man seit etwa 3000 v. Chr. Tempel mit Flachdach und durch Vor- und Rücksprünge gegliederten Mauern als reine Ziegelbauten. Das Dekorationssystem dieser Bauten ähnelt dem der Thinitengräber an den Ufern des Nils. Bald darauf erbaute man Tempel auf künstlichen Bergen, hoch über der in der fruchtbaren Ebene angelegten Stadt: So entstand die Zikkurat. Sie unterscheidet sich durch den Hochtempel auf der obersten Plattform, zu dem Treppen oder spiralförmig ansteigende Rampen führen, klar von der ägyptischen Pyramide. Städte, Festungen und Stadtmauern wurden vollständig aus ungebrannten Ziegeln erbaut; verschiedentlich war das Mauerwerk mit gebrannten, manchmal auch farbigen, glasierten Ziegeln verkleidet.

Parallel zu der Lehmarchitektur der Schwemmlandkulturen – am Tigris, Euphrat und Indus – entwickelte sich nach und nach am Ende des Neolithikums und während der Bronzezeit in ganz Europa eine Megalithbauweise. Gewaltige Bauten aus riesigen, kaum zugerichteten, aber sorgfältig gefügten Steinblöcken entstanden im 3. Jahrtausend v. Chr. auf Malta, in Südspanien, der Bretagne, England und Dänemark. Nahezu 50000 Menhire, Dolmen und Megalithheiligtümer bezeugen im Abendland das Vorhandensein eines gemeinsamen religiösen Systems und übereinstimmender Bestattungsweisen. Das erstaunlichste Denkmal aus jener Zeit ist das Rundheiligtum von Stonehenge bei Salisbury

A large number of Middle Eastern civilisations contemporary with ancient Egypt evolved extremely diverse architectures, some based on brick and others on freestone. As early as 3000 B.C. the Mesopotamians were erecting temples with redan walls built entirely of brick and covered with flat roofs. In their scheme of decoration these shrines were related to the Thinite tombs on the banks of the Nile. Soon they were being raised on gigantic bases, veritable artificial mountains (ziggurats) dominating the city in the fertile plain below. It was this raised temple, reached by means of flights of stairs or spiral ramps, that clearly distinguished the ziggurat from the Egyptian pyramid. Cities, fortifications and walls were built entirely of unfired brick with the occasional cladding of fired brick, perhaps glazed or polychromed in places.

Parallel to the mud architecture peculiar to the alluvial plains of the Tigris, Euphrates and Indus rivers a different, megalithic architecture spread gradually throughout prehistoric Europe in the late New Stone Age and during the Bronze Age. Colossal structures characterised by their use of enormous, virtually unhewn but carefully jointed stones were built in Malta and southern Spain as well as in Brittany, England and Denmark during the third millennium. Menhirs, dolmens and alignments, of which there must have been some 50,000 in the West, testify to the existence of a common religious system and identical burial customs. The most extraordinary monument of this period is the circular complex of Stonehenge, near Salisbury, England, which was built between 2700 and 1900 B.C. All this megalithic architecture is based on

Stonehenge, près de Salisbury, construit entre 2700 et 1900 avant notre ère. Toute cette architecture mégalithique repose sur le principe des voûtes en encorbellement et des dalles formant linteaux. La sépulture mycénienne dite «Trésor d'Atrée», qui date du XIVe siècle av. J.-C. constitue l'une de plus parfaites fausses coupoles, avec son appareil à jointoiement horizontal.

Le premier millénaire avant notre ère voit le recours à des formules plus élaborées au Moyen-Orient, avec l'avènement des formes propres à la Perse. Au VIe siècle, à Pasargades, capitale de Cyrus, et surtout à Persépolis, construite par Darius et Xerxès, de vastes salles d'apparat sont érigées au moyen de hautes colonnes de pierre qui supportent une couverture en grande poutraison de bois. Ces immenses salles hypostyles constituent des espaces internes tels que n'en avait connus aucune civilisation antérieure.

(zwischen 2700 und 1900 v.Chr.). Grundelemente der Megalithbauweise sind das Kraggewölbe und als Sturz verwendete Steinplatten. Eine der vollkommensten «falschen», also aus horizontalen Steinlagen gefügten Kuppeln überwölbt das «Schatzhaus des Atreus», ein mykenisches Grab aus dem 14. Jahrhundert v. Chr.

Im 1. Jahrtausend v. Chr. wurden im Mittleren Orient mit dem ersten Auftreten persischer Bauformen kompliziertere Lösungen entwickelt. Im 6. Jahrhundert entstanden in Pasargadai, der Hauptstadt des Kyros, und vor allem in Persepolis, das Darius und Xerxes erbauten, gewaltige prächtige Säle mit weitgespannten Holzdecken über hohen Steinsäulen. Innenräume von solchen Ausmaßen hatte bis dahin noch keine andere Kultur hervorgebracht.

the principle of corbelled vaults and slab lintels. The Mycenaean tomb known as the 'Treasury of Atreus', which dates from the fourteenth century B.C., is one of the most perfect examples of a false dome, with its horizontal jointing.

The first millennium B.C. saw the Middle East advance to more elaborate solutions with the advent of forms peculiar to Persia. In the sixth century, at Pasargadae, Cyrus's capital, and above all at Persepolis, which was built by Darius and Xerxes, vast ceremonial halls were erected with tall stone columns supporting a roof of enormous wooden beams. These immense hypostyles created internal spaces of a size no civilisation had ever known before.

1 Ensemble mégalithique de Stonehenge, détail des trilithes centraux (vers 1800 av. J.-C.).
2 Palais de Cnossos, en Crête, avec une partie des portiques à colonnes, tels qu'ils ont été reconstitués par Evans (XVIe s. av. J.-C.).
3 Frise des «Immortels» à la base de l'Apadana de Persépolis, construite par Darius Ier (vers 520 avant notre ère).

1 Stonehenge, Megalithisches Heiligtum, durch Sturzsteine verbundene Steinblöcke im Zentrum (um 1800 v.Chr.)
2 Knossos (Kreta), Teil der Säulenportiken nach der Rekonstruktion von Sir Arthur Evans (16. Jh. v. Chr.)
3 Persepolis, Fries der «Unsterblichen» am Fuß der Audienzhalle (Apadana) des Palastes (unter Darius I. erbaut, um 520 v.Chr.)

1 Stonehenge megalithic complex, detail of the central triliths (c.1800 B.C.).
2 Palace of Knossos, Crete, showing part of the columned porticoes as reconstructed by Sir Arthur Evans (sixteenth century B.C.).
3 Frieze of 'the Immortals' on the base of the apadana (audience hall), Persepolis, built by Darius I c. 520 B.C.

1

2

3

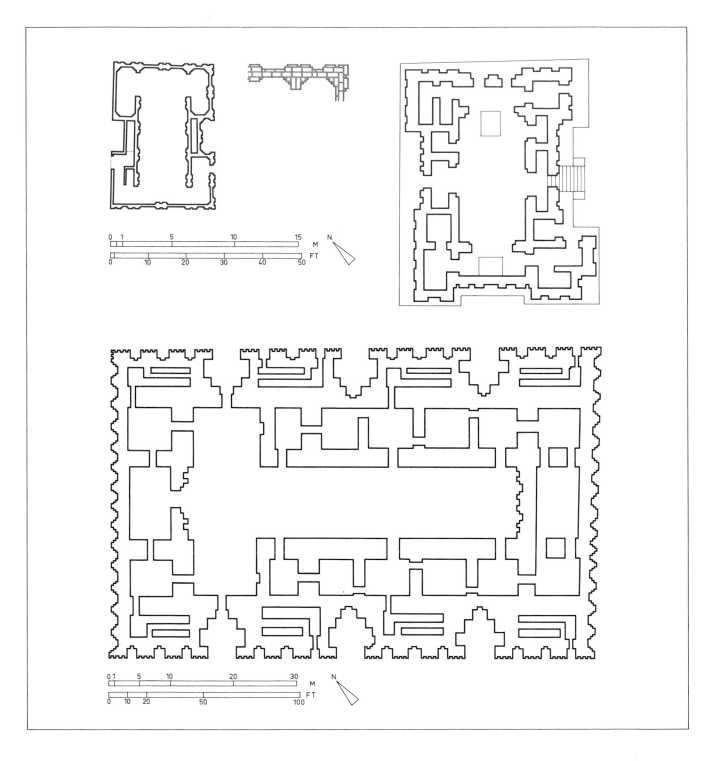

Architecture mésopotamienne: en haut, à gauche, **Temple nord de Tepe Gawra,** milieu du IVᵉ millénaire. Plan 1:300 et détail de l'appareil de brique. A droite, **Temple VII d'Eridu,** antérieur à 3000 avant notre ère. Plan 1:300. En bas, **Temple D à Uruk,** vers 3000 avant notre ère. C'est le plus grand des temples sumériens (50 × 80 m). Plan 1:600.

Mesopotamische Architektur: Oben links: **Tepe Gaura, Nordtempel,** Mitte des 4. Jahrtausends v. Chr. Grundriß 1:300; Detail des Mauerverbandes. Rechts: **Eridu, Tempel VII,** vor 3000 v. Chr. Grundriß 1:300. Unten: **Uruk, Tempel D,** um 3000 v. Chr. Dieser größte sumerische Tempel mißt 50 × 80 m. Grundriß 1:600.

Mesopotamian architecture: Top left, **North temple, Tepe Gawra,** middle of the fourth millennium. Plan 1:300 and detail of the brickwork. Right, **Temple VII, Eridu** before 3000 B.C. Plan 1:300. Below, **Temple D, Uruk,** c. 3000 B.C., largest of the Sumerian temples (80 m. by 50 m.). Plan 1:600.

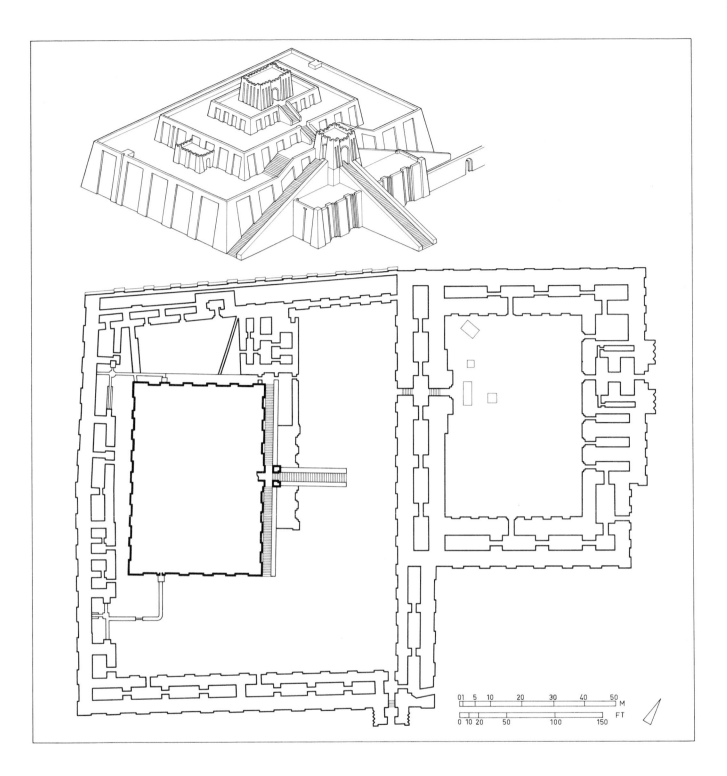

Ziggourat d'Ur, datant de 2100 à 1900 avant notre ère: axonométrie de la ziggourat avec ses quatre étages et son triple escalier d'accès au premier niveau. Plan de la ziggourat avec son «temenos» et sa cour d'entrée traités en murs redentés à la manière des fortifications contemporaines 1:1200. L'ensemble est édifié en brique crue, avec des parements et des sols en brique cuite.

Ur, Zikkurat, 2100–1900 v.Chr. Auf der obersten der drei Terrassen erhebt sich eine Cella; zur untersten führen drei Treppen. Die Mauern der Höfe sind wie beim gleichzeitigen Festungsbau durch Vor- und Rücksprünge gegliedert. Die Anlage ist aus ungebrannten Ziegeln errichtet, Wände und Böden sind mit gebrannten Ziegeln verkleidet. Grundriß mit Temenos und Vorhof 1:1200; Axonometrie.

Ziggurat of Ur, built 2100–1900 B.C. Axonometric projection of the ziggurat showing the four storeys and the triple stairway leading to the first level. Plan of the ziggurat showing the *temenos* and entrance courtyard with their buttressed walls, recalling the fortifications of the period, 1:1200. The building is of unfired brick with facings and floors of fired brick.

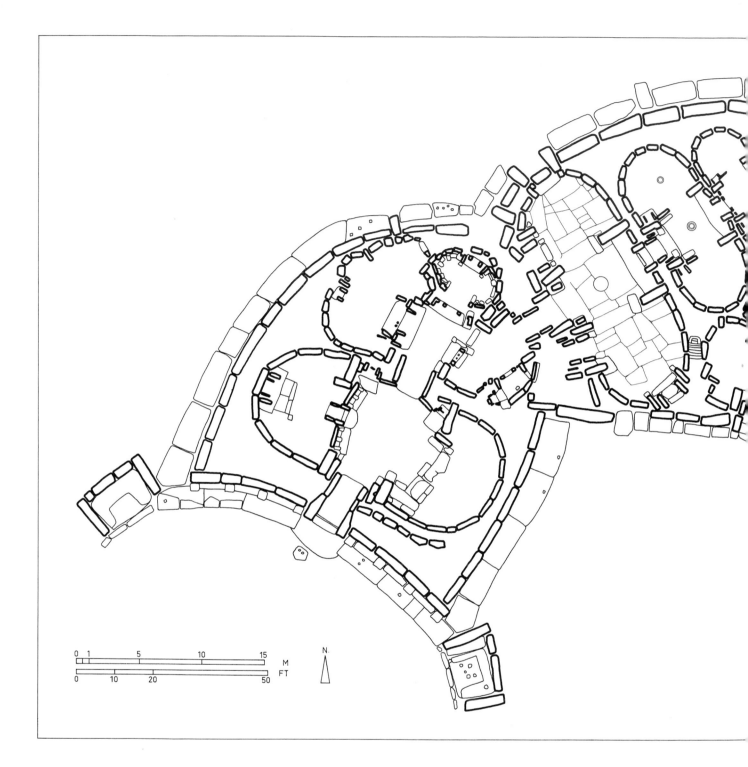

0 1   5   10   15   M
0   10   20   50   FT

N.

Groupe de Sanctuaires mégalithiques de Tarxien, île de Malte, construit entre 2100 et 1900 avant notre ère. Plan reconstitué 1:300. Ce complexe formé de trois sanctuaires est bâti à l'aide de grandes dalles formant parement. Les chambres ovales sont au nombre de deux ou trois pour chaque temple. Le plus ancien édifice est à gauche, le second à l'extrême droite, et le plus récent les réunit.

Tarxien (Malta), Megalith-Tempel, zwischen 2100 und 1900. Die Mauern dieser Tempelgruppe bestehen aus großen Steinplatten. Jeder der drei Tempel ist in zwei oder drei ovale Räume unterteilt. Links liegt der älteste Tempel, ganz rechts der zweite, der jüngste verbindet beide. Grundriß (Rekonstruktion) 1:300.

Tarxien group of megalithic shrines, Malta, built 2100–1900 B.C. Reconstructed plan 1:300. This complex of three shrines was built with the aid of large slabs as facing. There are two or three oval chambers to a temple. The oldest building is on the left, the second oldest on the extreme right, and the most recent lies between them.

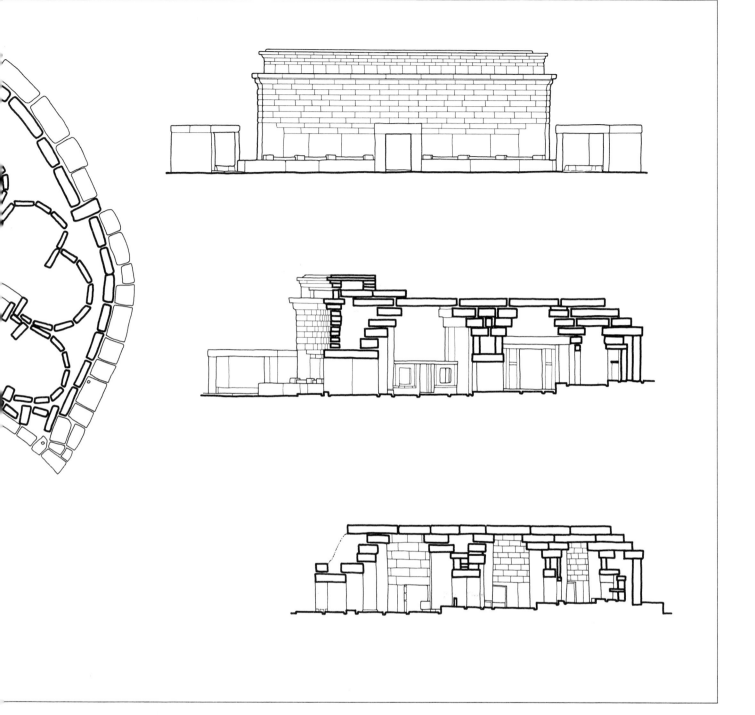

Elévation de la façade et coupe longitudinale du premier **Temple mégalithique de Tarxien, Malte.** Coupe longitudinale du **Temple central** 1:300. Le système de couverture est obtenu au moyen de grandes dalles en encorbellement. On remarque que le niveau du sol s'élève de l'entrée jusqu'au «saint des saints».

Tarxien (Malta), Megalith-Tempel. Die Bauten sind mit großen, überkragenden Steinplatten gedeckt. Der Boden steigt vom Eingang zum «Allerheiligsten» hin an. Fassadenaufriß und Längsschnitt des ältesten Tempels 1:300; Längsschnitt des zentralen, jüngsten Tempels 1:300.

Façade elevation and longitudinal section of the first **megalithic temple, Tarxien** (Malta); longitudinal section of the **middle temple** 1:300. The roofs are done with large corbelled slabs. Note how the floor level rises from the entrance towards the 'holy of holies'.

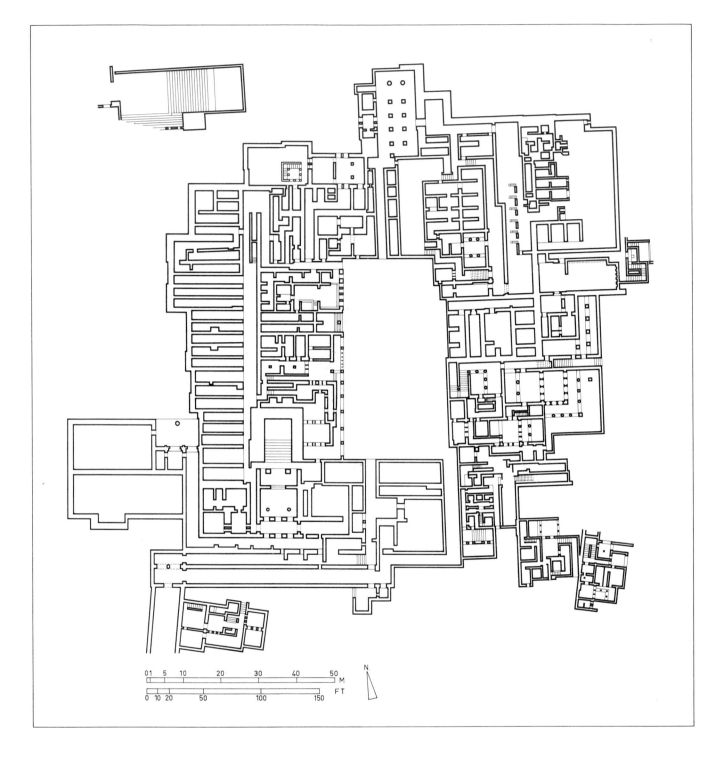

0 1 5 10   20   30   40   50 M

0 10 20   50   100   150 FT

N

Grand Palais de Cnossos, Crête, état aux XVIe et XVe siècles, avant sa destruction qui eut lieu vers 1400 av. J.-C. Plan d'ensemble 1:1000. Autour d'une vaste cour de 55 m de long sur 30 m de large s'organisent les différents espaces: appartements, salle du trône, mégaron, portiques et magasins, selon des circulations complexes qui ont donné naissance à la légende du labyrinthe.

Knossos (Kreta), Palast. Die Räume sind um einen 55 m langen und 30 m breiten zentralen Hof angeordnet: Kulträume, Wohnräume, Megaron, Magazine und ein kompliziertes System von Gängen, das vermutlich die Labyrinth-Sage entstehen ließ. Grundriß (Zustand im 16. und 15. Jh. v. Chr., vor der Zerstörung um 1400 v. Chr.) 1:1000.

Great Palace of Knossos, Crete, as it was in the sixteenth and fifteenth centuries prior to its destruction c.1400 B.C. Overall plan 1:1000. The vast courtyard measured 55 m. by 30 m., and around it were arranged the different elements—apartments, throne room, megaron, porticoes and store-rooms—making for the complex plan that gave rise to the labyrinth legend.

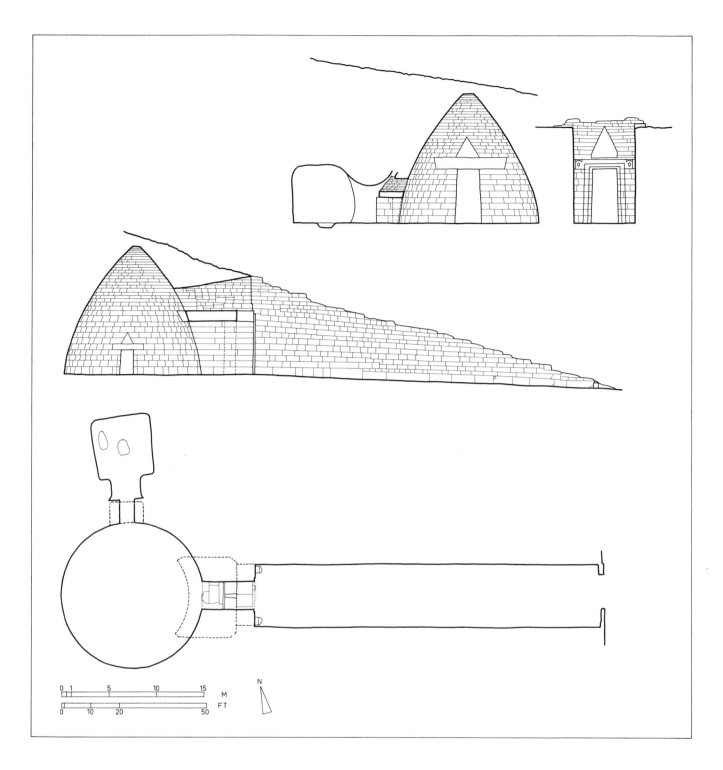

0 1   5   10   15   M
0   10   20   50   FT

N

Tombe mycénienne dite Trésor d'Atrée à Mycènes, datant d'environ 1325 av. J.-C. La chambre souterraine, circulaire et voûtée en encorbellement, est précédée d'un couloir à ciel ouvert ou dromos. Une chambre latérale est creusée directement dans le roc. Coupe transversale de la chambre voûtée et élévation de la porte, coupe longitudinale et plan 1:400.

Mykene, Schatzhaus des Atreus, um 1325 v. Chr. Der unterirdische Tholos dieses Kuppelgrabes ist als Kraggewölbe aus sorgfältig versetzten Quadern errichtet, die seitliche Grabkammer ist direkt in den Felsen geschnitten. Ein ungedeckter Gang (Dromos) führt zu dem Bau. Querschnitt durch Tholos und Kammer, Querschnitt durch den Dromos mit Portalaufriß, Längsschnitt, Grundriß 1:400.

Mycenaean tomb (the 'Treasury of Atreus'), Mycenae, built c. 1325 B.C. An unroofed corridor or *dromos* leads to the round, corbel-vaulted underground chamber. A side room is hollowed directly out of the rock. Cross section of the vaulted chamber and elevation of the gateway, longitudinal section and plan 1:400.

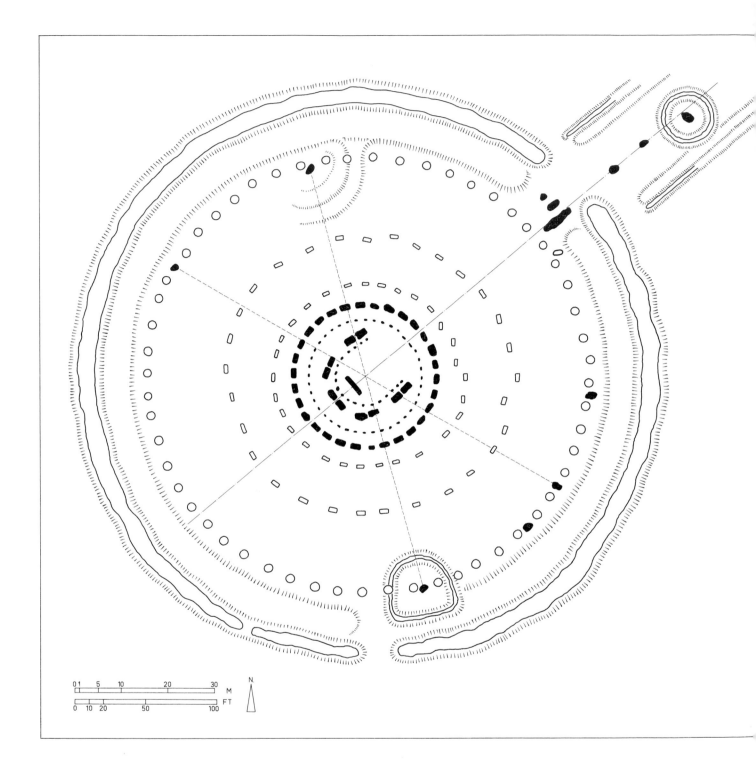

Ensemble mégalithique de Stonehenge (Grande-Bretagne). Plan d'ensemble 1:800. Le diamètre extérieur du fossé périphérique est de l'ordre de 125 m. En haut à droite, l'amorce d'une allée de 548 m de long. Le fossé et les trous qui le bordent à l'intérieur pourraient remonter au milieu du IIIᵉ millénaire, soit à la fin du néolithique. Le sanctuaire mégalithique central date de 1800 à 1500 av. J.-C.

Stonehenge (England), Megalithisches Heiligtum. Die Anlage, zu der eine 548 m lange Allee führt, hat, einschließlich des Grabens, einen Durchmesser von ca. 125 m. Der Graben und der innen umlaufende Kreis von Löchern könnten aus der Mitte des 3. Jahrtausends v. Chr. stammen; das zentrale megalithische Heiligtum entstand zwischen 1800 und 1500 v. Chr. Grundriß 1:800.

Stonehenge megalithic complex, England. Overall plan 1:800. The outer diameter of the peripheral ditch is about 125 m. At top right is the beginning of an avenue 548 m. long; the ditch and the holes just inside it may go back to the middle of the third millennium, i.e. the end of the New Stone Age. The central megalithic shrine dates from 1800–1500 B.C.

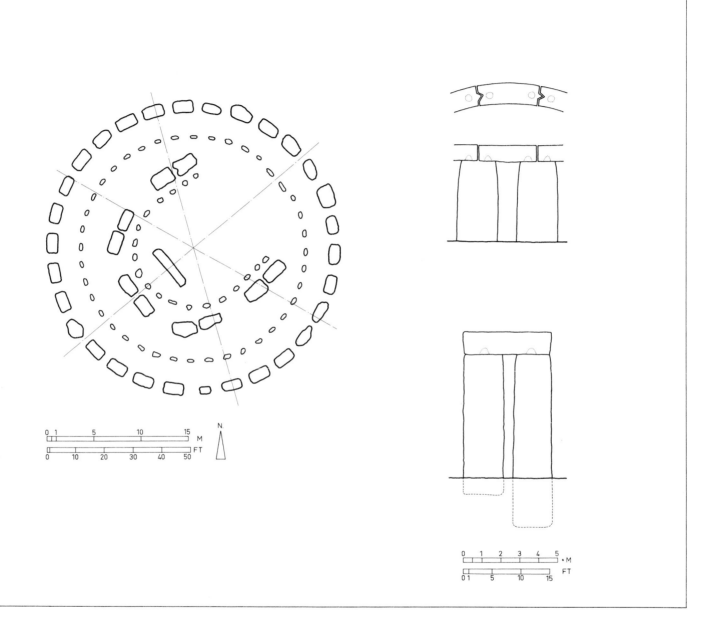

0 1   5   10   15
└┴┴┴┴┴┴┴┴┴┴┴┴┴┴┴┴┘ M

0   10   20   30   40   50
└┴┴┴┴┴┴┴┴┴┴┴┴┴┴┘ FT

N.

0 1 2 3 4 5
└┴┴┴┴┴┴┴┴┴┘ • M

0 1   5   10   15
└┴┴┴┴┴┴┘ FT

Détail du Sanctuaire mégalithique de Stonehenge 1:400. Le premier cercle de pierres dressées mesure 31 m de diamètre. Les blocs, hauts de plus de 4 m, sont réunis entre eux, deux à deux, par des blocs horizontaux formant linteaux. Des pierres plus petites forment un deuxième cercle à l'intérieur duquel se dressent cinq trilithes monumentaux de 6,70 m de haut, disposés en fer à cheval. Détails 1:200.

Stonehenge (England), Megalithisches Heiligtum, Zentrum und Details. Der äußere Kreis hat einen Durchmesser von 31 m, seine über 4 m hohen Steinblöcke sind durch Sturzbalken verbunden. Kleinere Steinblöcke bilden einen inneren Kreis, innerhalb dessen 5 Paare 6,70 m hoher, durch einen Sturz verbundener Steine ein zur Allee offenes Hufeisen bilden. Grundriß 1:400; Details 1:200.

Detail of megalithic shrine, Stonehenge, 1:400. The first circle of upright stones measures 31 m. across. The stones are more than 4 m. high and are linked by other stones forming lintels. Smaller stones form a second circle, inside which five monumental triliths measuring 6.7 m. in height stand in a horseshoe-shaped arrangement. Details 1:200.

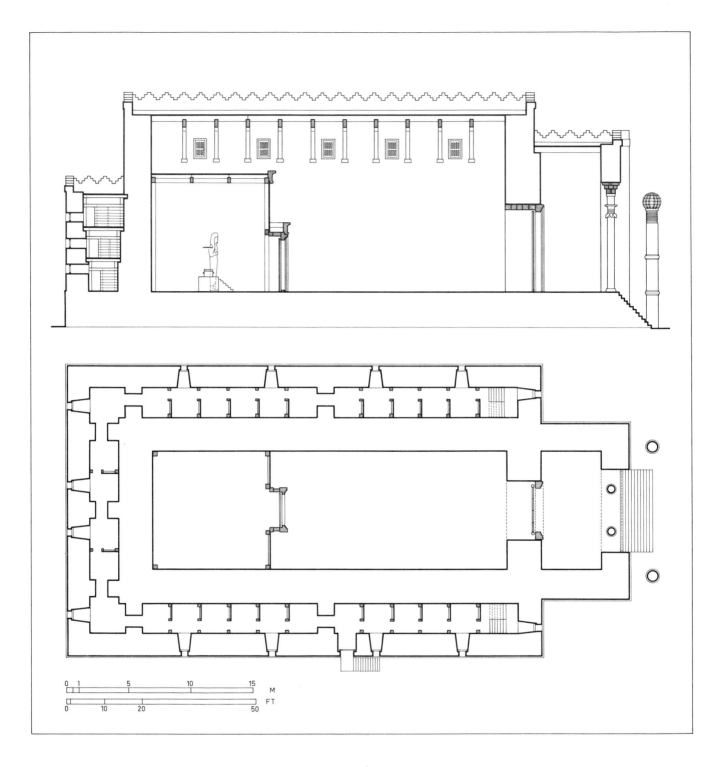

Temple de Salomon, à Jérusalem, vers 950 av. J.-C. Reconstitution par Th. Busink, coupe longitudinale et plan 1:300. Edifié en pierre, avec couverture supportée par une charpente en cèdre, cet édifice s'apparente au plan des temples assyriens du IIIᵉ millénaire. Le parvis à colonnes précédant la porte monumentale livre accès au sanctuaire dans lequel se trouve le naos ou «saint des saints».

Jerusalem, Tempel Salomonis, um 950 v. Chr.; Rekonstruktion von Th. Busink. Der Tempel ist ein fensterloser Steinbau, an dessen Rückwand das Allerheiligste liegt. Das Dach ruht auf einem Gebälk aus Zedernholz. Dem Portal mit mächtigen Flügeltüren ist eine Vorhalle mit säulengetragenem Eingang vorgelegt. Längsschnitt und Grundriß 1:300.

Solomon's Temple, Jerusalem, c. 950 B.C., as reconstructed by Th. Busink. Longitudinal section and plan 1:300. Built of stone with a roof supported by a cedar frame, this building was related in plan to third-millennium Assyrian temples. The columned courtyard in front of the monumental entrance gave access to the shrine containing the naos or 'holy of holies'.

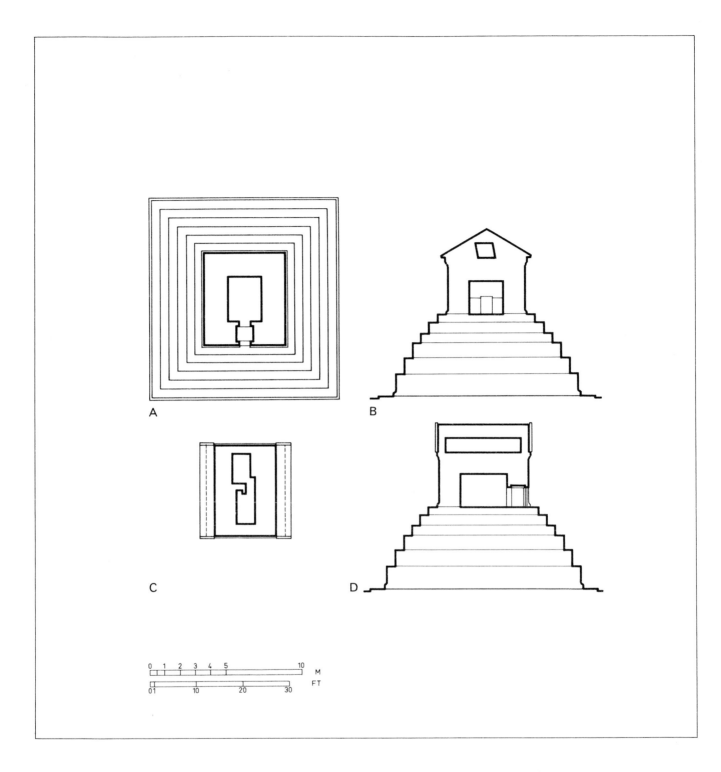

A   B

C   D

| 0 | 1 | 2 | 3 | 4 | 5 | | 10 | M |

| 0 1 | | 10 | | 20 | | 30 | FT |

Tombeau de Cyrus à Pasargades (Iran) vers 530 avant notre ère. Construite en appareil colossal, sur un socle à six degrés, la chambre funéraire, couverte d'un toit à double pente, s'apparente aux tombes de Gordion. Plan, coupe transversale, plan de la chambre de décharge et coupe longitudinale 1:250.

Pasargadai (Iran), Grab des Kyros, um 530 v. Chr. Die Grabkammer auf sechsstufigem Unterbau ist aus mächtigen Steinquadern errichtet und mit einem Satteldach gedeckt. Sie ähnelt den Gräbern von Gordion. Grundriß, Querschnitt, Plan der Entlastungskammer und Längsschnitt 1:250.

Tomb of Cyrus, Pasargadae (Iran), c. 530 B.C. Built of massive masonry on a six-stepped base, the burial chamber with its double-pitched roof recalls the tombs of Gordium. Plan, cross section, plan of the lumber room and longitudinal section 1:250.

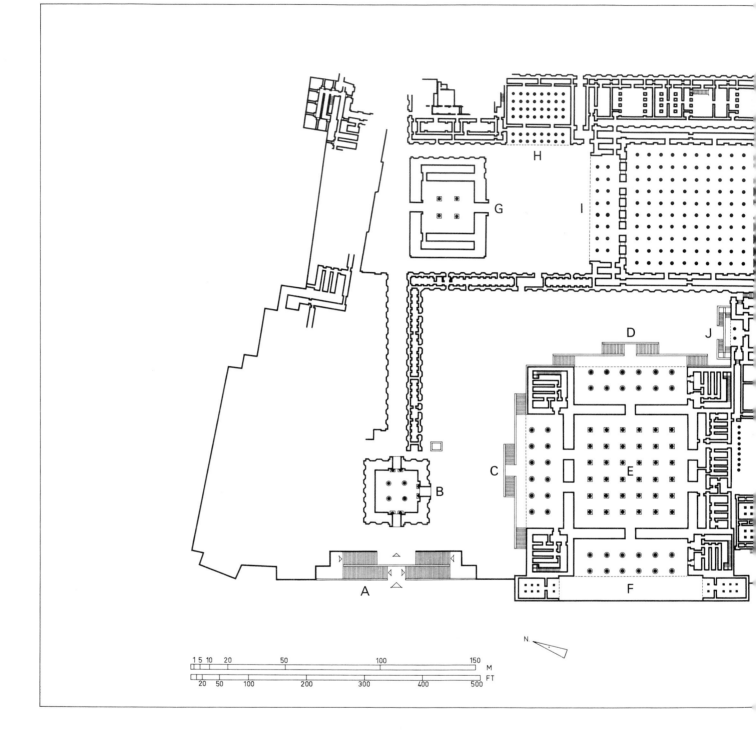

Palais de Persépolis (Iran), construit entre 518 et 330 av. J.-C. Plan d'ensemble 1:2000. C'est l'épanouissement de la grande architecture d'espaces internes, réalisée au moyen de salles hypostyles dont les colonnes supportent des couvertures en charpente. Ainsi la salle aux 36 colonnes de l'Apadana, hautes de 21 m, forme un hall de 3600 m².

Persepolis (Iran), Palast, zwischen 518 und 330 v. Chr. Die für diesen Palasttypus charakteristischen gewaltigen Innenräume sind als großartige vielsäulige, holzgedeckte Säle ausgebildet. Die Audienzhalle (Apadana) mit 36 je 21 m hohen Säulen bedeckt eine Fläche von 3600 m².

Palace of Persepolis (Iran), built 518 to 330 B.C. Overall plan 1:2000. This is the high point of a classic architecture of interior spaces, achieved by means of hypostyle halls with columns supporting wooden-framed roofs. The apadana (audience hall), for example, with 36 columns each standing 21 m. high, has a floor area of 3600 m².

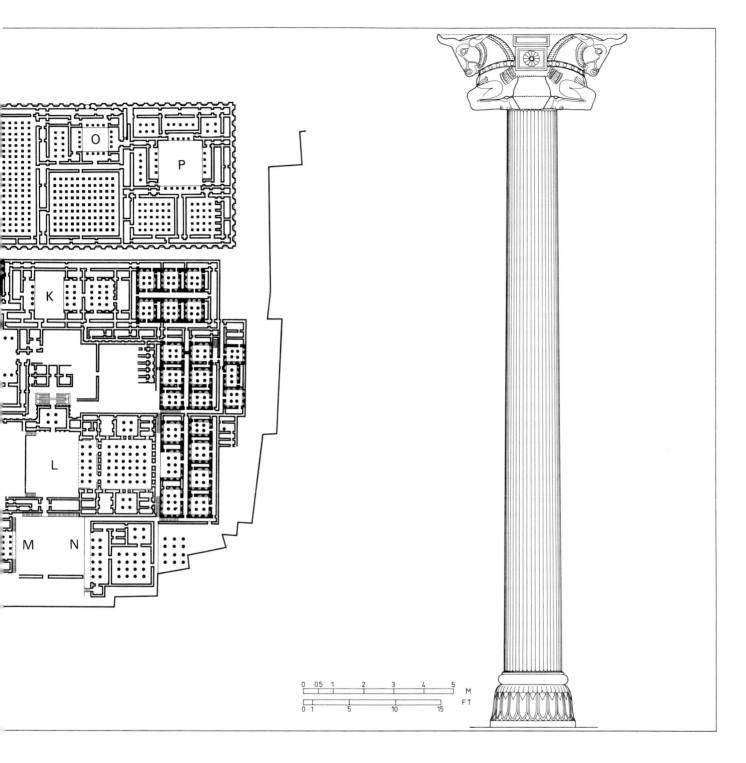

Persépolis: A) Grand escalier, B) Porte de Xerxès, C) et D) Escaliers de l'Apadana, E) Salle de l'Apadana, F) Portique en terrasse, G) Porte inachevée, H) Salle aux 32 colonnes, I) Portique et Hall aux 100 colonnes, J) Escaliers du Tripylon, K) Palais, L) Palais de Xerxès, M) Palais de Darius, N) Palais d'Artaxerxès III, O) Cour, P) Trésorerie. Colonne de l'Apadana 1:120.

Persepolis, Palast: A) große Treppe, B) Tor des Xerxes, C) und D) Treppen des Apadana, E) Audienzhalle (Apadana), F) Terrassenportikus, G) unvollendetes Tor, H) Saal der 32 Säulen, I) Portikus und Thronsaal, J) Aufgänge des Tripylons, K) Palast, L) Palast des Xerxes, M) Palast des Darius, N) Palast Artaxerxes' III., O) Hof, P) Schatzhaus. Grundriß 1:2000; Säule der Audienzhalle 1:120.

Persepolis. A) great stairway, B) gate of Xerxes, C & D) apadana stairways, E) apadana, F) terrace portico, G) unfinished gate, H) Hall of the 32 Columns, I) portico and Hall of the 100 Columns, J) tripylon stairways, K) palace, L) palace of Xerxes, M) palace of Darius, N) palace of Artaxerxes III, O) courtyard, P) treasury. Apadana column 1:120.

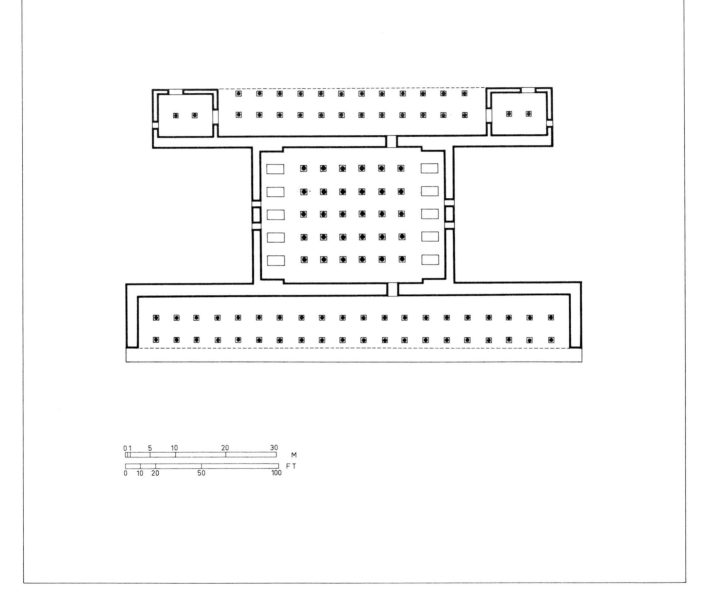

0 1 5 10   20   30
                              M
0 10 20   50   100 F T

Palais résidentiel de Cyrus II à Pasargades, construit vers 550 av. J.-C. 1:750. La formule du grand palais achéménide voit ici le jour: la salle centrale, une hypostyle de 30 colonnes couvrant 900 m², est flanquée de deux portiques à double rangée de colonnes, celui du sud s'étendant sur près de 80 m de long. L'association des fûts de pierre et des couvertures de bois est originale en Perse.

Pasargadai, Residenz Kyros' II., zentraler Saal, um 550 v.Chr. Hier entstand der Typus des Achämenidenpalastes. Der zentrale Saal mit 30 Säulen hat eine Grundfläche von 900 m². Er ist beidseits von zwei doppelreihigen Säulenportiken flankiert, der südliche ist fast 80 m lang. Die Verbindung von Steinsäulen mit einem Holzdach ist für Persien charakteristisch. Grundriß 1:750.

Palace residence of Cyrus II, Pasargadae, built *c.*550 B.C., 1:750. The classic Achaemenid palace formula: the central hall, a thirty-column hypostyle of 900 m², is flanked by two porticoes, each with a double row of columns, the southern one nearly 80 m. long. The combination of stone columns and wooden roofs was original for Persia.

Monde grec   Griechenland   Greece

Aux origines, comme en Egypte, l'habitation grecque est faite de torchis, la pierre étant réservée aux édifices sacrés et publics. D'ailleurs l'architecture grecque est essentiellement celle de la «polis», de la cité, en tant que centre religieux, politique et commercial enserré dans des fortifications et des murailles. L'agora, avec ses bâtiments publics, est le lieu de réunion des citoyens: temples des dieux protecteurs, portiques et marchés, auxquels s'ajouteront – souvent hors du centre proprement dit – le théâtre, le gymnase et les monuments funéraires. Dès l'époque hellénistique, on trouve des réalisations de prestige, destinées aux fastes du prince: palais et résidences d'apparat, mausolées grandioses, etc.

Au VIIe siècle avant notre ère, les principes essentiels du portique, de la colonnade péristyle, des colonnades intérieures, sont établis. Au début du VIe siècle, des édifices aux vastes proportions marquent une maîtrise des formes et des techniques de la pierre. Les différents styles (dorique, ionique, puis corinthien) sont nés, ainsi qu'en témoigne la «basilique» de Paestum. Le Ve siècle connaît l'épanouissement de l'architecture classique, faite de géométrie, de clarté et de volumétrie plus que d'espaces internes proprement dits: la cella des sanctuaires restant toujours très limitée n'est pas destinée aux rassemblements de foules; elle n'abrite que la statue de la divinité. On mentionnera le temple d'Aphaia à Egine, le temple de Héra à Paestum, le temple de Bassae, le Parthénon et le temple d'Athéna Nikè sur l'Acropole d'Athènes.

Avec le IVe siècle, les cités d'Asie Mineure connaissent un grand développement urbanistique (Priène, Milet) en même temps que s'affirme une archi-

Wie in Ägypten wurden auch in Griechenland Wohnbauten zunächst in Lehmbauweise errichtet; für Sakral- und Kommunalbauten ging man früh zum Steinbau über.

Die griechische Architektur ist im wesentlichen eine Architektur der «Polis», des von Mauern und Festungsanlagen umgrenzten religiösen, politischen und kommerziellen Zentrums. Die Agora war der Versammlungsort der Bürger, dort lagen die öffentlichen Bauten, die Tempel der Schutzgötter, Säulen- und Markthallen; dazu kamen – oft außerhalb des engeren Stadtzentrums – Theater, Gymnasium und Grabbauten, seit hellenistischer Zeit auch Prunkbauten der Herrscher: Paläste, stattliche Residenzen und großartige Mausoleen.

Die wichtigsten Elemente der griechischen Architektur – Vorhalle, Säulengang und Säulenhalle – waren im 7. Jahrhundert v. Ch. voll ausgebildet. Die großen Bauten vom Anfang des 6. Jahrhunderts zeigen bereits die völlige Beherrschung von Form und Technik des Steinbaus. Die verschiedenen Stile (dorisch, ionisch, später korinthisch) entwickeln sich. Das 5. Jahrhundert ist die große Zeit der klassischen Architektur, einer geometrisch klaren, von den Massen stärker als von den Innenräumen bestimmten Baukunst; denn die Cella des Tempels blieb stets klein, sie war nicht Versammlungsort, sondern beherbergte das Kultbild. Beispiele sind der Aphaia-Tempel auf Ägina, der Hera-Tempel in Paestum, der Apollon-Tempel von Bassai und der Nike-Tempel auf der Athener Akropolis.

Im 4. Jahrhundert blühten die großgriechischen Städte in Kleinasien auf (Priene und Milet); gleichzeitig entwickelte sich eine interessante Festungs-

Originally Greek domestic architecture, like Egyptian, used mud, stone being reserved for sacred and public buildings. Greek architecture is essentially that of the *polis*, the city as religious, political and commercial centre surrounded by walls and fortifications. The agora with its public buildings was the citizens' meeting-place, with the temples of the tutelary deities, porticoes, and markets. Later, often away from the centre proper, came the theatre, the gymnasium, and various funerary monuments. By the Hellenistic period we find prestige buildings—palaces, luxurious residences, grandiose mausoleums, and so on—being erected by more ostentatious rulers.

The key elements of portico, peristyle colonnade and interior colonnade had already emerged by the seventh century B.C. At the beginning of the sixth century various buildings of colossal proportions indicate that their architects were now masters of the forms and techniques of building in stone. This was when the different styles (Doric, Ionic, and then Corinthian) were born, as we see from the Basilica at Paestum. The fifth century was the heyday of classical Greek architecture—an architecture of volume and geometrical clarity rather than of interior spaces as such; the cella of the temple was invariably very small, being designed not for congregational assembly but purely to house the statue of the god. Among the finest examples are the temple of Aphaea on Aegina, the temple of Hera at Paestum, the temple of Bassae, and the Parthenon and the temple of Athena Nike on the Athens Acropolis.

From the fourth century the cities of Asia Minor began to expand enor-

tecture militaire d'un réel intérêt, dotée de murailles flanquées de tours à créneaux, de poternes et de donjons (Aegosthène, Eleuthères, Messène). C'est aussi l'époque où s'érigent les grands théâtres à ciel ouvert, adossés à leur colline dans laquelle est creusée la cavea (théâtres de Dionysos à Athènes, de Dodone, d'Epidaure). Jusque-là, la technique est fondée sur le jeu des supports et des architraves. Avec le IIIe siècle débute une diversification grâce à l'apport encore timide de la voûte (Nécromantéion d'Ephyra) et par l'enrichissement des programmes (grands ensembles de Pergame) qui annoncent l'art romain. Le gigantisme des temples (Didyméion de 120 m de long, avec colonnes ioniques de 19 m de haut) s'accompagne de vastes réalisations d'édilité (Stoa d'Attale, Athènes).

architektur: Stadtmauern mit zinnengekrönten Wehrtürmen, Ausfallpforten, Festungstürme (Aigosthena, Eleutherai, Messene). In dieser Zeit entstanden auch die großen Theater mit ihren unter freiem Himmel in Berghänge eingetieften Zuschauerrängen (Dionysos-Theater in Athen, Dodona, Epidaurus). Bis dahin waren Stütze und Gebälk die bestimmenden Elemente. Eine größere Vielfalt brachte das 3. Jahrhundert mit der vorerst zaghaften Einführung des Gewölbes (Nekromanteion in Ephyra) und durch Erweiterung der Bauprogramme (Pergamon), die bereits die römische Kunst ankündigen. Neben gigantischen Tempeln (Didymaion: 120 m Länge, Säulenhöhe ca. 19 m) errichtete man von nun an auch umfangreiche städtische Bauten (Stoa des Attalos in Athen, 135 v. Chr.).

mously (Priene, Miletus), and at the same time a really interesting military architecture emerged, featuring walls flanked by crenellated towers, posterns, and keeps (Aegosthena, Eleutherai, Messene). This is also the period of the great open-air theatres, built in the side of a hill from which the *cavea* or audience part was hollowed out (the theatre of Dionysus at Athens, and those at Dodona and Epidaurus). At this stage building technology was based on supports and architraves. The third century saw the beginnings of greater diversification with the use—tentative at first—of the vault (the Necromanteion at Ephyra) and with the more ambitious programmes (the great complexes at Pergamon) that already anticipated Roman architecture. Gigantic temples were built (the Didymeion is 120 m. long, its Ionic columns 19 m. high) as well as vast administrative buildings (the Stoa of Attalos, Athens, dating from *c.* 135).

1 Les colonnes fortement galbées de la «basilique» de Paestum (Italie), construite au troisième quart du VIe s. av. J.-C.
2 Le petit temple ionique d'Athéna Nikè, sur l'Acropole d'Athènes (425 av. J.-C.).
3 Détail de la cavéa du théâtre d'Epidaure, construit dans le dernier quart du IVe s. av. J.-C.
4 Donjon de la forteresse béotienne d'Aegosthène, sur le golfe de Corinthe (IVe s. av. J.-C.).

1 Paestum, Basilika, Säulen mit starker Entasis (3. Viertel 6. Jh. v. Chr.)
2 Athen, Akropolis, der ionische Tempel der Athena Nike (425 v. Chr.)
3 Epidaurus, Theater, Detail der Cavea (letztes Viertel 4. Jh. v. Chr.)
4 Aigosthena (Golf von Korinth), Festungsturm der böotischen Festung (4. Jh. v. Chr.)

1 The columns of the Basilica, Paestum, showing their pronounced entasis (third quarter of the sixth century B.C.).
2 The small Ionic temple of Athena Nike on the Acropolis, Athens (425 B.C.).
3 Detail of the *cavea* of Epidaurus theatre (last quarter of the fourth century B.C.).
4 Keep of the Boeotian fortress, Aegosthena, in the Gulf of Corinth (fourth century B.C.).

1

2

3

4

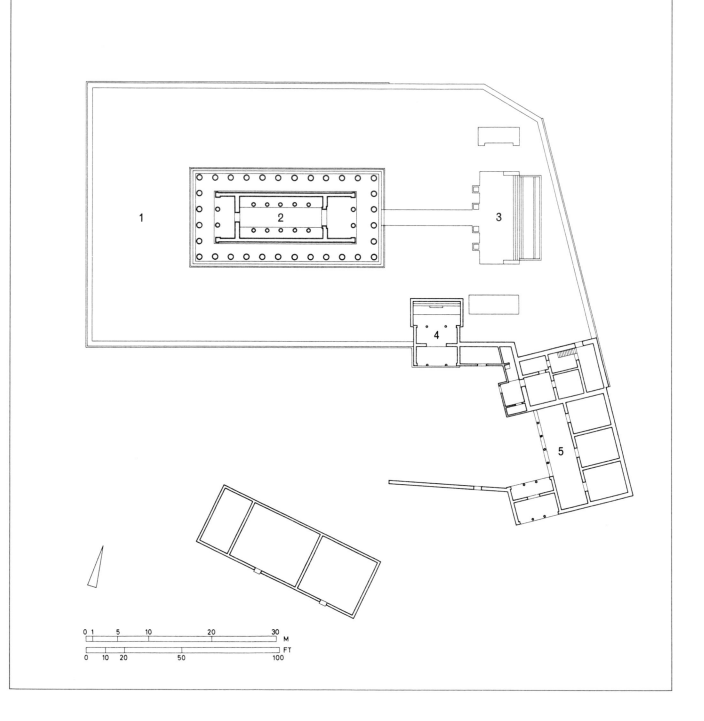

Temple d'Aphaia à Egine, vers 500 av. J.-C. Plan de situation 1:600. 1) Temenos, 2) Temple d'Aphaia, 3) Autel, 4) Propylées, 5) Logement des prêtres. Début de la formule classique du temple dorique périptère. Cella à double colonnade superposée supportant le plafond. L'espace interne exigu (12 × 6 m) contenait la statue de la divinité.

Ägina, Aphaia-Heiligtum, um 500 v. Chr. 1) Temenos, 2) Aphaia-Tempel, 3) Altar, 4) Propyläen, 5) Priesterwohnungen. Bei dieser ersten reinen Ausformung des dorischen Peripteraltempels tragen zwei Reihen in zwei Rängen übereinandergeordneter Säulen die Decke der Cella, in deren kleinem innerem Raum (12 × 6 m) die Statue der Gottheit stand. Lageplan 1:600.

Temple of Aphaea, Aegina, c.500 B.C. Site plan 1:600. 1) temenos, 2) temple of Aphaea, 3) altar, 4) propylaea, 5) priests' quarters. In this early example of the classic Doric peripteral temple formula the cella has a double superposed colonnade supporting the ceiling. The relatively small interior (12 m. by 6 m.) contained the statue of the deity.

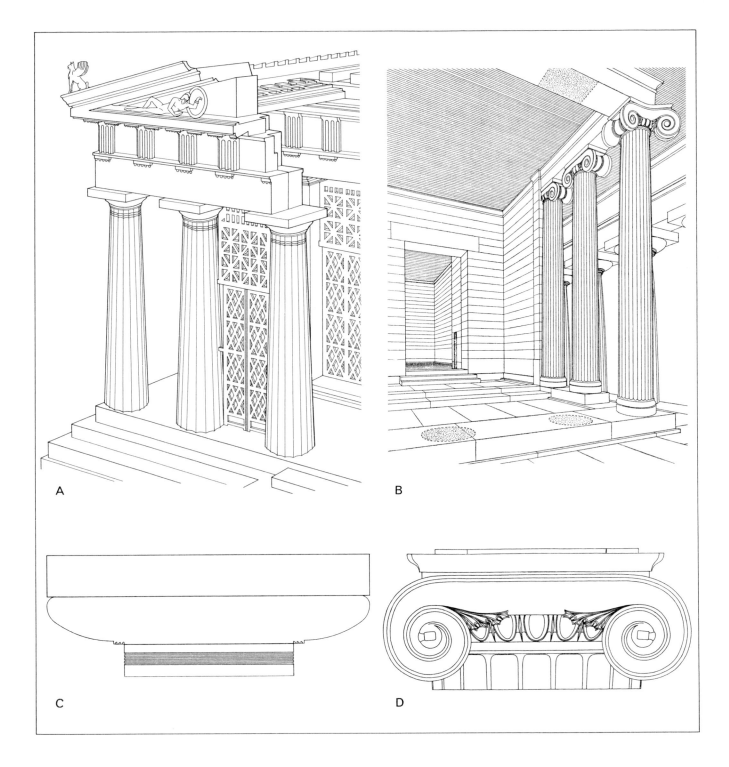

A   B

C   D

Le temple grec : A) Structure dorique du Temple d'Aphaia à Egine (500 av. J.-C.). Sur un revêtement de stuc, une polychromie vigoureuse animait les formes architectoniques. B) Mélange des ordres dorique et ionique au Temple d'Athéna de Paestum (vers 500 av. J.-C.). C) Chapiteau dorique vers la fin du VIe. D) Chapiteau ionique avec ses volutes et rangs d'oves.

Der griechische Tempel: A) Dorischer Tempel; die kräftigen Farben des bemalten Stucks heben die Architekturformen hervor: Ägina, Aphaia-Tempel, um 500 v. Chr. B) Verbindung dorischer und ionischer Elemente: Paestum, Athena-Tempel, um 500 v. Chr. C) Dorisches Kapitell, Ende 6. Jh. v. Chr. D) Ionisches Kapitell mit Voluten und Eierstab.

The Greek temple: A) Doric structure of the Temple of Aphaea, Aegina (c. 500 B.C.). Vigorous polychrome work on a stucco rendering enlivens the architectural forms. B) A blend of Doric and Ionic orders in the Temple of Athena, Paestum (c. 500 B.C.). C) Doric capital, late sixth century. D) Ionic capital with its volutes and ovolo mouldings.

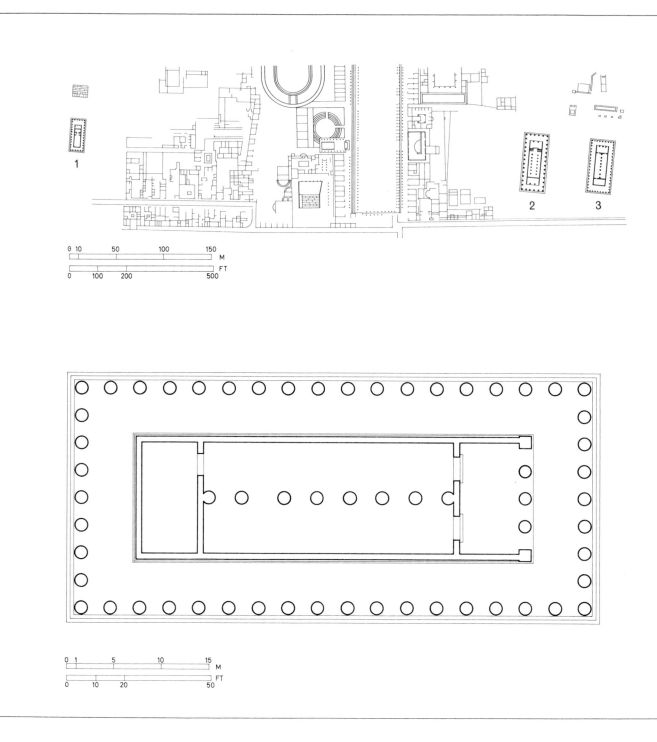

Paestum, plan général 1:4000. 1) Temple d'Athéna, 2) Temple de Héra (dit de Poséidon), 3) La «basilique». **La «basilique» de Paestum,** plan 1:400. Construit dans le troisième quart du VIe siècle, c'est le plus ancien temple de Paestum. Fait exceptionnel, il présente un nombre impair de colonnes en façade, de même que la cella possède une rangée de supports sur l'axe de symétrie.

Oben: **Paestum.** 1) Athena-Tempel, 2) Hera-Tempel (sog. Poseidon-Tempel), 3) Basilika. Lageplan 1:4000. Unten: **Paestum, Basilika,** drittes Viertel 6.Jh. Die Basilika ist der älteste Tempel in Paestum. Die Säulenreihe in der Symmetrieachse der Cella und die ungerade Säulenzahl an den Schmalseiten des Tempels sind ungewöhnlich. Grundriß 1:400.

Paestum (Italy). Overall plan 1:4000. 1) temple of Athena, 2) temple of Hera (temple of Poseidon), 3) Basilica. **Basilica, Paestum.** Plan 1:400. Built in the third quarter of the sixth century B.C., this is the oldest temple at Paestum. It is unusual in having an odd number of façade columns; also the cella has a row of supports along the axis of symmetry.

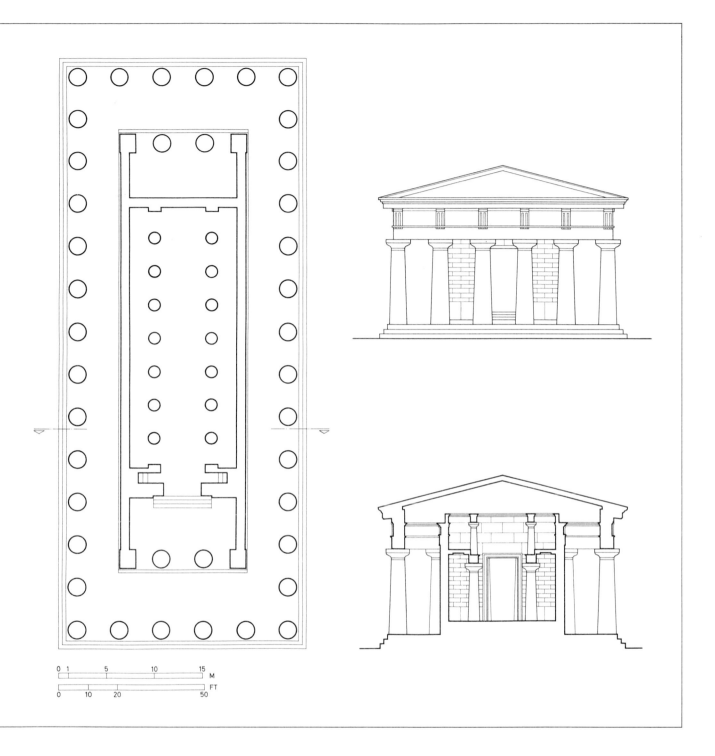

Temple de Héra Argiva, à Paestum, édifié entre 448 et 430 av. J.-C. Plan, élévation de la façade et coupe transversale montrant la double colonnade superposée de la cella 1:400. C'est le type du temple hexastyle classique dont les mesures sont ici 24,31 × 59,93 m avec 6 × 14 colonnes. L'espace intérieur de la cella ne dépasse pas 28 × 11 m.

Paestum, Tempel der Hera Argiva, 448 bis 430 v. Chr. Der Tempel ist ein klassischer Hexastylos (Peripteros mit sechssäuliger Front) mit 14 Säulen an den Langseiten; er mißt 24,31 × 59,93 m, das Innere der Cella 28 × 11 m. Grundriß, Aufriß der Fassade und Querschnitt mit den übereinanderstehenden Säulen der Cella 1:400.

Temple of Hera Argiva, Paestum, built between 448 and 430 B.C. Plan, façade elevation and cross section showing the double colonnade of the cella 1:400. A prime example of the classic hexastyle temple, it has 6 × 14 columns and measures 24.31 m. by 59.93 m. The interior of the cella is no more than 28 m. by 11 m.

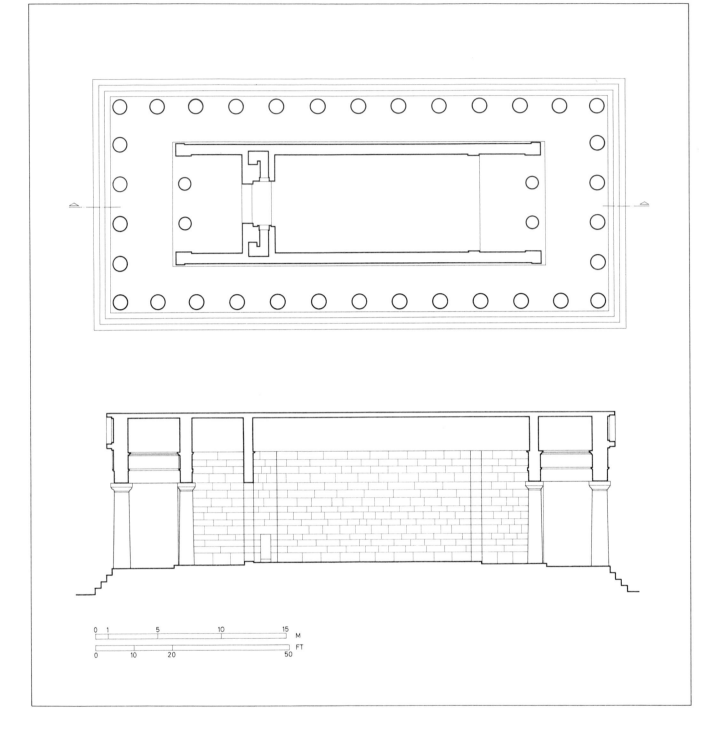

0 1   5   10   15   M
0   10   20   50   FT

Temple de la Concorde, à Agrigente, construit vers 430 av. J.-C. Plan et coupe longitudinale 1:300. C'est le plus récent des temples d'Agrigente. Hexastyle (6 × 13 colonnes), il a pour dimensions sur le stylobate 16,92 × 39,42 m. La cella ne présente pas de support interne. Exemple du style dorique à l'époque classique.

Agrigent, Tempel der Concordia, um 430 v. Chr. Dieser jüngste Tempel von Agrigent ist ein Hexastylos mit 13 Säulen an den Langseiten. Er mißt oberhalb des Stylobats 16,92 × 39,42 m. Die Cella hat keine innere Säulenstellung. Der Tempel ist ein Beispiel des dorischen Stils der klassischen Zeit. Grundriß und Längsschnitt 1:300.

Temple of Concord, Agrigentum, built *c.*430 B.C. Plan and longitudinal section 1:300. The most recent of the Agrigentum temples, this hexastyle (6 × 13 columns) exemplifies the classical period of the Doric style. It measures 16.92 m. by 39.42 m. on its stylobate, and the cella has no internal supports.

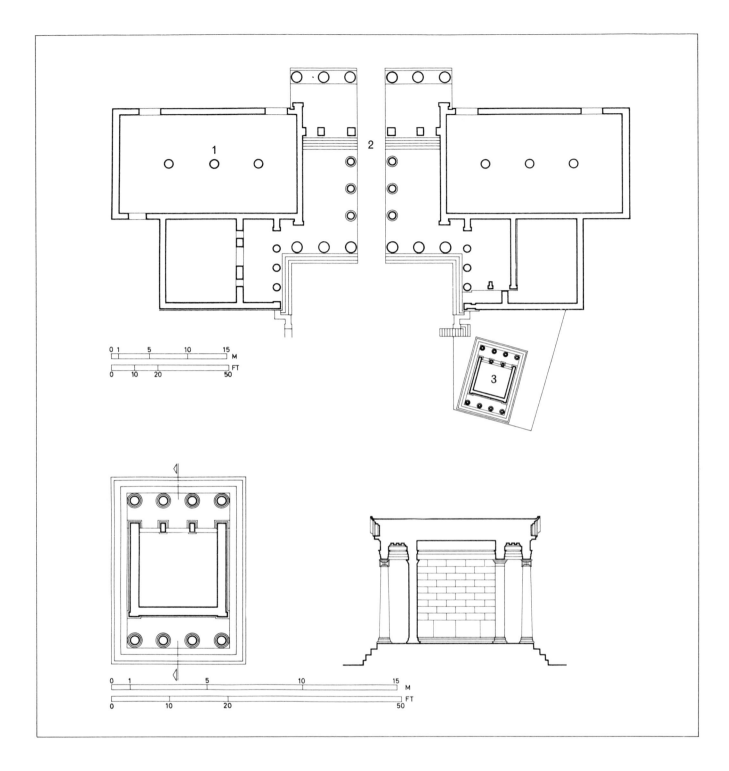

Les Propylées, sur l'Acropole d'Athènes, avec situation du **Temple d'Athéna Nikè.** Plan 1:500. Edifiées dès 437 av. J.-C. par Mnésiklès, elles sont précédées par la figure de proue du temple de Nikè. 1) Pinacothèque, 2) Propylées, 3) Temple d'Athéna Nikè. Plan et coupe longitudinale du temple ionique d'Athéna Nikè 1:200.

Athen, Akropolis, Propyläen und **Tempel der Athena Nike,** 437 v. Chr. begonnen. Den unter Mnesikles errichteten Propyläen ist einer Galionsfigur ähnlich der ionische Nike-Tempel vorgelagert. 1) Pinakothek, 2) Propyläen, 3) Tempel der Athena Nike. Lageplan 1:500; Grundriß und Längsschnitt des Nike-Tempels 1:200.

Propylaea on the Athens Acropolis, and site of the **Temple of Athena Nike.** Plan 1:500. Begun in 437 B.C. by Mnesicles, they are preceded by the 'figure-head' of the Nike temple. 1) Pinacotheca, 2) Propylaea, 3) temple of Athena Nike. Plan and longitudinal section of the Ionic temple of Athena Nike 1:200.

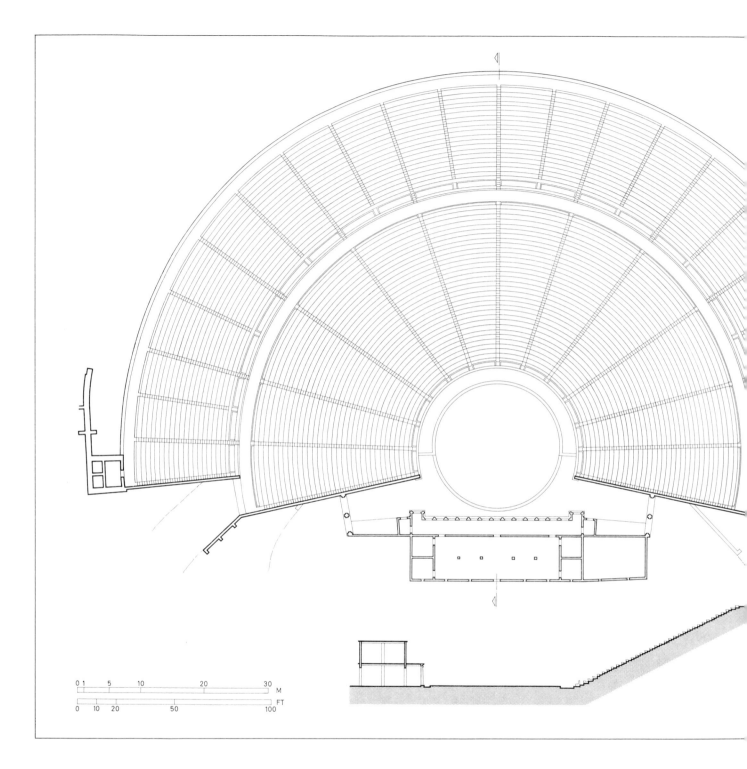

0 1   5   10   20   30
                                        M
0 10 20   50   100
                                        FT

Théâtre d'Epidaure, construit dans le dernier quart du IVᵉ s. av. J.-C. Plan général et coupe 1:600. Par l'harmonie de sa cavéa, son inscription dans le paysage où l'hémicycle est creusé à flanc de colline et la qualité de son accoustique, le théâtre d'Epidaure compte parmi les réussites du IVᵉ siècle. L'orchestra circulaire crée la liaison avec les bâtiments de scène.

Epidauros, Theater, letztes Viertel 4.Jh. v.Chr. Das Theater gehört dank seiner harmonisch in die Landschaft eingefügten, in den Hang eingeschnittenen Cavea und der ausgezeichneten Akustik zu den vollendetsten Bauten des 4.Jh. Zwischen dem Zuschauerraum und der Skene liegt die kreisrunde Orchestra. Grundriß und Schnitt 1:600.

Theatre, Epidaurus, built during the last quarter of the fourth century B.C. Overall plan and section 1:600. The harmony of its *cavea*, the way it 'sits' in the landscape with the semicircle hollowed out of the side of a hill, and the quality of its acoustics make the Epidaurus theatre one of the great architectural achievements of the fourth century. The circular orchestra provides the link with the stage buildings.

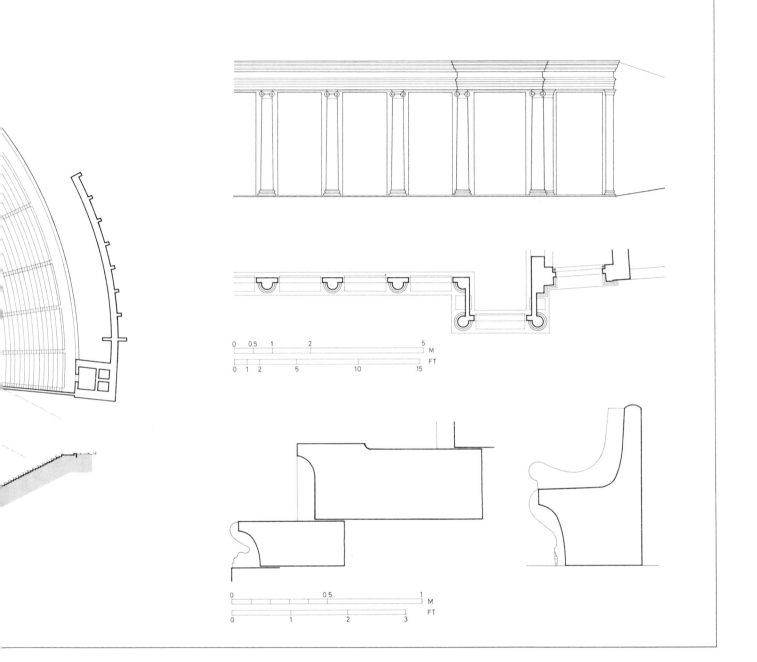

Détails du proskénion, ou mur de scène d'**Epidaure.** Elévation et plan 1:100, et détails des sièges 1:20. Le problème de la liaison entre la cavéa et le mur de scène a toujours été imparfaitement résolu dans l'architecture grecque. Il faudra attendre la période romaine pour qu'il trouve sa solution.

Epidauros, Proskenion des Theaters. Im griechischen Theaterbau ist die Verbindung zwischen Theatron und Skene immer etwas unbefriedigend geblieben. Das Problem wurde erst in römischer Zeit gelöst. Aufriß und Grundriß (Details) 1:100; Zuschauersitze 1:20.

Details of the *proskenion* or stage wall at **Epidaurus.** Elevation and plan 1:100; details of the seating 1:20. Greek architects never really solved the problem of the link between *cavea* and stage wall; it was not until the Roman period that a satisfactory solution was found.

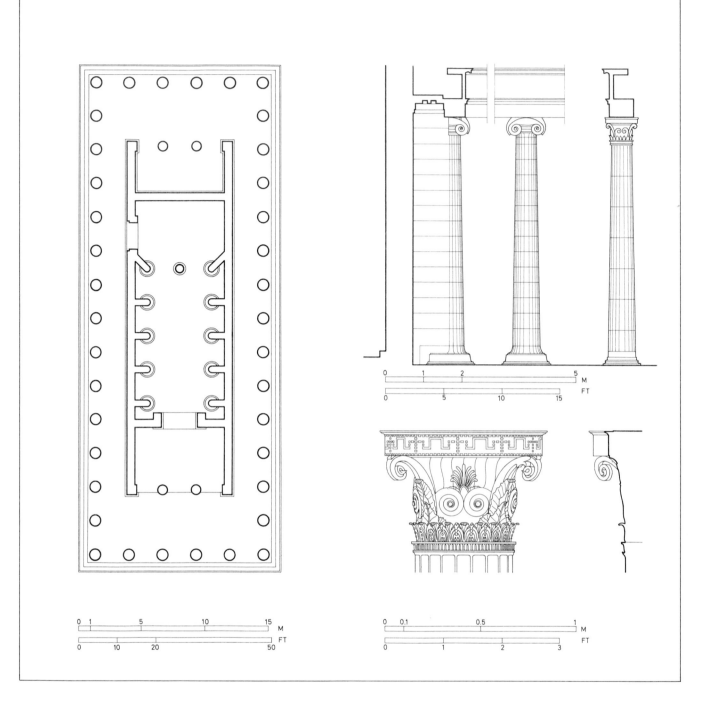

Temple d'Apollon à Bassae, Arcadie, construit vers 425 par Ictinos, architecte du Parthénon. Plan 1:300. Le temple hexastyle présente une curieuse disposition de l'aménagement de la cella, avec ses demi-colonnes ioniques engagées qui contrastent avec les fûts doriques du péristyle (6 × 15 colonnes) et sa colonne centrale à chapiteau corinthien. Détails des ordres intérieurs 1:100 et 1:20.

Bassai (Arkadien), Apollon-Tempel, um 425 v.Chr. Der von Iktinos, dem Erbauer des Parthenon, errichtete Hexastylos zeichnet sich durch die ionischen Halbsäulen in der Cella aus. Die Säulen der Ringhalle dagegen sind dorisch, die Mittelsäule der Cella hat ein korinthisches Kapitell. Grundriß 1:300; Details der Innensäulen 1:100 und 1:20.

Temple of Apollo, Bassae (Arcadia), built *c.*425 B.C. by Ictinos, the architect of the Parthenon. Plan 1:300. This hexastyle temple has an interesting cella design with its engaged Ionic half-columns, contrasting with the Doric columns (6 × 15) of the peristyle, and its middle column with Corinthian capital. Details of interior orders 1:100 and 1:20.

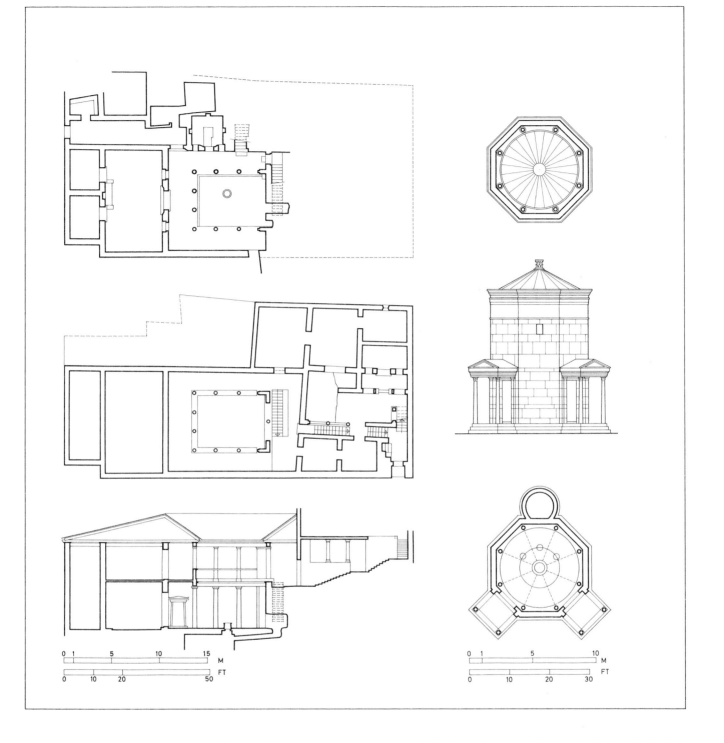

Maison dite de l'Hermès, à Délos, période hellénistique (IIIᵉ au IIᵉ s. avant notre ère). Plans du rez-de-chaussée et du premier étage, coupe longitudinale 1:400. Une cour à portique forme le centre de l'édifice. A droite, **Tour des Vents, à Athènes,** ou tour d'Andronikos. Plafond, élévation et plan 1:300. Il s'agit d'une horloge à eau d'époque hellénistique tardive.

Links: **Delos, Haus des Hermes,** hellenistisch, 3.–2. Jh. v. Chr. Der Bau ist um einen inneren Hof mit Säulenumgang angelegt. Grundriß des Erd- und des Obergeschosses und Längsschnitt 1:400. Rechts: **Athen, Turm der Winde** (Turm des Andronikos). Im Innern des späthellenistischen Turms gibt eine Wasseruhr die Zeit an. Dach, Aufriß und Grundriß 1:300.

'House of Hermes', Delos, Hellenistic period (third to second century B.C.). Ground floor and first floor plans, longitudinal section 1:400. A courtyard with a portico forms the centre of the building. Right, the **Tower of the Winds, Athens,** also known as the Andronicus Tower, a water clock of the late Hellenistic period. Ceiling, elevation and plan 1:300.

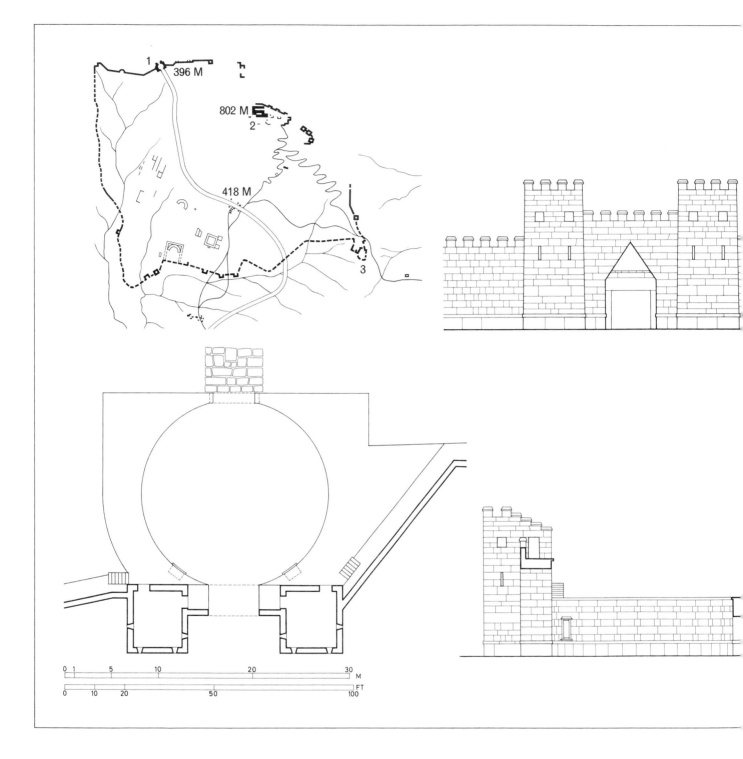

Architecture militaire: **Enceinte fortifiée de Messène** (Péloponèse), construite dans la première moitié du IVᵉ s. avant notre ère par Epaminondas. Situation de l'enceinte, magnifique muraille longue de 6 km: 1) Porte d'Arcadie, 2) Acropole du Mont Ithôme, 3) Porte de Laconie. **Porte d'Arcadie.** Plan, élévation et coupe 1:400.

Festungsbaukunst: **Messene (Peloponnes),** 1. Hälfte 4. Jh. Die großartige 6 km lange Stadtmauer wurde unter Epaminondas angelegt. Lageplan: 1) Arkadisches Tor, 2) Akropolis auf dem Ithome, 3) Lakonisches Tor; Grundriß, Aufriß und Längsschnitt des Arkadischen Tores 1:400.

Military architecture: **Fortified wall of Messene** (Peloponnesus), built by Epaminondas in the first half of the fourth century B.C. Site of the fortifications, comprising a magnificent wall 6 km. in length: 1) Arcadian gate, 2) Acropolis of Mount Ithome, 3) Laconian gate. Arcadian gate, plan, elevation and section 1:400.

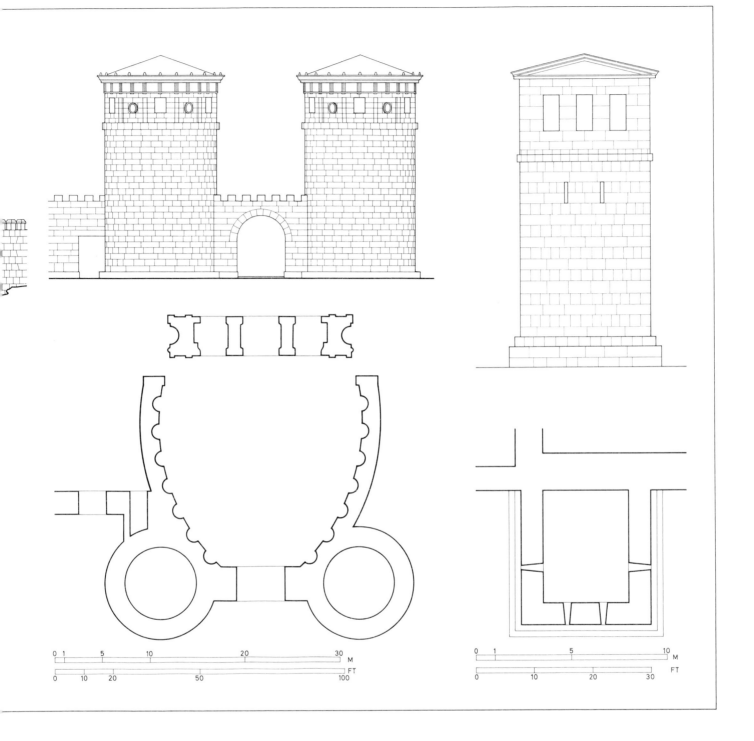

Porte monumentale de Pergè (Pamphylie), époque hellénistique. Elévation et plan 1:400. Cette énorme construction fortifiée de la ville basse précéda un arc triomphal d'époque romaine. A droite, **Tour carrée de l'enceinte de Pergè.** Elévation et plan 1:200. L'assise en saillie correspond au plancher de la salle supérieure, aménagée pour le tir des machines de guerre à travers les baies.

Links: **Perge (Pamphylien), Stadttor,** hellenistische Zeit. Das gewaltige Befestigungstor der Unterstadt ist einem römischen Triumphbogen vorgelagert. Aufriß und Grundriß 1:400. Rechts: **Perge, quadratischer Turm der Stadtmauer.** Das Gesims läuft in Fußbodenhöhe des oberen Saales um, durch dessen Schießscharten mit weitreichenden Schleudergeschützen geschossen werden konnte. Aufriß und Grundriß 1:200.

Monumental gate, Perga (Pamphylia), Hellenistic period. Elevation and plan 1:400. This enormous fortified structure in the lower town stands in front of a Roman triumphal arch. Right, **Square wall tower, Perga.** Elevation and plan 1:200. The projecting course corresponds to the floor of the room above, designed for firing war machines through the bays.

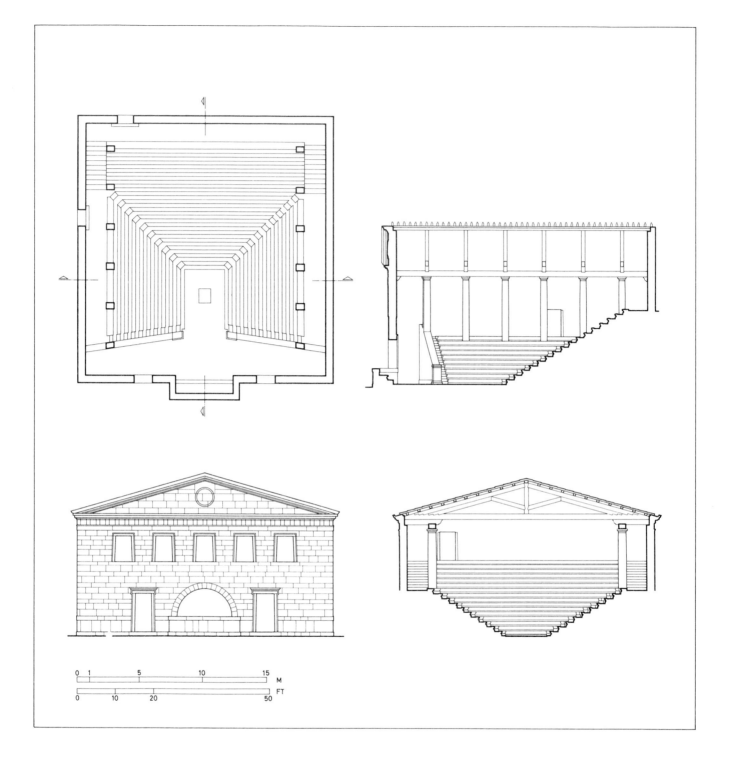

Bouleutérion de Priène, IVᵉ s. avant notre ère. Plan, élévation, coupe longitudinale et coupe transversale restituées avec les colonnes et les fermes de couverture 1:300. Cette salle du Conseil, avec ses gradins disposés sur trois côtés pour recevoir les membres de l'assemblée, revêt un style austère et dépouillée.

Priene, Buleuterion, 4. Jh. v. Chr. Der Stil des Ratssaales mit den auf drei Seiten ansteigenden Sitzreihen für die Ratsmitglieder ist streng und nüchtern. Grundriß und Aufriß; Längs- und Querschnitt mit Säulen und Dachstuhl (Rekonstruktion) 1:300.

Bouleuterion, Priene, fourth century B.C. Plan, elevation, longitudinal section and cross section, reconstructed with the columns and roof trusses 1:300. This council chamber, with tiered seats on three sides for the members of the Assembly, was built in a simple, austere style.

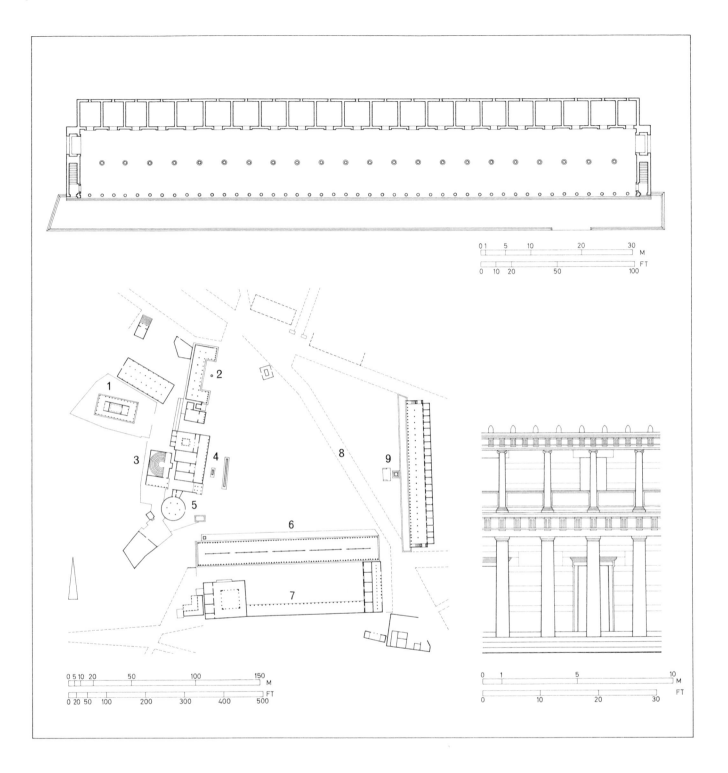

Stoa d'Attale à Athènes, construite vers 135 av. J.-C. par Attale III Philométor, dernier roi de Pergame. Plan du portique, rez-de-chaussée 1:750, plan de situation de l'agora hellénistique 1:3000. 1) Temple d'Héphaistos, 2) Stoa de Zeus, 3) Bouleutérion, 4) Métrôon, 5) Tholos, 6) Stoa centrale, 7) Stoa sud, 8) Voie des Panathénées, 9) Stoa d'Attale. Détail de la façace à double niveau 1:200.

Athen, Stoa des Attalos, um 135 v. Chr. unter Attalos III. Philometor, dem letzten König von Pergamon. Grundriß des Erdgeschosses 1:750; Lageplan der Agora 1:3000: 1) Hephaistos-Tempel, 2) Stoa des Zeus, 3) Buleuterion, 4) Metroon, 5) Tholos, 6) Mittlere Stoa, 7) Südliche Stoa, 8) Panathenäen-Straße, 9) Stoa des Attalos; Fassadenaufriß der Stoa des Attalos (Detail) 1:200.

Stoa of Attalos, Athens, built c. 135 B.C. by Attalos III Philometor, the last king of Pergamon. Plan of the portico, ground floor, 1:750; site plan of the Hellenistic agora 1:3000. 1) temple of Hephaistos, 2) stoa of Zeus, 3) bouleuterion, 4) metroon, 5) tholos, 6) middle stoa, 7) south stoa, 8) street of the Panathenians, 9) stoa of Attalos. Detail of the façade on two levels 1:200.

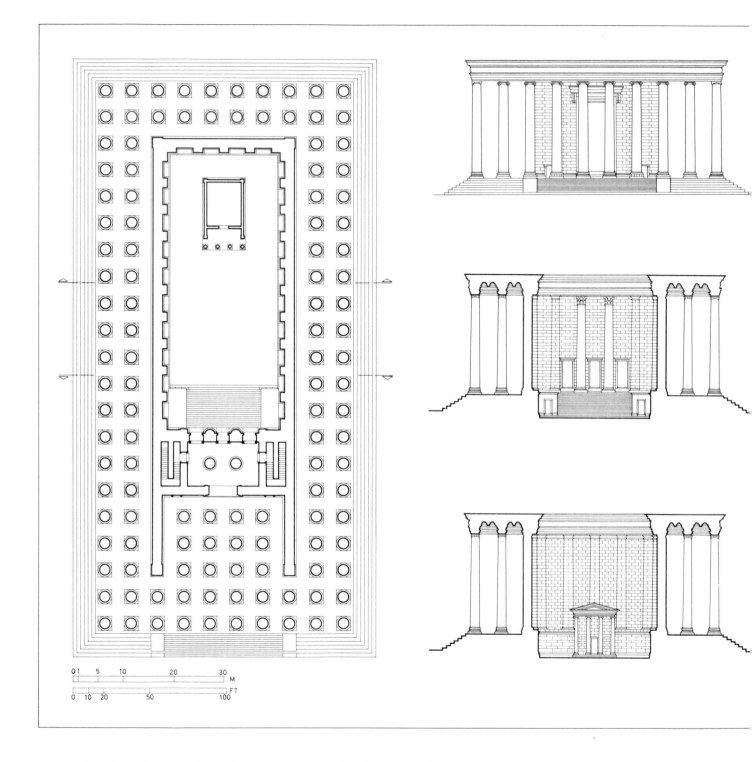

Temple d'Apollon à Didyme, datant du milieu du IIIᵉ s. av. J.-C. Plan, élévation et coupes transversales 1:750. Immense sanctuaire ionique à double colonnade périptère et à cour centrale à ciel ouvert contenant l'adyton, Didyme était un centre oraculaire célèbre en Asie Mineure. Les colonnes du péristyle culminent à 19,70 m.

Didyma, Apollon-Tempel, Mitte des 3.Jh.v.Chr. Das Orakel von Didyma war in ganz Kleinasien berühmt. In dem Innenhof des gewaltigen ionischen Dipteros steht ein kleiner Tempel für das Kultbild. Die Säulen der doppelten Ringhalle sind 19,70 m hoch. Grundriß, Aufriß und Querschnitte 1:750.

Temple of Apollo, Didyma, middle of the third century B.C. Elevation and cross sections 1:750. A vast Ionic shrine with a double peripteral colonnade and an open central courtyard containing the *adyton*. The peristyle columns are 19.7 m. high. Didyma was the site of one of the most famous oracles of Asia Minor.

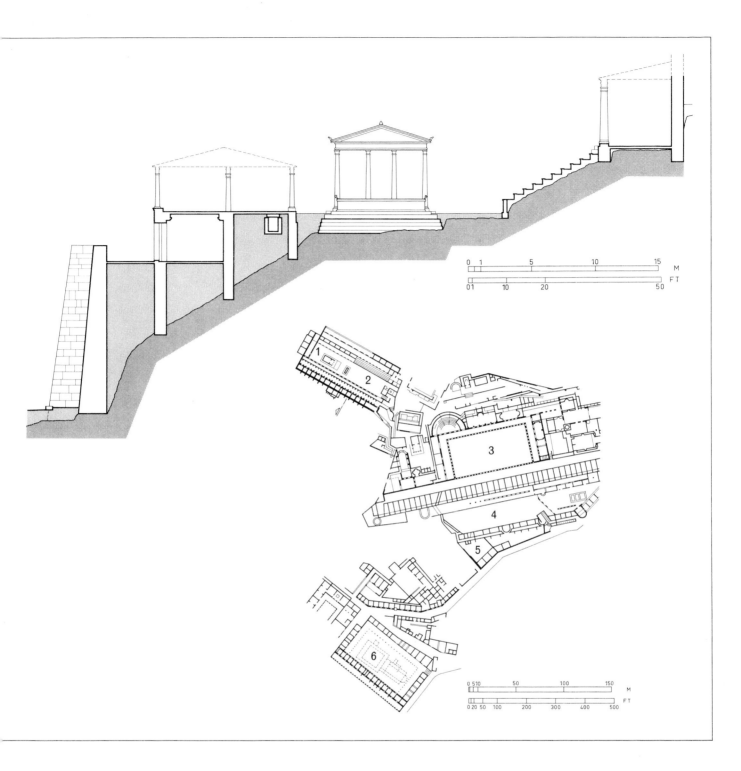

Agora de Pergame, datant de la fin de l'époque hellénistique (IIᵉ s. av. J.-C.). Coupe des stoai de la terrasse de Déméter, env. 1:300. Plan général de l'Agora de Pergame, 1) Temple de Déméter, 2) Terrasse de Déméter, 3) Gymnase supérieur, 4) Gymnase intermédiaire, 5) Gymnase inférieur, 6) Marché inférieur. Env. 1:4000. Les stoai modèlent le paysage et leurs fondations s'enfoncent jusqu'au rocher.

Pergamon, Agora, späthellenistisch, 2. Jh. v. Chr. Mit den Stoai, deren Fundamente im Fels verankert sind, wird der Hang geformt. Schnitt der Demeter-Terrasse mit den Stoai ca. 1:300; Lageplan der Agora ca. 1:4000: 1) Demeter-Tempel, 2) Demeter-Terrasse, 3) Oberes Gymnasium, 4) Mittleres Gymnasium, 5) Unteres Gymnasium, 6) Unterer Marktplatz.

Agora, Pergamon, late Hellenistic period (second century B.C.). Section of the *stoai* of the terrace of Demeter *c.*1:300. Plan of the Pergamon agora: 1) temple of Demeter, 2) terrace of Demeter, 3) upper gymnasium, 4) middle gymnasium, 5) lower gymnasium, 6) lower market. *C.*1:4000. The *stoai* model the landscape and their foundations go down as far as the rock.

71

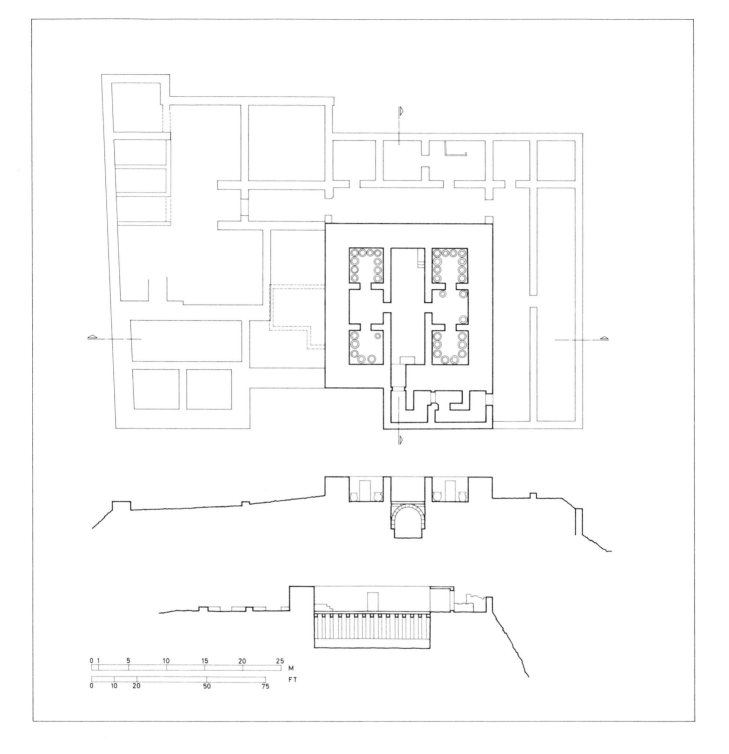

Nécromantéion d'Ephyra (ou Méso-
potamon), en Epire, sanctuaire souter-
rain de divination, construit vers le
milieu du IIIᵉ s. av. J.-C. La salle souterraine de consultation oraculaire présente un système de voûte en plein
cintre que renforcent des arcs doubleaux très rapprochés. Cet espace voûté
annonce les réalisations du monde romain. Plan, coupes transversale et longitudinale 1:500.

**Ephyra (Epiros), Nekromanteion (Meso-
potamon),** um Mitte des 3. Jh. v. Chr.
Ein Tonnengewölbe mit engen Bogen-
stellungen überspannt den unterirdischen Orakelraum des Heiligtums. Hier
kündigen sich bereits die römischen
Gewölbebauten an. Grundriß, Längs-
und Querschnitt 1:500.

Necromanteion, Ephyra (or Mesopota-
mon), in Epirus, an underground shrine
and oracle built around the middle of
the third century B.C. The underground
chamber where the oracle was consulted
has a semicircular vault system reinforced by transverse arches placed very
close together, a construction that foreshadows the achievements of the Roman world. Plan, cross section and
longitudinal section 1:500.

Empire romain   Das römische Reich   The Roman Empire

Poursuivant dans la tradition des solutions et des styles instaurés par la Grèce classique et la période hellénistique, Rome va amplifier encore le caractère urbain de l'architecture (forums immenses) et développer considérablement la création d'espaces internes. C'est par le recours à l'arc, la voûte et la coupole que les différents types de couvertures qui en découlent permettront aux réalisations romaines d'atteindre des proportions colossales à l'époque finale de l'Empire d'Occident, c'est-à-dire aux IIIᵉ et IVᵉ siècles de notre ère.

Auparavant, l'architecture romaine se caractérise par la diversification des programmes qui sont traités en dur. Outre les temples – qui recourent généralement au style corinthien et sont édifiés sur un soubassement –, les palais et les théâtres, on voit naître des formes nouvelles : amphithéâtre en ellipse, basilique civile – lieu de réunion qui supplante le bouleutérion exigu de l'époque grecque –, et surtout innombrables constructions utilitaires sont dorénavant bâties en pierre de taille, en brique ou en blocage de mortier formant béton. On citera en particulier des créations telles qu'aqueducs, crypto-portiques, fabriques diverses (huileries et moulins), ensembles de marchés (nous dirions supermarchés!) et surtout les îlots d'habitation et de commerce que présentent, sur plusieurs étages, les cités nouvelles dont se couvre le monde antique.

C'est avec la réalisation d'immenses salles voûtées que l'architecture romaine donne toute sa mesure sur le plan technologique. L'exemple le plus frappant est la coupole à oculus du Panthéon de Rome, construite sous Hadrien, dont le diamètre est de 43,30 m.

Die Römer behielten die durch die griechische – einschließlich der hellenistischen – Architektur eingeführten Techniken und Stile bei, legten aber einerseits das Hauptgewicht auf die städtische Architektur (riesige Foren), entwickelten andererseits neue Möglichkeiten für die Gestaltung von Innenräumen. Die Verwendung von Bogen, Gewölbe und Kuppel erlaubte in der Spätzeit des Weströmischen Reiches, also im 3. und 4. Jahrhundert n.Chr., Bauten von kolossalem Maßstab. Schon zuvor zeichnete sich die römische Architektur durch die Vielfalt ihrer Bautypen aus. Neben den meist in korinthischem Stil auf einem Podium errichteten Tempeln, den Palästen und Theatern stehen neue Formen: das elliptische Amphitheater, die Basilika als Versammlungsort anstelle des engen griechischen Buleuterions, vor allem aber die zahllosen Zweckbauten aus Werkstein, Ziegel oder dem römischen Gußbeton, die Aquädukte, die überwölbten Gänge in den Untergeschossen von Säulenhallen oder künstlichen Terrassen, Fabriken wie Ölmühlen und Mühlen, Marktanlagen (die wir heute «Supermärkte» nennen würden) und die «Insulae», mehrstöckig überbaute Wohn- und Geschäftsviertel in den neuen Städten, die allenthalben in der neuen Welt angelegt wurden.

Die technische Meisterschaft der römischen Architekten zeigt sich besonders deutlich an den riesigen überwölbten Sälen. Das großartigste Beispiel ist die mit einer Lichtöffnung (Opaion) im Scheitel versehene Kuppel des unter Hadrian errichteten Pantheons in Rom, die 43,30 m überspannt. Nicht zu vergessen sind die gewaltigen Thermen (Caracalla-Thermen, Diokletians-Ther-

Continuing the technical and stylistic tradition of ancient Greece and the Hellenistic period, Rome was to expand the urban character of architecture (immense forums) while at the same time taking the creation of interior spaces a great deal further. New kinds of roofing system based on the arch, the vault and the dome eventually enabled architects in the final period of the Western Empire (third and fourth centuries A.D.) to erect buildings of colossal proportions.

Earlier Roman architecture was characterised by a new diversity in the use of stone. Besides temples (which generally followed the Corinthian style and were built on a raised base), palaces and theatres there were also new forms: the oval amphitheatre, the secular basilica (the meeting place that replaced the tiny *bouleuterion* of the Greek period), and above all countless utilitarian structures were henceforth built of freestone, brick, or rubble-and-mortar concrete. Prominent among the latter were such buildings as aqueducts, cryptoporticus, various factories (oil and grain mills), market complexes, and the multi-storeyed residential and commercial blocks that sprang up in all the cities of the ancient world.

But it was with their enormous vaulted halls that Rome's architects really showed what they could do. The most striking example is the oculus dome of the Pantheon in Rome; built under Hadrian, it has a diameter of 43.3 m. Also worthy of mention are the vast bathing establishments (Thermae of Caracalla, Diocletian, etc.) with halls of between 1500 and 2000 m². Only the Basilica of Maxentius (Basilica of Constantine) in Rome, built in the fourth

Mais on se gardera d'omettre les énormes complexes des thermes (Caracalla, Dioclétien, etc.), avec leurs salles de 1500 à 2000 m². Seule une œuvre du IVe siècle, la basilique de Maxence, à Rome, avec ses 80 × 55 m, totalisant donc 4400 m², dépassera ces proportions, représentant ainsi la plus vaste salle voûtée de l'Antiquité.

Mais c'est dans les palais impériaux que s'affirme l'extraordinaire esprit créateur de l'architecture romaine et l'imagination spatiale qui nourrira Byzance, la Renaissance et surtout le Baroque. En effet, tant la Villa Hadriana, à Tivoli, que la fantastique Villa de Piazza Armerina, en Sicile, marquent l'aboutissement d'une science spatiale prodigieuse associée à une totale liberté d'expression plastique.

men usw.) mit Sälen von 1500 bis 2000 m² Fläche. Nur ein Werk des 4. Jahrhunderts, die Maxentius-Basilika in Rom, übertrifft mit einer Grundfläche von 4400 m² diese Maße; sie ist der größte überwölbte Raum der Antike.

Vor allem in den Kaiserpalästen kommen die außerordentliche Schöpferkraft, die der römischen Architektur zugrunde liegt, und eine Raumvorstellung zum Ausdruck, die zunächst auf Byzanz und später auf Renaissance und Barock weiterwirkten. Sowohl die Villa Hadriana in Tivoli als auch diejenige des Kaisers Maximianus Herculius in Piazza Armerina auf Sizilien sind Beispiele vollendeter Raumbeherrschung verbunden mit völliger Freiheit des plastischen, körperhaften Gestaltens.

century, exceeded these measurements; its dimensions of 80 m. by 55 m. gave a floor area of 4400 m² to make it the largest vaulted hall in the ancient world.

It was the imperial palaces, however, that brought out the extraordinarily creative spirit of Roman architecture and the spatial imagination that inspired Byzantium, the Renaissance, and above all Baroque. Such buildings as the Villa Hadriana at Tivoli and the fantastic villa near Piazza Armerina in Sicily represent the culmination of a prodigious mastery of space allied to complete freedom of plastic expression.

1 Temple de Bacchus à Baalbek, les colonnes engagées cannelées à chapiteau corinthien de la cella (milieu du IIe s. de notre ère).
2 La coupole du Panthéon d'Hadrien, à Rome, avec son oculus et ses structures à caissons (entre 120 et 123 de notre ère).
3 Le théâtre de Sabratha (Libye), avec son mur de scène restauré (début du IIIe s. de notre ère).

1 Baalbek, Bacchus-Tempel, die kannelierten korinthischen Wandsäulen der Cella (Mitte 2. Jh. n. Chr.)
2 Rom, Pantheon, die kassettierte Kuppel mit zentraler Lichtöffnung (unter Hadrian erbaut, 120–123 n. Chr.)
3 Sabratha (Libyen) die rekonstruierten Szenenbauten des Theaters (Anfang 3. Jh. n. Chr.)

1 Temple of Bacchus, Baalbek: the fluted engaged columns with Corinthian capitals in the cella (mid-second century A.D.).
2 The dome of Hadrian's Pantheon, Rome, showing the oculus and the coffered construction (A.D. 120–3).
3 Theatre of Sabrata (Libya) with its restored stage wall dating from the early third century.

1

2

3

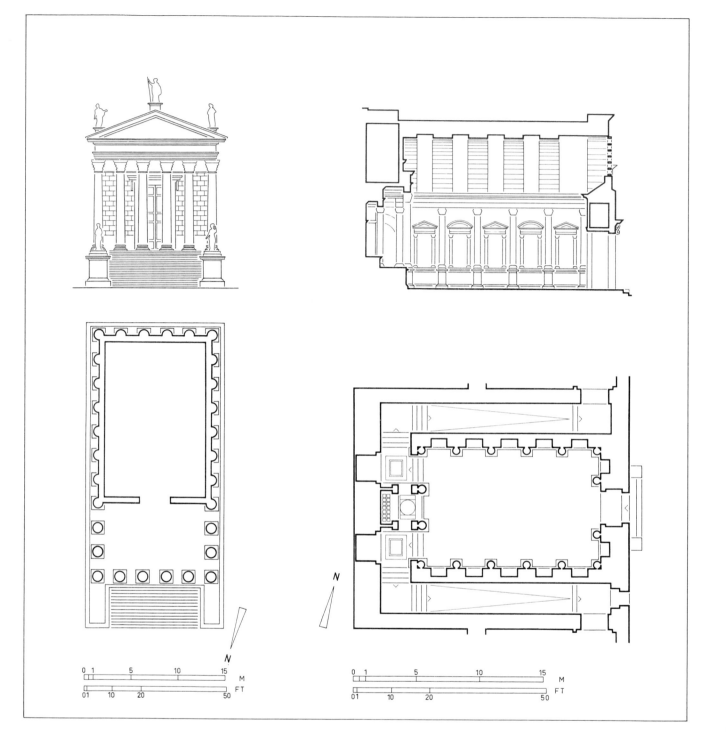

Temple dit Maison Carrée, à Nîmes, entre 20 et 15 av. J.-C. Elévation et plan 1:400. Temple pseudo-périptère (les colonnes latérales sont engagées) de l'époque classique augustéenne. A droite, **Temple de Diane à Nîmes,** de la fin du Ier s. de notre ère. Coupe longitudinale et plan 1:300. La formule de la salle voûtée annonce les basiliques du IIe siècle.

Links: **Nîmes, Maison Carrée,** Tempel, 20–15 v. Chr. Pseudoperipteros; die Säulen bilden keinen Umgang, sondern stehen im Verband mit der Cella-Mauer. Aufriß und Grundriß 1:400. Rechts: **Nîmes, Diana-Tempel,** Ende des 1. Jh. n. Chr. In der Wölbung des Saales kündigt sich bereits der Basilika-Typus des 2. Jh. n. Chr. an. Längsschnitt und Grundriß 1:300.

'Maison Carrée', Nîmes, built between 20 and 15 B.C. Elevation and plan 1:400. A pseudo-peripteral temple (the side columns are engaged) dating from the classic Augustan period. Right, **Temple of Diana, Nîmes,** late first century B.C. Longitudinal section and plan 1:300. The vaulted interior foreshadows the second-century basilica.

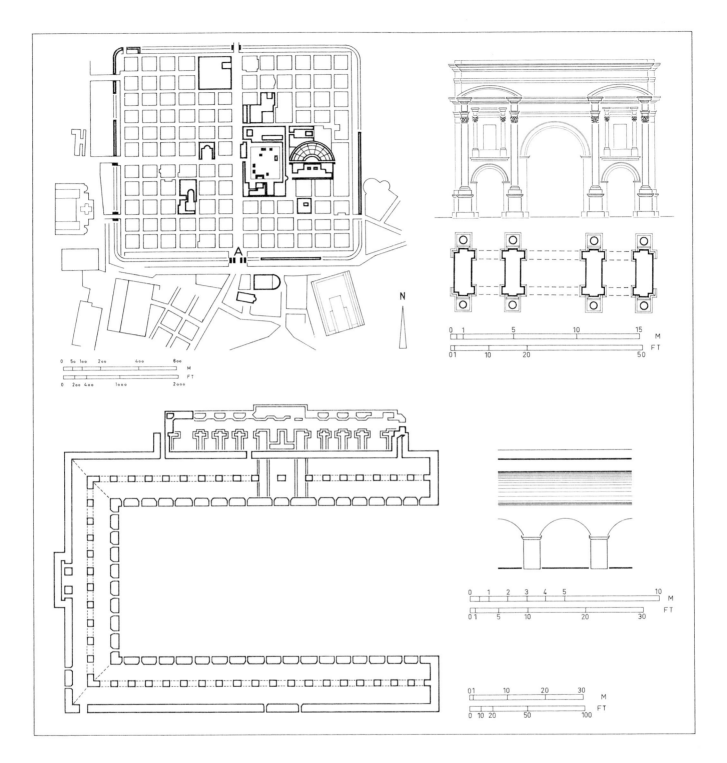

Timgad (Afrique du Nord). Plan de la ville fondée en 100 apr. J.-C. par Trajan. 1:20000. Exemple caractéristique d'une cité militaire romaine. A) Emplacement de l'Arc de Trajan. A droite, élévation et plan de l'**Arc de Trajan** 1:300. En bas, **Cryptoportiques d'Arles,** magasins souterrains construits vers 30 av. J.-C. Plan 1:1000 et détail des voûtes 1:200.

Oben links: **Timgad (Nordafrika).** Die von Trajan 100 n. Chr. gegründete Stadt ist ein typisches Beispiel einer römischen Militärsiedlung. Lageplan 1:20000: A) Trajansbogen. Oben rechts: **Trajansbogen.** Aufriß und Grundriß 1:300. Unten: **Arles, Kryptoportiken,** um 30 v. Chr. Diese unterirdischen Anlagen dienten als Magazine. Grundriß 1:1000; Details der Gewölbe 1:200.

Timgad (North Africa), founded by Trajan in A.D. 100, a typical example of a Roman garrison town. Plan 1:20,000. A) situation of Trajan's arch. Right, **Trajan's arch.** Elevation and plan 1:300. Below, **Cryptoporticus, Arles,** underground store-rooms built c. 30 B.C. Plan 1:1000; detail of the vaulting 1:200.

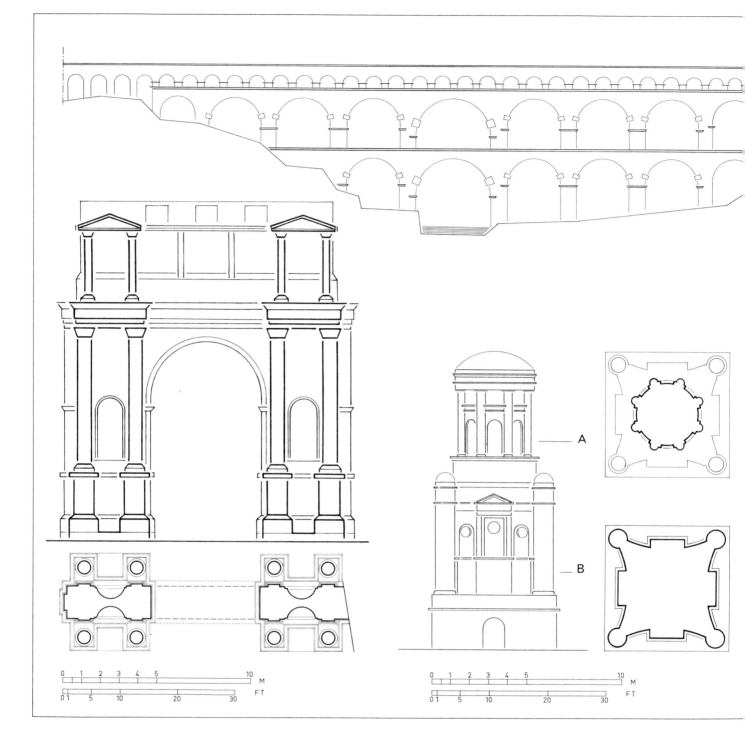

0 1 2 3 4 5 10 M
0 1 5 10 20 30 FT

A

B

0 1 2 3 4 5 10 M
0 1 5 10 20 30 FT

En haut, **Aqueduc et pont dit Pont du Gard,** construit vers 30 av. J.-C. Elévation 1:1000. Trois ordres d'arcades superposées, franchissant le cours du Gard pour amener l'eau à Nîmes. Longueur 230 m. En bas, à gauche, **Arc de Caracalla, à Cuicul** (Jemila). Elévation et plan 1:200. A droite, **Mausolée dit la Conocchia de Capoue.** Elévation et coupes horizontales (A, B) 1:200.

Oben: **Pont du Gard** (Aquädukt und Brücke), um 30 v.Chr. Die drei übereinandergestellten Bogenreihen von 230 m Länge überspannen das Tal des Gard. Sie führten ursprünglich Wasser nach Nîmes. Aufriß 1:1000. Unten links: **Cuicul (heute Djemila), Caracalla-Bogen.** Aufriß und Grundriß 1:200. Unten rechts: **Capua, Mausoleum (Conocchia).** Aufriß und Horizontalschnitte in A und B 1:200.

'Pont du Gard', near Nîmes, an aqueduct and bridge built *c.*30 B.C. Elevation 1:1000. Three storeys of arcades cross the valley of the Gard to supply Nîmes with water. Length 230 m. Below left, **Arch of Caracalla, Cuicul** (Djemila). Elevation and plan 1:200. Right, **'La Conocchia' mausoleum, Capua.** Elevation and horizontal sections (A,B) 1:200.

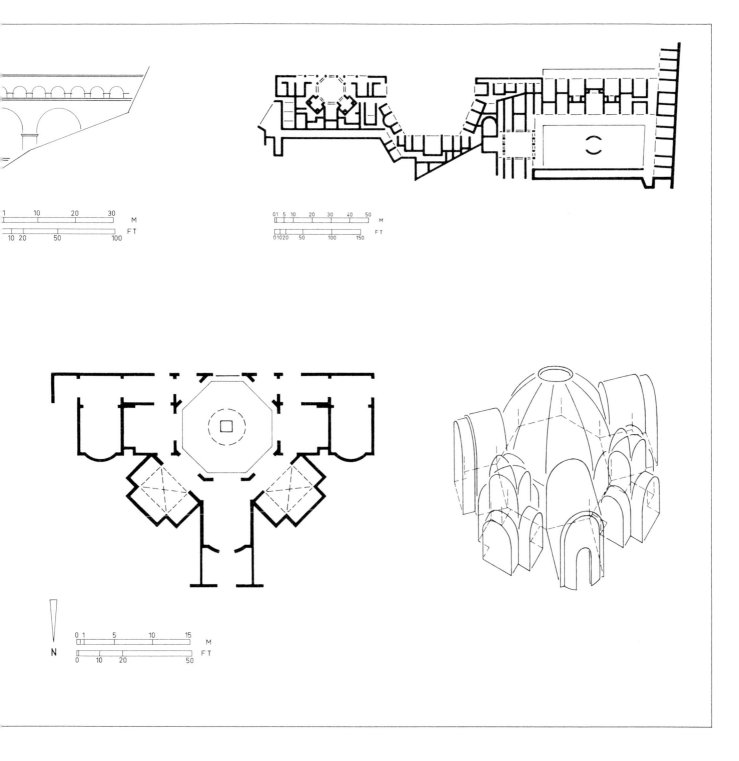

M

FT

M

FT

N

M

FT

Palais dit la Maison d'Or (Domus Aurea) **de Néron, à Rome,** édifié vers 60 apr. J.-C. Plan général 1:2000, plan de la salle octogonale 1:500 et axonométrie. Œuvre novatrice des ingénieurs et architectes Severus et Celer, la salle octogonale avec sa coupole de 14 m de diamètre, surmontée d'un oculus, annonce les grandes réalisations des IIᵉ et IIIᵉ siècles.

Rom, Domus Aurea (Goldenes Haus des Nero), um 60 n.Chr. Die 14 m überspannende Kuppel des achteckigen Saals hat im Scheitel eine runde Lichtöffnung. In dem Palast, einem fortschrittlichen Werk der Ingenieure und Architekten Severus und Celer, kündigen sich die großen Bauten des 2. und 3. Jh. an. Grundriß des Palastes 1:2000; Grundriß des Kuppelsaals 1:500; axonometrische Ansicht.

'Golden Palace' of Nero (Domus Aurea), Rome, built c.A.D. 60. Overall plan 1:2000; plan of the octagonal hall 1:500 and axonometric projection. A pioneering achievement by the engineers and architects Severus and Celer. The octagonal hall with its dome 14 m. across culminating in an oculus heralds the great buildings of the second and third centuries.

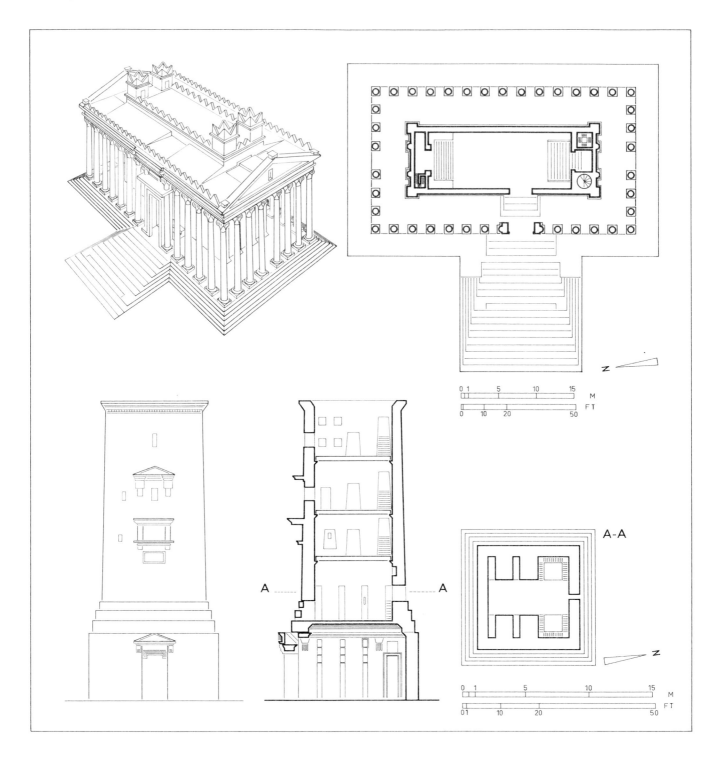

Temple de Bel, à Palmyre (Syrie), construit sous le règne de Tibère (14–37 apr. J.-C.). Vue et plan 1:500. Temple périptère avec entrée latérale précédée d'un grand escalier. En bas, Tour funéraire de Jamlishu, à Palmyre. Elévation, coupe et plan 1:300. Chacune des chambres, dans les divers étages, contient des niches en columbarium, dont les compartiments étaient fermés par des stèles.

Oben: Palmyra, Baals-Tempel, Regierungszeit des Tiberius (14–37 n.Chr.). Zu dem seitlichen Eingang des Peripteros führt eine breite Freitreppe. Perspektivische Ansicht und Grundriß 1:500. Unten: Palmyra, Totenturm des Iamlichos. In jedem Geschoß sind in die Wände des Raumes Grabnischen eingetieft, die durch Stelen verschlossen waren. Aufriß, Schnitt und Grundriß 1:300.

Temple of Bel, Palmyra (Syria), built in the reign of Tiberius (A.D. 14–37). View and plan 1:500. A peripteral temple with a side entrance and a great stairway leading up to it. Below, Burial tower of Iamblichus, Palmyra. Elevation, section and plan 1:300. Each of the rooms on the various storeys contains columbarium niches, their compartments closed by means of steles.

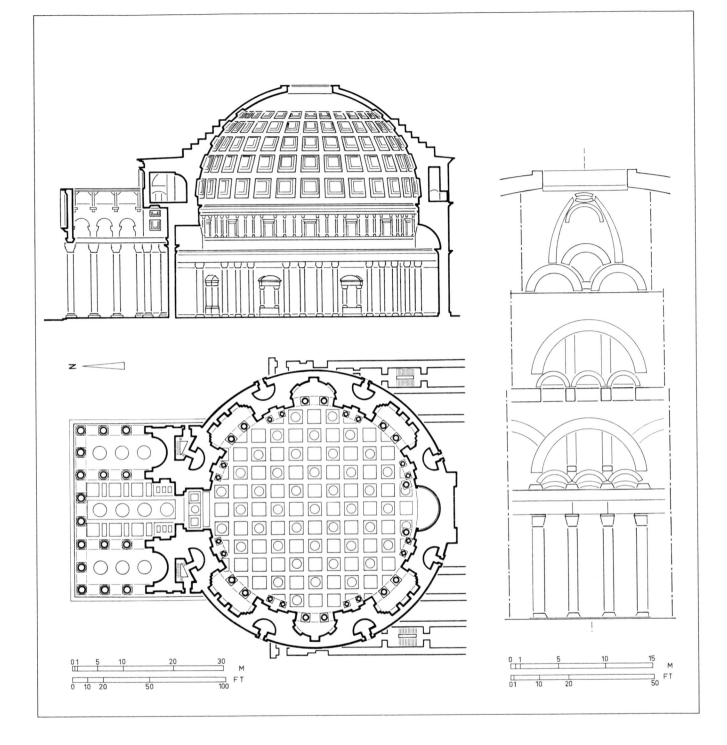

0 1	5	10		20			30	M
0 10 20			50					100	FT

0 1		5		10	15	M
01	10		20			50	FT

Panthéon, à Rome, construit sous le règne d'Hadrien, entre 120 et 123. Coupe longitudinale et plan 1:750, développement des structures de la coupole 1:400. La cella est une énorme rotonde de brique de 43,30 m de diamètre, surmontée d'une coupole à oculus culminant à une hauteur égale et construite, dans sa partie supérieure, en assises horizontales de tuf, sans contre-butement.

Rom, Pantheon, 120–123 n.Chr. (unter Hadrian). Die Cella ist ein Rundbau aus Ziegelmauerwerk mit einem Durchmesser von 43,30 m. Die Höhe bis zum Scheitel der Kuppel mit zentraler Lichtöffnung beträgt ebenfalls 43,30 m. Die Kuppel ist in ihrem oberen Teil aus horizontalen Tuffsteinlagen und ohne Widerlagersystem erbaut. Längsschnitt und Grundriß 1:750; System des Kuppelaufbaus 1:400.

Pantheon, Rome, built between A.D. 120 and 123, in the reign of Hadrian. Longitudinal section and plan 1:750; structural development of the dome 1:400. The cella is an enormous brick rotunda measuring 43.3 m. across, which is also the height of the oculus dome above it. It is constructed in the upper part of horizontal courses of tuff without buttressing.

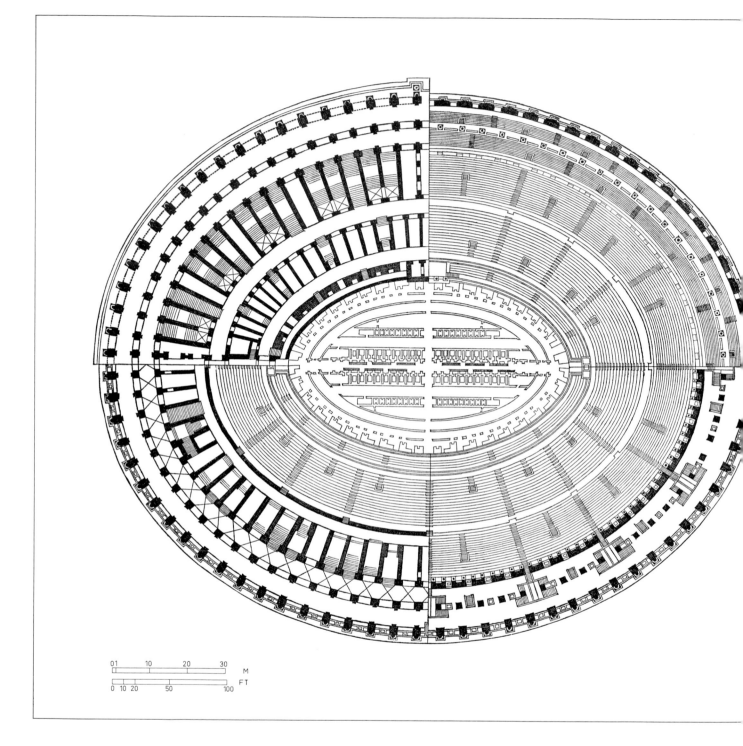

01 10 20 30
M
FT
0 10 20 50 100

Amphithéâtre Flavien, dit Colisée, à Rome, construit entre 75 et 80 apr. J.-C. Plan par quarts à divers niveaux 1:1000, et en page de droite, schéma des structures. La formule du «théâtre en rond», créée par les Romains, trouve ici sa forme la plus ample, avec des mesures dépassant 180 × 150 m sur les deux axes de l'ellipse et un savant système de contre-butement de voûtes.

Rom, Kolosseum, Flavisches Amphitheater, 75–80 n. Chr. Die von den Römern entwickelte Formel des «Rundtheaters» fand in diesem elliptischen Bau mit Durchmessern von mehr als 180 und 150 m und mit einem kunstvollen Widerlagersystem ihre eindrucksvollste Verwirklichung. Grundrisse in vier verschiedenen Ebenen 1:1000; Nebenseite: Konstruktionsschema.

Flavian amphitheatre, also known as the Colosseum, Rome, built between A.D. 75 and 80. Plan in quarters at various levels 1:1000. Opposite, structural diagram. The biggest ever 'theatre in the round'—a formula invented by the Romans—the Colosseum measures more than 180 m. by 150 m. along the two axes of the ellipse and uses a clever system of vault buttressing.

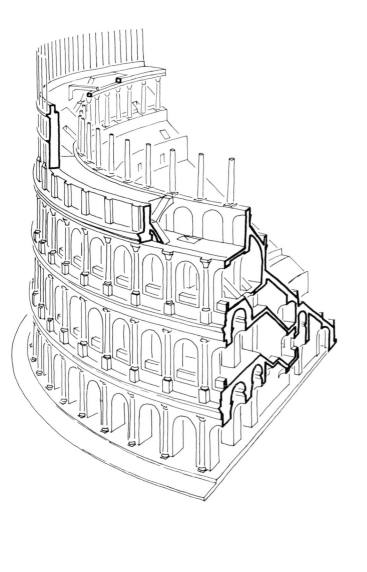

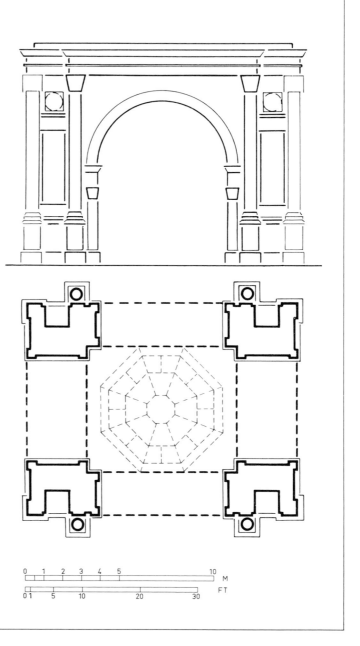

0 1 2 3 4 5   10   M

0 1   5   10   20   30   FT

Tétrapyle de Marc-Aurèle, à Tripoli, datant de 163 apr. J.-C. Elévation et plan env. 1:200. Comme les arcs de triomphe, auxquels ils s'apparentent par leur rôle dans la cité, les tétrapyles, situés à un carrefour urbain important, sont une création de l'architecture romaine. Celui de Tripoli est couvert d'une coupole octogonale en pierre de taille.

Tripolis, Tetrapylon des Mark Aurel, 163 n. Chr. Die an wichtigen Kreuzungen innerhalb der Städte errichteten Tetrapylone haben eine den Triumphbögen vergleichbare Funktion und sind wie sie Schöpfungen der römischen Baukunst. Der Tetrapylon von Tripolis ist mit einer Werksteinkuppel auf achteckigem Grundriß überwölbt. Aufriß und Grundriß ca. 1:200.

Tetrapylon of Marcus Aurelius, Tripoli, A.D. 163. Elevation and plan c. 1:200. The tetrapylon played a role similar to that of the triumphal arch in Roman urban architecture: both Roman inventions, they were placed at important city crossroads. The one at Tripoli is roofed with an octagonal dome of freestone.

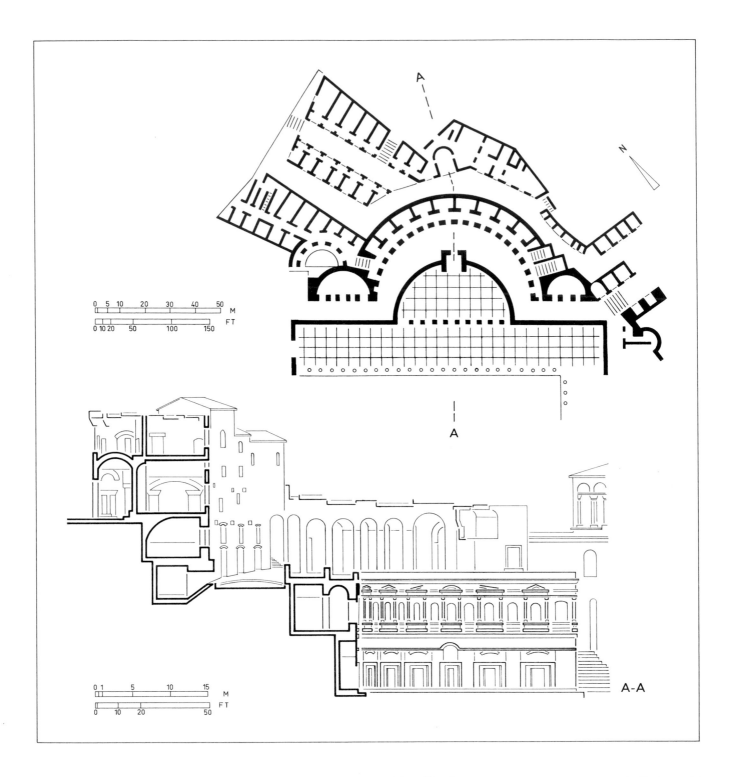

Marchés de Trajan, à Rome, par l'architecte Apollodore de Damas, construits en 106 de notre ère, Plan 1:1500 et coupe 1:500. Occupant un grand hémicycle qui domine le Forum, ces Marchés font partie du nouveau forum édifié par le vainqueur des Daces. L'innovation que constitue une façade concave est traitée à la manière des volumes convexes des théâtres et amphithéâtres.

Rom, Trajans-Markt, 106 n.Chr. Der von dem Architekten Apollodorus von Damaskus erbaute Markt liegt in einem großen Halbkreis oberhalb des Forums und bildet einen Teil des neuen Trajans-Forums. Die konkave Fassade, eine Neuerung, wurde den konvexen Fassaden der Theater und Amphitheater entsprechend behandelt. Grundriß 1:1500; Schnitt 1:500.

Trajan's markets, Rome, built A.D. 106 by the architect Apollodorus of Damascus. Plan 1:1500; section 1:500. Occupying a large semicircle that overlooks the Forum, these markets formed part of the new forum built by the conqueror of the Dacians. The pioneering concave façade is treated in the same way as the convex volumes of theatres and amphitheatres.

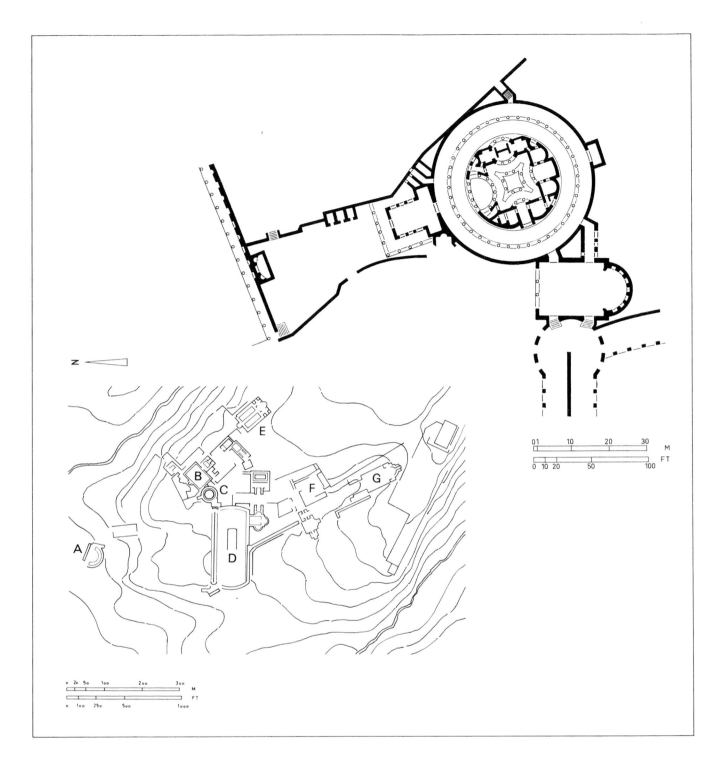

Villa Hadriana, à Tivoli (Tibur), datant de 120 environ apr. J.-C. Plan du **Théâtre maritime** 1:1000 et situation 1:10000. Cet immense ensemble de palais impériaux qui couvre 150 hectares annonce les formules de l'époque baroque. A) Théâtre, B) Bibliothèque, C) Théâtre maritime, D) Poecile, E) Piazza d'Oro, F) Thermes, G) Canope.

Tivoli (röm. Tibur), Villa Hadriana, um 120 n.Chr. Die gewaltige, 150 Hektar bedeckende kaiserliche Villenanlage zeigt bereits «barocke» Züge. Lageplan 1:10000: A) Theater, B) Bibliothek, C) Teatro marittimo, D) Poikile, E) Piazza d'Oro, F) Thermen, G) Kanopus. **Teatro marittimo** (C). Grundriß 1:1000.

Villa Hadriana, Tivoli (Tibur), built *c*.120. Plan of the **Maritime theatre** 1:1000 and site: 1:10,000. This vast complex of imperial palaces covering 150 hectares (nearly 400 acres) contains various anticipations of the 'baroque' style in Roman architecture. A) theatre, B) library, C) Maritime theatre, D) poecile, E) Piazza d'Oro, F) thermae, G) canopeum.

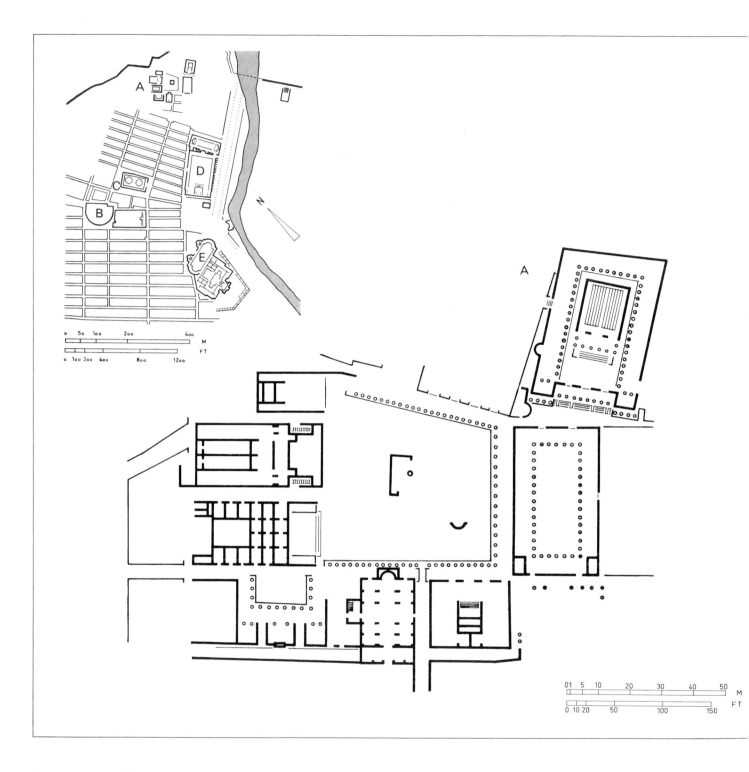

Lepcis Magna (Libye). Situation 1: 12000. A) Vieux Forum, B) Théâtre, C) Marché, D) Nouveau Forum, E) Thermes. Détail du **Vieux Forum** (A), datant du Ier s. de notre ère, 1:1200. Autour d'une place trapézoïdale se groupent des édifices civils, tels que temple, marchés et basilique, qui forment le centre administratif de la cité.

Leptis Magna (Libyen). Lageplan 1: 12000: A) Altes Forum, B) Theater, C) Markt, D) Neues Forum, E) Thermen. **Altes Forum** (A), 1. Jh. n. Chr. Um einen trapezförmigen Platz sind die öffentlichen Gebäude – Tempel, Märkte und Basilika – gruppiert. Hier lag das Verwaltungszentrum der Stadt. Grundriß 1:1200.

Leptis Magna (Libya). Site plan 1:12,000. A) Old forum, B) theatre, C) market, D) New forum, E) thermae. Detail of the **Old forum** (A), first century A.D., 1:1200. Grouped around a trapezoid are the various civic buildings —temple, markets, basilica—that made up the administrative centre of the city.

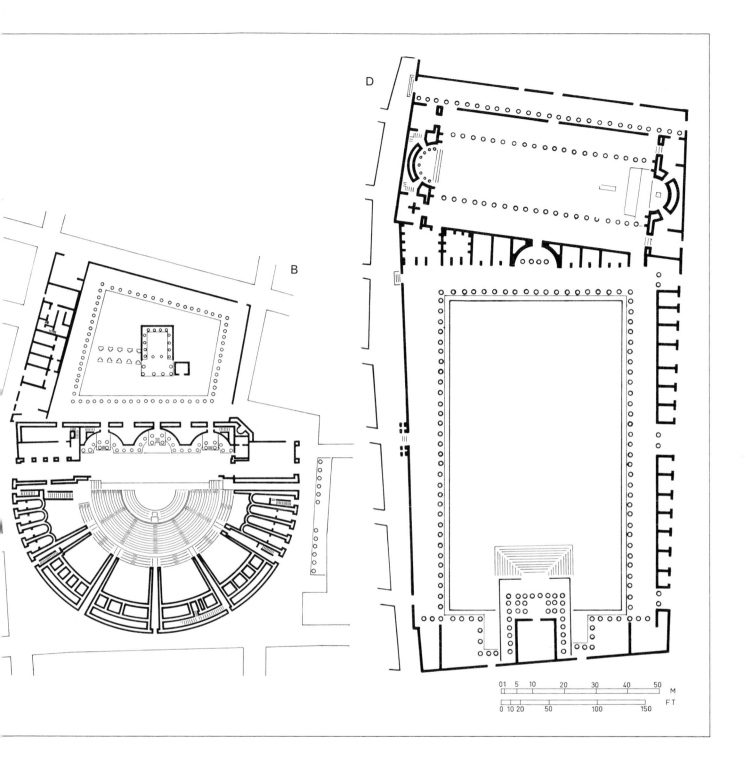

D

01 5 10   20   30   40   50   M

                                    FT
0 10 20   50   100   150

Théâtre de Lepcis Magna (B), inauguré en 35–36 de notre ère. 1:1200. La cavéa, partiellement excavée, fait face à un mur de scène traité en trois profonds hémicycles à colonnes que précède une place à portiques au centre de laquelle s'élève un temple des souverains divinisés. **Nouveau Forum** (D) 1:1200. Commencé à la fin du IIe et terminé au IIIe siècle, il entoure une vaste basilique civile à double abside.

Links: **Leptis Magna, Theater** (B), 35/36 n.Chr. eingeweiht. Gegenüber der Cavea die in drei halbrunde Nischen mit Säulenstellungen gegliederte Szenenwand, an deren Rückseite ein Platz mit Säulenportiken, in dessen Mitte ein Tempel der vergöttlichten Herrscher. Grundriß 1:1200. Rechts: **Neues Forum** (D), Ende 2.–3.Jh.n.Chr. An einer Schmalseite liegt eine Basilika mit zwei Apsiden. Grundriß 1:1200.

Theatre, Leptis Magna (B), inaugurated A.D. 35–6, 1:1200. The partially excavated *cavea* faces a stage wall treated in three deep columned semicircles. In front of this is a porticoed square, and in the centre of the square stands a temple dedicated to the deified rulers. **New forum** (D), 1:1200. Begun in the second and completed in the third century, this contains a vast two-apsed civic basilica.

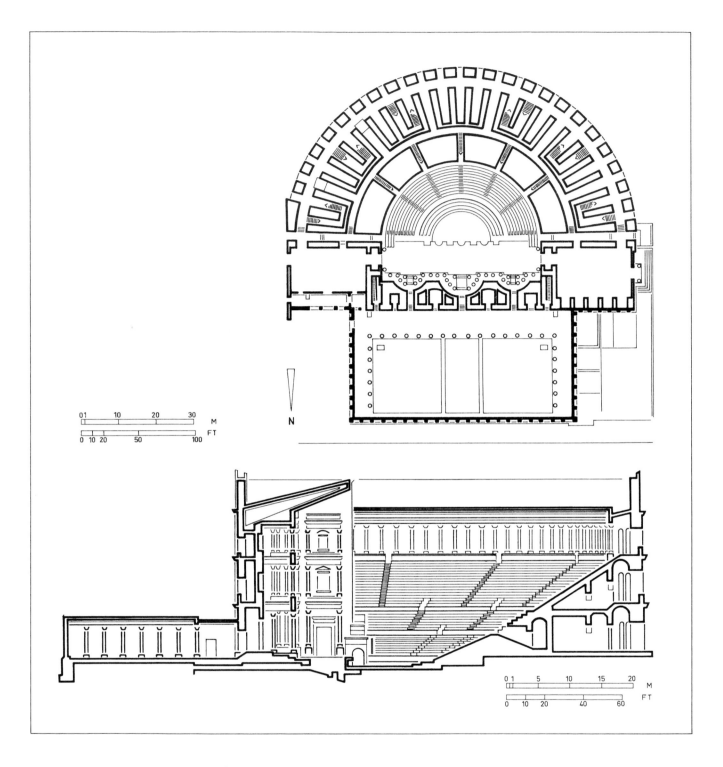

01 10 20 30 M
FT
0 10 20 50 100

N

0 1 5 10 15 20 M
FT
0 10 20 40 60

Théâtre de Sabratha, construit au début du IIIᵉ s., sous la dynastie sévérienne. Plan 1:1000 et coupe longitudinale 1:600. Comme à Lepcis Magna, le théâtre est accolé à une place à portiques au revers du mur de scène. Ce dernier présente aussi les avancées et retraits en colonnades superposées qui caractérisent le dynamisme baroque des façades de la Rome impériale.

Sabratha, Theater, Anfang 3. Jh. n. Chr. Wie in Leptis Magna schließt an die Rückseite der Szenenbauten ein Platz mit Säulenportiken an. Das Proszenium ist wie dort mit Nischen und Säulenstellungen gegliedert, Zeichen der «barokken» Dynamik römischer kaiserzeitlicher Architektur. Grundriß 1:1000; Längsschnitt 1:600.

Theatre, Sabrata, built in the early third century under the Severian dynasty. Plan 1:1000; longitudinal section 1:600. As at Leptis Magna, this theatre adjoins a porticoed square behind the stage wall. Again the latter has the in-and-out movement of superposed colonnades characteristic of the 'baroque' dynamism of imperial Roman façades.

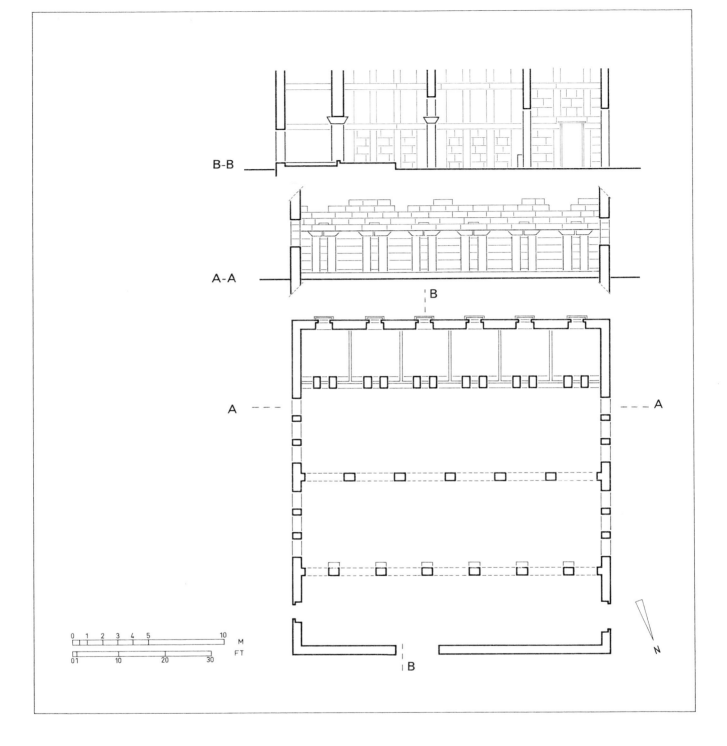

B-B

A-A

A - - -　　　　　　- - - A

B

0 1 2 3 4 5　　　　10　M
　　　　　　　　　　FT
0 1　　10　　　20　　30

N

B

Huilerie à Brisgane (Afrique du Nord), début du IIIᵉ s. de notre ère. Coupe longitudinale, coupe transversale et plan 1:250. Ces édifices utilitaires, destinés à l'activité économique et à l'exploitation des terres sous forme de monoculture, se développent à la fin de l'Empire, avec la création de vastes latifundia. C'est de l'architecture fonctionnelle avant la lettre.

Brisgane (Nordafrika), Ölmühle, Anfang 3.Jh.n.Chr. Am Ende der Kaiserzeit, mit der Schaffung der Latifundien, entstanden Zweckbauten, die der Wirtschaft und dem Landbau in Monokultur dienten: funktionelle Bauten ehe es den Begriff der «funktionellen Architektur» gab. Längsschnitt, Querschnitt und Grundriß 1:250.

Oil-mill, Brisganum (North Africa), early third century A.D. Longitudinal section, cross section, and plan 1:250. Such utilitarian buildings emerged under the late Empire with the creation of vast *latifundia* practising monoculture farming. They were an early form of functional architecture.

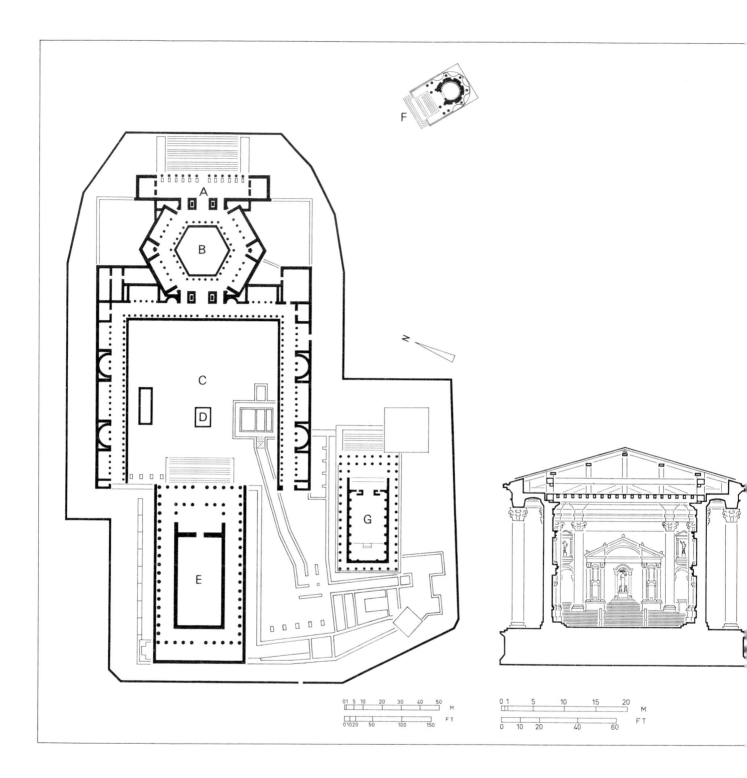

Scales:

01 5 10 · 20 · 30 · 40 · 50 M
01020 · 50 · 100 · 150 FT

0 1 · 5 · 10 · 15 · 20 M
0 · 10 · 20 · 40 · 60 FT

Ensemble cultuel de Baalbek (Liban), datant du milieu du IIe s. Situation 1:2000. A) Propylées, B) Cour hexagonale, C) Grande cour de l'autel, D) Autel, E) Temple de Jupiter héliopolitain, F) Temple de Vénus, G) Temple de Bacchus. L'ensemble, sur son temenos, couvre près de 200 × 300 m. Le Temple de Vénus (F) date du IIIe siècle, et constitue l'une des réalisations baroques de l'art romain.

Baalbek (Libanon), Heiligtum, Mitte des 2.Jh.n.Chr. Die von der Temenosmauer umschlossene Fläche hat eine Länge von fast 300 m und eine größte Breite von ca. 200 m. Plan 1:2000: A) Propyläen, B) Vorhof, C) Großer Altarhof, D) Altar, E) Tempel des Jupiter Heliopolitanus, F) Venus-Tempel, G) Bacchus-Tempel. Der Venus-Tempel (F), 3.Jh.n.Chr., ist ein Beispiel «barocker» römischer Architektur.

Temple complex, Baalbek (Lebanon), mid-second century A.D. Site 1:2000. A) propylaea, B) hexagonal courtyard, C) main altar courtyard, D) altar, E) temple of Jupiter Heliopolitanus, F) temple of Venus, G) temple of Bacchus. Grouped on a *temenos*, the complex covers an area of nearly 200 m. by 300 m. The temple of Venus (F) dates from the third century and is an example of the 'baroque' style of Roman architecture.

0 1   5   10   15
M
01   10   20   50
FT

0 1   5   10   15   20
M
0   10   20   40   60
FT

N

Temple de Bacchus à Baalbek, vue de l'Adyton. Coupe transversale et plan 1:600, coupe longitudinale 1:400. L'édifice périptère présentait une vaste cella couverte à l'aide de fermes. Des colonnes engagées cannelées, à riches chapiteaux corinthiens, créent de profondes niches en retrait, qui abritaient des statues.

Baalbek, Bacchus-Tempel. Die geräumige Cella des Peripteros war mit einem offenen Dachstuhl überdeckt. Zwischen den kannelierten Wandsäulen mit reichen korinthischen Kapitellen standen Statuen in Nischen. Perspektivische Ansicht des Adyton; Längsschnitt 1:400; Grundriß 1:600; Nebenseite: Querschnitt 1:600.

Temple of Bacchus, Baalbek. View of the *adyton.* Cross section and plan 1:600; longitudinal section 1:400. A peripteral structure, it had a vast cella roofed with the aid of trusses. Fluted engaged columns with elaborate Corinthian capitals flank deep niches that originally contained statues.

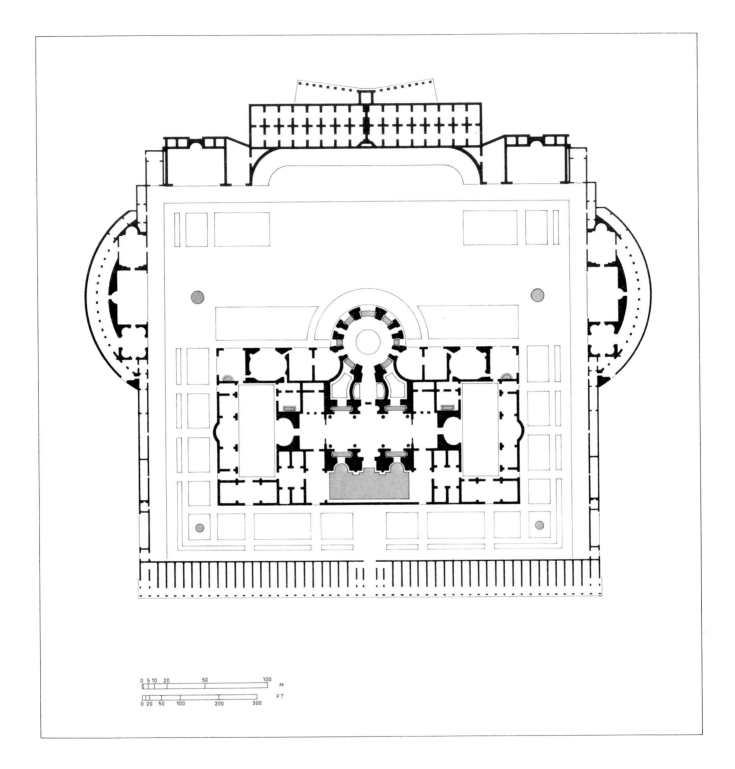

0 5 10 20   50   100 M

0 20 50 100   200   300 FT

Thermes de Caracalla, à Rome, vers 216. Plan 1:3000. Couvrant une surface de 20 hectares, cette immense réalisation impériale marque, par les gigantesques espaces internes qu'elle réalise, l'un des sommets des techniques architecturales romaines. La grande aula centrale mesure à elle seule 65 × 25 m, au sein d'un édifice thermal de 214 × 110 m.

Rom, Caracalla-Thermen, um 216 n. Chr. Die gewaltige, ca. 20 Hektar bedeckende Anlage bildet mit ihren riesigen Innenräumen einen der Höhepunkte römischer Baukunst. Die Cella Media des 214 × 110 m messenden Gebäudes ist allein 65 × 25 m groß. Grundriß 1:3000.

Thermae of Caracalla, Rome, c.216. Plan 1:3000. Covering 20 hectares (50 acres), this vast complex with its gigantic interiors represents one of the high points of Roman architectural engineering. The great central *aula* alone measures 65 m. by 25 m., and it lies at the heart of a building occupying an area 214 m. by 110 m.

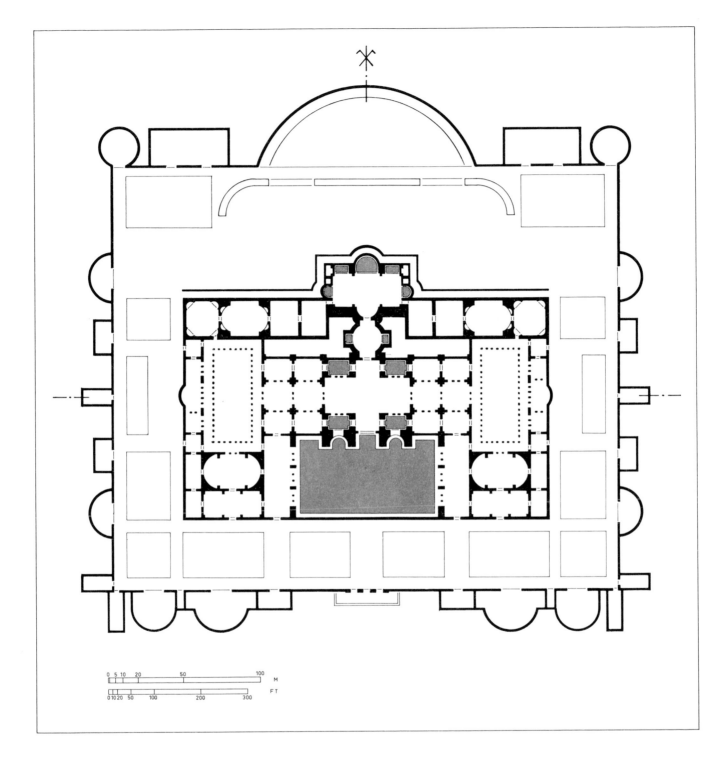

Thermes de Dioclétien, à Rome, construits entre 298 (mis en chantier par Maximien) et 306 (mort de Constance Chlore). Plan 1:2500. Dans un espace un peu moins vaste que celui des Thermes de Caracalla se développent des bâtiments thermaux encore plus énormes: 244 × 144 m. Les voûtes de l'aula centrale dépassent 30 m de hauteur.

Rom, Diokletians-Thermen, zwischen 298 (Baubeginn unter Maximian) und 306 (Tod des Constantius Chlorus). Die Gesamtanlage ist etwas kleiner als die der Caracalla-Thermen, der Bau selber jedoch mit 244 × 144 m noch größer. Der Gewölbescheitel der Cella Media lag über 30 m hoch. Grundriß 1:2500.

Thermae of Diocletian, Rome, begun in A.D. 298 under Maximian and completed in A.D. 306 (after the death of Constantius Chlorus). Plan 1:2500. On a site slightly smaller than that of the Thermae of Caracalla, the thermal buildings are even more enormous, measuring 244 m. by 144 m. The vaults of the central *aula* are more than 30 m. high.

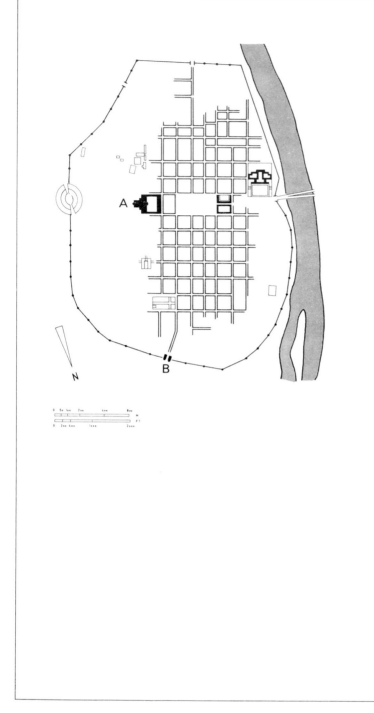

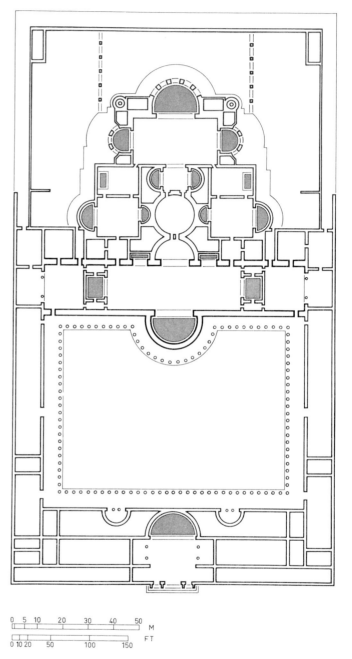

Trèves. Plan de la ville romaine 1:30000. A) Thermes impériaux, B) Porta Nigra ou porte noire. En bordure de la Moselle, la cité, bâtie sur un plan rigoureusement orthogonal, est ceinte de murs. Plan des **Thermes** 1:1500, avec leur vaste cour à portiques précédant des bâtiments thermaux dont le plan se développe selon une formule baroque.

Trier. Die römische Stadt am Ufer der Mosel war nach streng rechtwinkligem Plan angelegt und von einer Mauer umgeben. Lageplan 1:30000: A) Kaiserliche Thermen, B) Porta Nigra. **Thermen.** Vor dem in bewegten Formen gegliederten Bau liegt ein Hof mit Säulenportiken. Grundriß 1:1500.

Trier. Plan of the Roman city 1:30,000. A) imperial thermae, B) Porta Nigra or 'Black Gate'. Built on the banks of the Moselle, the walled city of Augusta Trevirorum followed a strictly rectangular plan. Plan of the **Thermae** 1:1500. A vast porticoed courtyard fronted thermal buildings that were built on a characteristically 'baroque' plan.

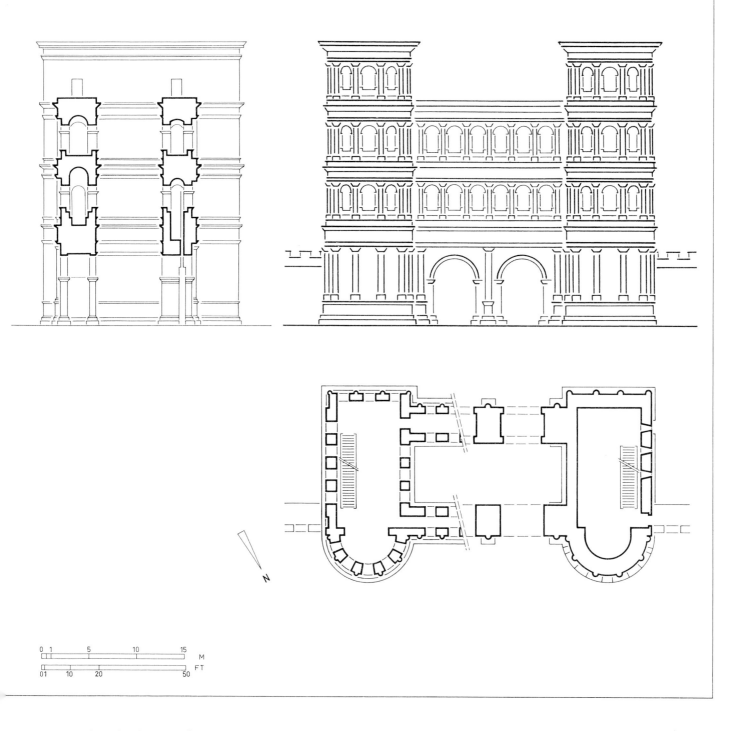

0 1   5   10   15
                        M
                        FT
01   10   20   50

Porta Nigra, à Trèves, entrée monumentale de la cité, datant d'une période située entre le IIe et le IVe s. Coupe, élévation et plan 1:400. Issue de la tradition de l'architecture militaire hellénistique, cette réalisation annonce pourtant les fortifications de l'époque médiévale.

Trier, Porta Nigra, zwischen 2. und 4. Jh. n. Chr. Das monumentale Stadttor entspricht in den wesentlichen Teilen der hellenistischen Festungsarchitektur, nimmt aber gewisse frühmittelalterliche Lösungen voraus. Querschnitt, Aufriß und Grundriß 1:400.

Porta Nigra, Trier, the monumental entrance to the city, built between the second and fourth centuries. Section, elevation and plan 1:400. Arising out of the Hellenistic tradition of military architecture, the 'Black Gate' heralds the fortifications of the medieval period.

95

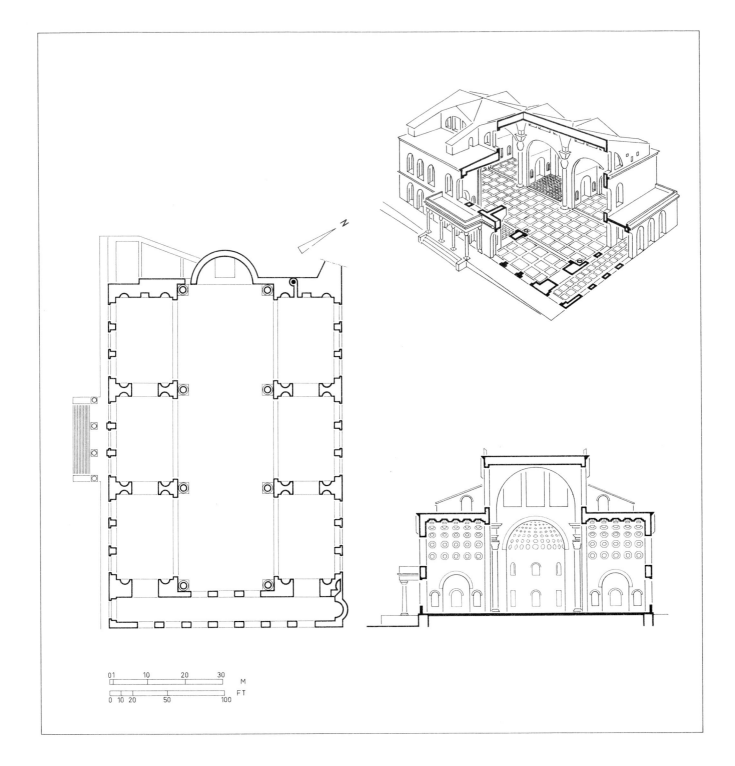

01   10   20   30   M
                            F T
0 10 20   50   100

Basilique de Maxence, à Rome, construite entre 306 et 312. Plan et coupe 1:1000 et vue des structures. Dernière basilique civile impériale, cet édifice présente une aula qui dépasse celles des plus vastes thermes romains: la nef seule mesure 80 × 25 m, couverte de trois voûtes d'arêtes. C'est la plus grande salle de l'Antiquité qui annonce les églises du règne de Constantin.

Rom, Maxentius-Basilika, 306–312 n. Chr. Der gewaltige Bau ist die letzte profane Basilika der Kaiserzeit. Das von drei Kreuzgratgewölben überspannte Schiff ist mit 80 × 25 m größer als die zentralen Räume der Thermen und damit der größte Raum der Antike. Hier kündigen sich die großen Kirchenbauten der konstantinischen Zeit an. Grundriß und Querschnitt 1:1000; Konstruktionsschema.

Basilica of Maxentius (Basilica of Constantine), Rome, built between A.D. 306 and 312. Plan and section 1:1000, and structural view. Imperial Rome's last secular basilica had a larger *aula* than even the largest Roman thermae, the nave alone measuring 80 m. by 25 m., covered with three groin vaults. This was the largest interior in the ancient world and foreshadowed the great churches of the reign of Constantine.

Byzance   Byzanz   Byzantium

Avec le règne de Constantin, et en particulier l'édit de Milan (313), proclamant la paix de l'Eglise et la fin des persécutions contre les chrétiens, débute une ère nouvelle au IVe siècle. La fondation de Constantinople (330), puis la division définitive de l'Empire en 395, à la mort de Théodose, marquent l'avènement du monde byzantin en Orient. Cette coupure historique n'est en revanche guère sensible sur le plan architectural: on construit, en même temps que la première Sainte-Irène et le grand palais sur le Bosphore, un hippodrome qui perpétue les mœurs et les jeux de Rome. Les techniques romaines sont toujours en usage, et les espaces ne se modifient que lentement lorsque la basilique civile se mue en lieu de réunion des chrétiens.

L'architecture du premier christianisme perpétue donc celle de Rome. La basilique de Saint-Pierre qu'édifie Constantin – en même temps que le Saint-Sépulcre – avec son atrium et ses cinq nefs à fermes, atteint d'emblée des proportions grandioses: 210 m de long. La solution structurale sera reprise dans tout l'Empire. Elle ne sera que progressivement remplacée par les couvertures voûtées.

Dès 532, à Constantinople, la grande église de Sainte-Sophie marque l'apogée de la formule à coupole, avec son fantastique dôme de 30 m de diamètre, contre-buté par deux demi-coupoles, qui forment ainsi un espace de plus de 70 m de longueur sans support. Les articulations sont traitées de manière fluide, sans arêtes nettes, et la décoration rutilante des mosaïques estompe encore les transitions.

Désormais l'architecture byzantine va se développer en obéissant à une re-

Im 4. Jahrhundert, mit der Regierung Konstantins und dem Mailänder Toleranzedikt (313), das die Religionsfreiheit sicherte und den Christenverfolgungen ein Ende machte, begann eine neue Epoche. Von der Gründung Konstantinopels im Jahr 330 an und der endgültigen Reichsteilung 395 nach dem Tod Theodosius' setzte der Aufstieg des Byzantinischen Reiches ein. Diese Zäsur ist in der Architektur freilich kaum spürbar: Gleichzeitig mit dem ersten Bau der Hagia Irene und dem großen Palast am Bosporus entstand ein Hippodrom, in dem römische Bräuche und römische Spiele weitergeführt wurden. Man behielt die römischen Bautechniken bei, und der Raumcharakter änderte sich nur allmählich mit dem Wandel der profanen Basilika zum Versammlungsort der Christen.

Die frühchristliche Architektur stand also ganz in der römischen Tradition. Die Ausmaße der von Konstantin gleichzeitig mit der Grabeskirche errichteten Basilika St. Peter in Rom, eines fünfschiffigen Baus mit offenem Dachstuhl und vorgelagertem Atrium, waren bei einer Länge von 210 m gewaltig. Dieser Bautypus setzte sich im ganzen Reich durch und wurde erst nach und nach von dem überwölbten Kirchentypus abgelöst.

Mit der 532 begonnenen Hagia Sophia erreichte der Kuppelbau in Konstantinopel seinen Höhepunkt: Die herrliche, mehr als 30 m überspannende Kuppel bildet zusammen mit den als Widerlager dienenden Halbkuppeln einen mehr als 70 m langen, stützenlosen Raum. Die einzelnen Elemente gehen ohne scharfe Grenzen ineinander über; die strahlenden Mosaiken verschleiern zusätzlich die Übergänge.

The reign of Constantine, and in particular his Edict of Milan (313) proclaiming peace with the Christian churches and an end to their persecution, marked the beginning of a new era. The foundation of Constantinople (330) and the final division of the Empire on the death of Theodosius in 395 ushered in the Byzantine world of the Eastern Empire. The historical rupture hardly found expression on the architectural level, however; contemporaneous with the first St. Irene and the great palace on the Bosphorus, a hippodrome perpetuated the customs and sports of Rome. Roman techniques remained in use, and interiors changed only slowly as the basilica was adapted as a place of Christian worship.

Early Christian architecture was thus an extension of that of Rome. The Basilica of St. Peter with its atrium and its five wooden-roofed aisles was built by Constantine at the same time as the Church of the Holy Sepulchre, and achieved the impressive length of 210 m. This structure was adopted throughout the Empire, and it was only gradually that vaulted roofs came in.

The great church of Hagia Sophia in Constantinople, begun in 532, marks the culmination of the dome formula; its fantastic dome, over 30 m. across, is buttressed by two half-domes, the whole arrangement roofing a space more than 70 m. long without intermediate support. The connections are treated in a fluid manner, with no sharp angles, and gleaming mosaics further obscure them.

From this point on, Byzantine architecture coherently developed the vault solution, but on a smaller scale. Volumes were subdivided around a central-

97

cherche cohérente du voûtement, mais à une échelle moindre. Autour de l'espace central, les volumes se subdivisent: Saint-Vital de Ravenne, Sainte-Sophie de Salonique, Saint-Luc de Phocide. La grande majorité des églises sont construites sur un plan à peu près carré, à trois absides, précédé d'un narthex et surmonté d'une coupole centrale sur tambour.

Une province éloignée du monde chrétien, le royaume d'Arménie, élabore un style particulier, fondé sur le blocage d'inspiration romaine, mais revêtu d'un magnifique parement de pierres de taille souvent richement sculpté. Les formes dures, géométriques, compactes, la richesse des formules de voûtement, où ils témoignent d'une étonnante imagination, font des œuvres créées par les Arméniens l'un des creusets de l'architecture médiévale.

In der Folge entwickelte Byzanz den Gewölbebau systematisch, jedoch in bescheideneren Ausmaßen weiter. Mittelraum und anliegende Nebenräume werden wieder deutlich getrennt: San Vitale in Ravenna, die Sophienkirche in Saloniki und die Kirchen des Lukasklosters in Phokis. Die meisten dieser Kirchen haben einen annähernd quadratischen Grundriß, drei Apsiden, eine zentrale Tambourkuppel und einen vorgelagerten Narthex.

Das Königreich Armenien, ein Gebiet am Rand der christlichen Welt, entwickelte einen eigenen Stil: Bruchsteinmauerwerk nach römischer Art erhielt eine großartige, oft reich skulptierte Werksteinverblendung. Bauten mit klaren, geometrischen, kompakten Formen und der Reichtum an Wölbungssystemen – Zeichen einer erstaunlichen Phantasie und Vorstellungskraft – zeigen Armenien als einen Schmelztiegel der mittelalterlichen Architektur.

ised space: S. Vitale, Ravenna; Hagia Sophia, Salonika; Hosios Lukas, Phocis. The vast majority of churches were built on a more or less square plan with three apses, preceded by a narthex and crowned with a central dome on a drum.

One remote outpost of the Christian world, the kingdom of Armenia, worked out a style of its own based on Roman-type rubble-work but clad with a magnificent freestone facing that was often richly carved. The hard, compact, geometrical forms used by the Armenians and the wealth of vault types, testifying to an astonishing imagination, make these buildings one of the main meeting points of medieval architectural trends.

1 Coupole de Sainte-Sophie de Constantinople, dont le diamètre dépasse 31 m, construite en 532 par Anthémios de Tralles et Isidore de Milet.
2 Façade du sanctuaire de Saint-Siméon le Stylite, à Qalat Siman, en Syrie, datant de 460.
3 Eglise Sainte-Irène, à Constantinople, datant de 740. Au centre, les degrés du synthronon.

1 Konstantinopel, Hagia Sophia, die Kuppel mit einem Durchmesser von mehr als 31 m (Anthemios von Thralles und Isidor von Milet, 532–537)
2 Qalaat Seman (Syrien), Fassade der Kirche des hl. Symeon Stylites (460 begonnen)
3 Konstantinopel, Hagia Irene; in der Apsis das Synthronon des Bischofs und der Geistlichen (740)

1 Dome of Hagia Sophia, Constantinople. More than 31 m. in diameter, it was built by Anthemius of Tralles and Isidorus of Miletus in 532.
2 Façade of the sanctuary of St. Simeon Stylites, Kalaat Saman (Syria; 460).
3 S. Irene, Constantinople (740). In the centre are the steps of the *synthronon* or joint throne for bishop and presbyters.

1

2

3

99

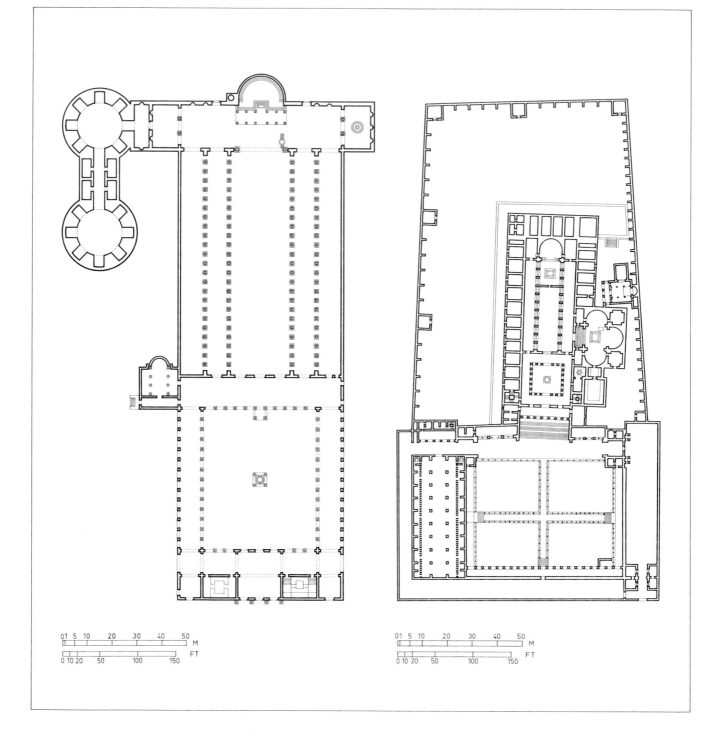

01 5 10 20 30 40 50 M
0 10 20 50 100 150 FT

01 5 10 20 30 40 50 M
0 10 20 50 100 150 FT

Première **Basilique Saint-Pierre de Rome.** Plan restitué 1:1500. Cette immense basilique à cinq nefs, précédée d'un vaste atrium à portiques, a été édifiée dès 324 par Constantin et inaugurée vers 336. L'édifice, détruit à la Renaissance, était couvert à l'aide de fermes. A droite, **Eglise et monastère de Tébessa (Algérie),** construits entre le IVe et le VIe siècle. Plan 1:1500.

Links: **Rom, Alt St. Peter,** 324 begonnen, um 336 geweiht. Der unter Konstantin begonnenen fünfschiffigen Basilika mit offenem Dachstuhl war ein Atrium mit Antiportikus vorgelagert. Die Kirche wurde durch den heutigen Bau von St. Peter ersetzt. Grundriß (Rekonstruktion) 1:1500. Rechts: **Tebessa (Algerien), Kirche und Kloster,** 4.–6. Jh. Grundriß 1:1500.

First **Basilica of St. Peter, Rome.** Reconstructed plan 1:1500. This immense five-aisled basilica, fronted by a vast porticoed atrium, was begun by Constantine in 324 and dedicated around 336, but was destroyed at the Renaissance. The building was roofed with trusses. Right, **Church and monastery of Tebessa** (Algeria), built between the fourth and sixth centuries. Plan 1:1500.

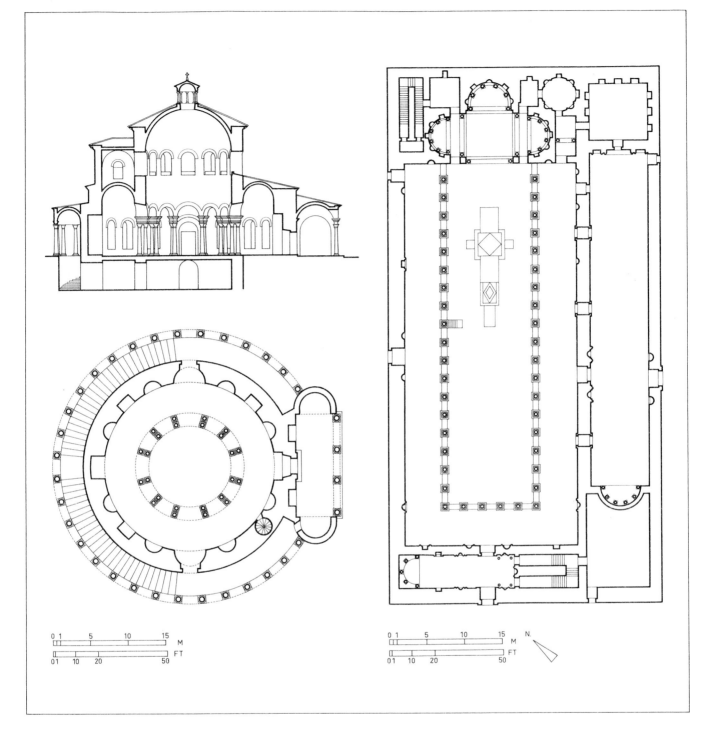

Eglise-rotonde (dite Mausolée) de Sainte-Constance, à Rome. Plan 1:500. Edifice à plan centré avec crypte, datant de 340 à 355. Un déambulatoire circulaire à portiques extérieurs fait le tour du bâtiment à coupole. A droite, Monastère Blanc, à Deir-el-Abiad, près de Sohag, en Egypte, bâti vers 460. Plan 1:500. Ce couvent est l'œuvre du moine et «prophète» copte Chenouté.

Links: Rom, Sta. Costanza (Mausoleum), 340–355. Um den inneren, überhöhten, kuppelgewölbten Raum führt ein tonnengewölbter Umgang. An die Vorhalle schließt beidseits ein Säulenumgang an. Grundriß 1:500. Rechts: Deir-el-Abiad (bei Sohag, Ägypten), Weißes Kloster, um 460. Ein Werk des koptischen Mönchs und Propheten Schenute. Grundriß 1:500.

Round church (or 'Mausoleum') of S. Costanza, Rome, built 340–355. Plan 1:500. A domed centralised structure with a crypt is surrounded by a circular ambulatory with external porticoes. Right, the White Monastery, Dayr al-Abiad (near Sohag, Egypt), built c. 460. Plan 1:500. The architect was the Coptic monk and 'prophet' Shenute.

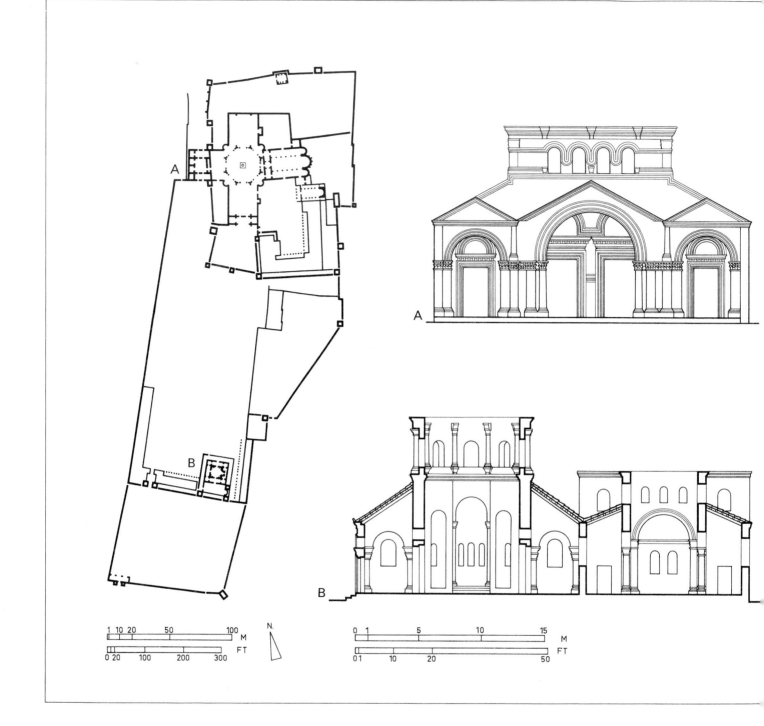

Couvent et forteresse de Saint-Siméon le Stylite (Qalat Siman), en Syrie du Nord, construit dès 460. Situation au Xe s. 1:3000. A) Eglise Saint-Siméon, B) Baptistère. A droite en haut, façade méridionale de l'église Saint-Siméon. Elévation 1:300. En bas, coupe du baptistère et de la chapelle attenante, 1:300. L'ensemble est en blocs soigneusement appareillés avec toiture en charpente.

Links: **Qalaat Seman, Festung und Heiligtum des Symeon Stylites,** 460 begonnen. Die Bauten mit sorgfältigem Steinschnitt tragen offene Dachstühle. Plan des Zustandes im 10. Jh. 1:3000: A) Kirche des hl. Symeon, B) Baptisterium. Rechts: A) Südfassade der Kirche, Aufriß 1:300; B) Schnitt durch das Baptisterium und die angrenzende Kapelle 1:300.

Monastery and fortress of St. Simeon Stylites (Kalaat Saman), north Syria, begun in 460. Site in the tenth century 1:3000. A) church of St. Simeon, B) baptistry. Above right, south façade of the church of St. Simeon, elevation 1:300. Below, section of the baptistry and the adjoining chapel 1:300. The complex is built of carefully jointed masonry with wooden roofs.

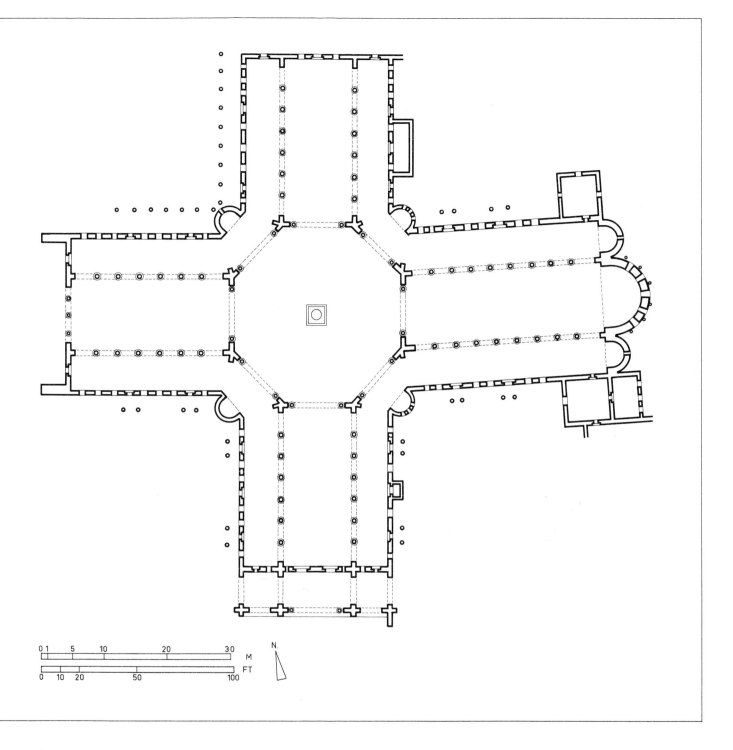

0 1	5	10	20	30	
					M
0	10 20		50	100	FT

N.

Eglise **Saint-Siméon le Stylite**, sanctuaire cruciforme. Plan 1:600. Au centre de l'octogone se dressait la colonne sur laquelle avait vécu l'anachorète. L'octogone, que d'aucuns considèrent comme un atrium, semble plutôt avoir été couvert d'une coupole en bois, d'un type analogue à celle du Dôme du Rocher à Jérusalem. La longueur de la nef avoisine 100 m.

Qalaat Seman, Kirche des hl. Symeon Stylites. Im Zentrum des kreuzförmigen Baues liegt ein Oktogon, in dessen Mitte die Säule stand, auf der der Anachoret lebte. Entgegen der Theorie, dieses Oktogon sei ein Atrium, scheint es mit einer hölzernen Kuppel überdacht gewesen zu sein, ähnlich der des Felsendomes in Jerusalem. Das Schiff ist fast 100 m lang. Grundriß 1:600.

Cruciform **Church of St. Simeon Stylites.** Plan 1:600. At the centre of the octagon stood the pillar on which the anchorite had lived. This octagon, which some authorities regard as an atrium, in fact appears to have been roofed with a wooden dome of the kind used for the Dome of the Rock, Jerusalem. The nave is c.100 m. long.

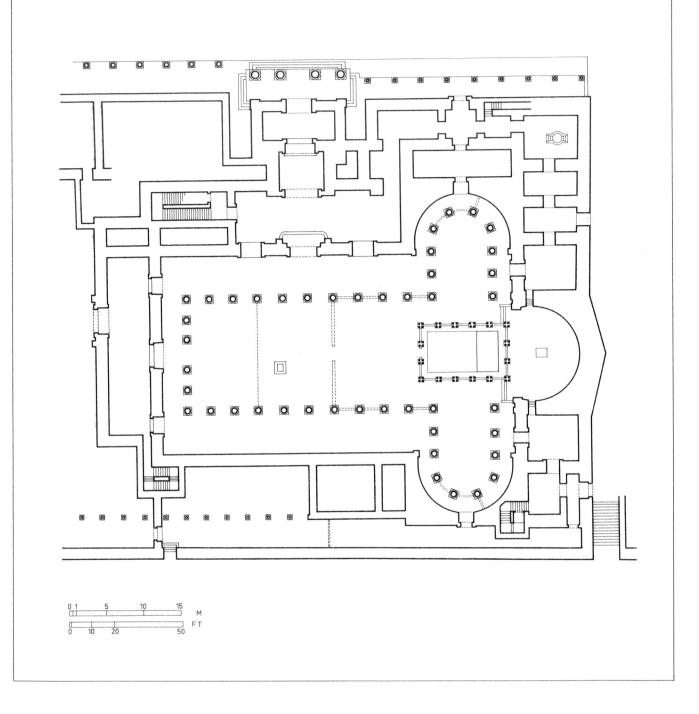

0 1   5   10   15   M
0   10   20   50   F T

Cathédrale d'Hermopolis (Ashmuneim), en Egypte, construite vers 440. Plan 1:500. L'architecture copte se caractérise souvent par cette formule du chœur triconque, ainsi que par les arcades intérieures faisant le tour de la nef, comme au Monastère Blanc de Sohag.

Hermopolis (heute Ashmunein, Ägypten), Kathedrale, um 440. Die Dreikonchen-anlage des Chores und die innen umlaufende Säulenstellung charakterisieren viele koptische Kirchen, so auch die des Weißen Klosters von Sohag. Grundriß 1:500.

Hermopolis Cathedral (Ashmunein, Egypt), built c.440. Plan 1:500. Coptic architecture often used a three-apsed chancel as well as an interior arcade round the nave (cf. the White Monastery, near Sohag).

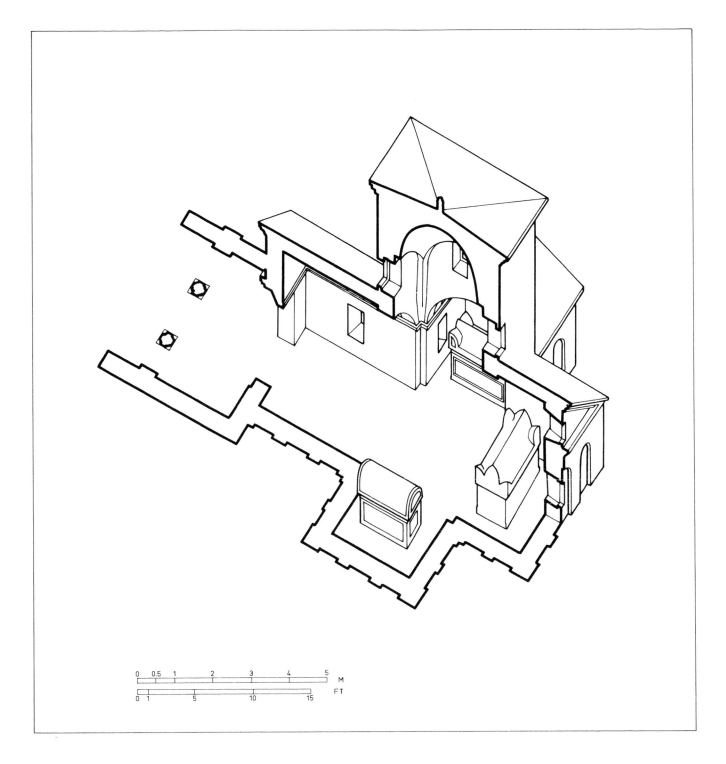

```
0   0.5   1      2      3      4      5
├───┼───┼──────┼──────┼──────┼──────┤   M
├───┼──────────┼──────────────┼──────┤   F T
0   1          5              10            15
```

Eglise, dite Mausolée de Galla Placidia, à Ravenne, construite vers 450. Axonométrie ouverte 1:100. Edifiée par la fille de Théodose I er et de Galla, cette petite église entièrement voûtée et décorée intérieurement d'admirables mosaïques est caractérisée par son plan cruciforme.

Ravenna, Mausoleum der Galla Placidia, um 450. Die kleine, von der Tochter Theodosius' I. und der Galla erbaute kreuzförmige Kirche ist vollständig überwölbt und mit herrlichen Mosaiken geschmückt. Axonometrie 1:100.

Mausoleum of Galla Placidia, Ravenna, built c.450 by the daughter of Theodosius I. Open axonometric projection 1:100. Cruciform in plan, this little church is vaulted throughout and decorated inside with magnificent mosaics.

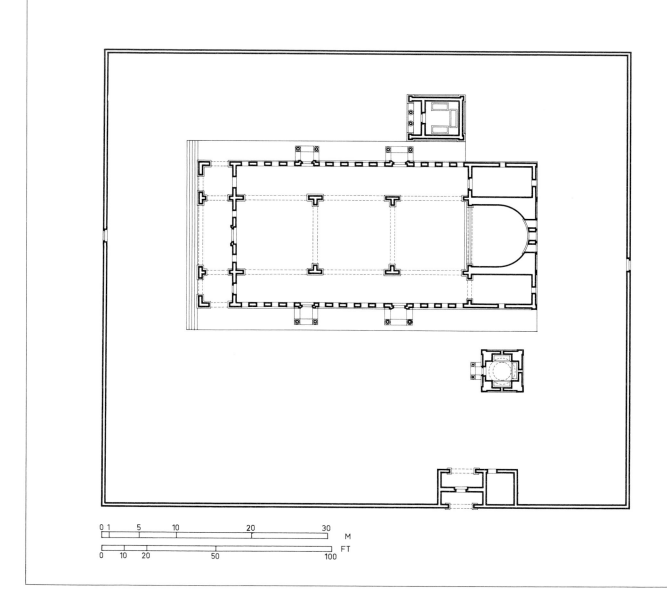

| 0 1 | 5 | 10 | 20 | 30 | M |
| 0 | 10 20 | | 50 | 100 | FT |

Eglise de Bizzos, à Roueïha (Syrie). Plan de situation de l'église et des deux tombeaux à l'intérieur de l'enceinte ou péribole, VIᵉ s. 1:500. Cette église à trois nefs et à triple arcade longitudinale était couverte à l'aide de fermes. Le chœur semi-circulaire, avec voûte en cul-de-four, est légèrement surélevé.

Ruweha (Syrien), Bizzos-Kirche, 6. Jh. Die dreischiffige, dreijochige Kirche hatte einen offenen Dachstuhl. Der gewölbte, halbrund geschlossene Chor liegt einige Stufen erhöht. Grundriß der Kirche mit den beiden Gräbern und der Umfassungsmauer 1:500.

Bizzos church, Roueiha (Syria), sixth century. Site plan of the church and the two tombs in the middle of the enclosing *peribolos* 1:500. This three-aisled church with a triple longitudinal arcade was roofed with the aid of trusses. The semicircular apse with its half-dome is slightly raised.

106

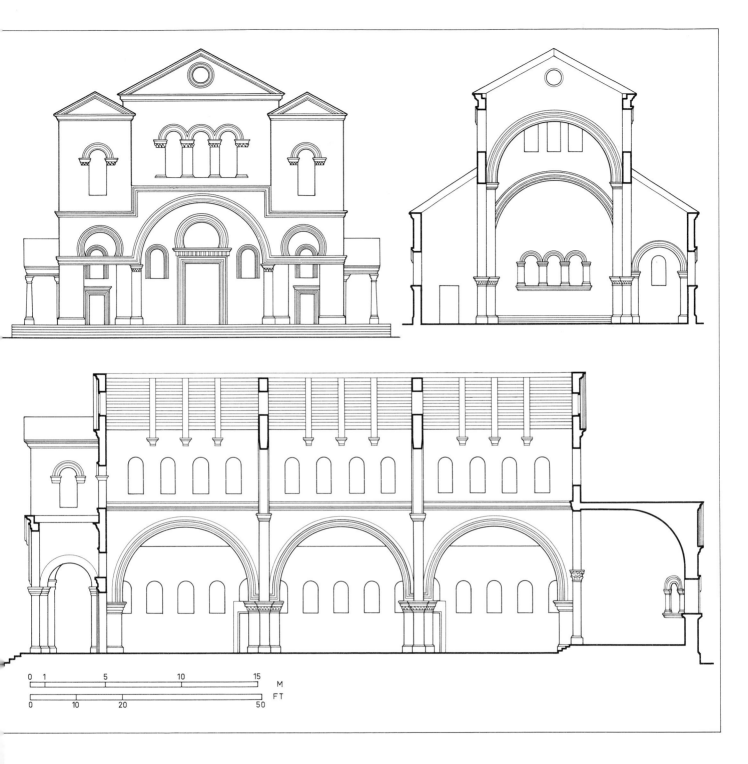

0 1   5   10   15   M
0   10   20   50   FT

Eglise de Bizzos, à Roueïha. Elévation de la façade, coupe transversale et coupe longitudinale 1:250. Cette architecture chrétienne de Syrie se caractérise par la qualité de sa stéréotomie et par les modénatures continues qui enserrent toute les faces de l'édifice. Les grandes arcades de 9 m de portée et la double rangée de fenêtres laissent largement pénétrer la lumière dans la nef centrale.

Ruweha (Syrien), Bizzos-Kirche. Die syrischen Kirchenbauten zeichnen sich durch die Qualität des Steinschnittes und durch die um den ganzen Bau umlaufenden profilierten Gesimse aus. Das Mittelschiff erhält dank der doppelten Fensterreihen und der großen Spannweite der Arkaden (9 m) viel Licht. Fassadenaufriß, Quer- und Längsschnitt 1:250.

Bizzos church, Roueiha. Façade elevation, cross section and longitudinal section 1:250. The Early Christian architecture of Syria was distinguished by the quality of its stereotomy and by the continuous cornices running round all sides of the building. The large arcades (span 9 m.) and the double row of windows admit plenty of light to the nave.

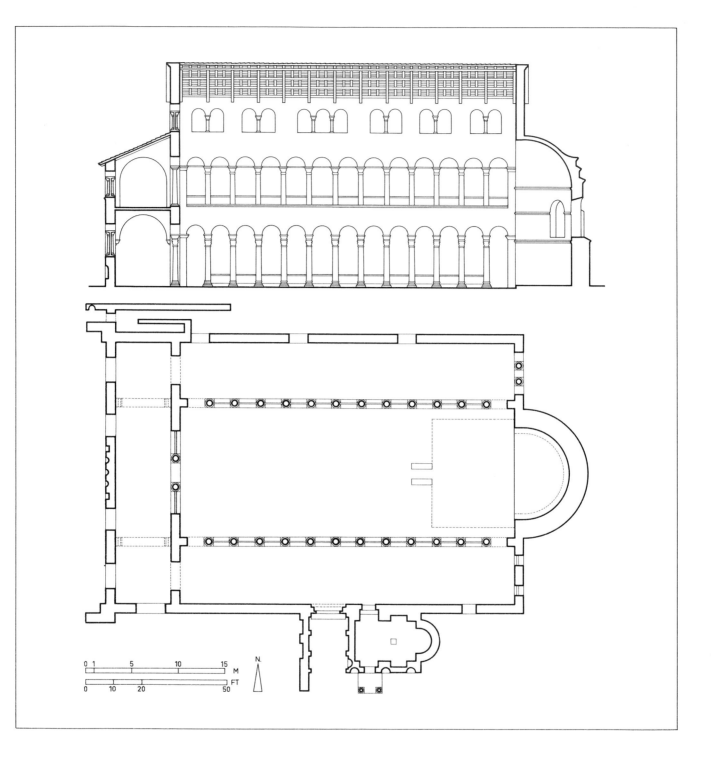

Eglise de l'Acheiropoeitos, à Salonique, construite vers 470. Coupe longitudinale et plan 1:400. Cette église, avec ses deux rangées d'arcades superposées, son narthex et son chœur surmonté d'une voûte en cul-de-four, ainsi que sa couverture à fermes, est un exemple typique de la première architecture chrétienne, dont on retrouve les solutions à Saint-Apollinaire le Neuf de Ravenne.

Saloniki, Archeiropoietos-Kirche, um 470. Der Aufbau der Mittelschiffswände ist dreizonig. Vor der Kirche liegt ein Narthex. Der halbrunde Chor ist mit einer Halbkuppel überwölbt, das Schiff hat einen offenen Dachstuhl. Der Bau ist für die frühchristliche Architektur typisch, ähnliche Lösungen zeigt S. Apollinare Nuovo in Ravenna. Längsschnitt und Grundriß 1:400.

Church of the Acheiropoeitos, Salonika, built *c.*470. Longitudinal section and plan 1:400. With its two superposed arcades, narthex, half-domed chancel and truss roof, this is a typical example of Early Christian architecture. The same features were used for S. Apollinare Nuovo, Ravenna.

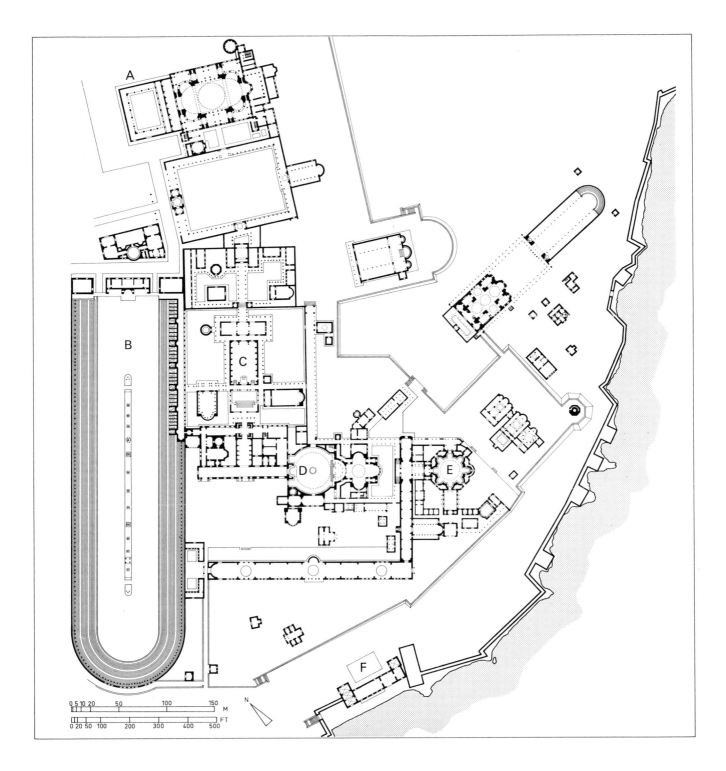

Constantinople à l'époque byzantine. Plan d'ensemble du quartier des palais 1:4000. A) Eglise Sainte-Sophie, B) Hippodrome, C) Palais impérial, D) Triconque, E) Chrysotriklinos, F) Maison dite de Justinien. La cité, bordée de fortifications sur la rive de la mer de Marmara (comme sur toutes ses autres faces: murailles terrestres et Corne d'Or), dominait les détroits de sa splendeur.

Konstantinopel in byzantinischer Zeit. Die am Marmarameer wie auch am Goldenen Horn und auf der Landseite befestigte Stadt beherrschte mit ihrer Pracht die Meerenge. Plan des Palastviertels 1:4000: A) Hagia Sophia, B) Hippodrom, C) kaiserlicher Palast, D) Trikonchos, E) Chrisotriklinos, F) sogenanntes Haus des Justinian.

Constantinople in the Byzantine period. Overall plan of the palace quarter 1:4000. A) Hagia Sophia, B) hippodrome, C) Imperial palace, D) triconch, E) chrysotriklinos F) house of Justinian. The city, bounded by fortifications along the Sea of Marmara shore as well as along its other sides (land walls and Golden Horn), dominated the strait with its splendour.

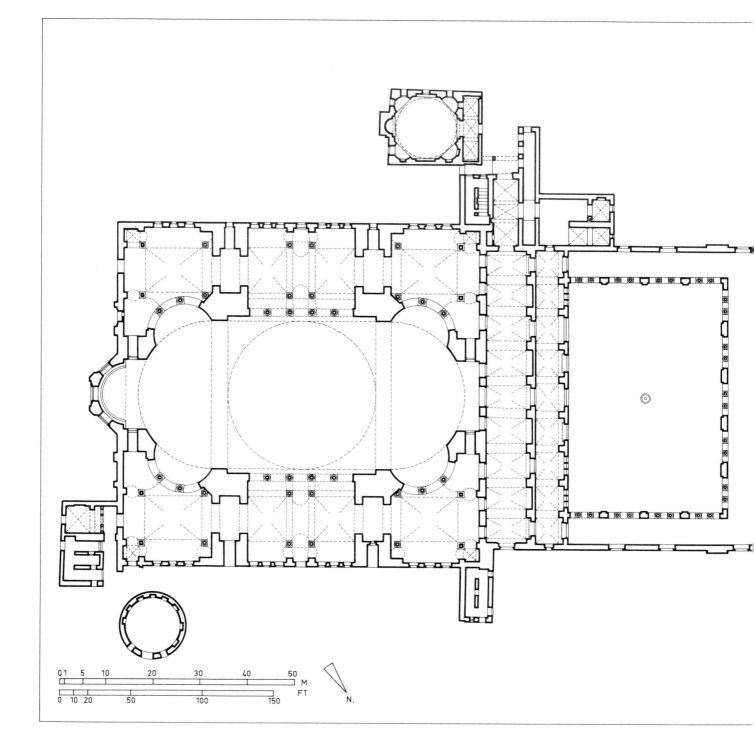

0 1 5 10 20 30 40 50 M
0 10 20 50 100 150 FT

N.

Sainte-Sophie de Constantinople, édifiée par l'empereur Justinien entre 532 et 537. Plan avec l'atrium restitué 1:800. Œuvre des architectes Anthémios de Tralles et Isidore de Milet, cette immense église, dont la coupole centrale dépasse 31 m de diamètre, contre-butée par deux demi-coupoles, elles-mêmes flanquées de deux petites niches à colonnes, est une expérience totalement neuve.

Konstantinopel, Hagia Sophia, 532–537. Die Kirche wurde unter Justinian I. durch Anthemios von Thralles und Isidor von Milet erbaut. Die Kuppel mit mehr als 31 m Durchmesser wird in der Längsachse von zwei Halbkuppeln begleitet, an die seitlich je zwei kleine Säulennischen mit Halbkuppeln anschließen: eine völlig neue Lösung. Grundriß mit rekonstruiertem Atrium 1:800.

Hagia Sophia, Constantinople, built by Justinian 532-7. Plan showing the reconstructed atrium 1:800. Designed by the architects Anthemius of Tralles and Isidore of Miletus, this vast church, with its central dome measuring more than 31 m. in diameter, buttressed by two half-domes that are themselves flanked by small columned niches, was a totally new architectural development.

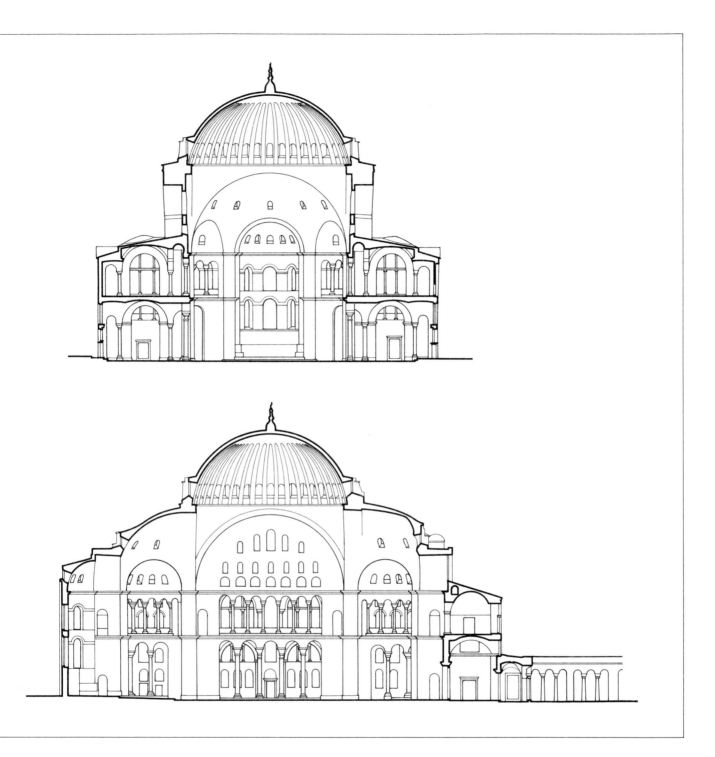

Eglise Sainte-Sophie, à Constantinople. Coupe transversale et coupe longitudinale 1:800. L'énorme espace, dont la coupole centrale culmine à 56 m du dallage, présente deux étages de bas-côtés qui contre-butent la poussée du dôme sur les énormes arcs surmontant les tympans latéraux, largement ajourés. Des rangées de fenêtres percent la base de la coupole.

Konstantinopel, Hagia Sophia. Der Scheitel der Hauptkuppel liegt 56 m über dem Boden. Die zweigeschossigen Seitenschiffe dienen als Widerlager für den Druck der Kuppel auf die Bögen der reich durchfensterten seitlichen Schildwände. Ein Fensterkranz durchbricht den Kuppelfuß. Quer- und Längsschnitt 1:800.

Hagia Sophia, Constantinople. Cross section and longitudinal section 1:800. The enormous central space, with the dome rising to a height of 56 m. above the floor, is flanked by two storeys of side aisles taking the thrust of the dome on huge arches that frame generously windowed tympani. A further row of windows runs round the base of the dome.

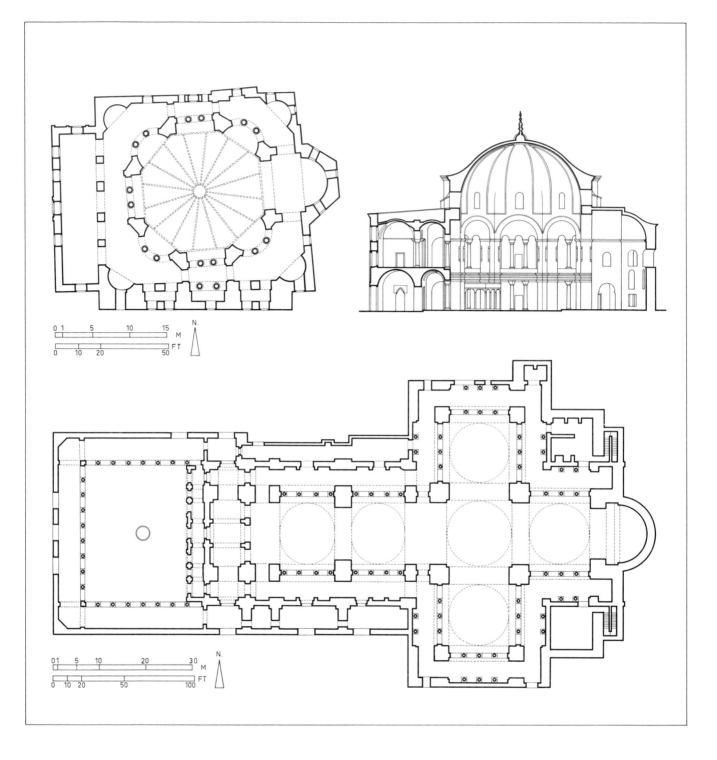

Eglise Saints-Serge-et-Bacchus, à Constantinople, édifiée entre 527 et 536. Plan et coupe longitudinale 1:500. Eglise byzantine typique à coupole centrale et déambulatoire. En bas, **Basilique d'Ephèse,** consacrée à Saint-Jean-le-Théologien, achevée en 565. Plan 1:800. L'édifice, sans l'atrium, dépasse 100 m de longueur. Le voûtement comporte six coupoles de 14 m.

Oben: **Konstantinopel, St.Sergios und Bakchos,** 527–536. Die zentrale Kuppel und der Umgang sind für byzantinische Kirchen typisch. Grundriß und Längsschnitt 1:500. Unten: **Ephesus, Johannes-Basilika,** 565 vollendet. Die Kuppelbasilika ist (ohne Atrium) über 100 m lang, die Kuppeln haben ca. 14 m Durchmesser. Grundriß 1:800.

SS. Sergius and Bacchus, Constantinople, a typical Byzantine church with a central dome and an ambulatory, built 527–36. Plan and longitudinal section 1:500. Below, **Basilica of St.John the Divine, Ephesus,** completed in 565. Plan 1:800. Not counting the atrium, the building is more than 100 m. long. It is vaulted with six 14 m. domes.

0 1 5 10 20 30 M
0 10 20 50 100 FT
N.

Eglise Saint-Vital, à Ravenne, construite entre 530 et 547. Coupe longitudinale et plan 1:500. Edifice octogonal à plan centré, dont le narthex décalé par rapport à l'axe devait être précédé d'un atrium rectangulaire, Saint-Vital témoigne d'un style constantinopolitain. Contemporaine de Sainte-Sophie, cette église influera sur la chapelle palatine d'Aix.

Ravenna, San Vitale, 530–547. Oktogonaler Zentralbau mit aus der Achse verschobenem Narthex, vermutlich war ein Atrium vorgelagert. Die gleichzeitig mit der Hagia Sophia entstandene Kirche ist ein Beispiel byzantinischer Architektur im weströmischen Reich; beim Bau der Aachener Pfalzkapelle wurde dieser Baugedanke wieder aufgegriffen. Längsschnitt und Grundriß 1:500.

S. Vitale, Ravenna, built 530–47. Longitudinal section and plan 1:500. The narthex of this octagonal centrally-planned church lies off the axis and was to have been fronted by a rectangular atrium. Contemporary with Hagia Sophia and reflecting the style of Constantinople, the influence of S. Vitale can be seen in the Palatine Chapel, Aachen.

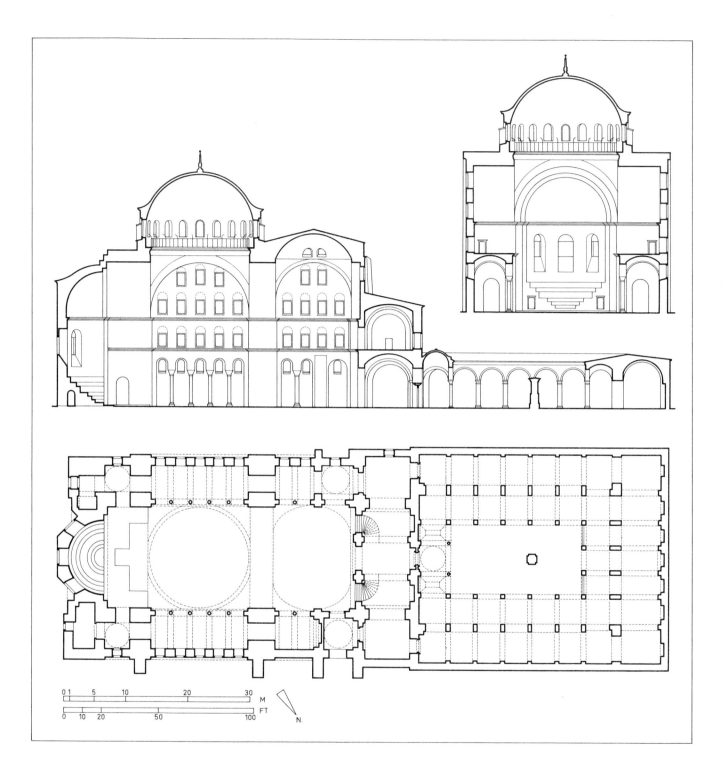

Eglise Sainte-Irène, à Constantinople,
bâtie par Constantin V Copronyme en
740 sur les ruines de l'église justinienne
incendiée une première fois en 532, puis
en 564, et dévastée par un séisme en
740. Coupe longitudinale et coupe transversale, plan 1:600. Basilique à coupoles précédée d'un atrium à double
arcade. Dans l'abside, le synthronon
destiné au clergé.

Konstantinopel, Hagia Irene, 740. Konstantin V. Kopronymos ließ die Kuppelbasilika über den Ruinen einer justinia-
nischen, 532 und 564 durch Brand,740
durch Erdbeben zerstörten Kirche er-
bauen. In der Apsis das Synthronon der
Geistlichkeit; das Atrium hat auf drei
Seiten eine doppelte Arkadenreihe.
Längs- und Querschnitt, Grundriß
1:600.

S.Irene, Constantinople, built in 740 by
Constantine V Copronymos, on the
ruins of the Justinian church that had
burned down once in 532, a second
time in 564, and had been destroyed in
an earthquake in 740. Longitudinal
section, cross section and plan 1:600.
A domed basilica is fronted by an
atrium with a double arcade. The apse
contains the *synthronon*, reserved for
the clergy.

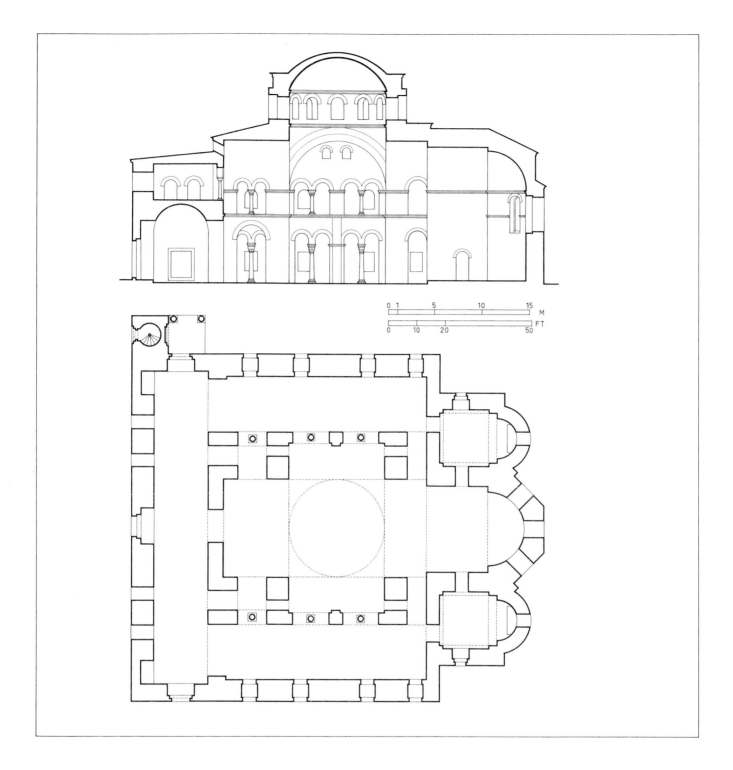

Sainte-Sophie de Salonique, construite dans la seconde moitié du VIIIᵉ s. Coupe longitudinale et plan 1:400. Plan à croix grecque inscrite, entourée de la galerie formée par les collatéraux et le narthex, qui constitue l'espace byzantin typique. La coupole trapue marque encore une formule qui évoluera vers une plus grande légèreté.

Saloniki, Sophienkirche, 2. Hälfte 8. Jh. Um den inneren Raum in Form eines griechischen Kreuzes läuft ein durch die Seitenschiffe und den Narthex gebildeter Umgang – ein typisch byzantinischer Raum. In der flachen Kuppel kündigen sich leichtere architektonische Lösungen an. Längsschnitt und Grundriß 1:400.

Hagia Sophia, Salonika, built in the second half of the eighth century. Longitudinal section and plan 1:400. Built on a Greek cross plan, the church is surrounded by the gallery formed by side aisles and narthex, making a typically Byzantine interior. The squat dome was another solution that was to evolve in the direction of greater lightness.

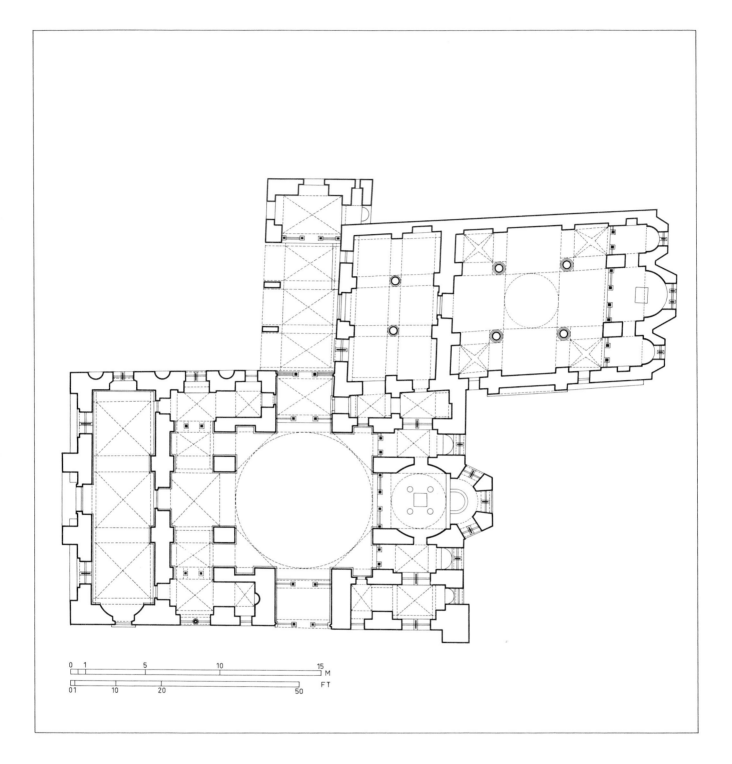

Scale bar:
0 1 ... 5 ... 10 ... 15 M
01 ... 10 ... 20 ... 50 FT

Eglises du Monastère Saint-Luc de Pho-cide, présentant, en haut du plan, le sanctuaire de Théotokos, de la fin du Xᵉ s., à coupole supportée par quatre colonnes, et en bas, l'église conven-tuelle ou Catholicon, datant du début du XIᵉ s., avec coupole sur trompes, 1:250. Issue de Perse, la trompe d'angle fait ici sa première apparition en Grèce, vraisemblablement sous le règne de Basile II.

Phokis, Kirchen des Lukasklosters. An die Kirche des Theotokos (oben), Ende 10.Jh., deren Kuppel auf vier Säulen ruht, schließt die Klosterkirche – das Katholikon – an (unten), Anfang 11.Jh. Die Kuppel dieses Baues ruht auf Trompen. Hier wurde – wohl unter Basilios II. – zum ersten Mal in Grie-chenland die aus Persien stammende Ecktrompe verwendet. Grundriß 1:250.

Churches of the monastery of Hosios Lukas, Phocis. Plan 1:250. Above is the shrine of Theotokos, late tenth century, with a dome supported by four col-umns; below is the monastery church or 'Catholicon', early eleventh century, with a dome on squinches. A Persian import, the squinch was here making its first appearance in Greece, probably in the reign of Basil II.

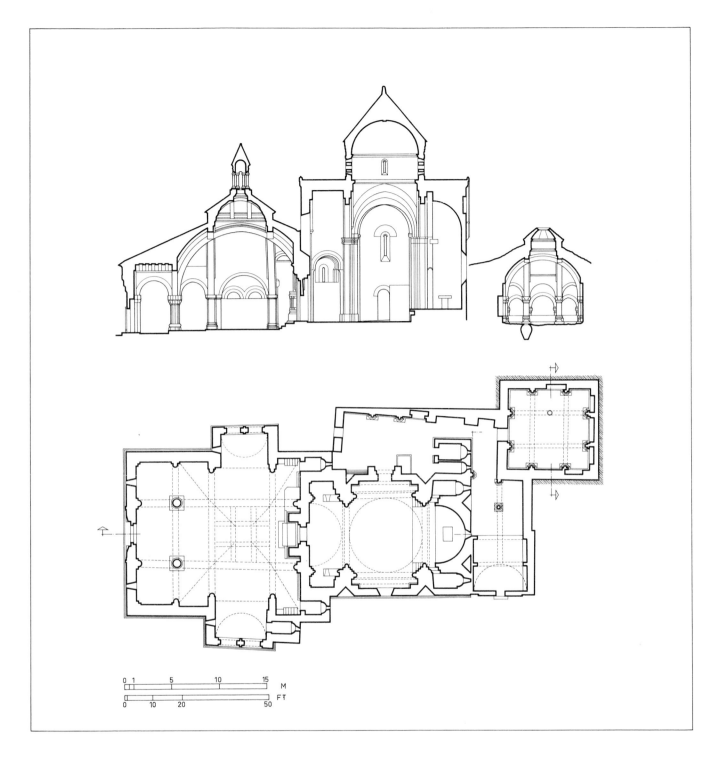

Complexe monastique de Haghbat, en Arménie, datant de 991. Coupe longitudinale et plan 1:400. L'architecture arménienne constitue une province particulière de l'art byzantin: absides inscrites dans l'épaisseur des murs, arcs entrecroisés, faisceaux de colonnes, stéréotomie savante la caractérisent. De gauche à droite: narthex, église conventuelle et bibliothèque.

Haghbat (Armenien), Kloster, 991. Die armenische Architektur bildet innerhalb der byzantinischen Kunst eine eigene Gruppe: in die Mauern eingetiefte Apsiden, Kreuzbögen, Säulenbündel, ein sehr sorgfältiger Steinschnitt. Längsschnitt und Grundriß 1:400: von links nach rechts: Narthex, Kirche, Bibliothek.

Monastic complex, Haghbat (Armenia), built 991. Longitudinal section and plan 1:400. Armenia developed its own version of Byzantine architecture, characterised by apses recessed in the thickness of the wall, intersecting arches, clustered piers and skilful stone-cutting. From left to right: narthex, monastery church and library.

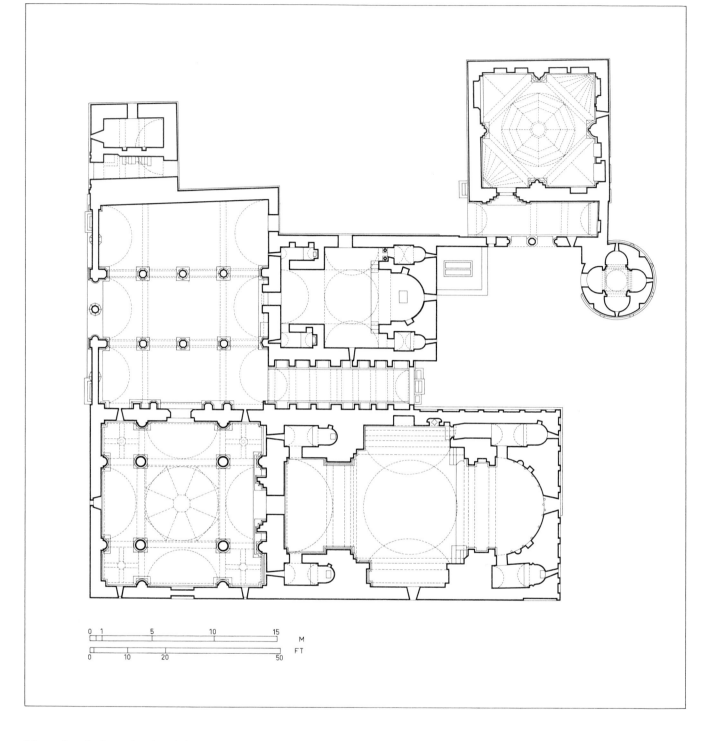

0 1   5   10   15   M

0   10   20   50   FT

Monastère de Sanahin, Arménie, complexe conventuel édifié du Xe au XIIIe s. Plan 1:300. Ensemble caractéristique de l'art arménien à son apogée, avec, à gauche, les narthex à colonnes des églises de Marie (en haut) et du Saint-Sauveur (en bas). A l'extrême droite en haut, la bibliothèque et la chapelle Saint-Grégoire, en croix tréflée.

Sanahin (Armenien), Kloster, 10.–13. Jh. Der Komplex ist für die Blütezeit der armenischen Architektur typisch. Die Marienkirche (oben) und die Erlöserkirche (unten) liegen Seite an Seite, vor jeder ein Narthex mit Säulenstellungen. An die Marienkirche anschließend (oben rechts) die Bibliothek und die Kapelle St. Gregor mit kleeblattförmigem Innenraum. Grundriß 1:300.

Sanahin monastery (Armenia), a monastic complex built in the tenth to thirteenth century. Plan 1:300. Left, the columned narthices of S. Maria (above) and St. Saviour (below); top right-hand corner, the library and the St. Gregory chapel, forming a trefoil cross. Sanahin typifies the great age of Armenian architecture.

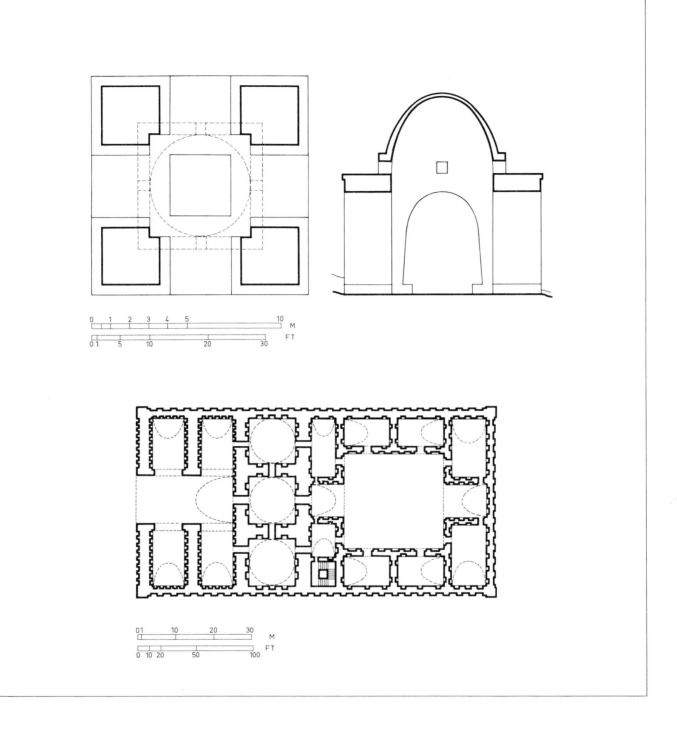

0 1 2 3 4 5   10   M

0 1   5   10   20   30   FT

01   10   20   30   M

FT
0 10 20   50   100

Architecture sassanide: en haut, **Tchahar-Tak de Neisar,** autel du feu datant de 229 apr. J.-C. Plan et coupe transversale 1:200. La voûte passe insensiblement du plan carré au plan circulaire. En bas, **Grand Palais de Firouzabad** (230). Plan 1:1000. Cet édifice aux murs redentés est entièrement couvert de voûtes et de coupoles sur trompes, caractéristiques des constructions de la Perse.

Sassanidische Architektur: oben: Neisar, **Tschahar Tak, Feueraltar,** 229. Das Gewölbe beginnt auf quadratischem Grundriß und geht unmerklich in ein Rund über. Grundriß und Querschnitt 1:200. Unten. **Firuzabad, Großer Palast,** 230. Die Mauern sind mit Vor- und Rücksprüngen gegliedert, der ganze Bau ist mit Gewölben und Trompenkuppel überspannt. Axonometrie; Grundriß 1:1000.

Sassanid architecture: Above, **Chahar-Tak, Neisar,** a fire altar dating from A.D. 229. Plan and cross section 1:200. The vault passes imperceptibly from a square to a circular plan. Below, **Great Palace, Firozabad,** built 230. Plan 1:1000. The building has ribbed walls and is roofed throughout with vaults and with the squinch domes typical of Persian architecture.

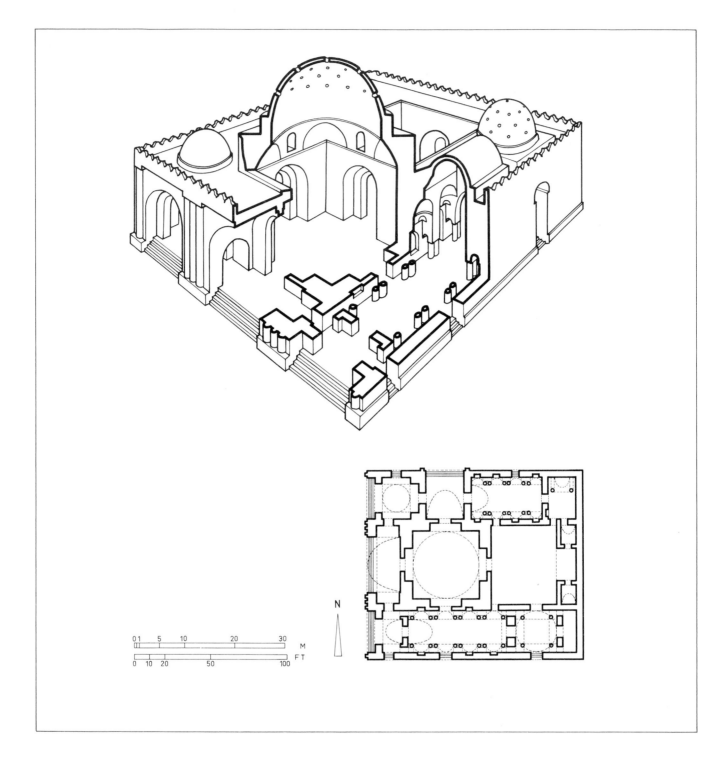

Palais sassanide de Sarvistan, datant de 420–430 de notre ère. Coupe axonométrique, plan 1:750. Comme à Firouzabad, on voit paraître ici la notion d'iwân d'entrée combiné avec une salle voûtée, dont l'architecture islamique de la Perse fera largement usage et qui dérive lointainement des portiques de Persépolis.

Sarwistan, Sassanidenpalast, 420–430. Wie in Firuzabad – und häufig in der islamischen Architektur Persiens – ist hier der Eingangs-Liwan mit einem Kuppelraum kombiniert. Diese Form geht letztlich auf die Portiken von Persepolis zurück. Axonometrie; Grundriß 1:750.

Sassanid palace, Sarvistan, built A.D. 420–30. Axonometric section, plan 1:750. Again, as at Firozabad, we find the idea of an entrance *iwan* combined with a vaulted hall of which Persia's Moslem architects were to make such extensive use. It is distantly derived from the porticoes of Persepolis.

Haut Moyen Age

Frühes Mittelalter

The Early Middle Ages

Lorsque l'Occident est submergé par les vagues d'invasions barbares et que l'Empire romain bascule dans le chaos, l'architecture se modifie profondément. Certes, l'héritage paléochrétien survit en partie, quand, la tourmente passée, on recommence à bâtir au VIIe siècle. Ce bref élan sera brisé au sud par la conquête arabe de l'Espagne et du midi de la France (722), et plus au nord par les raids des Vikings (dès 790) et des Hongrois à l'est (début Xe s.).

Mais dans tout l'Occident «les grands édifices publics romains restent debout, tout en changeant de fonction: les thermes deviennent résidences de seigneurs, les entrepôts monastères, les arènes forteresses». L'Eglise est l'unique institution qui survit à la mort de l'Empire. C'est elle qui, monopolisant l'administration, la justice et l'éducation, va être le principal bâtisseur, en attendant que le pouvoir se raffermisse, en Espagne du Nord avec la cour asturienne, en Europe centrale avec l'Empire carolingien.

C'est en Espagne que les édifices les plus nombreux ont subsisté, pour la période du Haut Moyen Age. Héritiers des réalisations visigothiques, les monuments asturiano-mozarabes forment un tout cohérent, caractérisé par l'échelle réduite des constructions, par le cloisonnement des espaces et par le recours fréquent aux arcs outrepassés. Poursuivant le courant créé par San Juan de Baños, San Frutuoso de Montelios et San Pedro de la Nave (VIIe s.) et qu'interrompt brutalement l'invasion islamique, toute une architecture va renaître aux IXe et Xe siècles dans le nord de la péninsule, avec des églises comme San Julian de los Prados à Oviedo, San Miguel de Lillo, Santa Cris-

Als die Völkerwanderung über das Abendland zog und das Weströmische Reich unterging, vollzog sich in der Architektur ein tiefgreifender Wandel. Im 7. Jahrhundert, nachdem eine Beruhigung eingetreten war, begann man wieder zu bauen. Damals war das frühchristliche Erbe noch mancherorts lebendig. Die neuen Ansätze wurden im Süden durch die Eroberung Spaniens und Südfrankreichs durch die Araber (722), im Norden durch die Wikingerzüge (ab 790) und im Osten durch den Einfall der Ungarn (Anfang 10. Jahrhundert) jäh unterbrochen.

Im ganzen Abendland waren die großen öffentlichen Bauten der Römer intakt geblieben, dienten aber neuen Zwecken: Thermen wurden zu Palästen der Landesherren, Lagerhäuser zu Klöstern, Arenen zu Festungen. Die Kirche überlebte als einzige Institution den Untergang des Römischen Reiches. Verwaltung, Rechtsprechung und Erziehung waren in ihrer Macht, und sie wurde zum wichtigsten Bauherrn, bis in Nordspanien – durch den Hof von Asturien – und in Mitteleuropa mit dem karolingischen Reich die weltliche Macht wieder erstarkte.

Die größte Anzahl frühmittelalterlicher Bauten ist in Spanien erhalten geblieben. Die auf westgotischer Tradition fußenden asturisch-mozarabischen Bauten bilden ein in sich geschlossenes Ganzes; sie sind durch geringe Größe, Raumunterteilung und -trennung und häufige Verwendung des Hufeisenbogens charakterisiert. Die Entwicklung wurde durch San Juan de Baños, San Frutuoso de Montelios und San Pedro de la Nave (7. Jahrhundert) eingeleitet. Nach der jähen Unterbrechung durch die arabische Invasion

As the West was swamped by successive waves of barbarian invasions and the Roman Empire toppled into chaos, architecture underwent a profound change. The Early Christian heritage did of course survive in part when, the turmoil over, Europe began building again in the seventh century. But this brief recovery was interrupted; in the south by the Arab conquest of Spain and southern France (722), in the north by Viking raids (from 790 onwards), and in the east by Hungarians (early tenth century).

Throughout the West, however, 'the great Roman public buildings remained standing, though they altered their function: thermae became noble residences, warehouses became monasteries, arenas became fortresses' (André Corboz). The only institution to survive the death of the Empire was the Church. It was the Church, monopolising the fields of administration, justice and education, that was the principal source of architectural commissions until the secular power was able to re-establish itself with the Asturian court in northern Spain and the Carolingian Empire in Central Europe.

It is in Spain that the largest number of buildings has survived from the early medieval period. Influenced by the Visigoths, the monuments of Mozarabic Asturias form a coherent whole, distinguished by their reduced scale, by the way in which they partition space, and by their frequent recourse to horseshoe arches. Continuing the tradition of S. Juan de Baños, S. Frutuoso de Montelios, and S. Pedro de la Nave (seventh century), a tradition that was rudely interrupted by the Moslem invasion, a whole architecture was reborn in

tina de Lena et surtout San Miguel de Escalada (913) et San Cebrian de Mazote (916), ainsi que des palais de souverains asturiens, dont Santa Maria de Naranco est un exemple exceptionnellement bien conservé.

Dans le centre de l'Europe, la renaissance carolingienne donne lieu à une remarquable réussite avec la chapelle palatine d'Aix (777), apparentée au plan de Saint-Vital de Ravenne. On citera aussi l'immense abbaye de Corvey (822), dont la formule se perpétue à l'époque ottonienne avec Saint-Cyriakus de Gernrode et Saint-Michel de Hildesheim. Un groupe alpin a conservé également des traditions très anciennes, tant en Suisse à Müstair et à Mistail, qu'en Italie à Santa Maria in Valle («Tempietto longobardo»), où sont perceptibles des réminiscences paléochrétiennes et ravennates.

entfaltete sich im 9. und 10. Jahrhundert im Norden der Iberischen Halbinsel eine reiche Bautätigkeit mit Kirchen wie San Julian de los Prados in Oviedo, San Miguel de Lillo, Santa Cristina de Lena und vor allem San Miguel in Escalada (913) und San Cebrian in Mazote (916) sowie mit den Bauten der asturischen Herrscher, für die die Königshalle von Santa Maria de Naranco ein außerordentlich gut erhaltenes Beispiel ist.

In Mitteleuropa entstanden während der karolingischen Renaissance so großartige Werke wie die Aachener Pfalzkapelle (777) – in der Anlage San Vitale in Ravenna ähnlich – und die große Abtei von Corvey (822), die auf die ottonischen Bauten von Sankt Cyriakus in Gernrode (989 voll.) und Sankt Michael in Hildesheim (1033 voll.) weiterwirkte.

Eine Gruppe alpenländischer Bauten steht in einer weit zurückreichenden Tradition: in der Schweiz die Kirchen von Mistail und Müstair, in Norditalien Santa Maria in Valle («Tempietto longobardo»), wo sich Anklänge an frühchristliche und ravennatische Formen finden.

the northern part of the Iberian peninsula in the ninth and tenth centuries with such churches as S. Julian de los Prados, Oviedo, S. Miguel de Lillo, S. Cristina de Lena, and above all S. Miguel de Escalada (913) and S. Cebrian de Mazote (916) as well as with the palaces of the Asturian rulers, of which S. Maria de Naranco is an exceptionally well preserved example.

In Central Europe the Carolingian renaissance produced a remarkable achievement in the Palatine Chapel at Aachen (777), which in plan was related to S. Vitale, Ravenna. Another noteworthy piece of architecture from this period was the vast abbey at Corvey (822), which found echoes during the Ottonian period in St. Cyriakus, Gernrode, and St. Michael, Hildesheim. Certain buildings in the Alps also preserved very old traditions, at Müstair and Mistail in Switzerland and at S. Maria in Valle (the 'Tempietto longobardo') in Italy, with definite reminiscences of Ravenna and Early Christian architecture.

1 Eglise visigothique de San Pedro de la Nave, à El Campillo (Espagne), datant de 680 env.
2 Palais asturien dit Santa Maria de Naranco, près d'Oviedo (Espagne), construit en 842.
3 Eglise San Miguel de Escalada, près de León (Espagne) datant de 913, la nef vue de l'iconostase.
4 La chapelle palatine à Aix-la-Chapelle (Allemagne), construite pour Charlemagne de 777 à 794 par Eudes de Metz.

1 El Campillo (Spanien), die westgotische Kirche San Pedro de la Nave (um 680)
2 Santa Maria de Naranco bei Oviedo, asturischer Königspavillon (842)
3 Escalada bei León (Spanien), San Miguel, Blick von den Chorschranken auf das Schiff (913)
4 Aachen, Pfalzkapelle, von Odo von Metz für Karl den Großen erbaut (777–794)

1 Visigothic church of S. Pedro de la Nave, El Campillo (Spain; c. 680).
2 Asturian palace of S. Maria, Naranco, near Oviedo (Spain; 842).
3 S. Miguel de Escalada, near Leon (Spain; 913): the nave seen from the iconostasis.
4 Palatine Chapel, Aachen (Germany), built for Charlemagne by Eudes of Metz in 777–94.

1

2

3

4

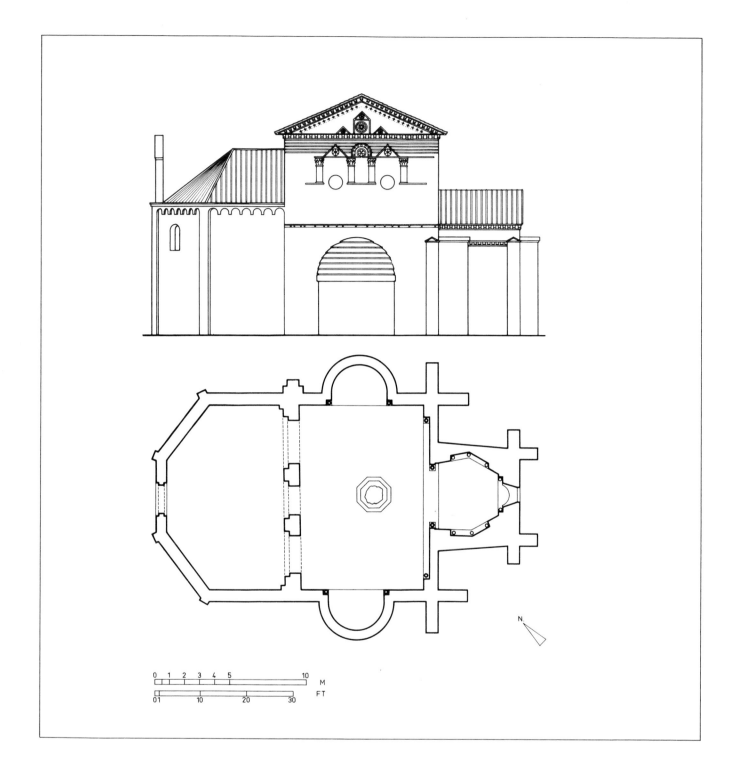

Baptistère Saint-Jean, à Poitiers (France), édifice construit entre le milieu du IVe s. et la fin du Xe s. Elévation latérale et plan 1:250. Du premier état restent la piscine et les trois murs de la salle baptismale. Restauration en 507. A la fin du Xe siècle un narthex polygonal remplace le narthex et son pronaos original; des absidioles semi-circulaires sont édifiées.

Poitiers, Baptisterium Saint-Jean, Mitte des 4.Jh. bis Ende 10.Jh. Vom ersten Bau stammen das Taufbecken und die drei Mauern der Taufkapelle. 507 wurde das Baptisterium restauriert. Ende 10.Jh. wurde der polygonale Narthex anstelle des ursprünglichen und einer Vorhalle erbaut, ebenso die halbrunden Apsidiolen. Aufriß einer Seite und Grundriß 1:250.

Baptistry of St.Jean, Poitiers (France), built in several stages between the mid-fourth and late tenth centuries. Side elevation and plan 1:250. Still original are the piscina and the three walls of the baptismal room. Restoration in 507. Towards the end of the tenth century a polygonal narthex replaced the original narthex and pronaos; semicircular apsidioles were erected.

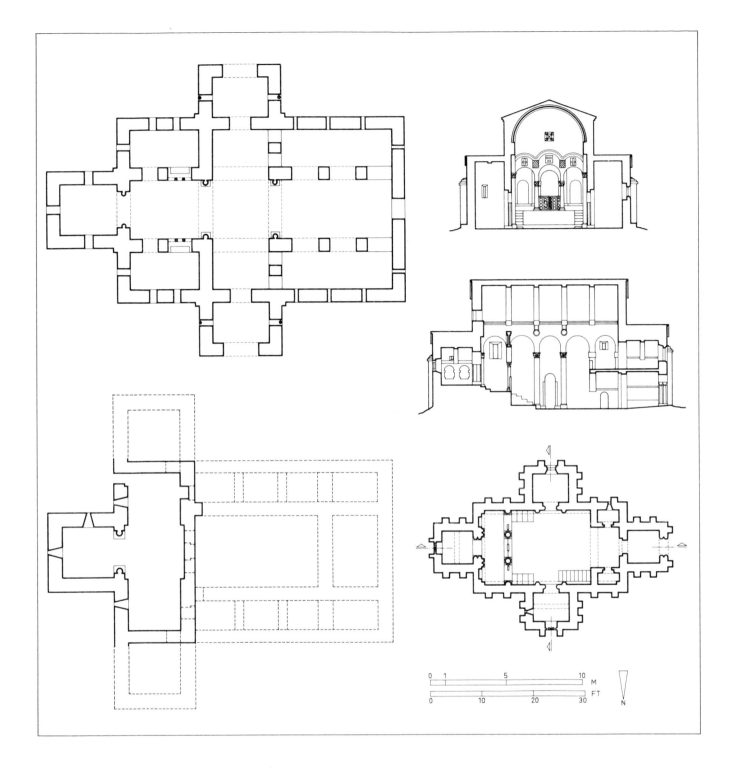

Eglise San Pedro de la Nave, à El Campillo, près de Zamora (Espagne), datant des environs de 680. Plan 1:250. Construction visigothique antérieure à la conquête arabe. En bas: **Chevet de l'église Santa Maria de Lara, à Quintanilla de las Viñas,** près de Burgos (Espagne), vers 690–700. Plan 1:250. A droite, **Eglise Santa Cristina de Lena, à Vega del Rey** (Espagne), construite vers 850. Coupes et plan 1:250.

Links oben: **El Campillo (bei Zamora, Spanien), San Pedro de la Nave,** um 680. Westgotischer, vor-arabischer Bau. Grundriß 1:250. Links unten: **Quintanilla de las Viñas (bei Burgos, Spanien), Santa Maria de Lara, Chorhaupt,** um 690–700. Grundriß 1:250. Rechts: **Vega del Rey (Spanien), Santa Cristina de Lena,** um 850. Schnitte und Grundriß 1:250.

S. Pedro de la Nave, El Campillo (near Zamora, Spain), built c. 680. Plan 1:250. A Visigothic building dating from before the Arab conquest. Below, **Apse of S. Maria de Lara, Quintanilla de las Viñas** (near Burgos, Spain), c. 690–700. Plan 1:250. Right, **S. Cristina de Lena, Vega del Rey** (Spain), built c. 850. Sections and plan 1:250.

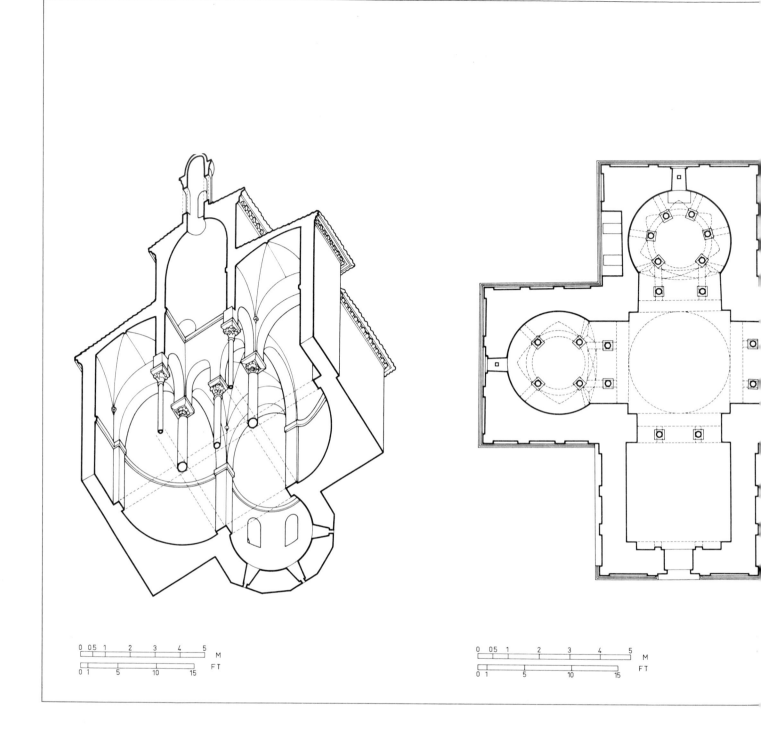

Baptistère San Miguel de Tarrasa, près de Barcelone (Espagne), construit vraisemblablement vers 650. Axonométrie env. 1:150. Edifice constitué d'un seul espace très obscur, que domine une coupole sur trompes, soutenue par huit colonnes à diamètres alternés. Plan cruciforme avec abside polygonale. La date est controversée, mais paraît antérieure à l'invasion musulmane.

Tarrasa (bei Barcelona), Baptisterium San Miguel, wahrscheinlich um 650. Der kreuzförmige Bau mit polygonaler Apsis bildet einen einzigen, ziemlich dunklen Innenraum mit einer zentralen Trompenkuppel auf acht Säulen von verschiedenen Durchmessern. Die Datierung ist strittig: vermutlich vor der arabischen Invasion. Axonometrie ca. 1:150.

Baptistry of S. Miguel, Tarrasa (near Barcelona, Spain), probably built c.650 (there is some argument about the date, but it appears to have been before the Moslem invasion). Axonometric projection c.1:150. The interior is a single very dark space covered by a dome on squinches, these being supported by eight columns of alternating diameters. The plan is cruciform with a polygonal apse.

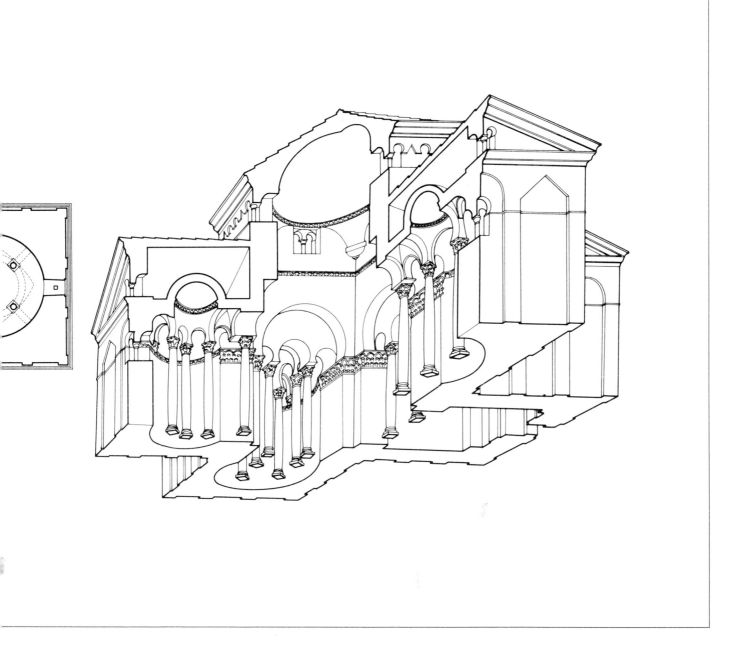

Eglise San Frutuoso de Montelios, à Braga (Portugal), édifiée en 665. Plan 1:125 et axonométrie. Ce petit sanctuaire de plan cruciforme, avec ses trois bras en absides outrepassées à colonnettes, est entièrement voûté. Entre la coupole centrale (reconstituée) et les bras, des murs diaphragmes à triple arcade. Le volume extérieur s'apparente au Mausolée de Galla Placidia à Ravenne.

Braga (Portugal), San Frutuoso de Montelios, 665. Die kleine Kirche mit kreuzförmigem Grundriß hat drei hufeisenförmige einbeschriebene Apsiden mit innerem Säulenumgang. Der kuppelgewölbte (Rekonstruktion) Mittelraum ist von jedem der vier Arme durch eine Drillingsarkade getrennt. Das Äußere ähnelt dem Mausoleum der Galla Placidia in Ravenna. Grundriß 1:125; Axonometrie.

S.Frutuoso de Montelios, Braga (Portugal), built in 665. Plan 1:125 and axonometric projection. This small cruciform shrine has three arms with horseshoe apses and small columns and is vaulted throughout. Diaphragm walls with a triple arcade separate the central dome (reconstructed) and the arms. The shape of the exterior recalls the Mausoleum of Galla Placidia, Ravenna.

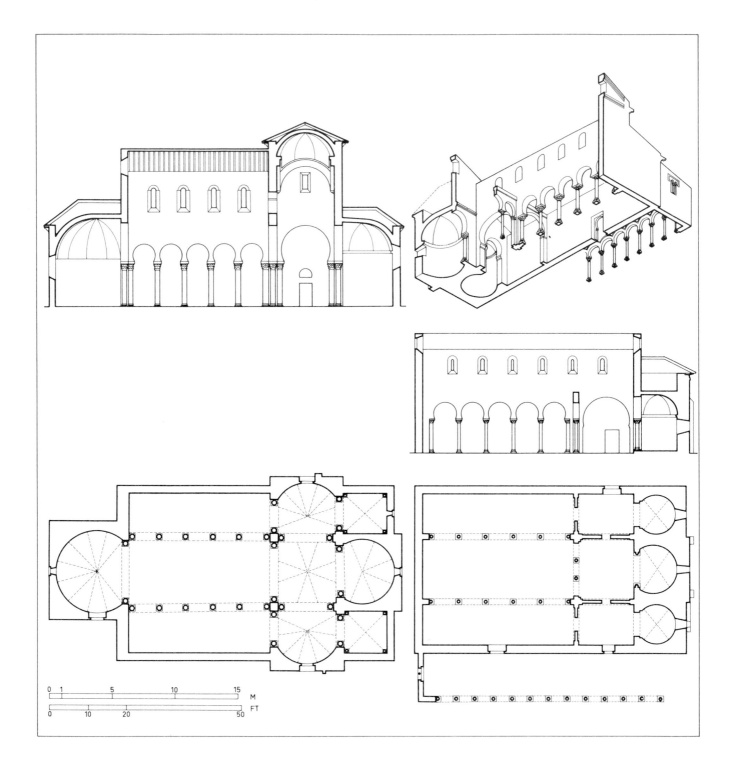

0 1   5   10   15   M
0   10   20   50   FT

Eglise San Cebrian de Mazote (Espagne), bâtie en 916. Coupe longitudinale et plan 1:300. Edifice caractéristique de l'art mozarabe, avec ses arcs outrepassés, tant en plan qu'en élévation. A droite, **Eglise San Miguel de Escalada, près de Leon** (Espagne), construite en 913. Axonométrie, coupe longitudinale et plan 1:300. Sanctuaire à trois absides à plan outrepassé. Au centre, l'iconostase.

Links: **Mazote (Spanien), San Cebrian** 916. Die Hufeisenform der Bögen im Grundriß und Aufriß ist für mozarabische Architektur charakteristisch. Längsschnitt und Grundriß 1:300. Rechts: **Escalada (bei León, Spanien), San Miguel,** 913. Die drei Apsiden sind hufeisenförmig, eine Schranke trennt Schiff und Chor. Axonometrie, Längsschnitt und Grundriß 1:300.

S. Cebrian, Mazote (Spain), built in 916. Longitudinal section and plan 1:300. A good example of Mozarabic architecture with its horseshoe arches both in plan and elevation. Right, **S. Miguel, Escalada** (near Léon, Spain), built in 913. Axonometric projection, longitudinal section and plan 1:300. The church has three horseshoe apses and an iconostasis in the centre.

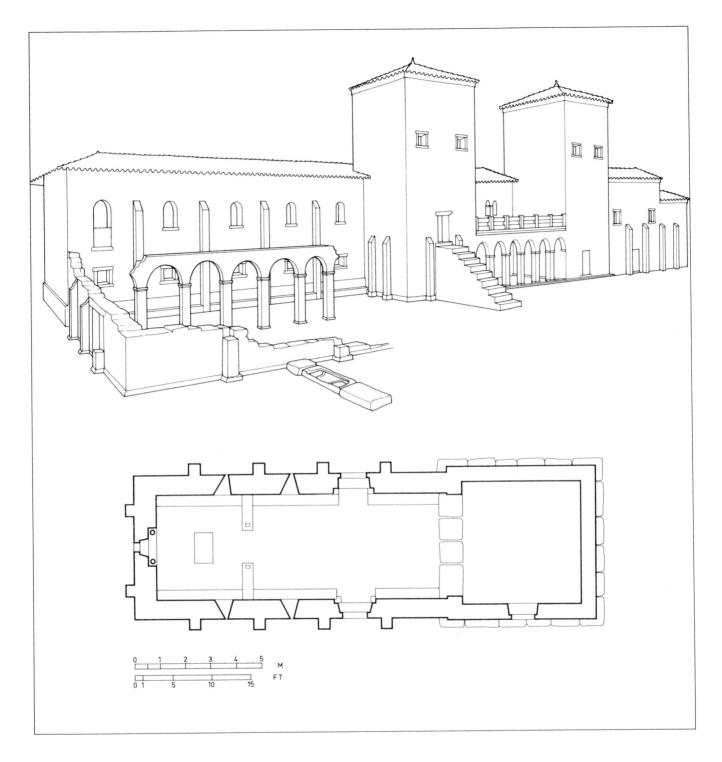

0 1 2 3 4 5 M
0 1 5 10 15 FT

Palais d'Alphonse II le Chaste, à Oviedo (Espagne), vers 800, restitution et **Camara Santa d'Oviedo.** Plan 1:150. La Camara Santa d'Oviedo forme la partie située à l'extrême droite de la restitution du palais royal asturien et présente des analogies avec l'étage inférieur du palais dit Santa Maria de Naranco.

Oben: **Oviedo (Spanien), Palast Alfons II. des Keuschen,** um 800. Rekonstruktion. Unten: **Oviedo, Camara Santa.** Der Bau zeigt gewisse Analogien zu Sta. Maria de Naranco, einem königlichen Palast. Die Camara Santa liegt am äußersten Ende des Palastes von Oviedo (rechts in der Rekonstruktion). Grundriß 1:150.

Palace of Alfonso II the Chaste, Oviedo (Spain), *c.* 800. Reconstruction, and **Camara Santa of Oviedo,** plan 1:150. The Camara Santa of Oviedo constitutes the extreme right-hand portion of the reconstructed Asturian royal palace and shows similarities to the palace known as S. Maria de Naranco.

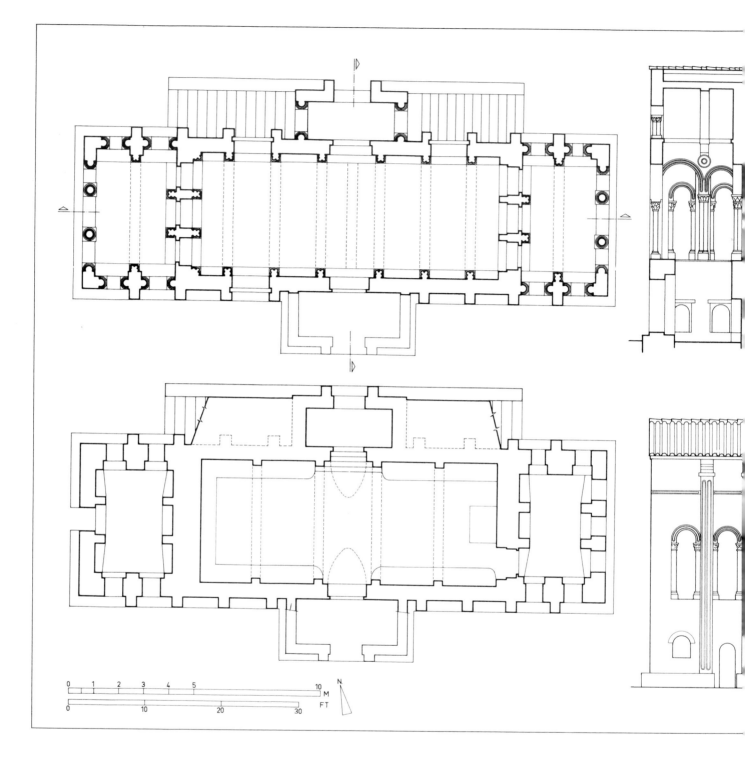

Palais asturien, dit Santa Maria de Naranco, près d'Oviedo (Espagne), construit en 842. Plan de l'aula regia, plan du rez-de-chaussée, coupe longitudinale, élévation nord, coupe transversale et élévation ouest 1:150. Pavillon royal de la monarchie asturienne régnant à Oviedo, cet édifice, avec ses deux belvédères et sa salle d'audience, est remarquablement conservé.

Santa Maria de Naranco (asturischer Königspavillon) bei Oviedo, 842. Der Königspavillon des in Oviedo residierenden Herrscherhauses von Asturien ist mit den beiden Belvedere und dem Audienzsaal bemerkenswert gut erhalten. Grundrisse der beiden Geschosse, Längsschnitt, Nordfassade, Querschnitt, Westfassade 1:150.

Asturian palace of S.Maria, Naranco (near Oviedo, Spain), built in 842. Plan of the *aula regia*, plan of the ground floor, longitudinal section, north elevation, cross section and west elevation 1:150. This was the royal pavilion of the Asturian monarchy which ruled from Oviedo: it has two belvederes and an audience hall and is remarkably well preserved.

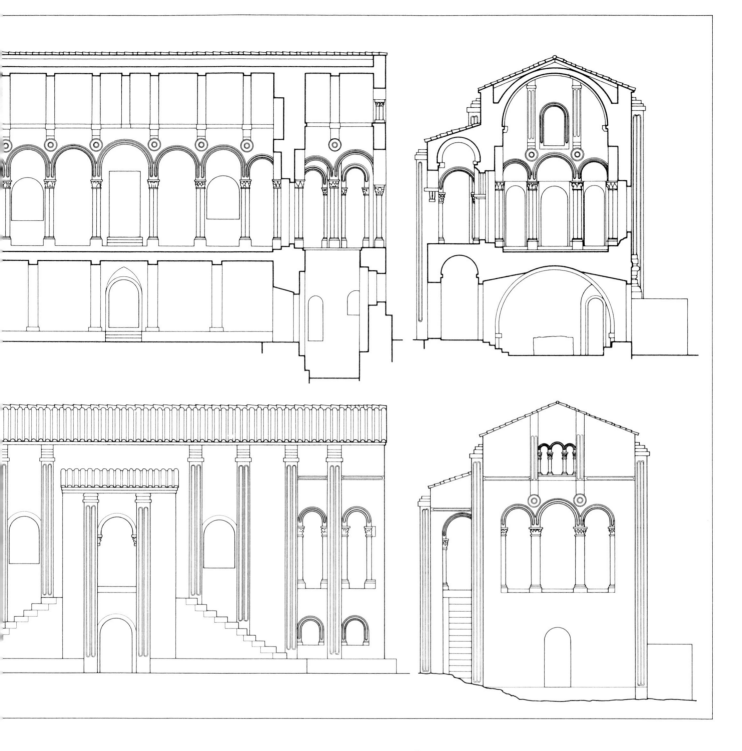

Doté de contreforts extérieurs auxquels correspondent à l'intérieur des pilastres décorés et des arcs doubleaux sur l'intrados de la voûte en plein cintre qui surmonte l'espace, ce bâtiment, avec sa double volée d'escaliers externes, relève d'un style très particulier. Les loggias, qui ouvrent par sept arcades sur le paysage, conservent pourtant au volume son unité.

Den Strebepfeilern des Äußeren entsprechen im Innern kannelierte Pilaster und Gurtbögen unter dem Tonnengewölbe. Der Bau mit seiner von zwei Seiten ansteigenden, zum Audienzsaal führenden Freitreppe hat einen ganz besonderen Stil. Die Arkaden-Loggien an beiden Seiten wahren die Geschlossenheit des Baukörpers.

With its double flight of external stairs and its outside buttresses matched on the interior by decorated pilasters and transverse arches on the intrados of the tunnel vault spanning the interior, this building has a style very much its own. Yet the loggias, opening on to the countryside through seven arches, give the volume unity.

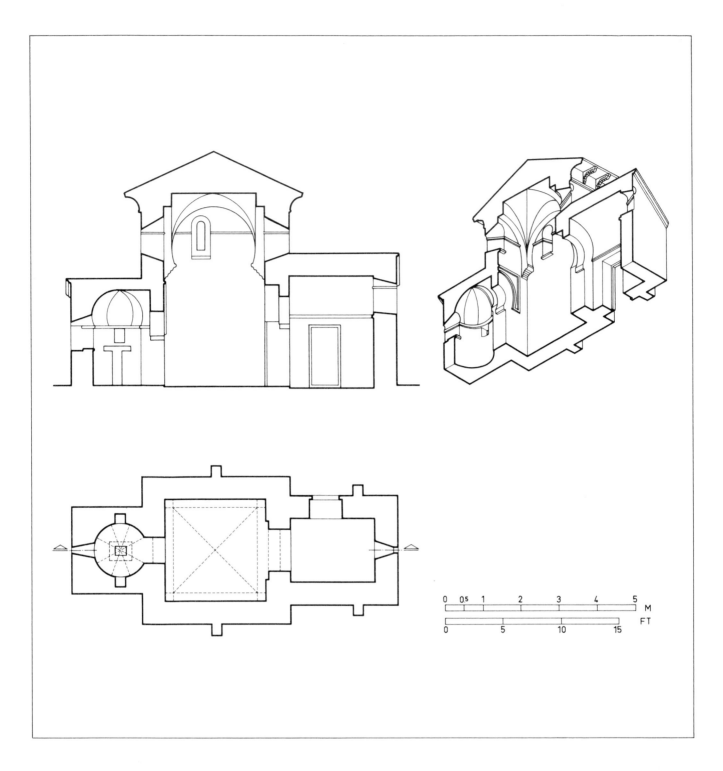

Oratoire San Miguel de Celanova (Espagne), construit vers 940. Coupe longitudinale (l'est à gauche), plan 1:100 et axonométrie. Ce petit ermitage, avec ses trois locaux en file, son espace central carré, voûté d'arêtes et sa petite abside à plan outrepassé, rappelle la volumétrie et le traitement de San Frutuoso, mais en plus simple.

Celanova (Spanien), Oratorium San Miguel, um 940. Die drei Räume der kleinen Einsiedlerkirche liegen in einer Achse, der quadratische Mittelraum hat ein Kreuzgratgewölbe, die Apsis ist hufeisenförmig. Das Oratorium erinnert in Gliederung und Ausführung an San Frutuoso in Braga, ist allerdings viel einfacher. Längsschnitt und Grundriß 1:100; Axonometrie.

Oratory of S. Miguel, Celanova (Spain), built c. 940. Longitudinal section (east is left), plan 1:100, and axonometric projection. With its three units in line, its square, groin-vaulted central space, and its small, horseshoe-plan apse, this hermitage resembles in volume and treatment a simpler version of S. Frutuoso.

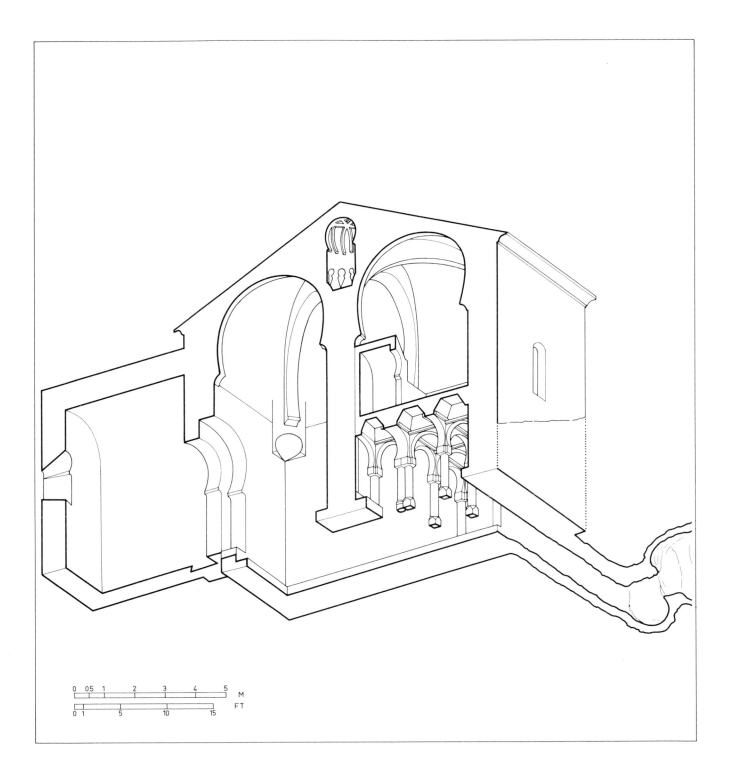

Eglise San Baudel de Berlanga (Espagne), construite au Xᵉ s. Axonométrie 1:125. Cet ermitage se caractérise par la présence d'une colonne centrale sur laquelle retombent les arcs de la coupole nervée (d'influence arabe?) avec une petite loge (∅ 1 m) en son sommet. Une tribune à arcades vient s'appuyer à cette colonne et supporte une minuscule chapelle.

Berlanga (Spanien), San Baudel, 10. Jh. Die Einsiedelei ist mit einer Kuppel überwölbt, deren Rippen von einer Mittelstütze mit kleinem Logenraum (∅ 1 m) aufgenommen werden; vielleicht eine arabisch beeinflußte Form. An diese Stütze schließt sich eine von Arkaden getragene Empore mit einer winzigen Kapelle an. Axonometrie 1:125.

S. Baudel, Berlanga (Spain), tenth century. Axonometric projection 1:125. A distinctive feature of this hermitage is the central column taking the arches of the ribbed dome (Arab influence?), which is topped by a lantern (diameter 1 m.). An arcaded gallery abuts this column and supports a tiny chapel.

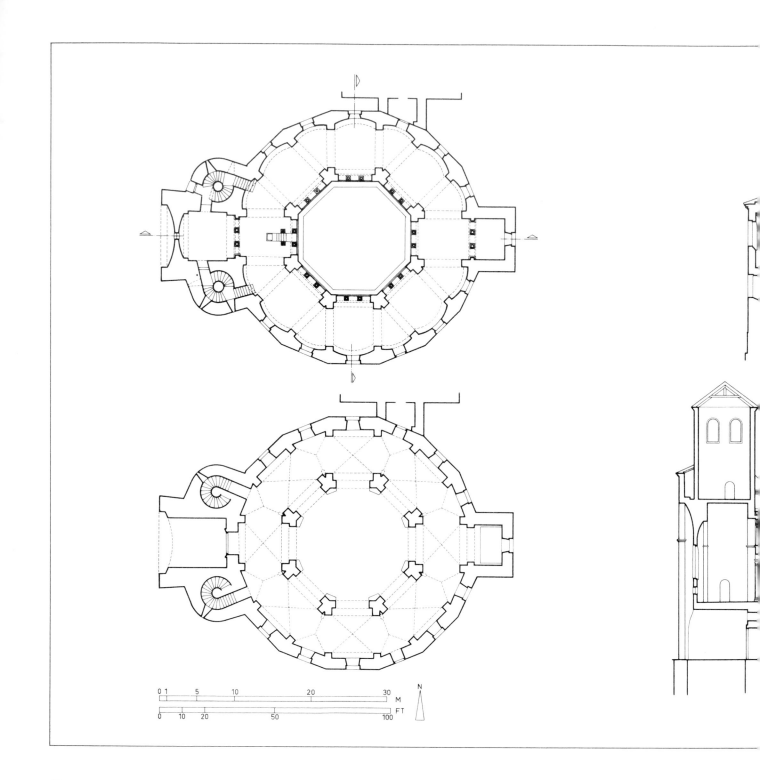

Chapelle palatine, à Aix-la-Chapelle (Allemagne), construite entre 777 et 794, état primitif conjectural. Plan de l'étage, plan du rez-de-chaussée, coupe transversale et coupe longitudinale, façade ouest et façade nord 1:500. Edifié pour l'empereur Charlemagne par l'architecte Eudes de Metz, ce sanctuaire impérial s'inspire du parti octogonal de Saint-Vital à Ravenne.

Aachen, Pfalzkapelle, 777–794. Die von Odo von Metz für Karl den Großen erbaute Kapelle steht in Beziehung zu San Vitale in Ravenna. Vermutlicher ursprünglicher Zustand: Grundrisse des Ober- und des Erdgeschosses 1:500.

Palatine Chapel, Aachen (Germany), 777–94. Conjectured original state, plan of first floor, plan of ground floor, cross section, longitudinal section, west façade and north façade 1:500. Built for Charlemagne by the architect Eudes of Metz, the Palatine Chapel was inspired by the octagonal solution of S. Vitale, Ravenna.

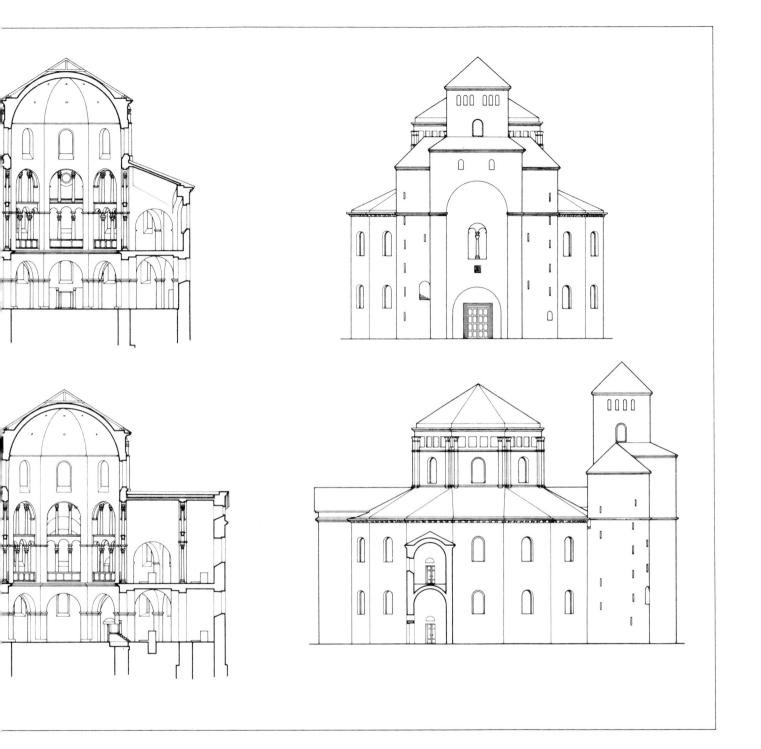

L'octogone à tribunes de la **Chapelle d'Aix** ménage en son centre un vide haut comme la nef de Notre-Dame de Paris. De part et d'autre de ce plan centré, l'architecte dispose à l'orient un chœur à chevet plat et à l'occident la formule récente du «Westwerk» propre aux édifices rhénans.

Aachen, Pfalzkapelle. Der von Emporen umgebene Mittelraum ist so hoch wie das Schiff der Notre-Dame von Paris. Die ursprüngliche Apsis war rechteckig, im Westen war dem Zentralbau ein Westwerk, wie es bei rheinischen Kirchen häufig ist, vorgelagert. Quer- und Längsschnitt, West- und Nordfassade 1:500.

The galleried octagon of the **Palatine Chapel, Aachen,** is as high at the centre as the nave of Notre Dame, Paris. The architect flanked this centrally planned part of his building with a shallow-apsed chancel in the east and, in the west, a westwork of the kind that had been developed recently in Rhineland churches.

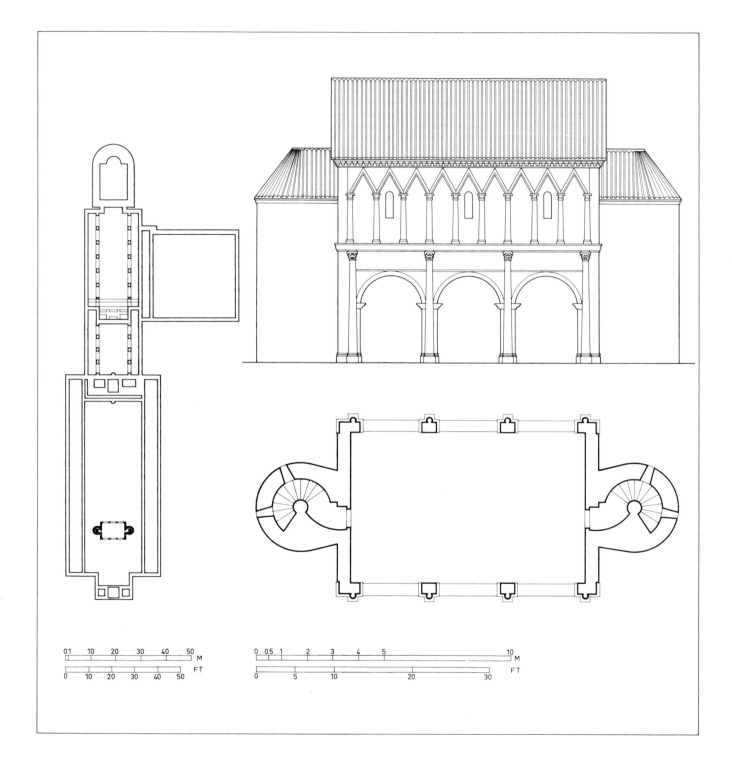

Porte triomphale à Lorsch, datant de 770. Plan d'ensemble du couvent 1:1500, élévation et plan 1:150. La Torhalle, ou porte, qui subsiste est traditionnellement considérée comme une chapelle Saint-Michel, les archanges jouant le rôle de sentinelles. Dans le style de la renaissance carolingienne, le décor des façades s'inspire de formules romaines.

Lorsch, Torhalle, 770. Die Torhalle, vermutlich eine Michaels-Kapelle, ist der einzige erhaltene Teil des Klosters. Der Fassadenschmuck zeigt die Merkmale der karolingischen Renaissance, die antike Anregungen aufnahm. Grundriß des Klosters 1:1500; Aufriß und Grundriß der Torhalle 1:150.

Triumphal gate, Lorsch (Germany), built 770. Overall plan of the monastery 1:1500; elevation and plan 1:150. The surviving *Torhalle* or gatehouse is traditionally regarded as a chapel to St. Michael, the archangels functioning as guards. Decorated in the style of the Carolingian renaissance, the façades drew their inspiration from Roman formulae.

136

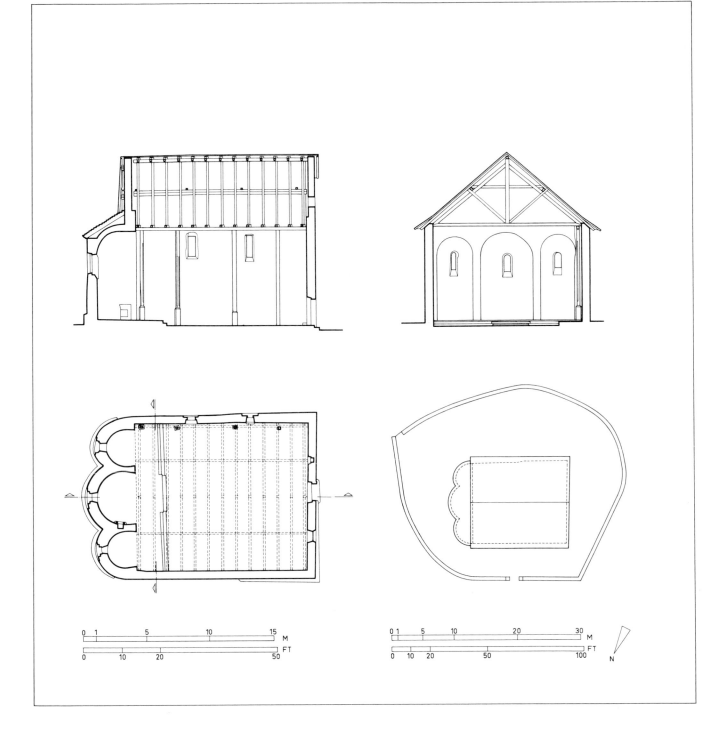

| 0 1 | 5 | 10 | 15 | M |
| 0 | 10 | 20 | | 50 | FT |

| 0 1 | 5 | 10 | 20 | 30 | M |
| 0 | 10 | 20 | 50 | 100 | FT |

N

Eglise St. Peter (Saint-Pierre), à Mistail, près de Tiefencastel (Suisse), datant de peu avant l'an 800, état primitif conjectural. Coupe longitudinale, plan et coupe transversale 1:300, situation 1:600. L'église à nef unique couverte de fermes présente trois absides accolées, légèrement outrepassées.

Mistail (bei Tiefencastel, Schweiz), Sankt Peter, kurz vor 800. Dreiapsidensaal mit hufeisenförmigen Apsiden und Holzdecke, vermutlicher ursprünglicher Zustand. Längsschnitt, Grundriß, Querschnitt 1:300; Lageplan 1:600.

St. Peter, Mistail (near Tiefencastel, Switzerland), built shortly before 800. Conjectured original state, longitudinal section, plan and cross section 1:300; site plan 1:600. This single-aisled church with a truss roof has three slightly horseshoe-shaped conjugate apses.

Santa Maria in Valle, à Cividale (Italie), édifice dit «Tempietto longobardo». Coupe longitudinale, plan et coupes transversales 1:200. La date, controversée, doit se situer entre la fin du VIIIᵉ et la fin du IXᵉ s. La chapelle, qui aurait eu une destination funéraire, s'orne de stucs admirablement conservés représentant la procession des saints.

Cividale (Italien), Santa Maria in Valle (Tempietto longobardo), 8.–9. Jh. Die Datierung ist strittig. Vielleicht handelt es sich bei diesem Bau um eine Grabkapelle. Der ausgezeichnet erhaltene Stuckdekor stellt eine Heiligenprozession dar. Längsschnitt, Grundriß und Querschnitte 1:200.

S. Maria in Valle ('Tempietto longobardo'), Cividale (Italy); its date is uncertain but must lie between the late eighth and late ninth centuries. Longitudinal section, plan and cross sections 1:200. Apparently designed for funerals, the chapel has some excellently preserved stuccos representing the procession of the saints.

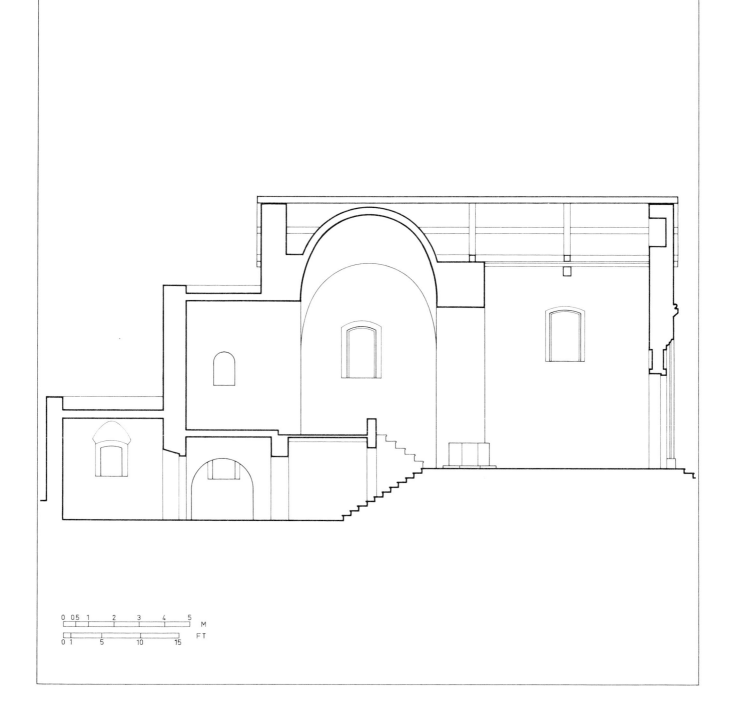

0 05 1   2   3   4   5
                                      M
0 1   5   10   15
                                      FT

Eglise San Salvatore, à Barzano, près de Côme, construite au IXᵉ s. Coupe longitudinale, env. 1:150. La coupe révèle les trois «niveaux cosmiques» de la crypte, à demi-enfoncée, et du presbytère surélevé par rapport à l'église proprement dite. Le plan inférieur est le séjour des morts, le plan de la nef, l'étage de la vie quotidienne, et le presbytère représente l'étage du ciel, avec coupole.

Barzano (bei Como, Italien), San Salvatore, 9. Jh. Die Räume liegen auf drei Ebenen: Die Krypta, als unterste Ebene, ist die Stätte der Toten, das Schiff liegt in der Alltags-Ebene, das erhöhte, kuppelüberwölbte Presbyterium entspricht dem himmlischen Bereich. Längsschnitt ca. 1:150.

S. Salvatore, Barzano (near Como, Italy), ninth century. Longitudinal section c. 1:150. The section shows the three 'cosmic levels' of the semi-sunken crypt, the raised presbytery, and the church itself in between. The lower level represents the abode of the dead, the nave is the level of everyday existence, and the domed presbytery stands for heaven.

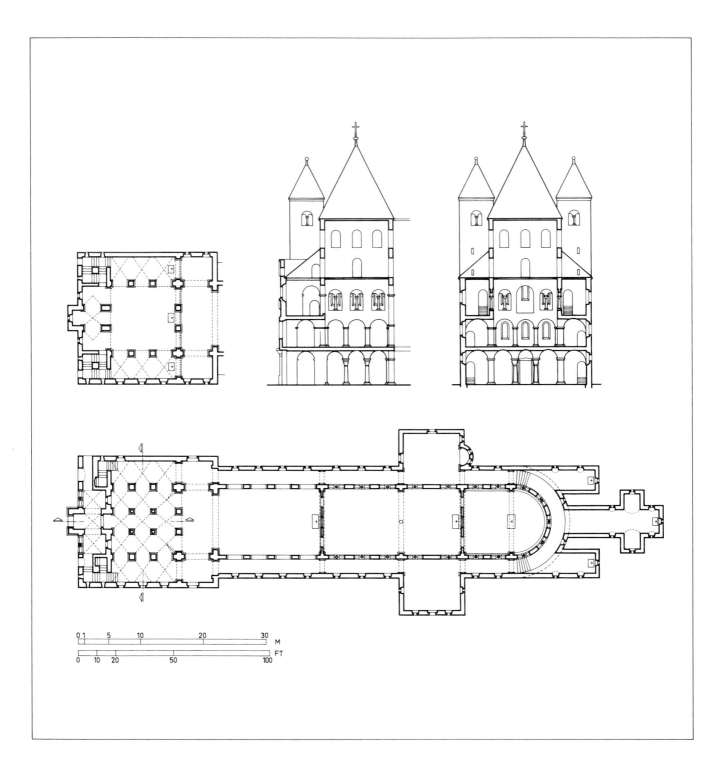

Abbaye bénédictine Nova Corbeia, à Corvey, près de Höxter (Allemagne), édifice commencé en 822 et consacré en 844. Plan de l'étage, coupe longitudinale et coupe transversale du Westwerk restitué, plan d'ensemble restitué 1:600. Le Westwerk, qui subsiste, est construit entre 873 et 875.

Corvey, Benediktinerabtei Nova Corbeia, 822 begonnen, 844 geweiht; das noch erhaltene Westwerk entstand zwischen 873 und 875. Rekonstruktionen des ursprünglichen Zustandes: Grundriß des Obergeschosses, Längs- und Querschnitt des Westwerks, Grundriß der Kirche 1:600.

Benedictine abbey of Nova Corbeia, Corvey (near Höxter, Germany), begun in 822 and consecrated in 844. Plan of the upper storey, longitudinal section and cross section of the reconstructed westwork, overall plan (reconstruction) 1:600. The westwork, which survives, was built 873–5.

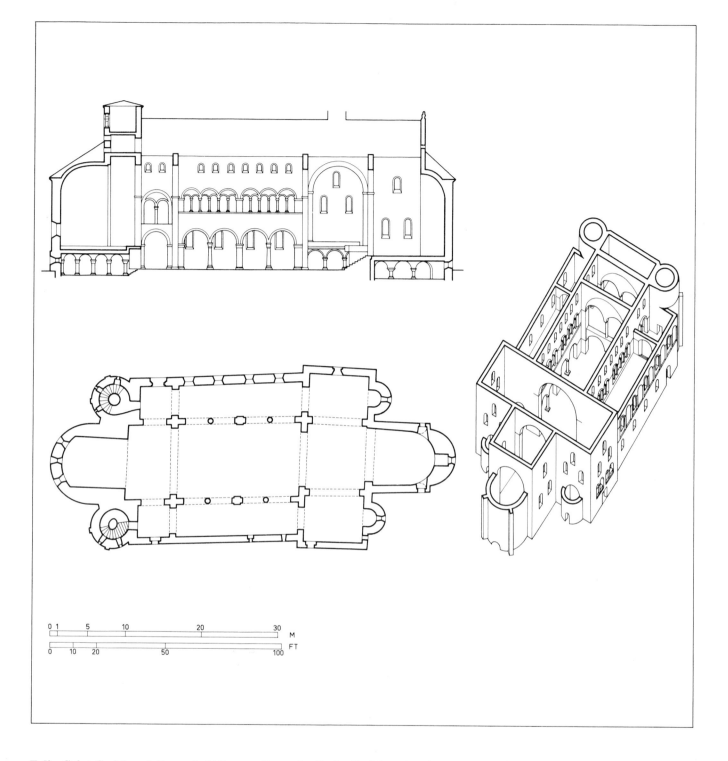

0 1   5   10   20   30   M

0   10   20   50   100   FT

Eglise Saint-Cyriakus, à Gernrode (Allemagne), fondée en 961. Coupe longitudinale et plan (état au XIIe s.) 1:500, axonométrie de l'état original. La contre-abside date du XIIe siècle. Les bas-côtés présentent des tribunes, lesquelles sont commandées par la fonction conventuelle, quand bien même la communication visuelle avec le chœur y est malaisée.

Gernrode, Sankt Cyriakus, 961 begonnen, Westapsis 12. Jh. Über den Seitenschiffen liegen die Nonnenemporen, die für eine Damenstiftskirche notwendig sind; der Chor war von dort aus nur schlecht einzusehen. Längsschnitt und Grundriß des Zustandes im 12. Jh. 1:500; Axonometrie des ursprünglichen Baues.

St. Cyriakus, Gernrode (East Germany), founded in 961. Longitudinal section and plan (twelfth-century building) 1:500; axonometric projection of the original building. The counter-apse is twelfth-century. The side aisles have galleries, as dictated by the church's monastic function, despite the fact that they impede visual communication with the chancel.

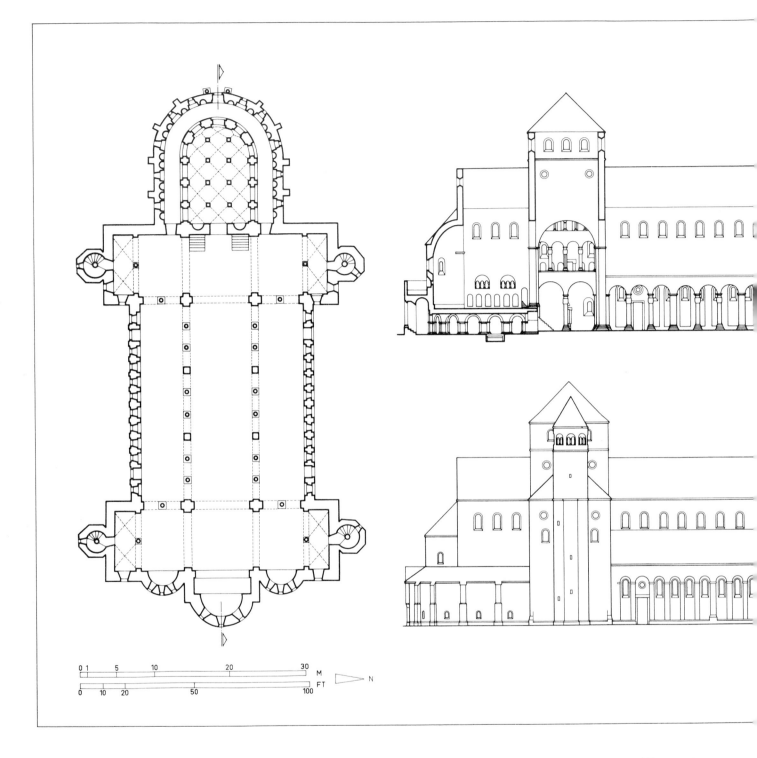

Eglise Saint-Michel de Hildesheim (Allemagne), plans conçus dès 993 par Bernward, conseiller de l'impératrice-régente Théophano et précepteur d'Otton III, et réalisés dès 1010. Consécration en 1022, et fin des travaux en 1033. Plan, coupe longitudinale, élévation sud 1:500, et coupe axonométrique.

Hildesheim, Sankt Michael, Planungsbeginn 993, Baubeginn 1010, Weihe 1022, vollendet 1033. Die Kirche wurde von Bernward, Bischof von Hildesheim, Ratgeber der Kaiserin Theophanu und Erzieher Ottos III., errichtet. Grundriß, Längsschnitt, Aufriß der Südseite 1:500; Axonometrie.

St. Michael, Hildesheim (Germany), planned in 993 by Bernward, adviser to Empress-Regent Theophano and tutor to Otto III, and begun in 1010; the church was consecrated in 1022 and work finally completed in 1033. Plan, longitudinal section and south elevation 1:500; axonometric section.

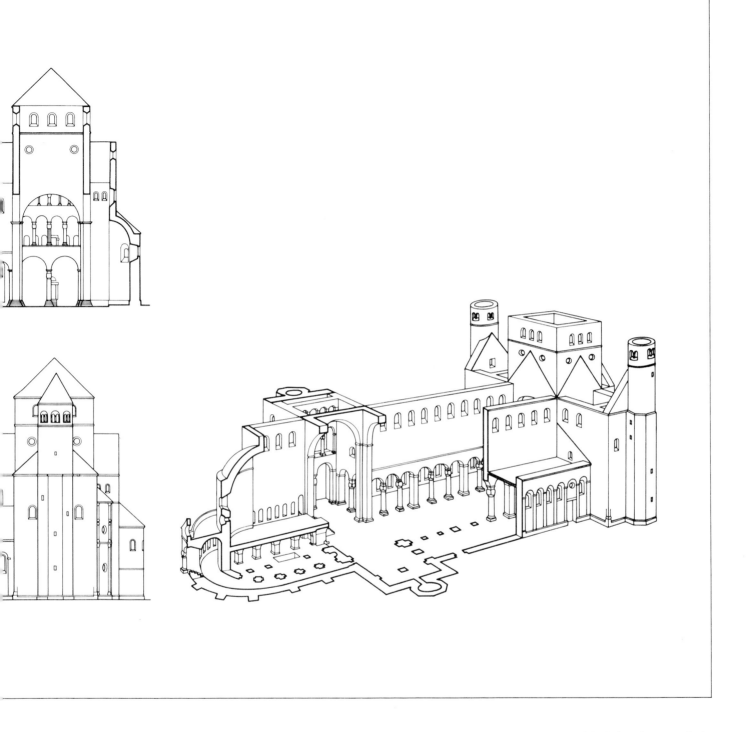

Saint-Michel de Hildesheim est une œuvre où l'architecte joue avec des éléments géométriques. Il crée un espace homogène à force de clarté dans la composition. On remarque l'alternance de deux colonnes, un pilier, deux colonnes dans la nef. Les tribunes se trouvent dans les transepts, qui comportent trois étages d'arcades.

Hildesheim, Sankt Michael. Der Baumeister hat durch eine klare geometrische Gliederung einen einheitlichen Bau geschaffen. Die Stützen sind im niedersächsischen Stützenwechsel – 1 Pfeiler, 2 Säulen – angeordnet. Die Emporen der dreigeschossigen Querschiffsarme öffnen sich in Arkaden.

St. Michael, Hildesheim, is a work in which the architect played with geometrical elements, creating a homogeneous interior by the clarity of his composition. Note the alternation of two columns and a pillar in the nave. The galleries are in the transepts, which feature three-tiered arcades.

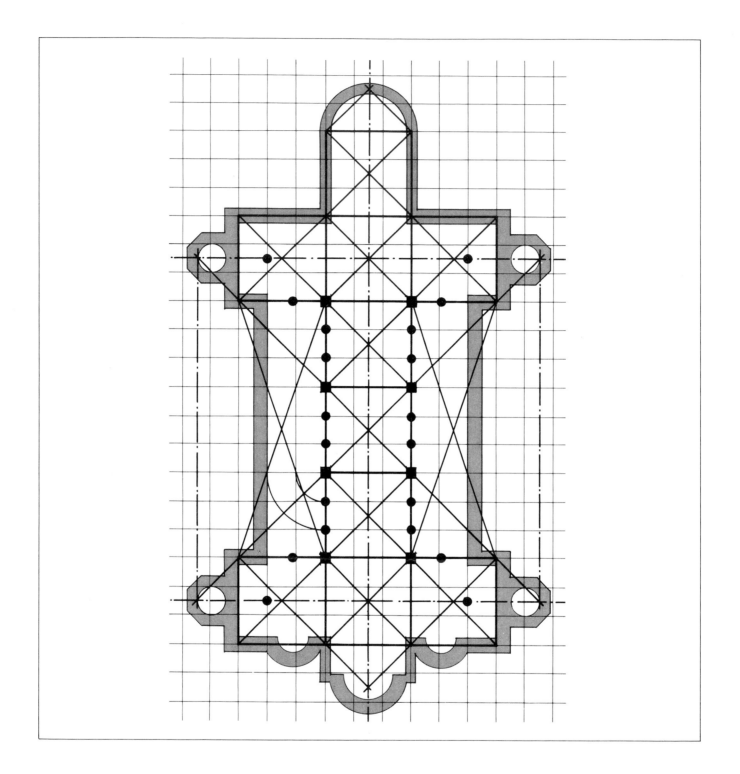

Tracé régulateur de **Saint-Michel de Hildesheim.** L'analyse schématique de la construction du plan démontre le propos rigoureusement géométrique de l'architecte: combinaisons de carrés et de diagonales qui régissent toute la composition, soulignant la valeur mathématico-phisolophique de l'œuvre, fondée sur le «De Arithmetica» de Boèce et les textes de Vitruve.

Hildesheim, Sankt Michael. Das Quadraturschema zeigt das geometrische System des Architekten, der den Grundriß aus Quadrat und Diagonale entwickelt hat. Hier kommt die mathematisch-philosophische Bedeutung des Baues, der auf Boëthius' «De arithmetica» und den Schriften Vitruvs fußt, deutlich zum Ausdruck.

St. Michael, Hildesheim. Diagram. Systematic analysis of the plan of the church reveals the architect's rigorously geometrical approach. Combinations of squares and diagonals govern the entire composition, stressing the mathematico-philosophical aspect of the building, which was based on Boethius' *De Arithmetica* and the writings of Vitruvius.

L'âge roman

Romanik

The Romanesque Period

Dès le Xᵉ et surtout au XIᵉ siècle, l'architecture connaît un extraordinaire essor, et l'Occident se couvre d'églises, en fonction de la stabilité retrouvée après les mouvements de populations de l'époque des invasions, de la paix et de la prospérité favorisant l'élévation générale du niveau de vie, et de la rupture du cloisonnement qui paralysait le négoce. La création de places de foire, l'échange de denrées provenant souvent de fort loin, l'ouverture des chemins de pèlerinage et le va-et-vient créé par les Croisades favorisent le commerce international ainsi que la diffusion des idées et des techniques.

La grande conquête de l'architecture religieuse romane repose sur le voûtement de pierre de la nef, en lieu et place des charpentes propres aux églises basilicales. Le recours généralisé au berceau, à la coupole, à la voûte d'arête et aux arcs en plein cintre aboutit à la création d'un style original qui se caractérise par la robustesse de la structure, le rôle plastique du mur, la volumétrie claire, géométrique, hiérarchisée, et l'importance du clocher.

Le rôle novateur de la Bourgogne, et des clunisiens en particulier, apparaît dans les solutions nouvelles au niveau du plan et de la couverture. Après l'éclosion du premier roman (Tournus, Payerne), l'apogée est marqué par une réduction de la massivité des murs et par l'apparition de parois rythmées au moyen de contreforts, par les nervures des arcs sous les arêtes des voûtements, par les arcades formant une armature interne divisée en travées, ainsi que par une augmentation des sources d'éclairage, une accentuation de la verticalité et une audace croissante dans les proportions. Le plus bel exemple de cette

Vom 10. Jahrhundert an und besonders im 11. erlebte die Architektur eine neue Blüte. Nach den Zeiten der Invasionen war wieder Frieden eingetreten, die Bevölkerung kam zur Ruhe, der Handel lebte auf, neue Märkte wurden gegründet, Wohlstand kehrte ein und das Abendland bedeckte sich von neuem mit Kirchen. Mit dem Warenaustausch über große Entfernungen, mit den Pilgerstraßen und den Kreuzzügen erfuhr nicht nur der Handel einen erheblichen Aufschwung, sondern ebenso auch der Austausch und die Verbreitung von Ideen und Techniken.

Die große Neuerung im romanischen Kirchenbau war die Wölbung des Kirchenschiffs anstelle des offenen Dachstuhls oder der Holzdecke früherer Bauten. Tonnengewölbe, Kuppel, Kreuzgratgewölbe und Rundbogen führen nun zu einem neuen Stil, der sich durch eine kräftige Struktur, die Betonung der geschlossenen Mauer, durch geometrisch klare, deutlich gegeneinander abgesetzte Baukörper und die Gewichtigkeit der Türme auszeichnet.

Die Bedeutung des Burgund und besonders der Cluniazenser äußert sich vor allem in neuen Lösungen für Grundrisse und Wölbungen. Gegenüber Bauten des 11. Jahrhunderts wie Tournus und Payerne wird in hochromanischer Zeit die Mauermasse reduziert, der Bau durch Strebepfeiler am Äußeren, durch Dienste und eine Gliederung in Traveen im Inneren rhythmisiert. Die Zahl der Fenster nimmt zu, die Vertikale wird betont, die Kirchen nehmen immer kühnere Ausmaße an. Das großartigste Beispiel dieser Blüte der Romanik muß wohl die heute zerstörte Kirche von Cluny III gewesen sein, in der zum ersten Mal weitgehend der

The tenth and above all the eleventh centuries saw an astonishing burst of architectural activity that left the West covered with churches. It was the natural outcome of a new-found stability following the population movements of the period of the invasions; Europe recovered after her long paralysis, and peace and prosperity brought a general rise in the standard of living. The creation of market-places, the exchange of commodities that often came from far away, the opening of pilgrimage routes and the comings and goings of the Crusades, besides promoting international trade, also furthered the dissemination of ideas and technology.

The big breakthrough of Romanesque religious architecture was to replace the wooden roof framework of the typical early basilican church with a stone vault over the nave. Increasingly widespread use of the barrel-vault, the dome, the groined vault, and the semicircular arch led to the creation of an original style characterised by robust construction, the plastic role of the wall, clear, geometrical, graded spatial organisation, and the importance of the bell-tower.

The pioneering role of Burgundy—and in particular of Cluny—crystallised in the form of fresh solutions with regard to plan and roofing. Following the initial flowering of Romanesque architecture at Tournus and Payerne, the culmination was marked by a reduction in the massiveness of the walls, the rhythmic use of buttresses, and the appearance of ribs continuing the line of the arches along the ridges of the ribs and of arcades constituting an interior framework divided into bays; it also brought an increase in the size and number of light sources, an emphasis on

apothéose romane devait être la grande église, aujourd'hui détruite, de Cluny III, dans laquelle apparaît pour la première fois l'usage généralisé de l'arc en tiers-point, dont l'architecture cistercienne fera un instrument de construction d'une rigueur fonctionnelle absolue.

En même temps que l'on suit ces progrès technologiques, la parure de l'architecture s'enrichit: chapiteaux et portails sculptés, modénature foisonnante, polychromie qui finit par recouvrir l'intérieur de l'édifice entier, comme à Saint-Savin, au moyen de fresques occultant entièrement l'appareil, sans parler des tissus, tapisseries et émaux.

Spitzbogen verwendet wurde, der dann auch zu einem wesentlichen Element der Zisterzienserarchitektur wurde.

Gleichzeitig mit diesem Wandel der Bauformen wurde der Bauschmuck ständig reicher: Kapitelle, Gesimse, Portale wurden reich skulptiert, das Innere der Kirche mit Fresken geschmückt, dazu kamen als weiterer Schmuck gewebte und gestickte Wandbehänge und prächtige Schreine mit Goldschmiede- und Emailarbeit.

the vertical, and a growing boldness of proportion. The finest example of the apotheosis of Romanesque must have been the great church (now destroyed) known as Cluny III. This was the first building to make general use of the pointed equilateral arch, which in Cistercian hands was to become a strictly functional constructional instrument.

These technological advances were paralleled by a growing richness of architectural ornamentation. Capitals and portals were sculptured, outlines became more elaborate, and polychrome work eventually covered the entire interior, as at St. Savin, where frescoes completely obscured the jointing and the effect was made richer still by textiles, tapestries and enamels.

1 Les voûtes en berceaux transversaux de l'abbatiale Saint-Philibert de Tournus, église consacrée en 1019.
2 Arcades du cloître de l'abbaye cistercienne de Fontenay, construit dès 1139.
3 La nef de l'église de la Madeleine de Vézelay, consacrée en 1130. Les arcs doubleaux à claveaux alternés soulignent le voûtement.

1 Tournus, Abteikirche Saint-Philibert, Blick in die Quertonnen des Mittelschiffs (Weihe 1019)
2 Fontenay, Zisterzienserabtei, Kreuzgang (1139 gegründet)
3 Vézelay, Sainte-Madeleine, Mittelschiff; die Form der Wölbung ist durch den Farbwechsel in den Gurtbogen betont (Weihe 1130)

1 The transverse tunnel vaults of the abbey church of St. Philibert, Tournus (consecrated 1019).
2 Cloister arcades of the Cistercian abbey, Fontenay (begun 1139).
3 The nave of La Madeleine, Vézelay (consecrated 1130). The transverse arches of alternate dark and light stones emphasize the vaulting.

1

2

3

Eglise de Vignory (France), construite avant 1050. Plan, axonométrie du chœur et coupe transversale de la nef 1:400. Cet édifice à nef non voûtée, mais couverte de fermes, selon la tradition carolingienne, présente un chœur en cul-de-four qu'entoure un déambulatoire voûté en berceau annulaire, sur piles alternées.

Vignory (Frankreich), Saint-Etienne, vor 1050. Das Langhaus ist entsprechend der karolingischen und ottonischen Tradition nicht gewölbt, sondern hat einen offenen Dachstuhl. Um den halbkuppelgewölbten Chor zieht sich ein tonnengewölbter Umgang mit Stützenwechsel. Grundriß, Axonometrie des Chors, Querschnitt durch das Langhaus 1:400.

St. Etienne, Vignory (France), before 1050. Plan, axonometric projection of the chancel and cross section of the nave 1:400. The nave is truss-roofed in the Carolingian tradition rather than vaulted, but the half-domed chancel is ringed by a curved ambulatory with a curved tunnel vault on alternating supports.

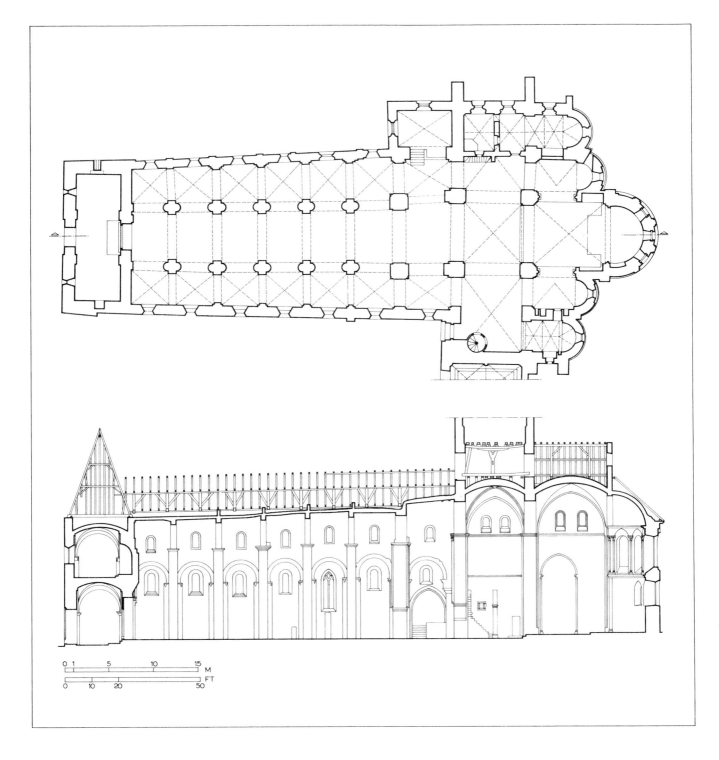

Eglise abbatiale de Payerne (Suisse), première étape de construction entre 1000
et 1050, deuxième campagne compre-
nant le chevet et la septième travée
avant 1080. Plan et coupe longitudinale
1:400. Structure de la nef: piles rectan-
gulaires, à demi-colonnes engagées, re-
cevant le berceau de la voûte, où les fenêtres hautes à pénétrations sont originales. Chœur à grande abside et quatre
absidioles.

Payerne (Schweiz), Abteikirche, 1. Bauabschnitt 1000–1050, 2. Bauabschnitt
(Chor und Querschiff) vor 1080. Die
Pfeiler des Langhauses tragen auf halbrunden Vorlagen die Arkaden, auf
rechteckigen die Gurtbogen des Ton-
nengewölbes. Die in das Langhausge-
wölbe eingeschnittene Fensterzone ist
eine Neuerung. Staffelchor mit fünf
Apsiden. Grundriß und Längsschnitt
1:400.

Abbey church, Payerne (Switzerland),
first stage built between 1000 and 1050,
second stage (apses and seventh bay)
before 1080. Plan and longitudinal
section 1:400. The nave consists of
rectangular piers with engaged half-
columns supporting a tunnel vault in
which the tall window-openings are
original. The chancel has a large apse
and four apsidioles.

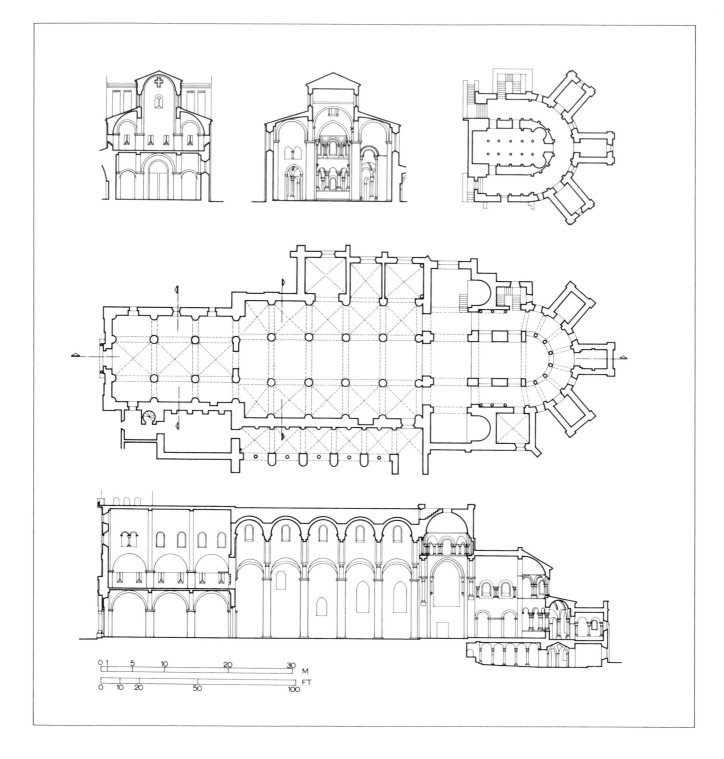

Abbatiale Saint-Philibert de Tournus (France). Après l'incendie qui ravage la première église en 1006, le nouvel édifice est consacré en 1019, puis remanié en 1033 et en 1120 avec nouvelle consécration. Coupes transversales du narthex et de la nef, plan de la crypte, plan général et coupe longitudinale 1:600. Après un puissant narthex, la nef est voûtée de berceaux transversaux.

Tournus (Frankreich), Abteikirche Saint-Philibert, Neubau nach Brand (1006), 1019 Weihe, 1033 und 1120 Umbau, neue Weihe. Das Mittelschiff des Langhauses ist mit quergestellten Tonnen überwölbt; vor dem Langhaus eine mächtige Vorkirche. Querschnitte durch Vorkirche und Langhaus, Grundriß der Krypta, Grundriß und Längsschnitt der Kirche 1:600.

Abbey church of St. Philibert, Tournus (France). Fire having destroyed the first church in 1006, the new building was consecrated in 1019, altered in 1033 and again in 1120, and reconsecrated. Cross sections of narthex and nave, plan of the crypt, overall plan and longitudinal section 1:600. After a powerful narthex, the nave is vaulted with transverse tunnels.

150

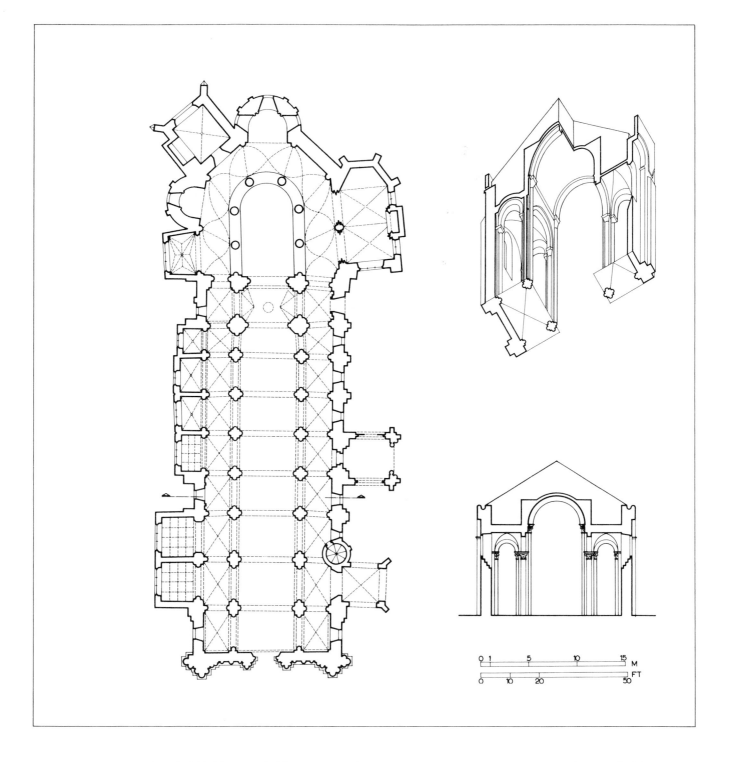

Eglise Notre-Dame-la-Grande, à Poitiers (France), mentionnée en 1090 comme collégiale. Plan, axonométrie d'une travée et coupe de la nef 1:400. Derrière une façade à la riche décoration, la nef en berceau et les collatéraux à voûtes d'arêtes sont austères. Une série de chapelles sont venues flanquer l'édifice aux XVᵉ et XVIᵉ s.

Poitiers (Frankreich), Notre-Dame-la-Grande, 1090 als Kollegiatkirche erwähnt. Die Fassade ist reich geschmückt; das tonnengewölbte Mittelschiff und die Seitenschiffe mit Kreuzgratgewölben wirken nüchtern. Die seitlichen Kapellen wurden im 15. und 16. Jh. erbaut. Grundriß, Axonometrie eines Jochs, Querschnitt durch das Langhaus 1:400.

Notre-Dame-la-Grande, Poitiers, mentioned in 1090 as a collegiate church. Plan, axonometric projection of a bay, and section of nave 1:400. Behind a richly decorated façade, the tunnel-vaulted nave and the groin-vaulted side aisles are of austere design. A row of chapels was put up round the building in the fifteenth and sixteenth centuries.

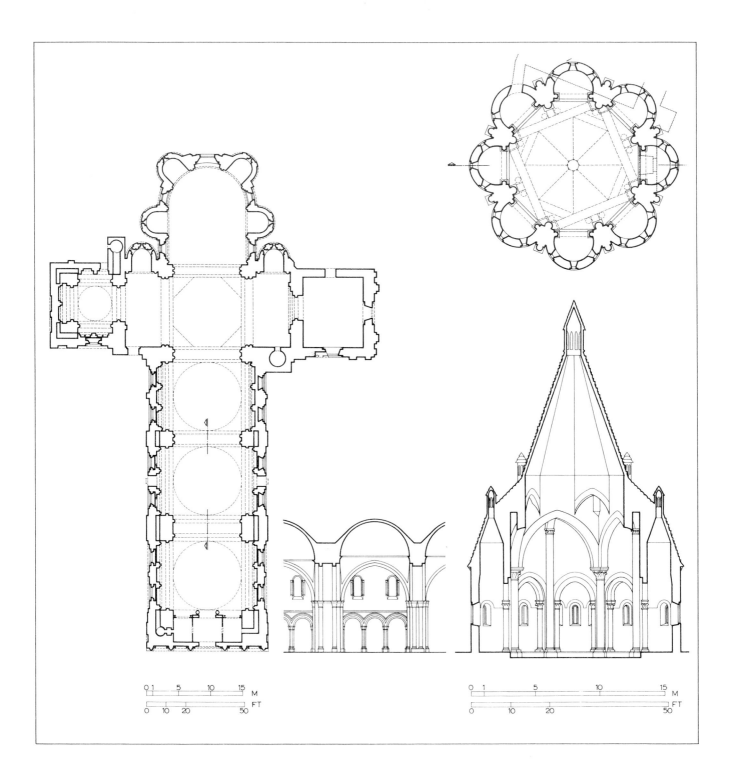

O 1   5   10   15
                      M
O   10   20   50
                      FT

O 1   5   10   15
                      M
O   10   20   50
                      FT

Cathédrale Saint-Pierre, à Angoulême (France), construite entre 1110 et 1128, date de la consécration. Plan et coupe longitudinale d'une travée 1:600. Nef couverte d'une rangée de trois coupoles (∅ 16 m). **Abbaye de Fontevrault** (France), **bâtiment des cuisines,** vers 1120. Plan de l'octogone et coupe 1:300. Construction exceptionnelle par sa structure complexe et élégante.

Links: **Angoulême (Frankreich), Kathedrale Saint-Pierre,** 1110–1128 (Weihe). Die drei Kuppeln des Langhauses haben 16 m Durchmesser. Grundriß und Längsschnitt (ein Joch) 1:600. Rechts: **Fontevrault (Frankreich), Küchenbau der Abtei,** um 1120. Ein durch seine geschlossene und elegante Struktur ungewöhnlicher Bau. Grundriß und Schnitt 1:300.

Cathedral of St. Pierre, Angoulême (France), begun 1110 and consecrated 1128. Plan and longitudinal section of a bay 1:600. The nave is roofed with three domes (diameter 16 m.) in a row. **Fontevrault Abbey** (France), **kitchen block,** c.1120. Plan of the octagon and section 1:300. The building is noteworthy for its complex and elegant structure.

152

Abbatiale Sainte-Foy, à Conques (France), datant de la seconde moitié du XIᵉ s. Plan 1:400. La nef à collatéraux est dotée de tribunes. Un clocher octogonal surmonte la croisée du transept coiffée d'une coupole. Le chevet est à déambulatoire et à chapelles rayonnantes. La formule se retrouve très semblable à Saint-Jacques de Compostelle.

Conques (Frankreich), Abteikirche Sainte-Foy, 2. Hälfte 11. Jh. Dreischiffige Emporenkirche mit Chorumgang und Kapellenkranz, über der Vierungskuppel ein achteckiger Turm. Eine ähnliche Lösung findet sich in Santiago de Compostela. Grundriß 1:400.

Abbey church of Ste. Foy, Conques (Aveyron, France), second half of eleventh century. Plan 1:400. The nave is accompanied by side aisles and galleries. An octagonal belfry rises above the domed transept crossing. The apse has an ambulatory and radial chapels. Altogether a solution very similar to that of Santiago de Compostela.

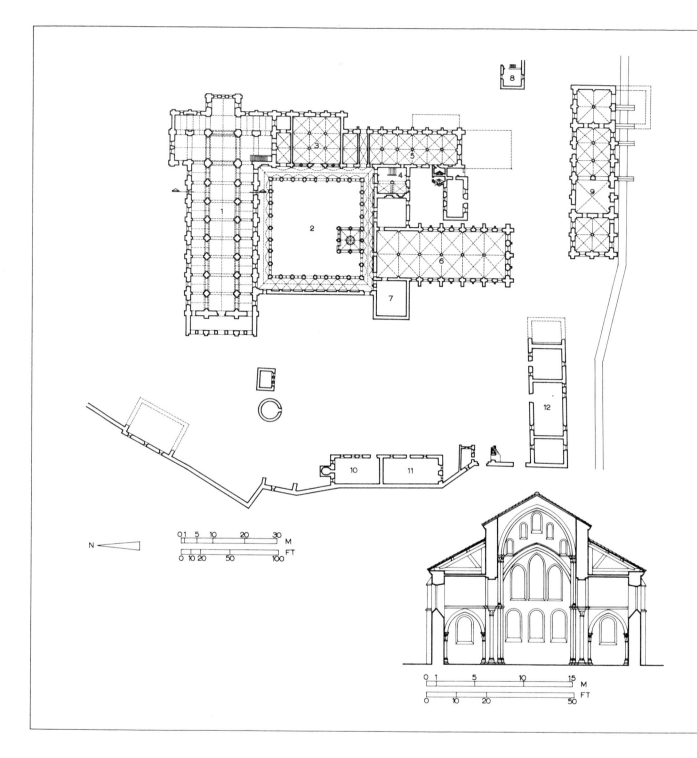

Abbaye cistercienne de Fontenay (France), édifiée par saint Bernard dès 1119. Plan général 1:1200 et coupe transversale de la nef 1:400. 1) Eglise, 2) Cloître, 3) Salle capitulaire, 4) Chauffoir, 5) Grande salle, 6) Réfectoire, 7) Cuisines, 8) Infirmerie, 9) Forge, 10) Boulangerie, 11) Chapelle des étrangers, 12) Hôtellerie. Une organisation rigoureuse préside à la disposition du plan cistercien.

Fontenay (Frankreich), Zisterzienserabtei, 1119 von Bernhard von Clairvaux gegründet. Die Zisterzienserklöster sind nach strengen Regeln angelegt. Lageplan 1:1200: 1) Kirche, 2) Kreuzgang, 3) Kapitelsaal, 4) Wärmestube, 5) Großer Saal, 6) Refektorium, 7) Küche, 8) Krankenstube, 9) Schmiede, 10) Bäkkerei, 11) Gästekapelle, 12) Gästehaus; Querschnitt der Kirche 1:400.

Cistercian abbey, Fontenay (France), designed by St. Bernard and begun in 1119. Overall plan 1:1200; cross section of the nave 1:400. 1) church, 2) cloister, 3) chapter-house, 4) calefactory, 5) main hall, 6) refectory, 7) kitchens, 8) infirmary, 9) forge, 10) bakery, 11) strangers' chapel, 12) guest quarters. Strict organisation governed the layout of a Cistercian monastery.

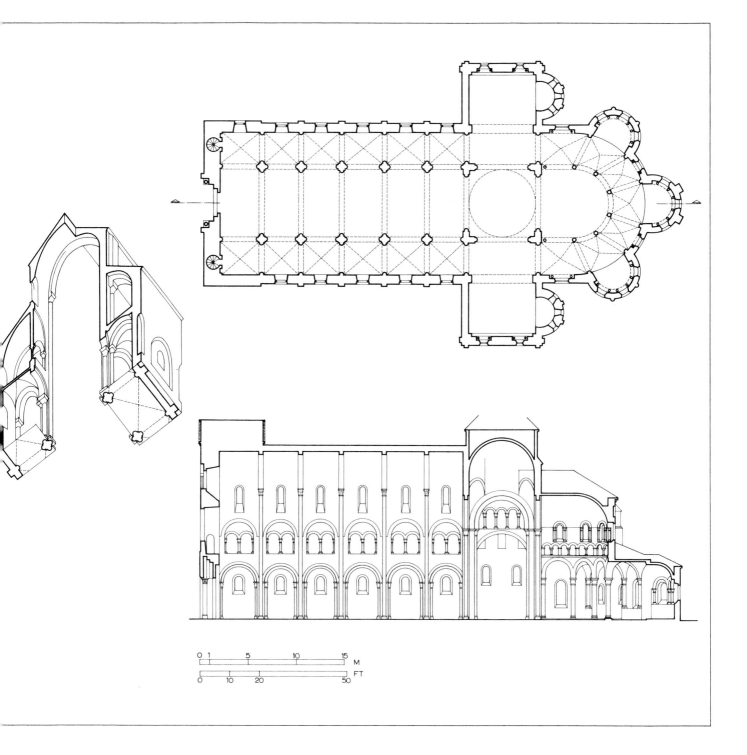

Eglise Saint-Etienne de Nevers (France), construite entre 1062 et 1097. Axonométrie d'une travée, plan et coupe longitudinale 1:400. La nef à trois étages, voûtée en berceau, est contre-butée par les demi-berceaux des tribunes. Le transept largement saillant précède un chœur à déambulatoire et chapelles rayonnantes.

Nevers (Frankreich), Saint-Etienne, 1062 bis 1097. Dem Tonnengewölbe des dreigeschossigen Mittelschiffs dienen die Vierteltonnen der Emporen als Widerlager. Zwischen dem Langhaus und dem Chor mit Umgang und Kapellenkranz ein weitausladendes Querhaus. Axonometrie eines Jochs, Grundriß und Längsschnitt 1:400.

St. Etienne, Nevers (France), built between 1062 and 1097. Axonometric projection of a bay, plan, and longitudinal section 1:400. The three-storeyed tunnel-vaulted nave is buttressed by the half-tunnels of the galleries. The wide transept is followed by a chancel with an ambulatory and radial chapels.

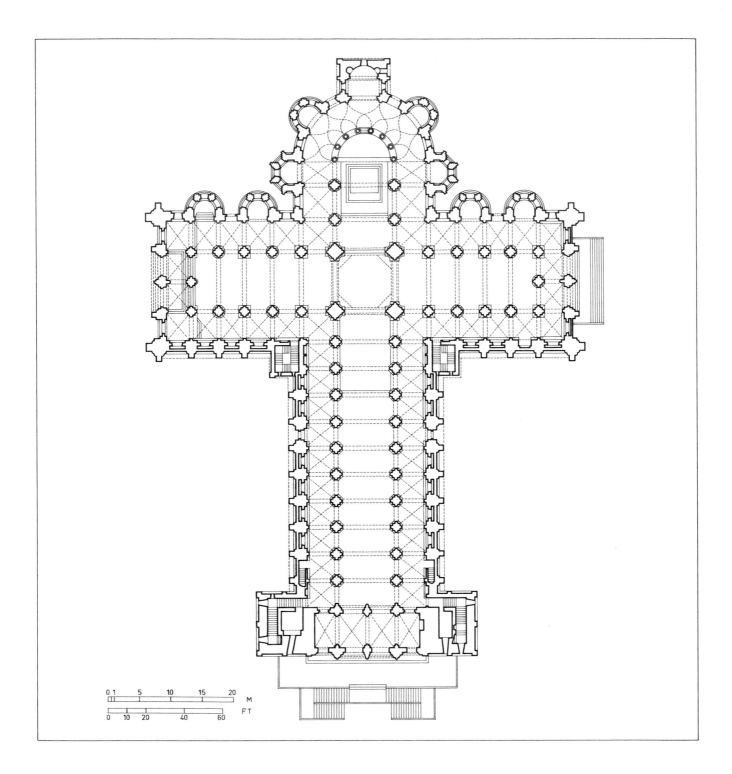

Cathédrale Saint-Jacques de Compostelle (Espagne), édifiée dès 1080 par Bernard, dit le Vieux, puis dès 1101 par Etienne, et encore inachevée en 1130. Plan 1:600. Cette vaste église de plus de 100 m de long, construite pour répondre à l'afflux des pèlerins de Saint-Jacques, semble avoir été bâtie par des architectes venant de France. L'analogie avec Sainte-Foy en fournit la preuve.

Santiago de Compostela (Spanien), Kathedrale, 1080 Baubeginn unter Bernhard d.Ä., weitergeführt 1101 unter Stefan, 1130 noch nicht vollendet. Die Baumeister der für den wachsenden Pilgerstrom errichteten, mehr als 100 m langen Kirche kamen vermutlich aus Frankreich, wie Übereinstimmungen mit Ste-Foy in Conques beweisen. Grundriß 1:600.

Cathedral of Santiago de Compostela (Spain), begun in 1080 by Bernard the Old, continued in 1101 by Etienne, still unfinished in 1130. Plan 1:600. This enormous church, more than 100 m. long and built in order to accommodate the influx of pilgrims to the tomb of St. James, appears to have been the work of French architects. Comparison with Ste. Foy would seem to prove this.

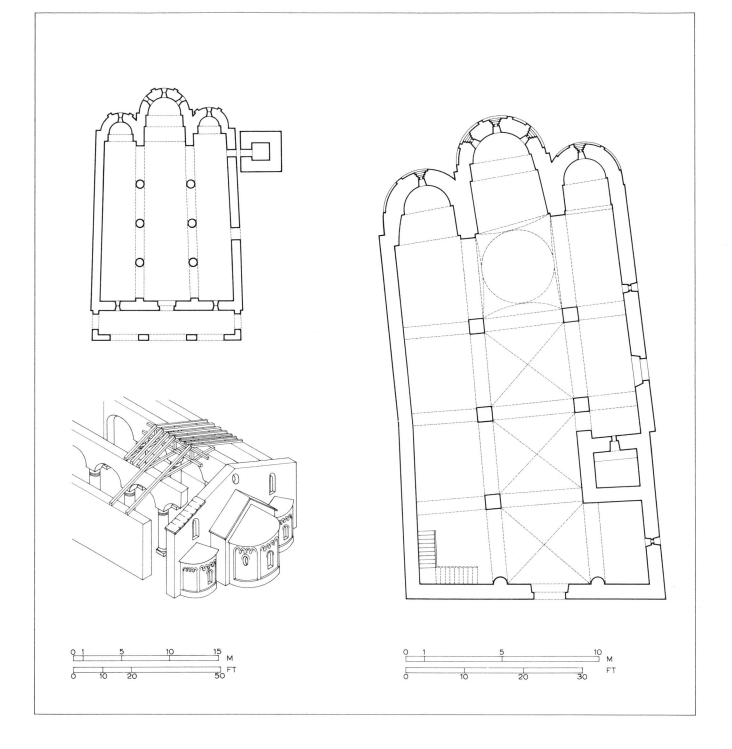

Eglise Saint-Clément de Tahull (Espagne), consacrée en 1123. Plan et axonométrie 1:400. De type basilical parfait, avec ses trois nefs, sa toiture de bois et ses trois absides, cette petite église constitue une survivance. Le clocher carré est séparé à la manière des campaniles. A droite, **Eglise Santa-Maria de Tahull,** datant de 1123 également. Plan 1:200.

Links: **Tahull (Spanien), San Clemente,** 1123 geweiht. In dieser kleinen dreischiffigen Kirche mit offenem Dachstuhl und drei Apsiden überlebt eine ältere Form. Der quadratische Glockenstuhl steht frei, in der Art eines Campanile. Grundriß und Axonometrie 1:400. Rechts: **Tahull, Santa Maria,** 1123. Grundriß 1:200.

S. Clemente, Tahull (Spain), consecrated 1123. Plan and axonometric projection 1:400. This perfect basilican church with its three aisles, wooden roof and three apses constitutes a relic of times past. The square belfry is separate, like the Italian campanile. Right, **S. Maria, Tahull,** also 1123. Plan 1:200.

Eglise San Tomaso, à Almenno San Bartolomeo (Italie), édifice circulaire bâti au XIᵉ s. Plan et coupe transversale 1:300. Cette église de pèlerinage présente des tribunes de déambulatoire formant de larges baies en plein cintre. A droite: **Cathédrale San Pietro de Tuscania,** qui relève de la tradition basilicale. Plan, plan de la crypte et coupe transversale 1:400.

Links: **Almenno San Bartolomeo (Italien), San Tomaso,** 11. Jh. Wallfahrtskirche; Umgang und Emporen des Rundbaus öffnen sich in großen Rundbogen zum Zentralraum. Grundriß und Querschnitt 1:300. Rechts: **Tuscania (Italien), Kathedrale San Pietro.** Der Bau führt die Tradition der Basilika weiter. Grundriß der Kirche, Grundriß der Krypta, Querschnitt 1:400.

S. Tomaso, Almenno San Bartolomeo (Italy), eleventh century. Plan and cross section 1:300. In this round pilgrimage church the ambulatory galleries form wide semicircular bays. Right, **Cathedral of S. Pietro, Tuscania** (Italy), built in the basilican tradition. Plan, plan of the crypt and cross section 1:400.

Abbatiale Santa Maria de Portonovo
(Italie), de formule romane authentique,
avec son voûtement systématique et ses
absides. Plan, coupe longitudinale et
coupe transversale 1:300 et situation
1:1500. A la croisée, une coupole sur
trompes. Les bas-côtés sont couverts en
voûtes d'arêtes.

**Portonovo (Italien), Abteikirche Santa
Maria.** Romanischer Bau mit strengem
Wölbungssystem und mehreren Apsiden; über der Vierung eine Trompenkuppel, Kreuzgratgewölbe in den Seitenschiffen. Grundriß, Längs- und
Querschnitt 1:300; Lageplan 1:1500.

Abbey church of S. Maria, Portonovo
(Italy), an authentic Romanesque structure with its systematic vaulting and
apses. Plan, longitudinal section and
cross section 1:300; site plan 1:1500.
The crossing is vaulted with a dome on
squinches, the side aisles with groin
vaults.

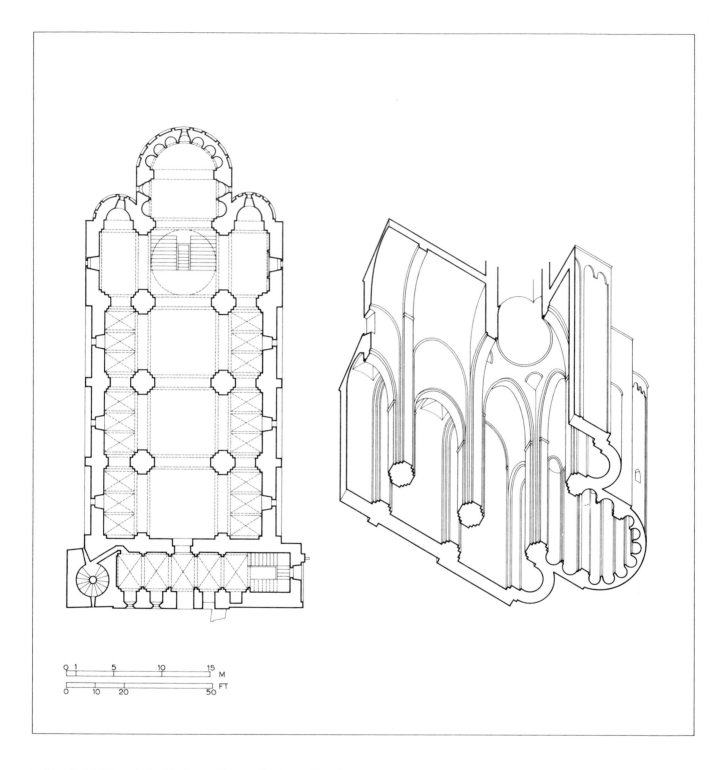

Eglise Saint-Vincent de Cardona (Espagne), dédicace en 1040. Plan et axonométrie ouverte du chœur 1:400. Eglise à plan basilical à trois nefs, avec transept surmonté d'un dôme et chevet triabsidal. Expression puissante de l'architecture aux traits austères, mais d'une saveur plastique vigoureuse.

Cardona (Spanien), San Vicente, 1040 geweiht. Dreischiffige Basilika mit einer Trompenkuppel über der Vierung und drei Apsiden. Der Bau ist durch seine knappe Formensprache und kräftige Plastizität eindrucksvoll. Grundriß, Axonometrie des Chors 1:400.

S. Vincente, Cardona (Spain), consecrated 1040. Plan and open axonometric projection of the chancel 1:400. This three-aisled basilican church has a domed transept and a three-apsed termination. It is a powerful piece of architecture, austere in design yet vigorously plastic.

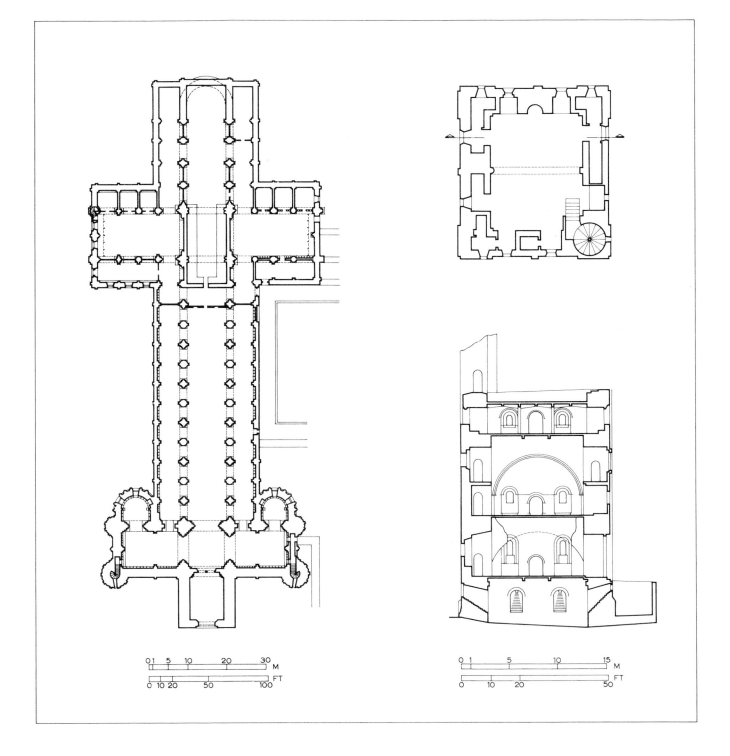

0 1 5 10 20 30 M
0 10 20 50 100 FT

0 1 5 10 15 M
0 10 20 50 FT

Cathédrale d'Ely (Grande-Bretagne), en construction vers 1080. Plan 1:1000. Ce vaste vaisseau est un exemple des églises normandes à élévation tripartite à piles alternées. Baie unique au rez-de-chaussée, double à l'étage des tribunes et triple au niveau de la claire-voie supérieure. A droite: **Donjon du château d'Hedingham.** Plan et coupe 1:400. Enorme tour à quatre étages de plan orthogonal.

Links: **Ely (England), Kathedrale,** um 1080 im Bau. Das Langhaus ist ein Beispiel für normannische Kirchen mit dreizonigem Aufbau und Stützenwechsel. Einer Arkade entspricht ein Zwillingsbogen im Emporengeschoß und in der Fensterzone eine Drillingsöffnung. Grundriß 1:1000. Rechts: **Hedingham (England), Donjon der Burg.** Grundriß und Schnitt 1:400.

Ely Cathedral (England), begun c.1080. Plan 1:1000. The huge nave is a typical example of the Norman three-tiered elevation with alternate piers; a single ground-floor bay becomes a double bay at gallery level and a triple bay at clerestory level. Right, **Keep of Hedingham Castle** (England), a vast four-storeyed tower on a rectangular plan. Plan and section 1:400.

161

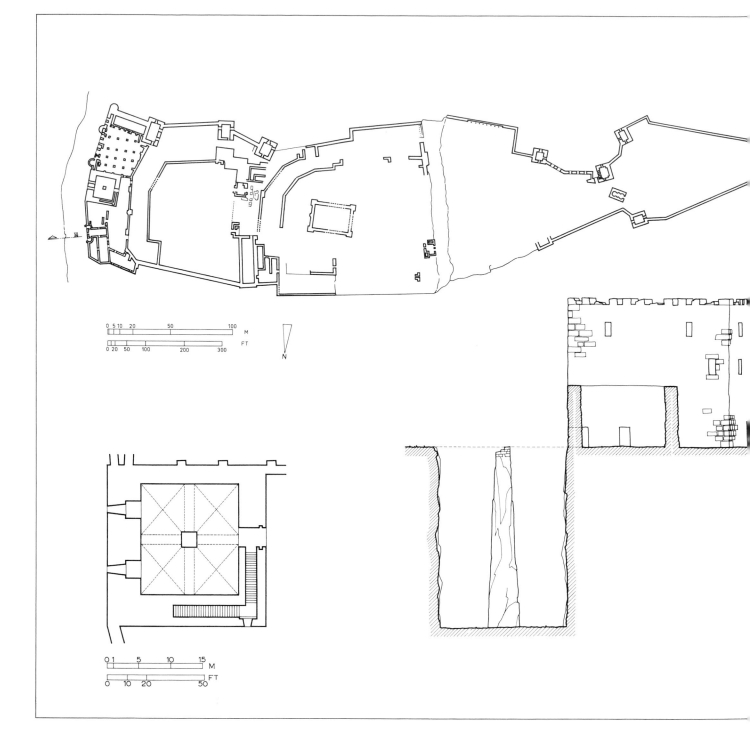

Château de Saone (Syrie), forteresse des Francs en Terre sainte mentionnée dès 1119. Plan général 1:3000, plan du donjon, coupe sur le grand fossé et élévation du donjon 1:600. Le fossé qui isole la forteresse construite entre deux cours d'eau, est taillé de main d'homme en pleine roche. Une aiguille de pierre est laissée en réserve pour supporter le pont-levis d'accès.

Saone (Syrien), Kreuzfahrerburg, 1119 erstmals erwähnt. Der Graben der zwischen zwei Flüssen angelegten Burg wurde aus dem gewachsenen Fels gehauen, als Stütze für die Zugbrücke ließ man dabei eine Felsnadel stehen. Lageplan 1:3000; Grundriß des Donjons, Schnitt durch den Burggraben mit Aufriß des Donjons 1:600.

Saone Castle (Syria), a Frankish fortress in the Holy Land mentioned first in 1119. Overall plan 1:3000; plan of the keep, section through the great moat, and elevation of the keep 1:600. The moat isolating the fortress, which is built between two rivers, was carved out of the solid rock, a single stone needle being left to support the drawbridge.

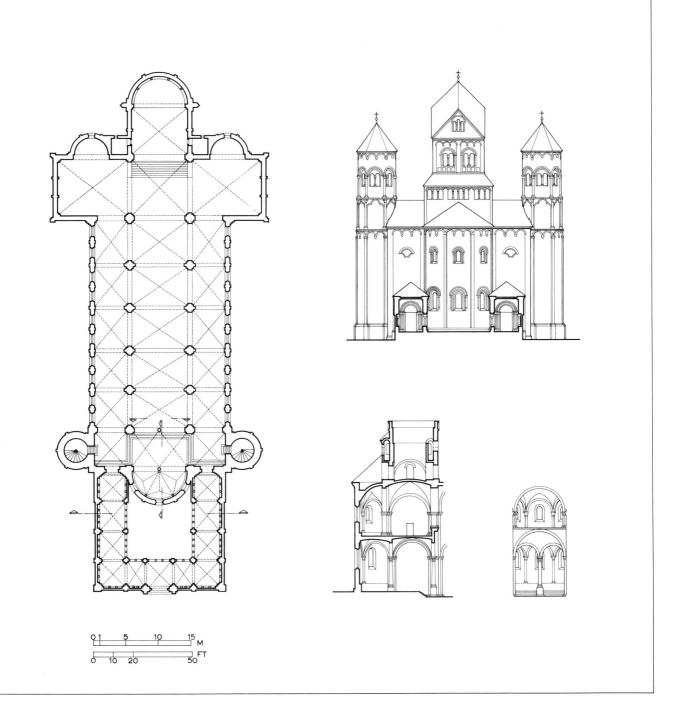

Abbatiale de Maria-Laach, dans l'Eifel (Allemagne), construite dès 1093 et jusqu'au début du XIIIᵉ s. Plan, élévation du chevet, coupe longitudinale et coupe transversale sur le chœur occidental 1:600. Partout les voûtes d'arêtes sont substituées aux plafonds de bois ottoniens. Des bandes lombardes ornent les murs extérieurs.

Maria Laach (Eifel), Abteikirche, 1093 bis Anfang 13. Jh. An die Stelle der ottonischen hölzernen Flachdecke sind Kreuzgratgewölbe getreten. Das Äußere der Kirche ist mit Blendbogen geschmückt. Grundriß, Aufriß des Ostchors, Längs- und Querschnitt durch den Westchor 1:600.

Abbey church of Maria Laach (in the Eifel, Germany), begun in 1093 and completed in the early thirteenth century. Plan, elevation of the apse, longitudinal section, and cross section through the west chancel 1:600. Throughout the building groin vaults took the place of the wooden ceilings of the Ottonian period. The exterior is decorated with Lombard bands.

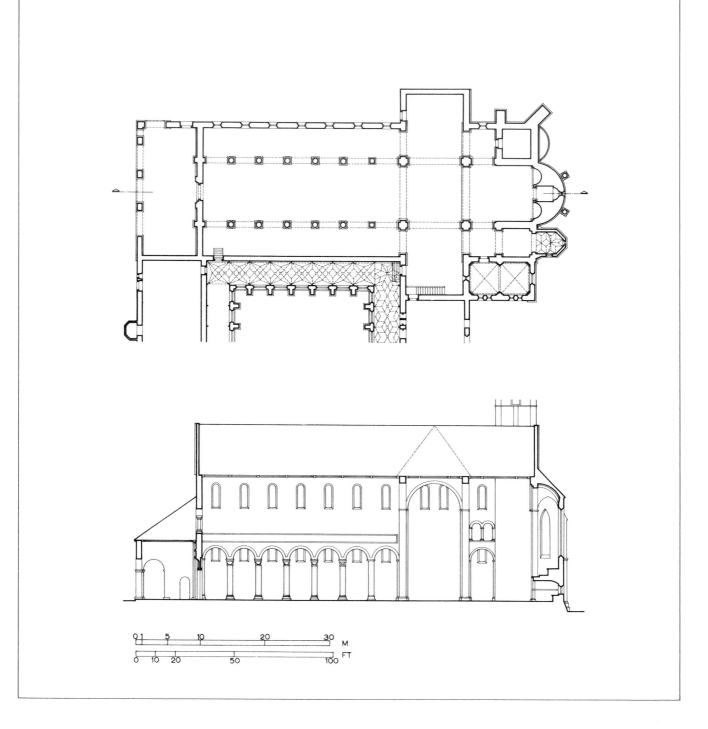

Abbaye bénédictine d'Alpirsbach, Souabe (Allemagne), fondée en 1095 par Adalbert von Zollern. Plan et coupe longitudinale 1:600. Cette église édifiée sur le thème basilical traditionnel, à massif porche occidental, est couverte de fermes et plafonds de bois qui perpétuent les formules ottoniennes. Quatre arcs diaphragmes marquent la croisée, et la nef ne présente pas de division en travées.

Alpirsbach, Benediktinerklosterkirche, 1095 von Adalbert von Zollern gegründet. Basilika mit westlicher, mächtiger Vorhalle; das Langhaus hat in Fortsetzung der ottonischen Tradition eine hölzerne Flachdecke und ist nicht in Joche unterteilt, die Vierung ist ausgeschieden. Grundriß und Längsschnitt 1:600.

Benedictine abbey, Alpirsbach (in the Black Forest, Germany), founded by Adalbert von Zollern in 1095. Plan and longitudinal section 1:600. A version of the traditional basilican design with a massive west porch, this church is roofed in the Ottonian manner with trusses and wooden ceilings. Four diaphragm arches mark the crossing, and the nave is not divided into bays.

164

Gothique   Gotik   Gothic

Se fondant sur les ultimes leçons des expériences romanes (Caen), et en particulier sur le recours au tiers-point et aux voûtes d'arêtes qui donnent naissance aux arcs ogives, la conception du style qui sera qualifié de gothique se fait jour en France avec la réalisation de l'église Saint-Denis, par l'évêque Suger, au milieu du XIIe siècle. La formule évolue à la suite d'une série de modifications progressives qui convergent en une mécanique nouvelle de l'architecture, que les grandes cathédrales (Chartres, Senlis, Laon, Reims, Bourges, Paris, Amiens) vont sans cesse perfectionner et parfaire, jusqu'à l'hypertrophie de Beauvais, au milieu du XIIIe siècle.

Les caractéristiques du style gothique sont: affaiblissement du rôle du mur qui perd de sa massivité, s'amincit, s'ouvre au moyen de hautes baies; renforcement des structures, par le jeu des contreforts, puis des arcs-boutants qui rejettent à l'extérieur de l'édifice les organes sur lesquels portent les efforts; création d'un système organique de piliers, de nervures et de croisées d'ogives possédant une statique propre, indépendamment des parois, lesquelles ne servent souvent que de remplissage; accentuation de la verticalité du vaisseau par haussement de la nef centrale; allègement des galeries en triphorium, d'abord aveugles, puis ouvertes sur l'extérieur. La proportion largeur/hauteur de la nef peut atteindre 1 à 3 à Reims, voire 1 à 3,5 à Beauvais, où elle culmine à 48 m.

Dans la nef, comme dans la croisée du transept, la lumière, tamisée par des vitraux multicolores, pénètre à flots. La différence est considérable par rapport à l'obscurité propice au recueillement du style roman. La cathédrale gothique est un vaisseau de lumière, une architec-

---

Als erster gotischer Bau kann die von Abt Suger in der Mitte des 12. Jahrhunderts erbaute Kirche von Saint-Denis angesehen werden. Ihre Voraussetzungen waren, neben Bauten wie den Kirchen von Caen, die Entwicklung des Spitzbogens und des Kreuzgewölbes. Durch stetige Modifikation dieser Formeln entstand ein neues Architektursystem, das in den großen Kathedralen (Chartres, Senlis, Laon, Reims, Bourges, Paris, Amiens) unaufhörlich verfeinert und vervollkommnet wurde, bis hin zu dem hypertrophen Bau von Beauvais in der Mitte des 13. Jahrhunderts.

Charakteristika des gotischen Stiles sind: geringere Bedeutung der Mauer, die von großen Öffnungen durchbrochen ist; Betonung der Struktur durch Strebepfeiler und Strebebogen und Ableitung des Gewölbedruckes und -schubs auf tragende Elemente außerhalb des Mauermantels; ein System von Stützen, Gurten und Kreuzrippen, das heißt, ein statisches System unabhängig von den oft nur noch als Füllung dienenden Mauern; stärkere Betonung der Vertikalen durch Steigerung der Mittelschiffshöhe; Einführung des zunächst blinden, dann durchfensterten Triforiums. Das Verhältnis Breite zu Höhe beträgt beim Mittelschiff der Kathedrale zu Reims 1:3, in Beauvais sogar 1:3,5 (Scheitelhöhe 48 m).

Durch vielfarbige Scheiben einströmendes Licht erhellt Langhaus und Vierung – ein auffälliger Gegensatz zum Dunkel der romanischen Kirchen. Die gotische Kathedrale ist von Licht erfüllt, ein scheinbar schwereloses Bauwerk, Symbol des Neuen Jerusalems der Apokalypse.

Von Frankreich ausgehend verbreitete sich die Gotik über ganz Europa. Man-

---

Based on the ultimate lessons of Romanesque experience (Caen) and particularly on the pointed equilateral arch and the groin vault, the style that came to be known as Gothic first emerged in France with the abbey church of St. Denis, built by Bishop Suger in the middle of the twelfth century. Progressive modifications had eventually produced a new kind of architectural engineering, which in France was further improved upon in the classic High Gothic cathedrals of Chartres, Senlis, Laon, Reims, Bourges, Paris and Amiens—right up to the extremes of Beauvais (mid-thirteenth century).

The distinctive features of the Gothic style are: a playing-down of the role of the wall, which became thinner and less massive as it was broken up into tall bays; increased structural strength through the use of buttresses and subsequently of flying buttresses, which removed the load-bearing structures to a position outside the actual building; the creation of an organic, statically autonomous system of pillars, arches, and intersecting ribs that often reduced the walls to mere filling; an emphasis on the vertical by increasing the height of the central nave; and a lightening of the gallery into a triforium, blind at first, then opening on to the exterior. The width-to-height ratio of the nave was as much as 1:3 at Reims—and at Beauvais it even reached 1:3.5, with the highest point of the nave 48 m. above the floor.

Nave and transept crossings were flooded with light from huge, multicoloured stained-glass windows—in marked contrast to the meditative semi-darkness of the Romanesque church. The Gothic cathedral was in fact a vessel of light, its immaterial architecture a

ture immatérielle qui traduit symboliquement l'apparition de la Jérusalem Nouvelle de l'Apocalypse.

De France, le Gothique s'étend à l'Europe entière, avec des variations locales parfois importantes: églises halles en Allemagne, où la nef et les bas-côtés s'élèvent au même niveau, comme le sud de la France avec les Jacobins de Toulouse l'avait esquissé dans une formule à deux nefs; foisonnement des nervures et des liernes qui envahissent toute la couverture dans les églises anglaises (Wells, Cambridge); luxuriance décorative au Portugal (Batalha, fin XVe s.). Enfin, une architecture militaire considérable de forts et de donjons s'épanouit avec l'âge des Croisades et à la suite des contacts avec l'Islam (Krak des Chevaliers, Carcassonne, Aigues-Mortes).

che Länder entwickelten charakteristische Sonderformen: Deutschland die Hallenkirchen mit gleicher oder annähernd gleicher Höhe von Mittel- und Seitenschiffen (eine ähnliche Lösung findet sich bei der zweischiffigen Jakobinerkirche von Toulouse aus dem 13. Jahrhundert); England ein System von das ganze Kircheninnere überwuchernden Gurten und Rippen (Wells, Cambridge); Portugal überquellenden Bauschmuck (Batalha, Ende 15. Jahrhundert). Im Zeitalter der Kreuzzüge und unter dem Einfluß der islamischen Welt entwickelte sich eine Militärarchitektur mit Festungen und Wehrtürmen. Beispiele sind Krak des Chevaliers (Qala'at al-Husn in Syrien), Carcassonne und Aigues-Mortes.

symbol of the New Jerusalem of the Apocalypse.

From France Gothic architecture spread throughout Europe, producing some important local variations: Germany built hall churches with nave and side aisles all of the same height, a solution already hinted at by the Jacobin friars at Toulouse with their two-naved formula; English architects filled the whole vault area with ribs, tiercerons, and liernes (Wells Cathedral; King's College Chapel, Cambridge); Portugal went in for luxuriant decoration (Batalha, late fifteenth century). Finally the Crusades and the resultant contacts with the Moslem world prompted military architects to produce some important fortresses and keeps (the Krak des Chevaliers, Carcassonne, Aigues-Mortes).

1 Le voûtement gothique: à gauche, travée double ou sexpartite avec alternance des piles fortes et faibles; à droite, travées à croisée simple (Cathédrale de Lausanne, Suisse, XIIIe s.).
2 Château de Castel del Monte (Italie), construit vers 1240 par Frédéric II de Hohenstaufen.
3 La nef d'Amiens (France), construite par Robert de Luzarches vers 1240, dont les voûtes culminent à 42 m.

1 Lausanne, Kathedrale, gotische Wölbung: links sechsteiliges Gewölbe mit verschieden starken Rippen, rechts zwei Kreuzrippengewölbe (13. Jh.)
2 Castel del Monte (Apulien, Italien), Jagdschloß Friedrich II. (um 1240)
3 Amiens, Kathedrale, Mittelschiff; der Gewölbescheitel liegt in 42 m Höhe (Robert de Luzarches, um 1240)

1 Gothic vaulting: left, double or sexpartite bay with alternate strong and weak piers; right, bay with simple intersecting ribs (Lausanne cathedral, Switzerland; thirteenth century).
2 Castel del Monte (Italy), built c. 1240 by Frederick II.
3 The nave of Amiens cathedral (France), built c. 1240 by Robert de Luzarches. The vaults reach a height of 42 m.

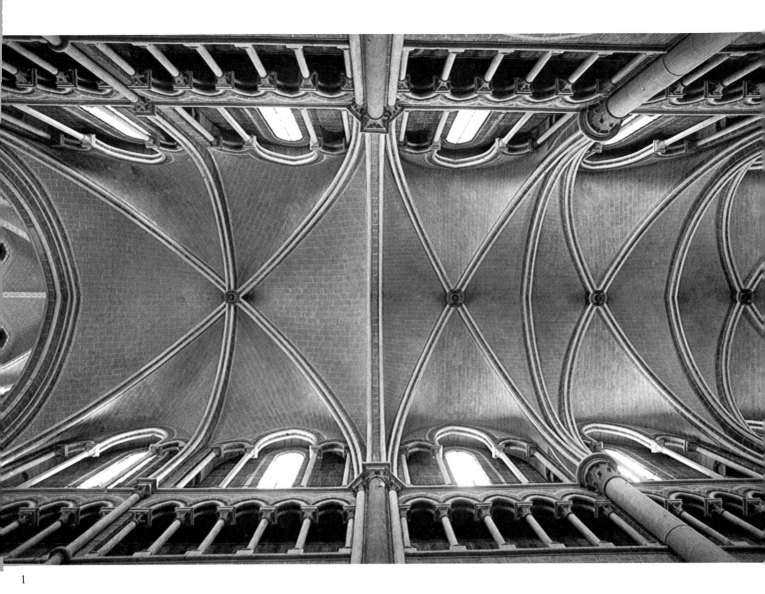

1

2

3

167

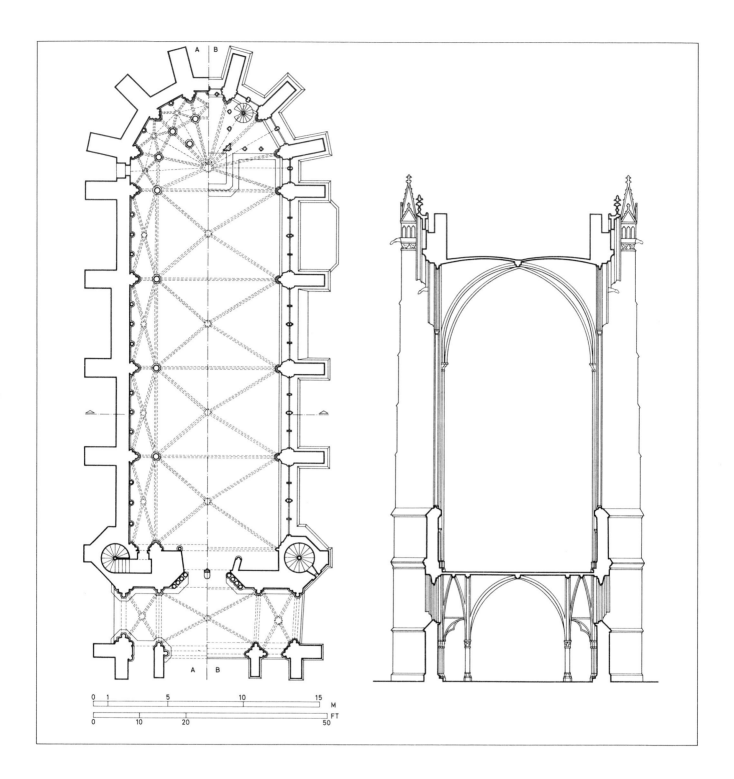

Sainte-Chapelle, Paris, construite par Jean de Chelles et Pierre de Montreuil pour le roi saint Louis, entre 1245 et 1248. Plan A) de l'église inférieure, et B) de l'église supérieure, coupe transversale 1:250. Joyau du gothique de l'Ile de France, contemporain de Notre-Dame de Paris, la chapelle palatine se caractérise par le remplacement de tout mur par des contreforts.

Paris, Saint-Chapelle, 1245–1248. Die Palastkapelle wurde für König Ludwig den Heiligen von Jean de Chelles und Pierre de Montreuil gebaut. Dieses «Juwel» unter den gotischen Bauten der Ile-de-France entstand gleichzeitig mit Notre-Dame in Paris. Das tragende Mauerwerk ist hier durch ein System von Strebepfeilern ersetzt. Grundriß 1:250: A) Unterkirche, B) Oberkirche.

Sainte-Chapelle, Paris, built 1245–8 by Jean de Chelles and Pierre de Montreuil for St. Louis, king of France. Plans a) of the lower church, b) of the upper church, and cross section 1:250. This jewel among the Gothic architecture of the Ile de France, built as a chapel palatine at the same time as Notre-Dame, is distinguished by the fact that the wall is entirely replaced by buttresses.

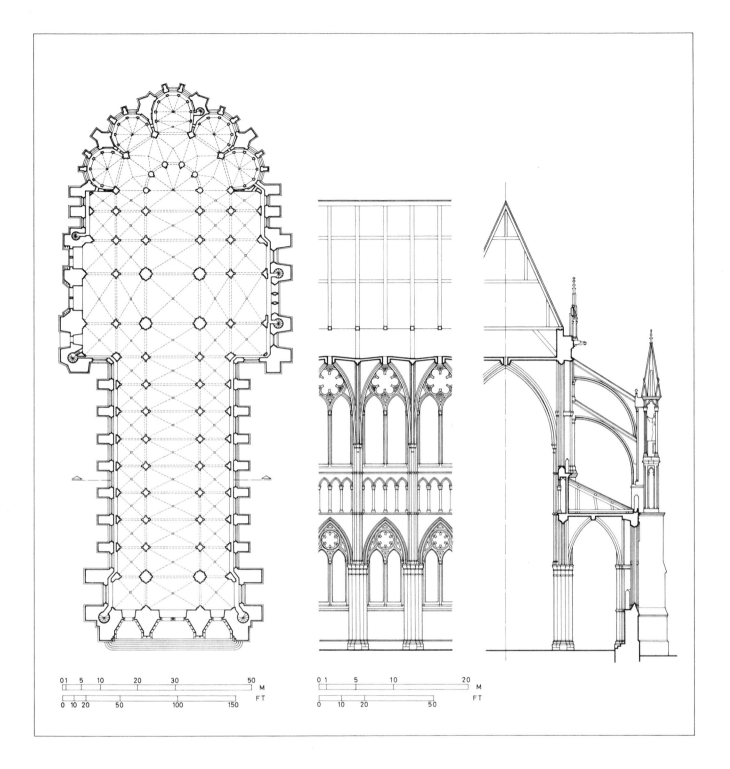

Cathédrale Notre-Dame, à Reims, bâtie par l'architecte Jean d'Orbais, mise en chantier en 1211, chevet, transept et deux travées achevés en 1241, façade de 1255 à 1291, achèvement du gros œuvre en 1311. Plan 1:1000, élévation intérieure d'une travée et coupe transversale de la nef 1:500. Edifice considéré comme le type le plus achevé du gothique français avec son savant jeu d'arcs-boutants.

Reims, Kathedrale Notre-Dame, Baumeister Jean d'Orbais, 1211 begonnen, Chor, Querhaus, zwei Joche 1241 vollendet, Fassade 1255–1291, Rohbau 1311 vollendet. Der Bau gilt dank seines wohldurchdachten Strebewerks als vollkommenste Ausprägung der französischen Gotik. Grundriß 1:1000; Aufriß eines Joches, Querschnitt durch das Langhaus mit Strebewerk 1:500.

Cathedral of Notre-Dame, Reims. Architect Jean d'Orbais. Begun 1211, apse, transept and two bays completed by 1241, façade 1255–91, main works completed by 1311. Plan 1:1000; interior elevation of a bay and cross section of the nave 1:500. Regarded as a prime example of French Gothic with its skilful use of flying buttresses.

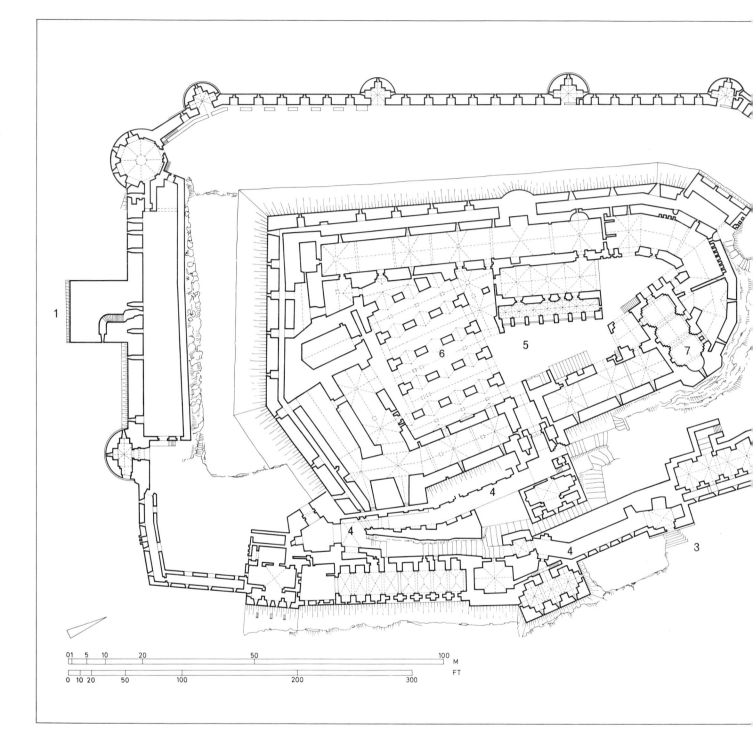

Forteresse dite Krak des Chevaliers, en Syrie, construite par les Hospitaliers entre 1170 et 1250. Plan général 1:1000. 1) Entrée latérale, 2) Barbacane, 3) Entrée principale, 4) Rampes d'accès, 5) Cour, 6) Grand'Salle, 7) Chapelle. L'un des plus puissants châteaux édifiés par les Croisés en Terre sainte, avec sa double enceinte et ses glacis.

Qala'at al Husn (Krak des Chevaliers; Syrien), 1170–1250. Diese Festung der Hospitalienbrüder ist mit ihrem doppelten Mauergürtel und dem Glacis eine der wehrhaftesten Kreuzfahrer-Burgen im Heiligen Land. Plan 1:1000: 1) Seiteneingang, 2) Barbakane, 3) Haupteingang, 4) Auffahrtsrampe, 5) Hof, 6) großer Saal, 7) Kapelle.

'Krak des Chevaliers' (Syria), built by the Hospitallers between 1170 and 1250. Overall plan 1:1000. 1) side entrance, 2) barbican, 3) main entrance, 4) access ramps, 5) courtyard, 6) great hall, 7) chapel. With its double wall and its glacis, this was one of the most powerful castles built by the Crusaders in the Holy Land.

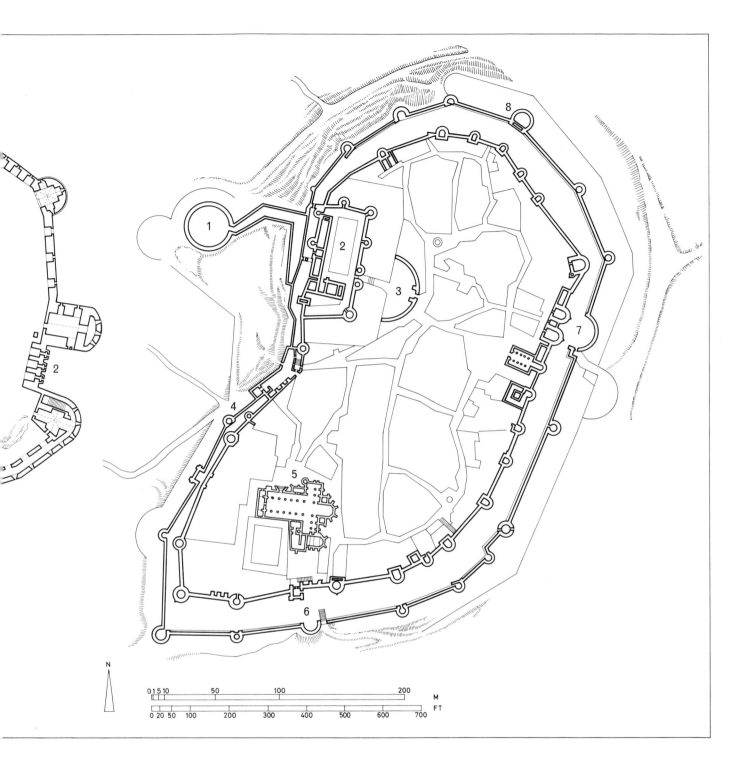

Cité forte de Carcassonne (France). Plan général 1:3000. Cette enceinte qui remonte à 1130 et fut renforcée après 1240 puis dès 1270 mesure, pour la muraille intérieure, 1286 m et présente 25 tours. La muraille extérieure qui mesure 1500 m compte 17 tours. 1) Barbacane démolie, 2) Château comtal, 3) Barbacane, 4) Porte d'Aude, 5) Eglise Saint-Nazaire, 6) Poterne, 7) Porte Narbonnaise, 8) Tour Notre-Dame.

Carcassonne (Frankreich), befestigte Stadt. Die Stadtmauern gehen auf 1130 zurück, wurden 1240 und ab 1270 verstärkt. Der innere Mauerring mit 25 Türmen mißt 1286 m, der äußere mit 17 Türmen 1500 m. Plan 1:3000: 1) Barbakane (zerstört), 2) gräfliche Burg, 3) Barbakane, 4) Porte d'Aude, 5) Kirche Saint-Nazaire, 6) Poterne Saint-Nazaire, 7) Porte Narbonnaise, 8) Tour Notre-Dame.

Fortified city of Carcassonne (France); fortifications begun 1130, reinforced after 1240 and begun again in 1270. Overall plan 1:3000. The inner wall measures 1286 m. and has 25 towers; the outer wall, with 17 towers, measures 1500 m. 1) demolished barbican, 2) Count's castle, 3) barbican, 4) Porte d'Aude, 5) St. Nazaire church, 6) postern, 7) Porte Narbonnaise, 8) Notre-Dame tower.

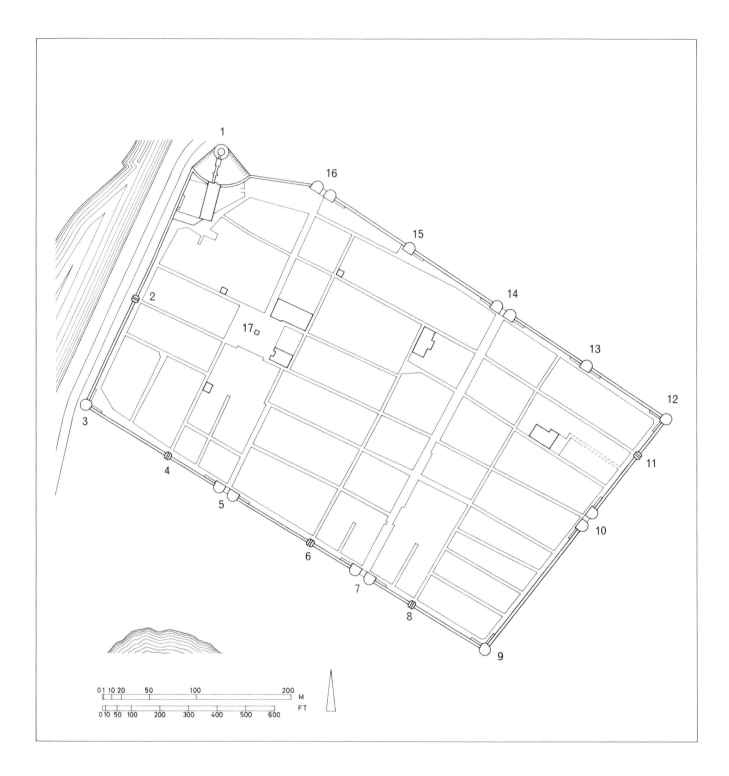

Cité forte d'Aigues-Mortes (France), édifiée par saint Louis en 1240. Plan d'ensemble 1:4000. Port d'embarquement de la Croisade, la cité est construite d'un seul jet. 1) Tour de Constance; 2, 4, 6, 8, 11) Poternes; 3, 9, 12, 13, 15) Tours; 5, 7, 10, 14, 16) Portes; 17) Place Saint-Louis.

Aigues-Mortes (Frankreich), befestigte Stadt, 1240. Die Stadt wurde unter Ludwig dem Heiligen als Kreuzfahrer-Hafen angelegt und in einem Zug erbaut. Grundriß 1:4000. 1) Tour Constance, 2) 4) 6) 8) 11) Poternen (Ausfallpforten), 3) 9) 12) 13) 15) Wehrtürme, 5) 7) 10) 14) 16) Tore, 17) Place St-Louis.

Fortified city of Aigues-Mortes (France), built 1240 by St. Louis in a single operation as a port of embarkation for his Crusade. Overall plan 1:4000. 1) Constance tower, 2, 4, 6, 8, 11) posterns, 3, 9, 12, 13, 15) towers, 5, 7, 10, 14, 16) gates, 17) Place Saint-Louis.

 0 1   5   10   20   30 M
0 10 20   50   100 FT

Eglise des Jacobins, à Toulouse (France), édifice commencé en 1260 et consacré en 1292. Plan, élévation intérieure d'une travée, structure axonométrique et coupe 1:600. Entièrement construite en brique, cette église est régie par les principes ascétiques de l'architecture propre aux ordres mendiants. Double nef à rangée de colonnes centrales, latéralement contre-butée par des dosserets.

Toulouse, Jakobinerkirche, 1260 begonnen, 1292 Weihe. Der Backsteinbau entspricht den asketischen Bauregeln der Bettelorden; er ist zweischiffig mit innerer Säulenstellung und mit Strebepfeilern. Grundriß, Aufriß und Axonometrie eines Joches, Querschnitt 1:600.

Jacobin church, Toulouse (France), begun 1260 and consecrated 1292. Plan, interior elevation of a bay, axonometric structure and section 1:600. Built of brick throughout, this church is governed by the ascetic architectural principles of the mendicant orders. The twin aisles, separated by a row of columns, are buttressed with piers at the sides.

Cathédrale Sainte-Cécile, à Albi (France), église-forteresse construite entre 1282 et 1480. Plan 1:1000, élévation intérieure d'une travée et coupe transversale de la nef 1:500, structure axonométrique. La nef unique que n'interrompent ni transept ni déambulatoire, est fondée sur le principe des dosserets internes contre-butant les voûtes et déterminant des chapelles latérales. Le jubé date du XVe s.

Albi (Frankreich), Kathedrale Sainte-Cécile, 1282–1480. Einschiffige befestigte Kirche ohne Querschiff und Umgang (Choreinbau später). Das Gewölbe ruht auf eingezogenen Strebepfeilern, dazwischen Seitenkapellen. Grundriß 1:1000; Innenaufriß eines Joches, Querschnitt durch das Langhaus 1:500; Axonometrie.

Cathedral of Ste. Cécile, Albi (France), a fortified church built between 1282 and 1480. Plan 1:1000; interior elevation of a bay and cross section of the nave 1:500; axonometric structure. The single aisle, with neither transept nor ambulatory, is based on the principle of internal piers buttressing the vaults and governing the side chapels. The choir-screen dates from the fifteenth century.

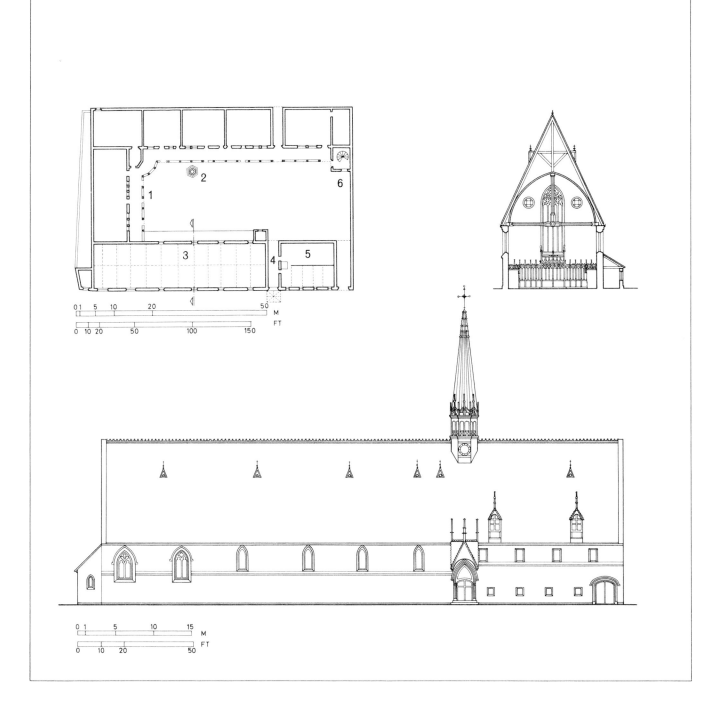

Hôtel-Dieu, à Beaune (France), établissement hospitalier créé en 1443. Plan 1:1000, façade et coupe de la salle des malades 1:500. Cet édifice de l'architecture civile du gothique tardif se caractérise par le voûtement de bois en carène de la salle des malades. 1) Cour d'honneur, 2) Puits, 3) Salle des malades et chapelle, 4) Porche et entrée, 5) Réfectoire, 6) Escaliers.

Beaune (Frankreich), Hôtel-Dieu, 1443 gegründet. Ein Beispiel spätgotischer Profanarchitektur; über dem Krankensaal ein hölzernes Schiffsgewölbe. Grundriß 1:1000: 1) Hof, 2) Brunnen, 3) Krankensaal mit Kapelle, 4) Eingangstor, 5) Refektorium, 6) Treppe; Fassadenaufriß, Querschnitt durch den Krankensaal 1:500.

Hôtel-Dieu, Beaune (France), a Hospitaller foundation dating from 1443. Plan 1:1000; façade and section of the sick room 1:500. The most distinctive feature of this piece of late Gothic secular architecture is the wooden keel vaulting over the sick room. 1) main courtyard, 2) well, 3) sick room and chapel, 4) porch and entrance, 5) refectory, 6) stairs.

Cathédrale Saint-Pierre de Beauvais (France). Commencé en 1247, par Milon de Nanteuil, le chœur à cinq nefs fut achevé en 1272, la nef ne fut jamais achevée. Coupe transversale 1:400. Le vaisseau qui culmine à 48 m de hauteur constitue une véritable hypertrophie du gothique. Les voûtes s'écrouleront en 1284. La tour surmontant la croisée atteignait 153 m et s'effondra à son tour en 1573.

Beauvais (Frankreich), Kathedrale Saint-Pierre, 1247 Baubeginn, Milon de Nanteuil; 1272 Vollendung des fünfschiffigen Chors, Langhaus nie ausgeführt. Die Kühnheit des Chorbaus mit einer Mittelschiffshöhe von 48 m grenzte an Vermessenheit, 1248 stürzten die Gewölbe ein. 1573 Einsturz des 153 m hohen Vierungsturms. Querschnitt 1:400.

Cathedral of St. Pierre, Beauvais (France), begun 1247 by Milon de Nanteuil; the five-aisled chancel was completed in 1272, but the nave remains unfinished. Cross section 1:400. The nave, 48 m. in height, represents the Gothic style at its most excessive. The vaults collapsed in 1284. The tower above the crossing was 153 m. high; it too collapsed in 1573.

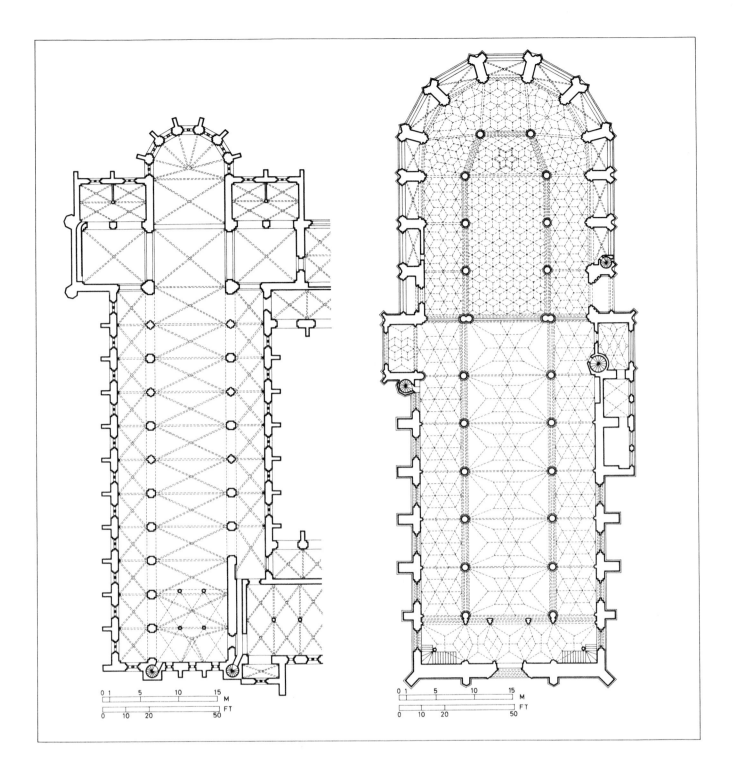

Eglise cistercienne de Chorin (Allemagne), abbatiale édifiée dans la Marche
de Brandebourg en 1274. Plan 1:500.
Bâtiment de brique à plan basilical
cruciforme. Consécration en 1334.
Eglise Sainte-Croix, à Schwäbisch
Gmünd, édifiée dès 1330, chœur dès
1351. Plan 1:500. Eglise halle où les
trois nefs sont de même hauteur. Architecte: Heinrich Parler.

Links: Chorin (Mark Brandenburg),
Zisterzienserklosterkirche, um 1274 begonnen, 1334 geweiht. Kreuzförmige
Backsteinkirche im basilikalen Typus. Grundriß 1:500. Rechts: Schwäbisch Gmünd, Stadtkirche Hl.Kreuz,
1330 begonnen, Chor ab 1351. Dreischiffige Hallenkirche mit gleichhohen
Schiffen; der Architekt war Heinrich
Parler. Grundriß 1:500.

Cistercian church, Chorin (East Germany), an abbey church in the Brandenburg March begun in c. 1274 and consecrated in 1334. Plan 1:500. The church
is built of brick on a cruciform basilican plan. Heiligkreuzkirche (Holy Cross
church), Schwäbisch Gmünd (Germany),
begun in 1330; chancel begun in 1351.
Plan 1:500. A hall church with three
aisles of the same height. The architect
was Heinrich Parler.

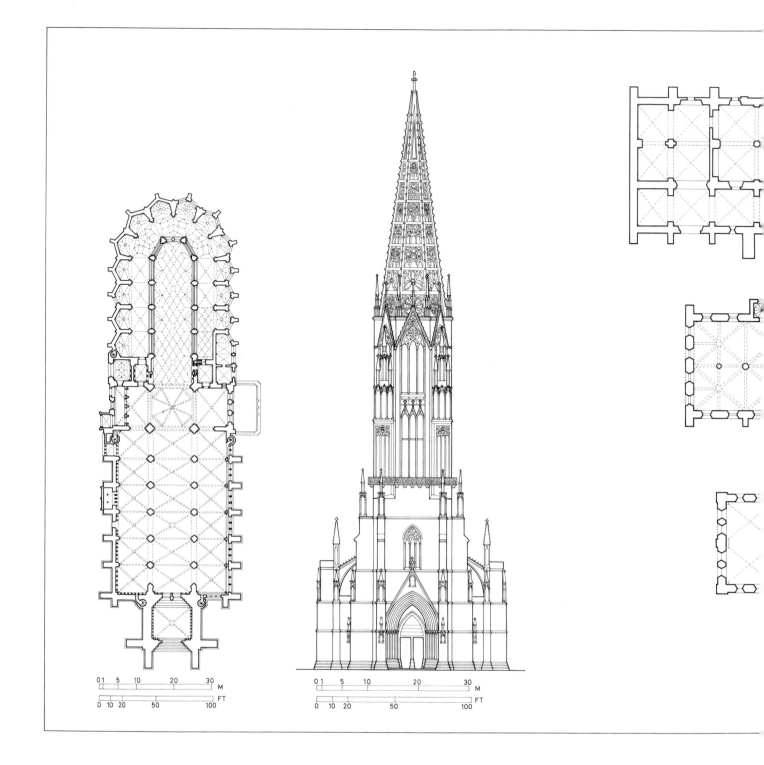

| 0 1 | 5 | 10 | 20 | 30 | M |
| 0 10 | 20 | | 50 | | 100 FT |

| 0 1 | 5 | 10 | 20 | 30 | M |
| 0 10 | 20 | | 50 | | 100 FT |

Cathédrale Notre-Dame, à Fribourg-en-Brisgau (Allemagne), bâtie dès le XIIIe s. Plan 1:1000 et élévation de la façade 1:750. Sur des parties datant du roman tardif, l'architecte gothique a apporté des transformations tant à la croisée qu'à la nef très élevée. La tour est réalisée jusqu'en 1301 par maître Gerhart, puis dès 1310 par Heinrich der Leiterer. Le chœur a été reconstruit en 1354.

Freiburg i. Br., Münster Unserer Lieben Frau, Baubeginn 13. Jh. Vom romanischen Bau sind das Querschiff und die Hahnentürme erhalten. Der gotische Baumeister des Schiffs änderte den Plan. Turmbau bis 1301 durch Meister Gerhart, ihm folgte Heinrich der Leiterer. Chorneubau ab 1354 durch Johannes von Gmünd. Grundriß 1:1000; Fassadenaufriß 1:750.

Freiburg-im-Breisgau Cathedral (Germany), begun in the thirteenth century. Plan 1:1000; façade elevation 1:750. To the parts dating from the late Romanesque period the Gothic architect made changes at the crossing and in the extremely high nave. The tower was begun before 1301 by Meister Gerhart and continued from 1310 by Heinrich der Leiterer. The choir was rebuilt in 1354.

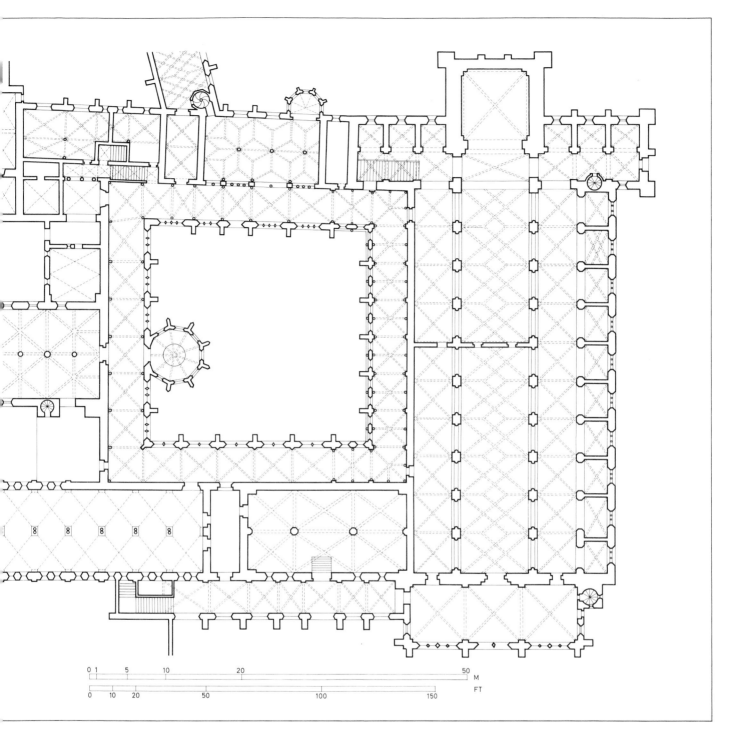

0 1   5   10   20   50   M
                                                                                      FT
0   10 20   50   100   150

Monastère cistercien de Maulbronn (Al-lemagne), abbaye édifiée en pays de Bade dès le roman en 1147, avec une première période gothique en 1210, une salle capitulaire du XIVᵉ et les voûtes à liernes de l'église datant du XVᵉ s. Plan 1:500. Le cloître occupe le centre de la partie réservée aux moines, selon une formule propre à de nombreux monastères cisterciens.

Maulbronn (Württemberg), Zisterzien-serabtei, 1147 begonnen, erster gotischer Bauabschnitt ab 1210, Kapitelsaal 14.Jh., Kreuzrippengewölbe der Kirche 15.Jh. In der Mitte des unter Klausur stehenden Klosterbereichs liegt, wie bei Zisterzienserklöstern üblich, der Kreuz-gang. Grundriß 1:500.

Cistercian monastery, Maulbronn (Ger-many), an abbey in Baden begun 1147 in the Romanesque style, a first Gothic period following in 1210; the chapter-house dates from the fourteenth century and the lierne vaults in the church from the fifteenth. Plan 1:500. The cloister occupies the centre of the part reserved for the monks in obedience to the for-mula adopted in many Cistercian houses.

179

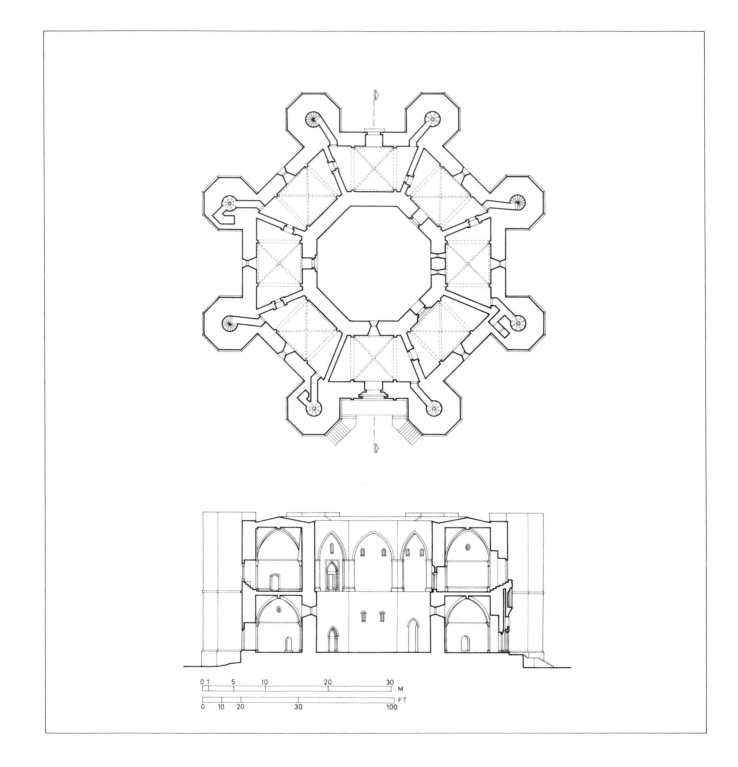

Château de Castel del Monte, en Apulie (Italie), construit par Frédéric II de Hohenstaufen vers 1240. Plan et coupe 1:600. De plan octogonal, régulier comme un cristal, ce château de chasse s'apparente à certains édifices seldjoukides, peut-être en raison de la présence d'architectes musulmans à la cour de l'empereur.

Castel del Monte (Apulien, Italien), um 1240. Das durch Kaiser Friedrich II. errichtete Jagdschloß, ein achteckiger Zentralbau von der Regelmäßigkeit eines Kristalls, ähnelt gewissen seldschukischen Bauten. Vielleicht geht dies auf die am kaiserlichen Hof tätigen islamischen Architekten zurück. Grundriß und Schnitt 1:600.

Castel del Monte (Apulia, Italy), built c.1240 by Frederick II. Plan and section 1:600. Octagonal in plan and as regular as a crystal, this hunting castle bears a resemblance to certain Seljuk buildings, possibly as a result of the presence of Moslem architects at the imperial court.

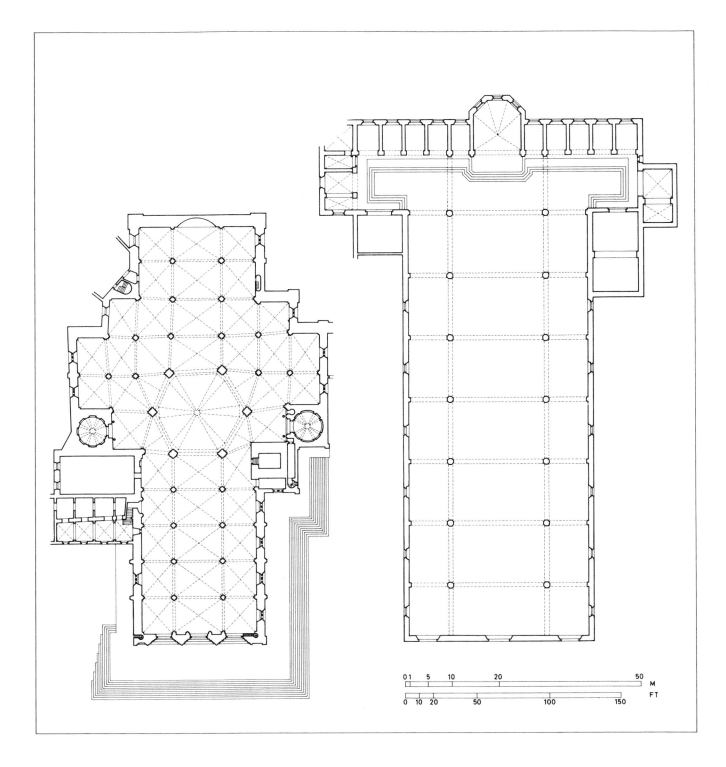

Cathédrale de Sienne (Italie), première campagne de 1196 à 1215, nef terminée en 1259, façade de 1284 à 1299, due à Giovanni Pisano, avec étage supérieur de Giovanni di Cecco datant de 1376. Plan 1:800. La coupole de la croisée est octogonale, à caissons avec lanterne. **Eglise Santa-Croce, à Florence** (Italie), sanctuaire de l'ordre mendiant des Franciscains, achevé en 1295. Plan 1:800.

Links: **Siena, Dom,** Erster Bauabschnitt 1196–1215, 1259 Vollendung des Langhauses, Fassade 1284–1299 (Giovanni Pisano) mit 1376 vollendetem Obergeschoß (Giovanni di Cecco). Über der Vierung eine oktogonale Kassettenkuppel. Grundriß 1:800. Rechts: **Florenz, Santa Croce,** 1295 vollendet. Franziskanerkirche. Grundriß 1:800.

Siena Cathedral (Italy), first stage of building 1196–1215; the nave was completed in 1259 and the façade built by Giovanni Pisano in 1284–99, with an upper storey added by Giovanni di Cecco in 1376. Plan 1:800. The crossing is surmounted by an octagonal coffered dome and a lantern. **S. Croce, Florence** (Italy), a church of the mendicant order of Franciscans, completed in 1295. Plan 1:800.

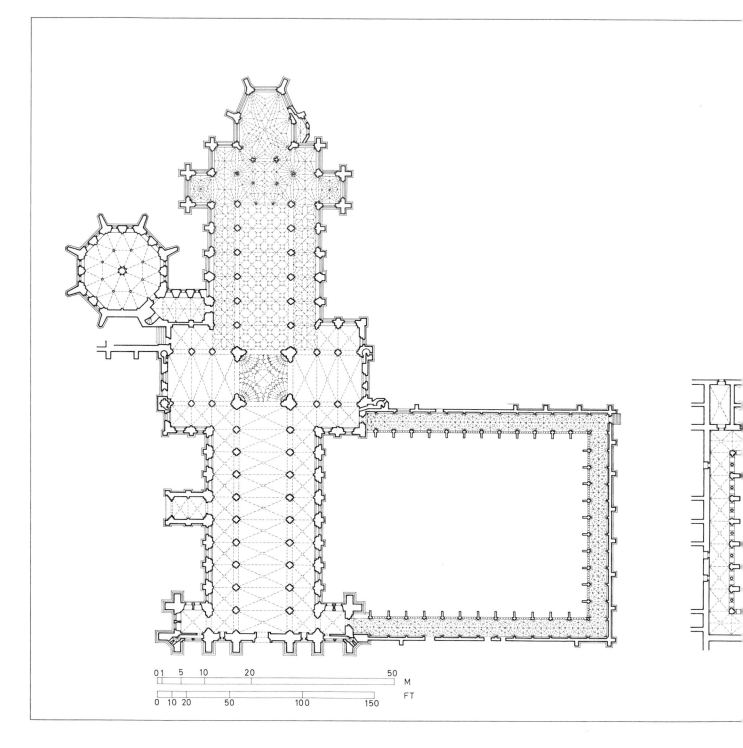

0 1 5 10   20   50
                                           M
                                           FT
0 10 20   50   100   150

Ensemble de la cathédrale de Wells (Grande-Bretagne), la cathédrale St-Andrew fut construite entre 1192 et 1230, avec la façade ouest érigée de 1220 à 1239 et les tours de 1367 à 1386 pour celle sise au sud et de 1407 à 1424 pour celle du nord. Plan général 1:800. Le carré de la croisée est supporté par des arcs entrecroisés construits en 1338. A gauche, la salle capitulaire octogonale de 1319.

Wells (England), Kathedrale St. Andrews, 1192–1230, Westfassade 1220 bis 1239, Südturm 1367–1386, Nordturm 1407–1424. Die quadratische Vierung ist durch 1338 eingezogene, sich kreuzende Bögen ausgeschieden. Der achteckige Kapitelsaal (links im Plan) wurde 1319 erbaut. Grundriß 1:800.

Wells Cathedral (England), dedicated to St. Andrew and built 1192–1230; the west front was built 1220–39, the south tower 1367–86, and the north tower 1407–24. Overall plan 1:800. The square of the crossing is braced by pairs of arches (one of each pair inverted) built in 1338. The octagonal chapterhouse on the left dates from 1319.

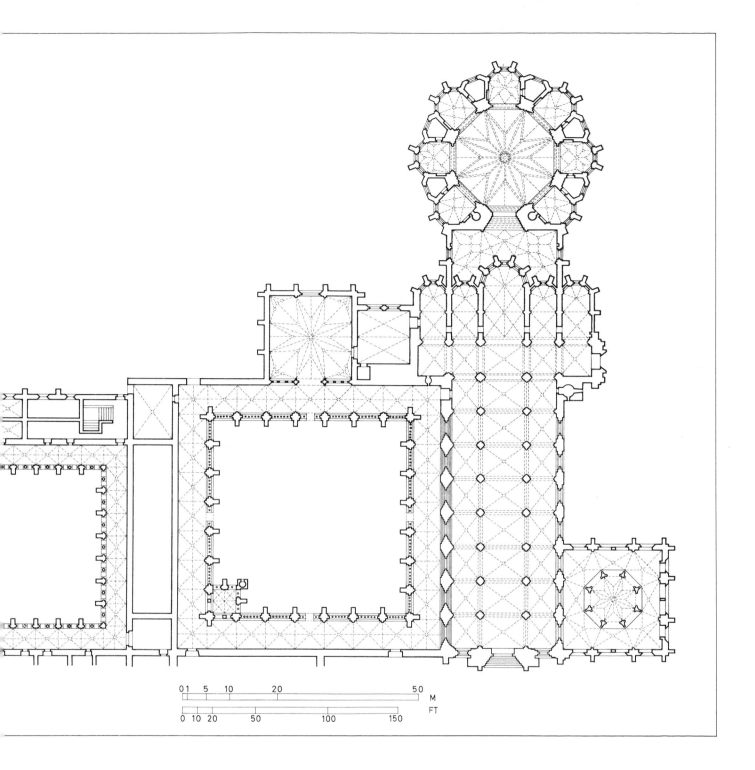

0 1 5 10   20   50
                                               M
                                             FT
0 10 20   50   100   150

Abbaye de Batalha (Portugal), monastère Sainte-Marie-de-la-Victoire édifié dès 1388 à la fin du XVe s. par l'architecte Alfonso Domingues, puis par Huguet dès 1402, pour l'église. Plan 1:800. Œuvre caractéristique du gothique flamboyant portugais dit manuélin, cet ensemble présente deux cloîtres d'une richesse extrême, bâtis par des architectes d'Evora entre 1438 et 1477.

Batalha (Portugal), Kloster Santa Maria da Victoria, Kloster 1388 von dem Baumeister Alfonso Domingues begonnen, Baubeginn der Kirche 1402, Vollendung der Gesamtanlage Ende 15. Jh. Das Dominikanerkloster ist ein charakteristisches Werk der portugiesischen Spätgotik (Manuelstil); die beiden Kreuzgänge wurden zwischen 1438 und 1477 von Architekten aus Evora erbaut. Grundriß 1:800.

Batalha Abbey (Portugal), the monastery of S. Maria da Victoria begun by the architect Alfonso Domingues in 1388, with Huguet taking over the church in 1402; work went on until the end of the fifteenth century. Plan 1:800. This building, a typical product of the flamboyant Portuguese Gothic style known as Manueline, has two luxuriantly decorated cloisters built by architects from Evora between 1438 and 1477.

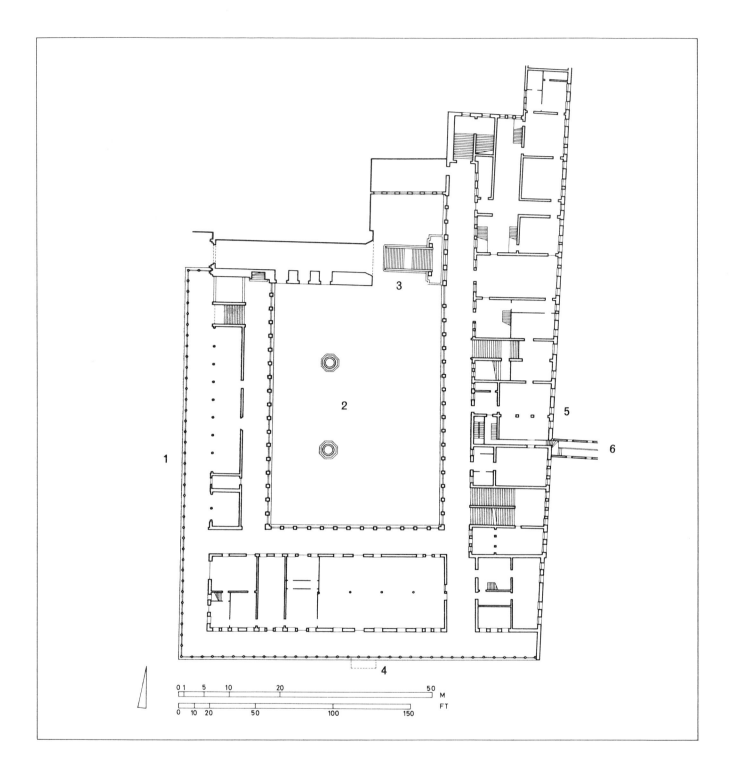

Palais des Doges, à Venise (Italie), construit entre 1309 et 1442, la façade côté canal datant de 1340–1419 et celle côté piazetta de 1424 à 1442, plan 1:750. 1) Façade sur la Placette St-Marc, 2) Cour du palais, 3) Escaliers des Géants, 4) Façade sur le canal St-Marc, 5) Canal du palais, 6) Pont des Soupirs. Solution hardie du palais gothique par la légèreté de la façade à sa base.

Venedig, Dogenpalast, 1309–1442; Fassade zum Canale Grande 1340–1419, Fassade zur Piazzetta San Marco 1424 bis 1442. Eine durch die Auflösung der unteren Geschosse in Arkaden besonders kühne Lösung im gotischen Palastbau. Grundriß 1:750: 1) Fassade zur Piazzetta S. Marco, 2) Hof, 3) Gigantentreppe, 4) Fassade zum Canale Grande, 5) Palastkanal, 6) Seufzerbrücke.

Doge's Palace, Venice (Italy), built 1309–1442; the canal façade dates from 1340–1419, the piazzetta façade from 1424–42. Plan 1:750. 1) Piazzetta S. Marco façade, 2) palace courtyard, 3) Giants' Stairs, 4) canal façade, 5) palace canal, 6) Bridge of Sighs. A bold solution for a Gothic palace by reason of the lightness of the lower part of the façade.

Renaissance

Renaissance

Renaissance

Par rapport au Gothique, le style renaissance marque une rupture brutale, même si les deux formes architecturales coexistent longtemps. Le mouvement débute en Italie, où le souvenir de l'Antiquité était resté vif. On cherche à redécouvrir l'âme de l'architecture romaine en étudiant les monuments et surtout le traité que Vitruve avait dédié à Auguste. Par là même, la Renaissance rend aux notions de module et de proportions leur importance et redonne vie aux ordres antiques: dorique, ionique et corinthien. Tout le vocabulaire des formes et du décor de l'Antiquité est repris aussi fidèlement que possible et celui du Gothique rejeté, en même temps que son verticalisme que remplace une ordonnance horizontale très accusée.

Mais ce mouvement repose sur un malentendu: le théoricien qu'était Vitruve se fondait sur l'architecture républicaine. Or le grand art romain ne s'épanouit qu'avec le monde impérial des IIe, IIIe et IVe siècles, et Vitruve ne l'a pas connu. C'est donc essentiellement le langage ornemental antique qui sert de modèle. Ceci d'autant plus que les programmes de la Renaissance diffèrent de ceux de Rome: on ne construit ni amphithéâtres, ni thermes, ni mausolées aux dimensions de celui d'Hadrien (Château Saint-Ange), mais des églises et des palais, ces derniers n'ayant aucun rapport avec ceux de Rome (Maison d'Or de Néron), et perpétuant plutôt l'organisation et la volumétrie des palais gothiques.

La Renaissance, avec ses théoriciens Alberti, Serlio, Vignole et Palladio, recherche la structure mathématique de la beauté, grâce à un système arithmétique, géométrique et harmonique.

Zwischen der Renaissance-Architektur und der gotischen Baukunst besteht eine klare stilistische Trennung, auch wenn beide Formen lange Zeit nebeneinander verwendet wurden. Die Renaissance begann in Italien. Dort war die Antike noch in gewisser Weise lebendig geblieben, und man bemühte sich – einerseits durch das Studium der Bauwerke, andererseits mit Hilfe des um 25 v. Chr. entstandenen Vitruvschen Werkes «De architectura» – das Wesen der römischen antiken Baukunst wieder zu erfassen. Die Bedeutung von Modul, Proportion und antiken Ordnungen – dorisch, ionisch, korinthisch – wurde der Renaissance erneut bewußt. Sie nahm den antiken Formenschatz so getreu wie möglich auf. Nicht nur die gotischen Formen verschwanden jetzt, sondern auch das Prinzip der Vertikalität, an dessen Stelle eine Betonung der Horizontalen trat.

Bei diesen Bemühungen um eine «Wiedergeburt der Antike» hat ein Mißverständnis eine nicht unwesentliche Rolle gespielt: Vitruvs Werk beruht auf der Architektur der Republik, die großen Bauten der Kaiserzeit, des 2., 3. und 4. Jahrhunderts, entstanden erst sehr viel später; das Studium seiner Werke konnte also nur einen Ausschnitt der römischen Antike vermitteln.

In erster Linie übernahm die Renaissance den ornamentalen antiken Formenschatz. Das lag nahe, denn ihre Bauprogramme waren sehr verschieden: Man baute weder Amphitheater, Thermen noch Mausoleen von den Ausmaßen des Hadrian-Mausoleums (Engelsburg), sondern Kirchen. Und die Paläste der Renaissance standen in Aufbau und Gliederung ihren gotischen

Seen in relation to Gothic, the architecture of the Renaissance represents a complete break with tradition, even though the two styles coexisted for a long time. The movement began in Italy, where the memory of classical antiquity had never died. Architects sought to rediscover the essence of Roman architecture by looking at its monuments and above all by studying the treatise that Vitruvius had dedicated to Augustus. The Renaissance put the idea of the module and the rule of proportion back at the heart of architecture and gave new life to the classical orders: Doric, Ionic and Corinthian. The whole classical vocabulary of form and decoration was taken up as faithfully as possible, and that of Gothic rejected; at the same time the verticalism of the latter was replaced by a markedly horizontal arrangement.

Unfortunately it was all based on a misunderstanding. The theoretician Vitruvius had been talking about Republican Rome, whereas the truly great Roman architecture only blossomed in the Imperial period of the second, third, and fourth centuries—long after Vitruvius' death. So it was essentially the decorative language of antiquity that the Renaissance took as its model. In any case its programmes were very different from those of Rome. Renaissance architects built neither amphitheatres, nor thermae, nor mausoleums on the scale of that of Hadrian (Castel S. Angelo) but churches and palaces. Moreover their palaces had nothing whatever to do with those of Rome (Nero's Golden Palace), continuing instead the spatial organisation of the Gothic palace.

The Renaissance, through its theoreticians Alberti, Serlio, Vignola and Pal-

Pour des raisons d'intelligibilité plastique, on accorde une grande importance au plan centré qu'avait négligé le Gothique: Tempietto de Bramante et projets de la nouvelle basilique Saint-Pierre. La gageure technologique que constitue l'immense coupole du dôme de Florence, par Brunelleschi, transforme presque l'église à nef en édifice centré.

A partir de la notion de villa, créée par les Romains, la Renaissance donne aux grands de ce temps des résidences fastueuses, articulées dans le paysage que modèle un art totalement neuf des jardins.

Bientôt, le style renaissance s'étend à toute l'Europe pour connaître des visages divers. Il se mue en style classique en France, alors que l'Italie et l'Allemagne susciteront le mouvement baroque.

Vorgängern sehr viel näher als antiken Bauten wie etwa dem Goldenen Haus des Nero.

Die Architektur-Theoretiker der Renaissance – Alberti, Serlio, Vignola und Palladio – bemühten sich mit Hilfe der Geometrie, Arithmetik und Harmonielehre das Wesen der Schönheit mathematisch zu erfassen. Der Zentralbau, der während der Gotik eine weniger wichtige Rolle gespielt hatte, erhielt nun – weil sein Baukörper leichter erfaßbar ist – neue Bedeutung: Bramantes Tempietto und die Entwürfe für St. Peter in Rom sind Beispiele. Brunelleschis Domkuppel in Florenz, eine technische Meisterleistung, gab diesem längsgerichteten Bau eine dem Zentralbau verwandte Wirkung.

Von der Idee der römischen Villa ausgehend ließen sich die Mächtigen der Renaissance prachtvolle, in Gärten eines ganz neuen Typus eingebettete Landsitze bauen.

Die Renaissance breitete sich von Italien her über ganz Europa aus und nahm in jedem Land eigene Formen an. In Frankreich entwickelte sich in der Folge der «klassische» Stil, in Italien und Deutschland der Barock.

ladio, pursued the mathematical structure of beauty by arithmetical, geometrical and harmonic means. For reasons of plastic intelligibility great importance was attached to the centralised plan, which Gothic architects had passed over. Examples are Bramante's Tempietto and the plans for a new basilica of St. Peter. The technological challenge of Brunelleschi's huge dome on Florence Cathedral virtually turned the aisled church into a centralised structure.

Drawing their inspiration from the Roman villa, Renaissance architects provided the great men of their time with luxurious residences in settings that were models for the wholly new art of landscape gardening.

The Renaissance style soon spread throughout Europe, undergoing various transformations. In France it became 'le style classique', whereas Italy and Germany fashioned it into the movement known as Baroque.

1 Chevet et dôme de la cathédrale Santa Maria del Fiore, à Florence, construite de 1417 à 1446 par Brunelleschi.
2 Vue interne de la coupole de Saint-Pierre de Rome, projetée par Michel-Ange et réalisée (modifiée) par Giacomo Della Porta et Domenico Fontana entre 1586 et 1593.
3 La Villa Almerico, dite Rotonda, à Vicence (1566), par Palladio.
4 Vue intérieure du Théâtre Olympique à Vicence (1580), par Palladio.

1 Florenz, Dom Santa Maria del Fiore, Chor und Kuppel (Brunelleschi, 1417–1446)
2 Rom, Sankt Peter, Inneres nach Entwurf von Michelangelo (Ausführung in veränderter Form durch Giacomo della Porta und Domenico Fontana, 1586 und 1593)
3 Vicenza, Villa Rotonda, auch: Villa Almerico Capra (Palladio, 1566)
4 Vicenza, Teatro Olimpico, Inneres (Palladio, 1580)

1 Apse and dome of S. Maria del Fiore (Florence cathedral), built 1417–46 by Brunelleschi.
2 Interior view of the dome of St. Peter's, Rome, designed by Michelangelo and built (in a modified form) by Giacomo della Porta and Domenico Fontana between 1586 and 1593.
3 Villa Almerico Capra, also known as La Rotonda, Vicenza, by Palladio (1566).
4 Interior view of the Olympic Theatre, Vicenza, by Palladio (1580).

1

2

3

4

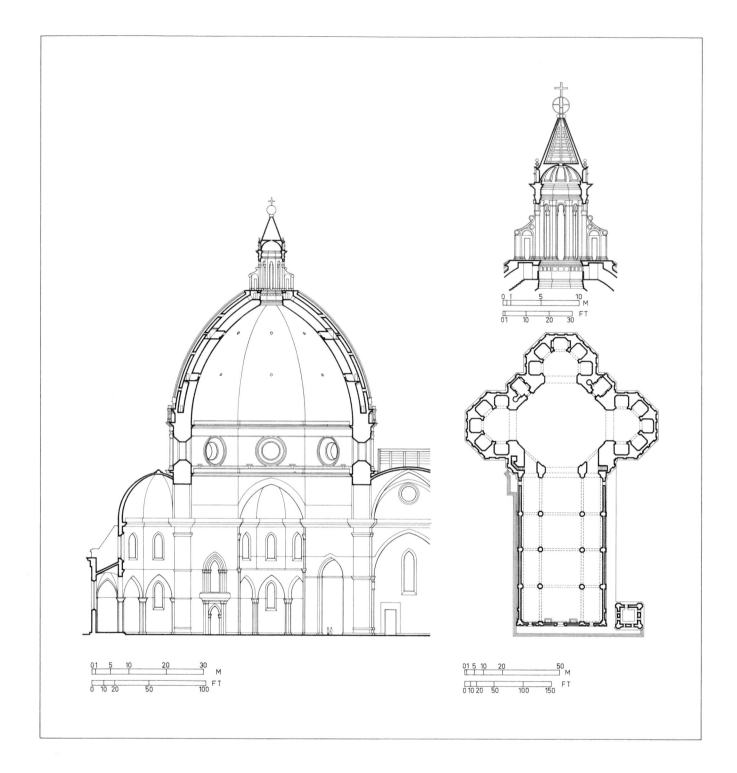

Cathédrale Santa Maria del Fiore, à Florence (Italie), coupole couvrant la croisée, par Brunelleschi, construite entre 1417 et 1446. Coupe longitudinale 1:1000, détail de la lanterne 1:500, et plan 1:2000. Cette énorme coupole à élévation elliptique de 43 m de diamètre (égale au Panthéon de Rome) qui culmine à 115 m de haut est construite sans cintre, en deux coques à nervures.

Florenz, Dom Santa Maria del Fiore, 1296 begonnen, Vierungskuppel 1417 bis 1446 von Brunelleschi. Die Kuppel mit elliptischem Querschnitt ist aus zwei Schalen mit Rippen, doch ohne Gurte konstruiert. Ihr Scheitel liegt 115 m hoch, ihr Durchmesser gleicht dem des Pantheon in Rom. Längsschnitt der Ostteile 1:1000; Detail der Laterne 1:500; Grundriß 1:2000.

Cathedral of S. Maria del Fiore, Florence (Italy), Brunelleschi's dome over the crossing, built 1417–46. Longitudinal section 1:1000; detail of the lantern 1:500; plan 1:2000. This vast elliptical dome—43 m. in diameter (the same as that of the Pantheon, Rome) and rising to a height of 115 m.—was erected in two ribbed shells without centring.

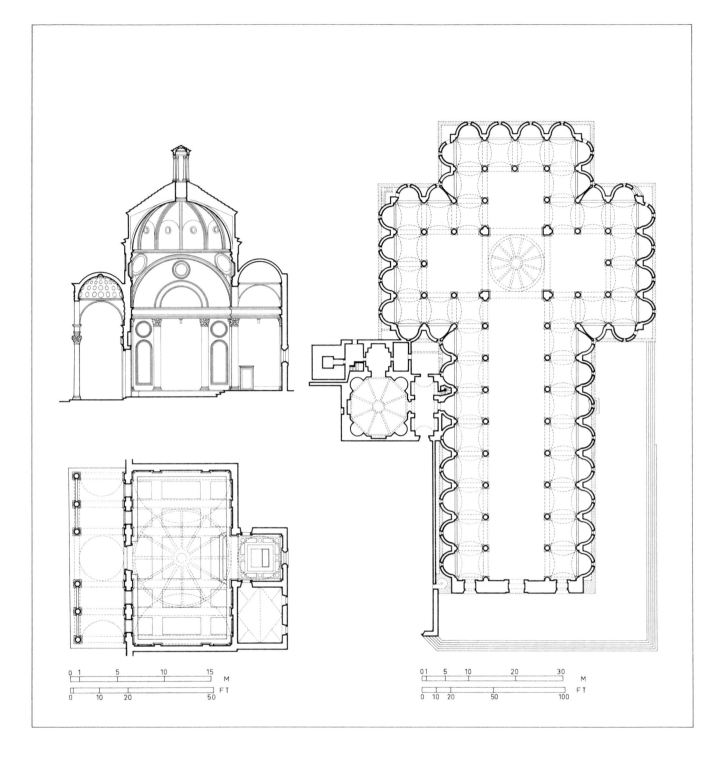

Chapelle des Pazzi, Santa Croce, à Flo-rence (Italie), construite entre 1430 et 1461 par Brunelleschi. Coupe longitu-dinale et plan 1:400. A droite, **Eglise Santo Spirito, Florence,** par Brunel-leschi, édifiée en 1444. Plan restituant l'idée originale de l'architecte 1:800. Les façades «ondulantes» dérivent de formules romaines, telles qu'on les trouve au temple de Minerva Medica.

Links: **Florenz, Capella dei Pazzi, Santa Croce,** 1430–1461, Brunelleschi. Längs-schnitt und Grundriß 1:400. Rechts: **Florenz, Santo Spirito,** 1444, Brunelle-schi. Der Grundriß zeigt den ursprüng-lichen Entwurf. Die «gewellten» Fas-saden widerspiegeln antike Baugedan-ken, wie sie z.B. am Tempel der Mi-nerva Medica ausgeführt wurden. Grundriß 1:800.

Pazzi Chapel, S. Croce, Florence (Italy), built 1430–61 by Brunelleschi. Longitu-dinal section and plan 1:400. Right, **S. Spirito, Florence,** built 1444, also by Brunelleschi. Plan showing the archi-tect's original idea 1:800. The 'wavy' façades stem from Roman formulae as used in the temple of Minerva Medica, Rome.

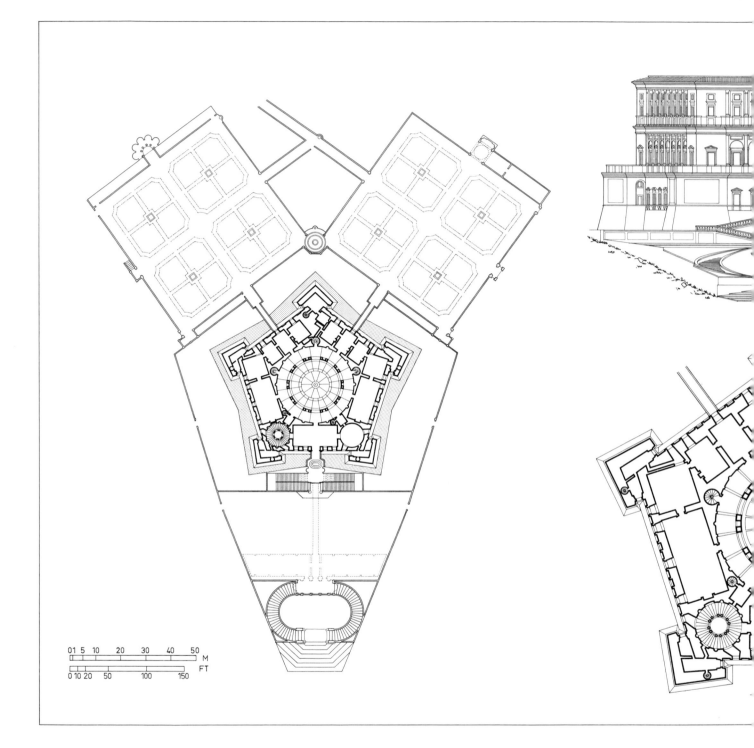

Villa Farnèse, à Caprarola (Italie), par Vignole, construite de 1559 à 1564. Situation 1:1500, élévation de la façade, plan du rez-de-chaussée, coupe longitudinale et plan de l'étage 1:750. Ce château pentagonal, dont le plan dérive d'une forteresse conçue par Antonio da Sangallo et Peruzzi, au début du XVIᵉ s., est édifié sur les bastions antérieurs.

Caprarola (Italien), Villa Farnese, 1559 bis 1564, Vignola. Das Schloß mit fünfeckigem Grundriß, der auf einen Festungsentwurf des frühen 16. Jh. von Antonio de Sangallo und Peruzzi zurückgeht, wurde über älteren Festungsanlagen errichtet. Lageplan 1:1500; Fassadenaufriß, Grundriß des Erdgeschosses, Längsschnitt, Grundriß des Obergeschosses 1:750.

Villa Farnese, Caprarola (Italy), built 1559–64 by Vignola. Site plan 1:1500; façade elevation, plan of the ground floor, longitudinal section and plan of the upper storey 1:750. The pentagonal palace, the plan of which derived from a fort designed by Antonio da Sangallo and Peruzzi at the beginning of the sixteenth century, was erected on the old bastions.

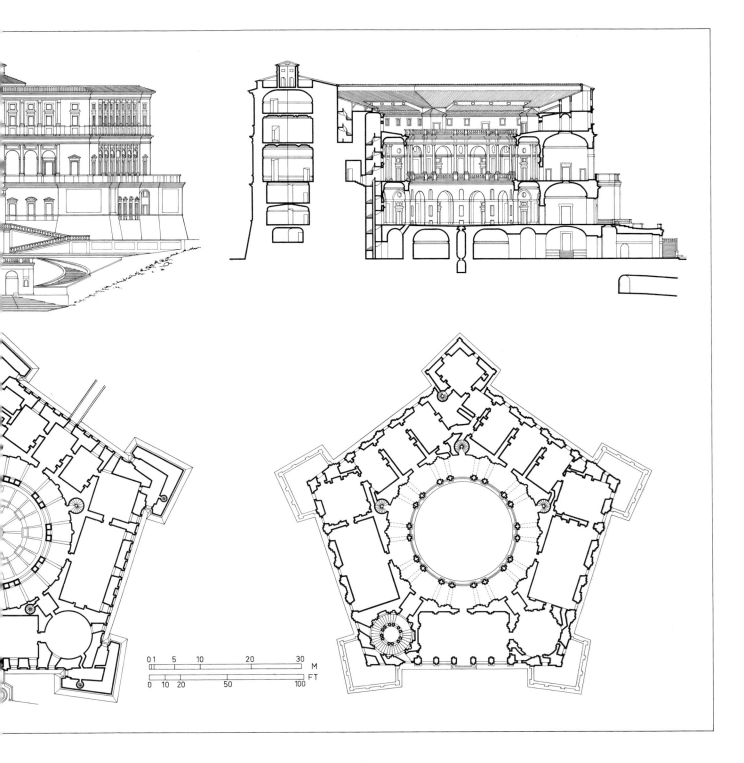

Le **Palais de Caprarola** est conçu à partir d'un polygone régulier qui présente à l'extérieur des façades austères au niveau du «podium» sur lequel repose l'édifice. Il s'allège aux niveaux supérieurs et surtout dans la cour circulaire aux rythmes alternés de paires de colonnes engagées et de baies en plein cintre.

Der Grundriß des Palastes von **Caprarola** ist ein regelmäßiges Fünfeck. Die Fassaden des Sockelgeschosses sind streng, die oberen Geschosse wirken leichter, besonders der runde Hof, in dem Paare von Säulenvorlagen mit Rundbogen wechseln.

Villa Farnese, Caprarola, based on a regular polygon. Austere at the level of the 'podium' on which the building rests, the façades become lighter in the upper storeys, particularly in the circular courtyard with its alternate rhythms of pairs of engaged columns and semicircular bays.

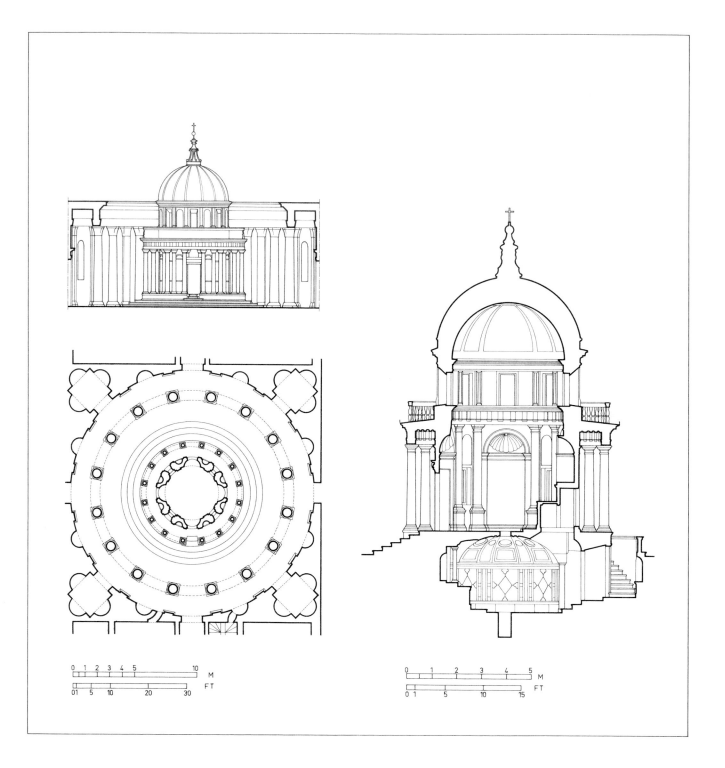

Tempietto de San Pietro in Montorio, à Rome, édifié en 1502 par Bramante. Elévation et plan de l'ensemble projeté 1:300, et coupe du bâtiment conçu comme un martyrium 1:150. Se fondant sur le temple de Vesta à Tivoli, Bramante dote l'édifice d'une crypte et d'un étage surmonté d'un dôme. L'entourage de la cour qui avait été prévu n'a jamais été réalisé.

Rom, Tempietto von San Pietro in Montorio, 1502, Bramante. Bei dem Entwurf ging Bramante von dem Vesta-Tempel in Tivoli aus; er gab der Kapelle eine Krypta und ein kuppelgewölbtes Obergeschoß. Der geplante umgebende Hof wurde niemals ausgeführt. Aufriß und Grundriß der geplanten Gesamtanlage 1:300; Schnitt durch die Märtyrerkapelle 1:150.

Tempietto of S. Pietro in Montorio, Rome, built by Bramante in 1502. Elevation and projected overall plan 1:300; section of the building, which was designed as a martyrium, 1:150. Drawing his inspiration from the temple of Vesta, Tivoli, Bramante gave his building a crypt and an upper storey surmounted by a dome. His plans for the courtyard were never carried out.

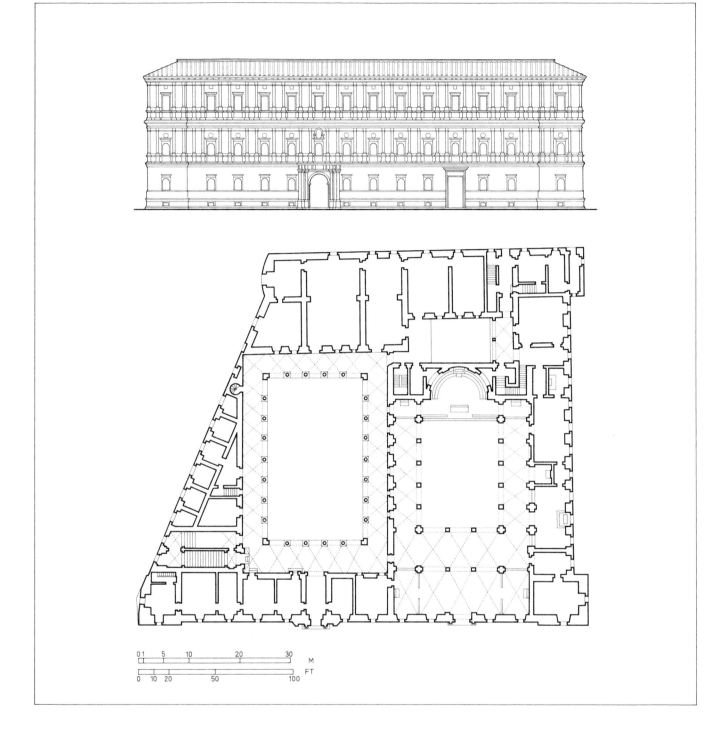

Palais de la Chancellerie, à Rome, qui fait corps avec l'église San Lorenzo in Damaso, construit de 1483 à 1517 par Bregno, puis par Bramante. Elévation de la façade principale et plan 1:750. Cet immense palais, édifié pour le cardinal Riario, devint la chancellerie papale. Sa façade est faite de travertin emprunté au Colisée. Les 44 colonnes de la cour viennent du théâtre de Pompée.

Rom, Palazzo della Cancelleria, 1483 bis 1517 von Bregno begonnen, von Bramante weitergeführt. Der gewaltige, für den Kardinal Riario erbaute Palast, der mit der Kirche San Lorenzo in Damaso einen Komplex bildet, wurde später päpstliche Kanzlei. Der Travertin der Fassade stammt vom Kolosseum, die 44 Säulen des Hofes aus dem Theater des Pompejus. Aufriß der Hauptfassade, Grundriß 1:750.

Chancellery Palace, Rome, adjoining S. Lorenzo in Damaso, built 1483–1517, first by Bregno and than by Bramante. Elevation of the main façade and plan 1:750. Designed for Cardinal Riario, this enormous palace became the papal chancellery. The façade is made of travertine taken from the Colosseum. The 44 columns of the courtyard came from the theatre of Pompeiy.

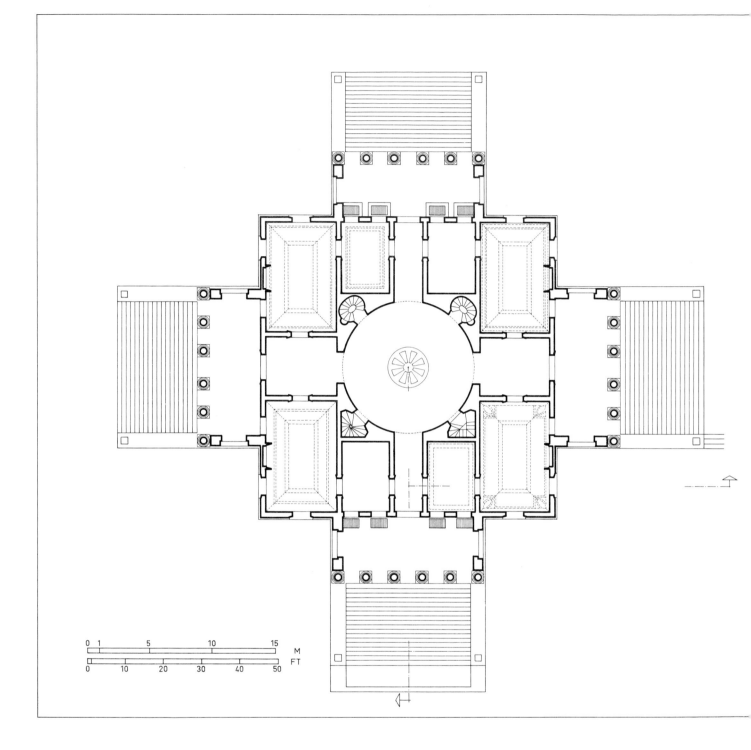

| 0 1 | 5 | 10 | 15 | M |
| 0 | 10 | 20 | 30 | 40 | 50 | FT |

Villa Almerico, dite la Rotonda, à Vicence (Italie), édifiée par Andrea Palladio en 1566. Plan 1:300. C'est la plus fastueuse des villas construites par Palladio. Elle est régie par un plan fondé sur une double symétrie que commandent quatre escaliers. Au centre de l'édifice rigoureusement carré, la rotonde, à laquelle le bâtiment doit son appellation.

Vicenza, Villa Rotonda (Villa Almerico Capra), 1566, Palladio. Die Rotonda ist wohl die großartigste unter den von Palladio erbauten Villen. Ihr Grundriß mit vier Freitreppen ist sowohl zur Längs- wie zur Querachse symmetrisch. Den Kern des quadratischen Baues bildet die Rotunde, die der Villa den Namen gab. Grundriß 1:300.

Villa Almerico Capra (also called La Rotonda), Vicenza (Italy), built by Andrea Palladio in 1566. Plan 1:300. This is the most sumptuous of Palladio's villas. Its plan is based on a double symmetry dictated by four flights of steps. At the centre of a perfect square is the rotunda that has given the building its name.

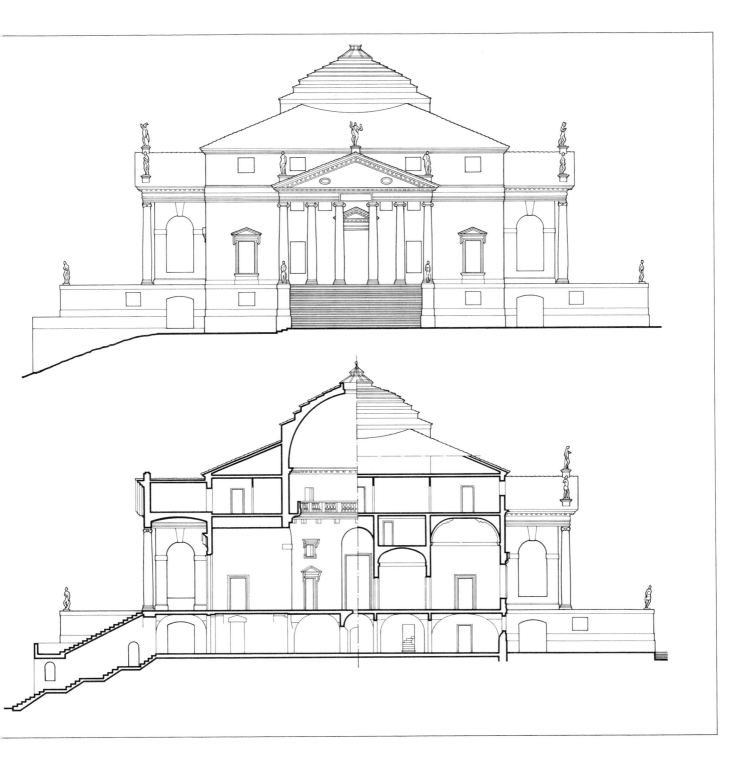

La Rotonda, avec ses porches à colonnes surmontés de frontons – c'est ainsi que Palladio se représentait les villas romaines – et sa salle centrale couverte d'une coupole. Elévation d'une façade (nord-ouest) et deux demi-coupes 1:300. C'est l'exemple de la rigueur et de l'équilibre propres à la Renaissance.

Wie die **Rotonda** mit ihren von Giebeln bekrönten Säulenfronten stellte sich Palladio römische Villen vor; die Rotunde ist mit einer Kuppel überwölbt. Die Villa zeigt beispielhaft die Strenge und Ausgewogenheit der Renaissancekunst. Aufriß der Nordwestfassade und zwei Halbschnitte 1:300.

La Rotonda, with its columned porches surmounted by pediments—this was how Palladio imagined Roman villas to have been—and its central domed hall. Elevation of one façade (north-west) and two half-sections 1:300. A perfect example of the rigour and balance that typified the Renaissance.

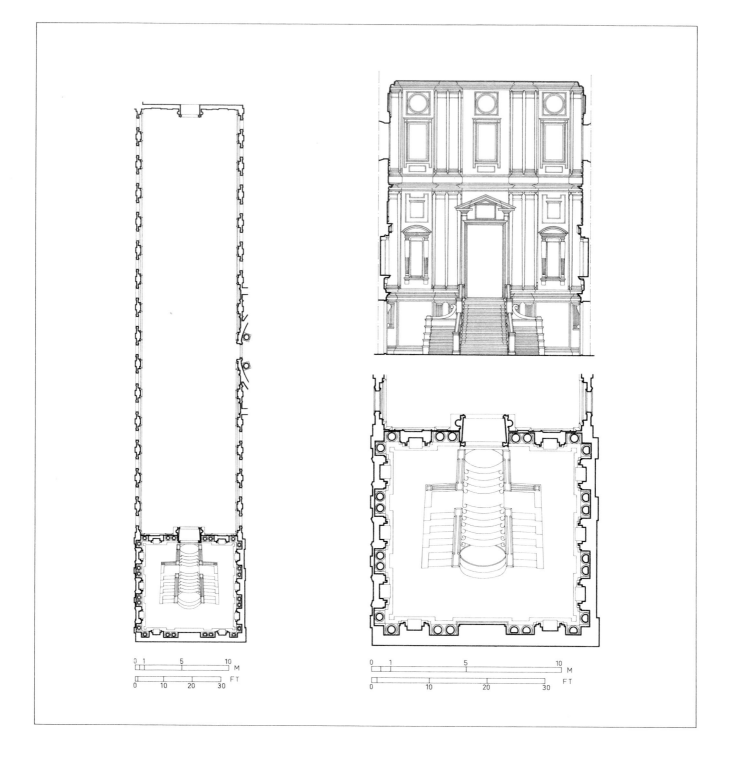

Bibliothèque Laurentienne, à Florence, édifiée par Michel-Ange entre 1524 et 1560, dans le complexe de l'église et de l'Ancienne Sacristie de Brunelleschi. Plan général 1:400, élévation de la façade de l'escalier et plan de l'escalier 1:200. L'escalier monumental qui relie le vestibule à la salle de lecture fut terminé après 1550 par Vasari et Ammannati.

Florenz, Biblioteca Laurentiana, 1524 bis 1560, Michelangelo. Der Bau bildet mit Brunelleschis Kirche San Lorenzo und mit der Alten Sakristei einen Komplex. Die gewaltige Treppe vom Vestibül zum Lesesaal wurde nach 1550 von Vasari und Ammannati vollendet. Grundriß 1:400; Fassadenaufriß und Grundriß des Vestibüls 1:200.

Laurentian Library, Florence (Italy), built by Michelangelo in 1524–60 as part of the complex including S. Lorenzo and Brunelleschi's Old Sacristy. Overall plan 1:400; elevation of the staircase façade and plan of the staircase 1:200. The monumental staircase linking the ante-room and the reading room was completed by Vasari and Ammannati after 1550.

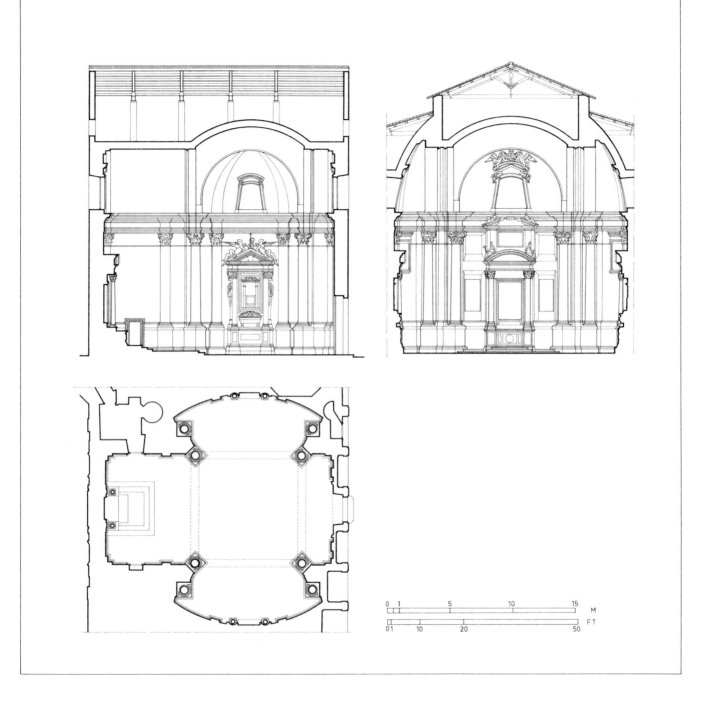

Eglise Sainte-Marie-Majeure, la Chapelle Sforza construite en 1564 par Michel-Ange. Coupe longitudinale, coupe transversale et plan 1:300. Dotée de faces latérales intérieures concaves et de colonnes disposées à 45° sous la retombée des voûtes, cette construction annonce les solutions spatiales du Baroque.

Rom, Santa Maria Maggiore, Sforza-Kapelle, 1564, Michelangelo. Die konkaven Seitenwände und die in einem Winkel von 45° unter dem Gewölbeansatz stehenden Säulen kündigen bereits barocke Raumlösungen an. Längsschnitt, Querschnitt, Grundriß 1:300.

Sforza Chapel, S. Maria Maggiore, Rome, built by Michelangelo in 1564. Longitudinal section, cross section and plan 1:300. The concave interior lateral faces and the columns set at 45° beneath the vault springers foreshadow Baroque spatial solutions.

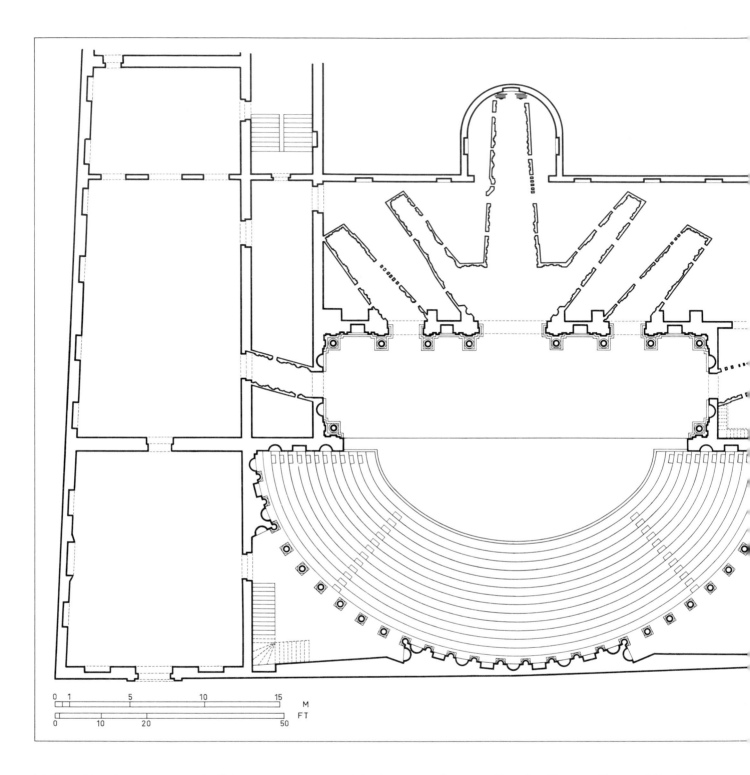

| 0 | 1 | 5 | 10 | 15 | M |
| 0 | 10 | 20 | | 50 | FT |

Théâtre Olympique, à Vicence (Italie), édifié par Palladio jusqu'à sa mort en 1580, puis achevé par Scamozzi. Plan 1:250. Sa cavea elliptique, que surmonte une galerie à colonnes dont la partie centrale est fermée par des niches, s'inspire du plan d'un amphithéâtre coupé en deux sur son axe longitudinal. En raison de sa couverture, ce théâtre récuse l'antique.

Vicenza, Teatro Olimpico, Entwurf von Palladio, ab 1580 von Scamozzi vollendet. Der elliptische Zuschauerraum schließt oben mit einer Kolonnade, deren Mitte zu Nischen ausgebildet ist. Der Raum entspricht einem in der Längsachse geteilten Amphitheater, seine Überdeckung widerspricht jedoch antiker Tradition. Grundriß 1:250.

Olympic Theatre (Teatro Olimpico), Vicenza (Italy), designed by Palladio and completed after his death in 1580 by Scamozzi. Plan 1:250. The elliptical *cavea*, surmounted by a columned gallery of which the central portion is closed with niches, was inspired by the plan of an amphitheatre cut in two along its longitudinal axis, but the theatre rejects antiquity by being roofed.

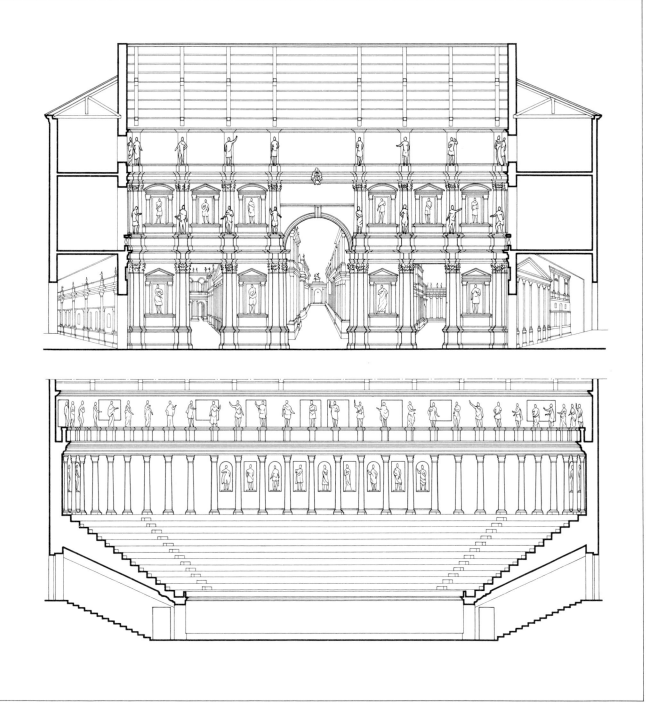

Par le décor, le **Théâtre Olympique** de Palladio évoque au contraire le mur de scène des édifices sévériens. Les ordres superposés, les niches à frontons contenant des statues, contribuent à l'illusion. Une innovation fascinante: les architectures en perspective très accentuée qu'offrent les ouvertures du mur de scène.

Die Bühnenarchitektur von Palladios **Teatro Olimpico** erinnert an die Szenenbauten severianischer Theater, vor allem durch die übereinandergestellten Säulenreihen und die giebelbekrönten Figurennischen. Eine faszinierende Neuerung sind die Architekturperspektiven in den Durchbrechungen der Bühnenfront.

The decoration of Palladio's **Olympic Theatre, Vicenza,** however, recalls the stage walls of Severian theatres. The superposed orders and the pedimented statue niches contribute to the illusion. A fascinating innovation were the enhanced perspective effects offered by the openings in the stage wall.

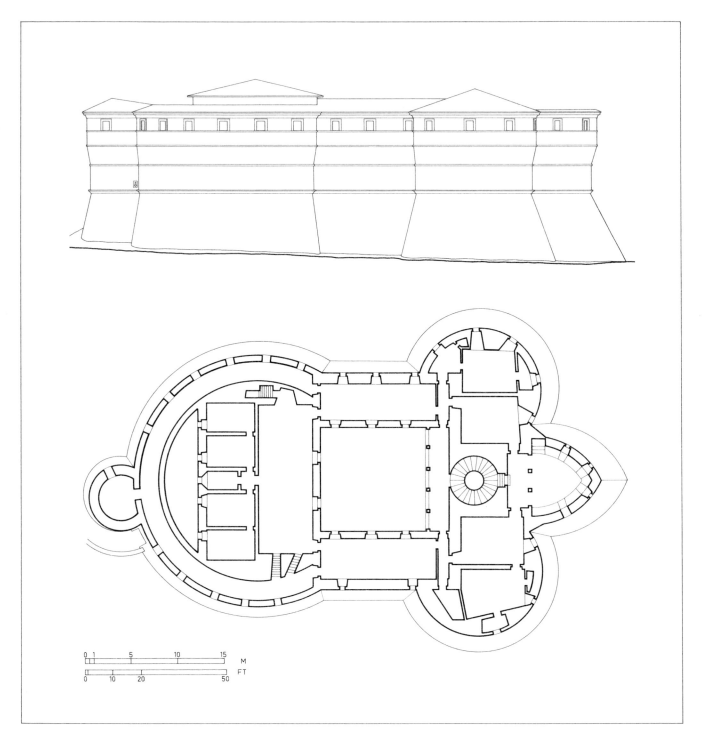

Forteresse de Sassocorvaro, dite «La Rocca», dans les Apennins (Italie), bâtie par Giorgio Martini de 1475 à 1480. Elévation latérale et plan 1:400. Ce castello puissant et massif qui se fonde sur les principes énoncés par Francesco di Giorgio, donne toute son importance au plan, et en particulier aux bastions triangulaires répondant aux progrès de l'artillerie.

Festung Sassocorvaro («La Rocca»; Apennin, Italien), 1475–1480. An dem mächtigen, wehrhaften Kastell, das nach den von Francesco di Giorgio Martini aufgestellten Prinzipien erbaut wurde, sind – entsprechend der Entwicklung der Artillerie – der Grundriß und vor allem die Dreiecksbastion von besonderer Bedeutung. Aufriß einer Seite, Grundriß 1:400.

'La Rocca' Fortress, Sassocorvaro (in the Apennines, Italy), 1475–80, by F. di Giorgio Martini. Side elevation and plan 1:400. The plan of this solidly powerful *castello*, based on the principles laid down by Francesco di Giorgio, is all-important, particularly as regards the triangular bastions dictated by advances in artillery.

Baroque: Italie et Europe centrale

Barock (Italien und die Länder nördlich der Alpen)

Baroque (Italy and Central Europe)

Le Baroque fait éclater les rigoureuses compositions de la Renaissance. Le Bernin, Guarino Guarini et Borromini en Italie (1620 à 1680) élaborent un langage neuf qui se lit tant dans le plan que dans l'élévation: courbes et contre-courbes, surfaces convexes et concaves, renflements et resserrements, éclatement de l'espace, jeux de tensions et effets de surprise dotent l'architecture de cette palpitation qui rejoint, par-delà les siècles, la prodigieuse invention spatiale de l'Empire romain au IVᵉ siècle.

Certes, le vocabulaire fondamental de la Renaissance n'a pas disparu: ordres, rythmes et proportions antiques sont toujours requis pour l'élaboration des formes baroques. Colonnes cannelées à chapiteaux corinthiens, pilastres, entablements et corniches ont pourtant changé de rôle: au lieu de la clarté dépouillée d'un mur de Michel-Ange ou de Palladio, c'est le sens du mystère qui surgit, détruisant la paroi et la remplaçant par des écrans de colonnes très rapprochées, par des pilastres décalés, par un foisonnement du décor. On crée des limites insaisissables, des jeux d'ombre et de lumière dramatiques. Le dessin des corniches est tourmenté et forme ces étranglements en pinces de crabe qu'affectionnent les architectes baroques. Les voûtements eux-mêmes ne sont plus formés de coupoles clairement délimitées, mais se muent en surfaces ondulantes, où règnent les ovales, les ellipses qui s'interpénètrent.

C'est avec le Baroque de l'Allemagne du Sud, et en particulier les frères Asam, Zimmermann, Fischer et Thumb, ainsi que le grand Balthasar Neumann qu'explosent ce grouillement tumultueux, ce décor torturé, cette notion du pathéti-

Im Barock wird die strenge Gliederung der Renaissance-Architektur aufgegeben. Im 17. Jahrhundert in Italien – im Hochbarock – schufen Bernini, Borromini und Guarino Guarini eine neue, sowohl im Grundriß wie im Aufriß klar ablesbare Formensprache: Kurven und Gegenkurven, konvexe und konkave Wandzonen, Schwellungen und Einzüge, durchbrochene und verschliffene Raumgrenzen. Spannung und Dynamik beherrschen die Architektur und verbinden sie über die Jahrhunderte hinweg mit den großartigen Raumschöpfungen der römischen Kaiserzeit.

Der Formenschatz der Renaissance blieb allerdings weiterhin erhalten, die barocken Formen wurden immer noch aus den antiken Ordnungen entwickelt. Doch die kannellierten Säulen mit korinthischen Kapitellen, die Pilaster und Gesimse spielen nun eine andere Rolle. An die Stelle der klaren Wandgliederung bei Michelangelo oder Palladio treten gitterartig wirkende, enge Säulenfolgen, gestaffelte Pilaster, übergreifender plastischer Schmuck und reiche, bewegte Gesimse. Das Spiel von Licht und Schatten wird damit vielfältiger und komplizierter, und die Raumgrenzen sind schwerer ablesbar. Die Wölbung geschieht kaum noch mit einfachen, klaren Kuppelformen, sondern mit sich verschleifenden Figurationen, in denen Oval und Ellipse vorherrschen.

Im süddeutschen Barock, in den Werken der Brüder Asam, Zimmermanns, Fischers, der Thumb, Balthasar Neumanns und anderer Meister, besonders in den großen Wallfahrtskirchen, erreicht dieser Stil seinen Höhepunkt. Bühnenartige Dekorationsformen und ein wahrer «horror vacui» führen zu

Baroque took the rigorous compositions of the Renaissance and tore them apart. Between 1620 and 1680 the Italians Bernini, Guarino Guarini, and Borromini wrote a whole new language of architecture, a language that can be read in both plan and elevation. Curves and counter-curves, convex and concave surfaces, swellings and constrictions, explosions of space, and extensive use of tension and surprise effects gave their architecture a kind of excitement that recalled the prodigious spatial inventiveness of the fourth-century Roman Empire.

The basic vocabulary of the Renaissance was still there; always underlying the forms of Baroque were the orders, rhythms and proportions of classical antiquity. Yet the fluted columns with their Corinthian capitals, the pilasters, entablatures, and cornices had undergone a change of role. Instead of the stripped-down clarity of a wall by Michelangelo or Palladio there was a looming sense of mystery; the wall as such was done away with; and replaced by screens of columns set very close together, or by staggered pilasters, or by a wealth of decoration. Baroque created intangible limits, set up dramatic plays of light and shade. Cornices became tormented in design, forming those crab-claw shapes so dear to Baroque architects. Vaults themselves abandoned the clearly defined domes of the Renaissance in favour of undulating surfaces dominated by interpenetrating ovals and ellipses.

It was in southern Germany, and in the hands particularly of such Baroque masters as the Asam brothers, Zimmermann, Fischer, Thumb, and of course the great Balthasar Neumann,

que propres aux grandes églises de pèlerinage. Théâtralité optique et refus du vide se combinent en une ornementation surabondante, où le stuc joue un rôle essentiel, avec sa polychromie aux tons éclatants ou aux nuances pastel. Colonnes torses ou salomoniques, guirlandes, modénatures surchargées, putti et fausses perspectives de la fresque qui ouvre des trous sur l'infini en lieu et place des voûtes compactes de la Renaissance, caractérisent cet épanouissement rococo, situé entre 1720 et 1780.

Dans le domaine des palais, le Baroque brise l'aspect monolithique des façades, les articule, les perce de baies, les hiérarchise en soulignant le «piano nobile». Dans l'urbanisme enfin, il se manifeste par la création de places conçues comme des scénographies, avec escaliers d'apparat, fontaines ou obélisques.

einem Schmuckreichtum, an dem der polychrome, kräftig leuchtende oder zart pastellfarbene Stuck wesentlichen Anteil hat. Gewundene Säulen, Girlanden, üppige Gesimse, Putten, aber auch illusionistische Fresken, die dort, wo die Renaissance eine solide Kuppel baute, den Blick in die Ewigkeit führen, sind wesentliche Ausdrucksmittel des späten Barock und des Rokoko bis etwa 1780.

Im Palastbau gliederte der Barock die Fassaden, öffnete sie durch große Fenster und Fenstertüren, betonte den «piano nobile» und damit die Hierarchie der Geschosse.

Im Städtebau schließlich schuf der Barock große, wie Bühnenbilder angelegte Plätze, eigentliche Platz-Räume, mit Prachttreppen, Brunnen und Obelisken.

that this teeming energy, this tortured decoration and this conception of pathos found its most explosive expression. In the great pilgrimage churches, visual theatricality and a rejection of the void combined to produce a superabundant decor in which stucco, painted either in sharp, bright colours or in pastel shades, played a key part. Barley-sugar columns, garlands, overloaded profiles, putti, and false perspectives (painted in fresco to open windows on infinity where the Renaissance had placed a solid vault) characterised this final, Rococo phase of the Baroque style between 1720 and 1780.

In palace architecture Baroque broke up the monolithic aspect of the façade, articulating it, perforating it with bays, and subdividing it by stressing the *piano nobile* or main floor. Finally, Baroque's contribution to town-planning was its creation of public squares treated as stage-sets with elaborate staircases, fountains and obelisks.

1 Coupole de l'église Saint-Laurent, à Turin, par Guarino Guarini, (construction de 1668–1687).
2 La Salle des Miroirs de l'Amalienburg, à Munich, par Cuvilliés (construction de 1734 à 1739).
3 La nef de l'église d'Ottobeuren, en Bavière, construite en 1748, par Johann Michael Fischer.
4 Une travée de l'église de pèlerinage de la Wies, en Bavière, par Zimmermann, datant de 1746.

1 Turin, San Lorenzo, Inneres der Kuppel (Guarino Guarini, 1668–1687)
2 München, Nymphenburg, Spiegelsaal der Amalienburg (François Cuvilliés, 1734–1739)
3 Ottobeuren, Abteikirche, Mittelschiff (Johann Michael Fischer, 1748)
4 Die Wies, Wallfahrtskirche, Emporenarkade im Chor (Dominikus Zimmermann, 1746 begonnen)

1 Interior view of the dome of S. Lorenzo, Turin, built 1668–87 by Guarino Guarini.
2 Hall of Mirrors in the Amalienburg, Munich, by Cuvilliès (1734–9).
3 The nave of Ottobeuren church, Bavaria, by Johann Michael Fischer (1748).
4 A bay of Die Wies pilgrimage church, Bavaria, by Zimmermann (begun 1746).

1

2

3

4

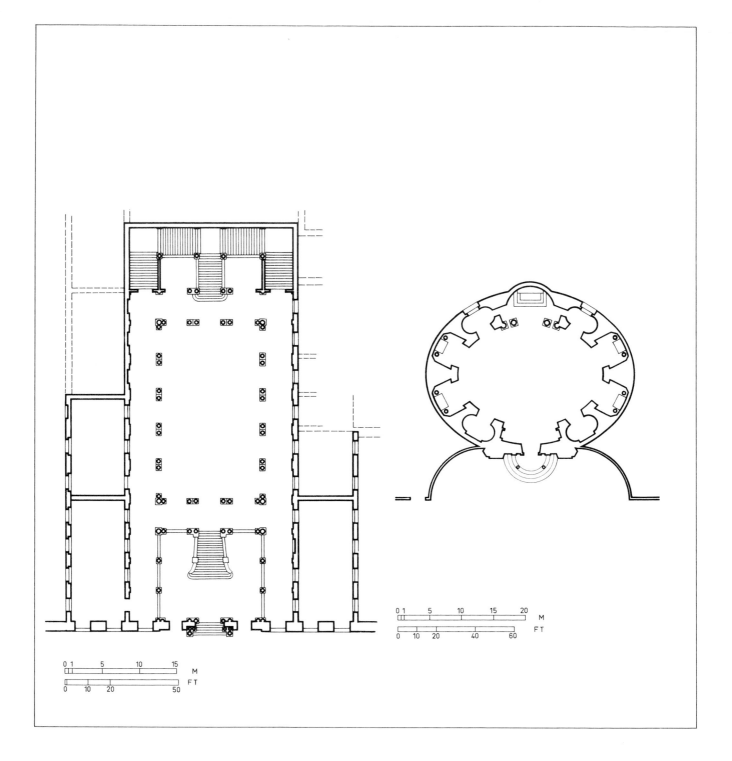

0 1   5   10   15   M
0   10   20   50   F T

0 1   5   10   15   20   M
0   10   20   40   60   F T

Université de Gênes (Italie), construite par Bartolomeo Bianco qui conçoit les plans en 1629, les soumet aux Jésuites en 1630 et fait débuter les travaux en 1634. L'édifice est terminé en 1645. Plan 1:500. Le jeu des escaliers marque l'avènement du premier Baroque. **Saint-André-du-Quirinal, à Rome,** édifié par le Bernin entre 1658 et 1670. Plan 1:600. Espace elliptique et façade concave.

Links: **Genua, Universität,** 1629 Entwurf von Bartolomeo Bianco, 1630 Vorlage bei den Jesuiten, 1634 Baubeginn, Vollendung 1645. Die Treppenanlage ist frühbarock. Grundriß 1:500. Rechts: **Rom, S. Andrea al Quirinale,** 1658–1670, Bernini. Der Raum ist ein Queroval, die Fassade konkav. Grundriß 1:600.

Genoa University (Italy), by Bartolomeo Bianco; planned 1629, plans submitted to the Jesuits 1630, built 1634–45. Plan 1:500. The staircase design marks the beginning of Baroque. **S. Andrea al Quirinale, Rome,** 1658–70, by Bernini. Plan 1:600. Elliptical interior and concave façade.

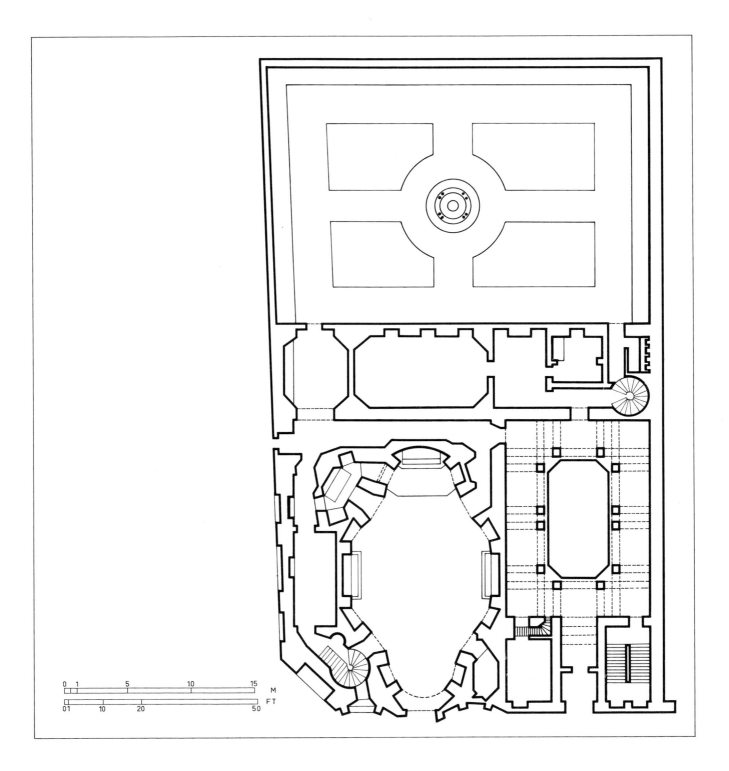

Saint-Charles-aux-Quatre-Fontaines, à Rome, bâti par Borromini entre 1638 et 1641. Plan de l'église et du cloître avec son jardin 1:300. Eglise en losange à double symétrie axiale et donc centrée, avec coupole ovale posée dans le sens de la longueur soulignant l'orientation que contredisent les deux autels latéraux.

Rom, San Carlo alle quattro Fontane 1638–1641, Borromini. Der rautenförmige Zentralbau hat zwei Symmetrieachsen, die längsgerichtete ovale Kuppel betont die Tiefe des Raums, die beiden Seitenaltäre stehen dagegen quer zur Raumrichtung. Grundriß der Kirche, des Kreuzgangs und des Gartens 1:300.

S. Carlo alle Quattro Fontane, Rome, 1638–41, by Borromini. Plan of the church and the cloister with its garden 1:300. This diamond-shaped church is symmetrical on both axes, i.e. it is centrally planned. The oval dome is placed lengthways in order to stress the orientation, which is then qualified by the two side altars.

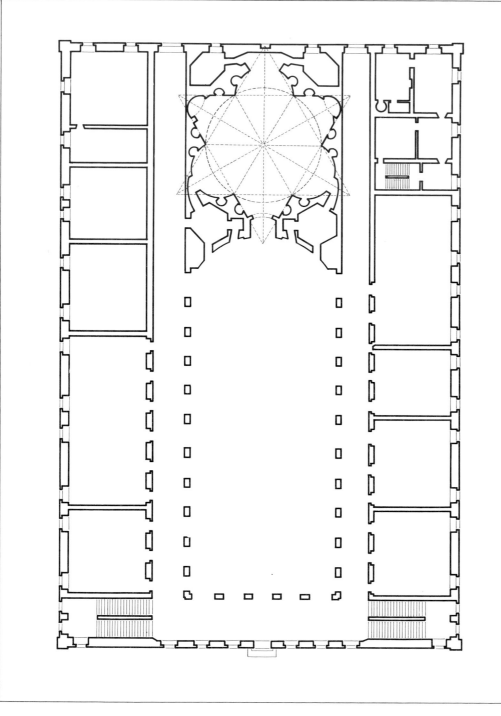

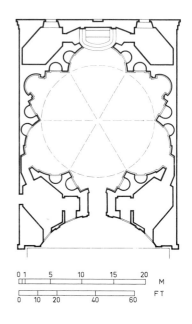

Palais de la Sapience, à Rome, édifice de style Renaissance réalisé en 1575 par Giacomo Della Porta, plan 1:600, dans lequel Borromini construit l'église **Saint-Yves-de-la-Sapience** de 1642 à 1650. Plan 1:600 et coupe transversale 1:450. Le plan de l'église découle d'un tracé opposant deux triangles équilatéraux enlacés. Toutes les lignes sont courbes.

Rom, **Palazzo della Sapienza,** 1575, Giacomo della Porta, mit der Kirche **S. Ivo della Sapienza,** 1642–1650, Borromini. Der Grundriß der Kirche ist aus einem sechsstrahligen Stern (zwei gleichseitigen Dreiecken) entwickelt, alle Linien sind geschwungen. Grundriß der Gesamtanlage und Grundriß der Kirche 1:600; Nebenseite: Querschnitt der Kirche 1:450.

Palazzo della Sapienza, Rome, a Renaissance-style building by Giacomo Della Porta erected in 1575. Plan 1:600. Here Borromini built the church of **S. Ivo della Sapienza,** 1642–50. Plan 1:600; cross section 1:450. The plan of the church is based on two interlocking equilateral triangles. All the lines in it are curved.

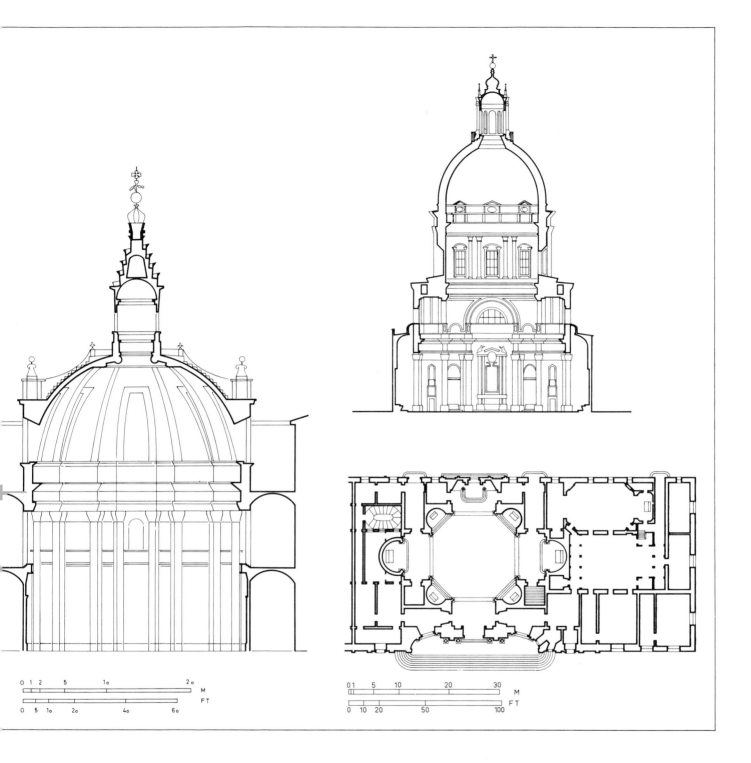

Sainte-Agnès à la place Navone, Rome, église commencée en 1652 par Girolamo Rainaldi et son fils Carlo, puis reprise en 1653 par Borromini, qui cède la place en 1657 à Carlo Rainaldi. Les tours seront achevées en 1666. Coupe transversale et plan 1:750. La coupole est surélevée grâce à un haut tambour, qui repose sur quatre voûtes en berceau.

Rom, Sant'Agnese in Piazza Navona, 1652 von Girolamo Rainaldi und seinem Sohn Carlo begonnen, 1653 von Borromini, 1657 von Carlo Rainaldi weitergeführt, Türme 1666 vollendet. Die Kuppel steigt über einem hohen Tambour auf, der auf vier Tonnengewölben ruht. Querschnitt und Grundriß 1:750.

S. Agnese in Piazza Navona, Rome, begun in 1652 by Girolamo Rainaldi and his son Carlo; a year later Borromini took over, to be replaced again by Carlo Rainaldi in 1657. The towers were completed in 1666. Cross section and plan 1:750. The dome is raised up on a high drum that rests on four tunnel vaults.

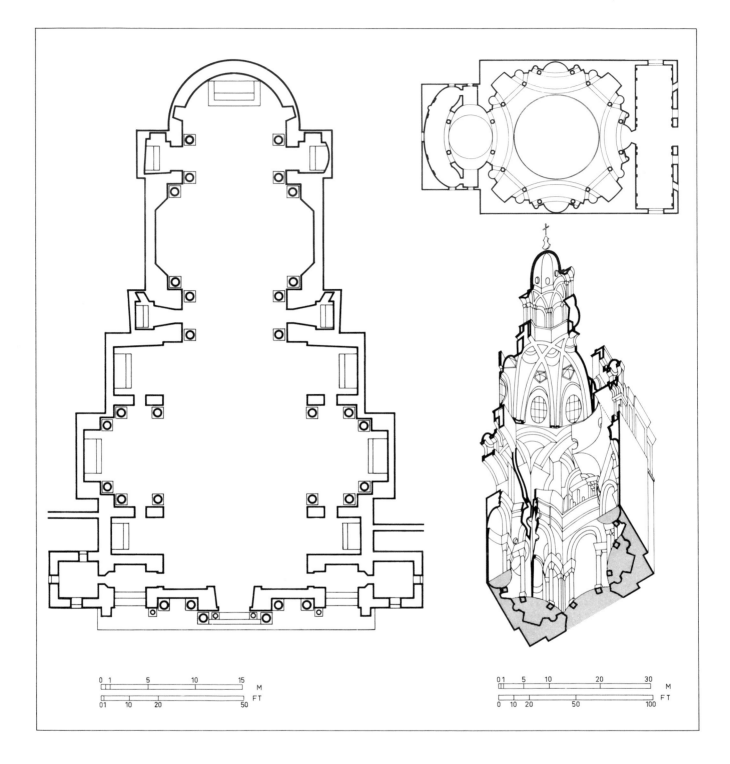

Scale bars (left plan):
0 1 5 10 15 M
01 10 20 50 FT

Scale bars (right):
0 1 5 10 20 30 M
0 10 20 50 100 FT

Eglise Santa Maria in Portico (ou in Campitelli), à Rome, édifiée de 1663 à 1667 par Carlo Rainaldi. Plan 1:400. Plan orthogonal, avec étranglement précédant la coupole devant le chœur. **Eglise Saint-Laurent, à Turin** (Italie), construite entre 1668 et 1687 par Guarino Guarini. Plan et vue axonométrique 1:750. Plan fondé sur un octogone et coupole nervée.

Links: **Rom, Santa Maria in Portico (S.M. in Campitelli),** 1663–1667, Carlo Rainaldi. Rechtwinkliges Grundrißsystem mit einer Einschnürung vor der Kuppel des Vorchors. Grundriß 1:400. Rechts: **Turin, San Lorenzo,** 1668–1687, Guarino Guarini. Der Grundriß ist aus einem Oktogon entwickelt; Kuppel mit sich kreuzenden Gurten. Grundriß und Axonometrie 1:750.

S. Maria in Portico (S. Maria in Campitelli), Rome, built 1663-7 by Carlo Rainaldi. Plan 1:400. The rectangular plan narrows before the dome that precedes the chancel. **S. Lorenzo, Turin** (Italy), built 1668-87 by Guarino Guarini. Plan and axonometric view 1:750. Here a basically octagonal plan is surmounted by a ribbed dome.

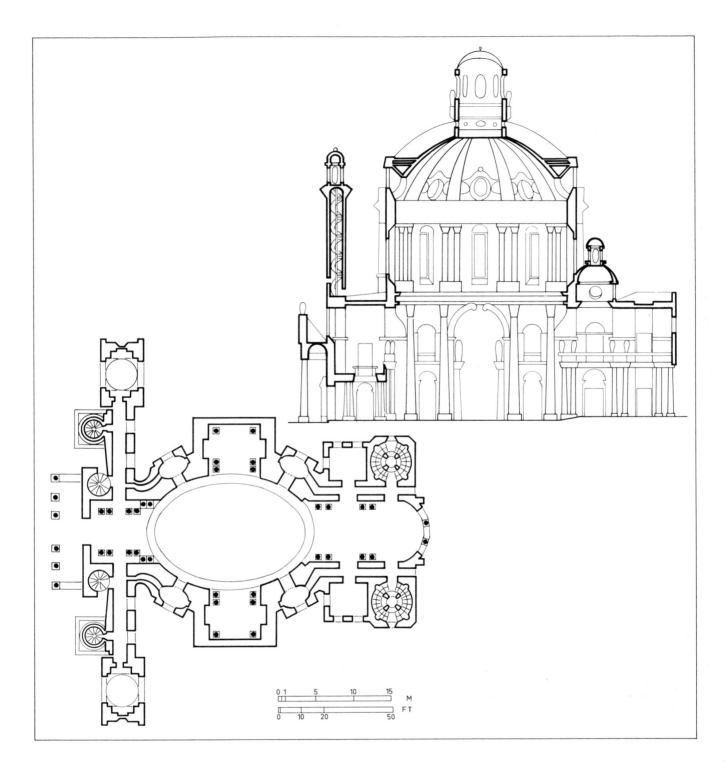

Eglise Saint-Charles-Borromée, à Vienne (Autriche), bâtie de 1716 à 1729 par J.-B. Fischer von Erlach. Coupe longitudinale et plan 1:500. Devant une façade aussi large que l'église est longue se dressent deux colonnes inspirées de la colonne Trajane. L'église à nef elliptique et à transept comporte un chœur profond. Elle est surmontée d'une coupole ovale de 24 m de diamètre.

Wien, Karlskirche, 1716–1729, Johann Bernhard Fischer von Erlach. Vor der Fassade, deren Breite gleich der Gesamtlänge der Kirche ist, und im Verband mit ihr zwei von der Trajans-Säule beeinflußte Säulen. Das elliptische Schiff mit querhausartigen Armen und tiefem Chor ist von einer ovalen Kuppel (größter Durchmesser 24 m) gekrönt. Längsschnitt und Grundriß 1:500.

Karlskirche (St. Charles Borromeus), Vienna, built 1716–29 by J.B. Fischer von Erlach. Longitudinal section and plan 1:500. A façade as wide as the church is long is fronted by two columns inspired by Trajan's Column in Rome. The church has an elliptical nave, a transept and a deep chancel. It is surmounted by an oval dome 24 m. in diameter.

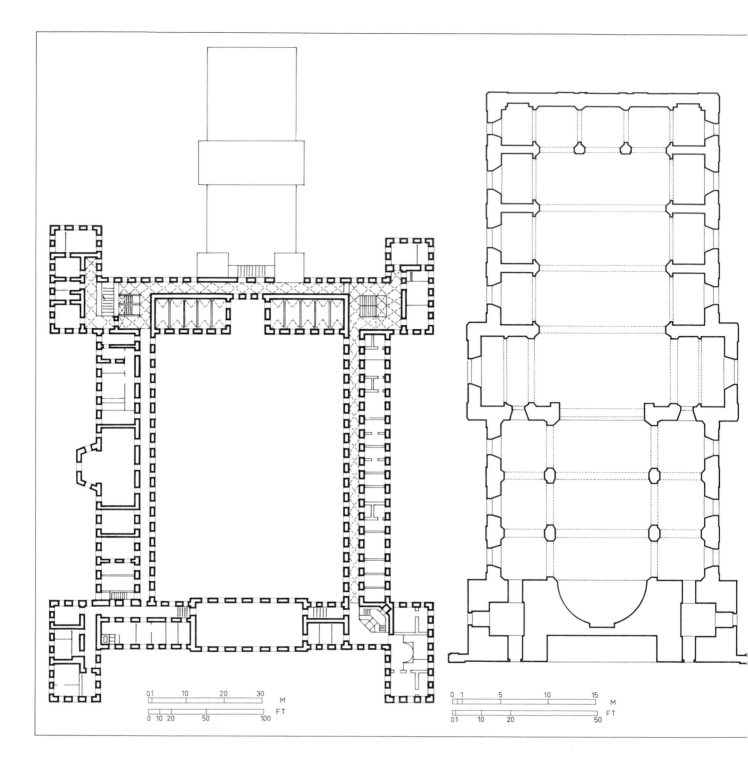

Abbaye d'Obermarchtal, en Souabe (Allemagne). L'église abbatiale est construite de 1686 à 1692 sous la direction de Michel Thumb, puis de son frère Christian et de son cousin Fr. Beer. Plan d'ensemble avec situation de l'abbatiale 1:1000, et plan de l'abbatiale 1:400. Distribution orthogonale avec tribunes rectilignes et puissants «Wandpfeiler».

Obermarchtal (Schwaben), Prämonstratenserabtei, Klosterkirche 1686 begonnen, Rohbau 1692 vollendet, Michael Thumb (†1690), nach dessen Tod sein Bruder Christian und sein Vetter Franz Beer. Rechtwinkliges Grundrißsystem mit kräftigen Wandpfeilern und gerade geführten Emporen. Grundriß des Klosters 1:1000; Grundriß der Kirche 1:400.

Obermarchtal Abbey (in Swabia, Germany). The abbey church was built 1686–92 under the direction first of Michael Thumb and subsequently of his brother Christian and his cousin Franz Beer. Overall plan showing the site of the abbey church 1:1000; plan of the abbey church 1:400. A rectangular arrangement with straight galleries and powerful *Wandpfeiler*.

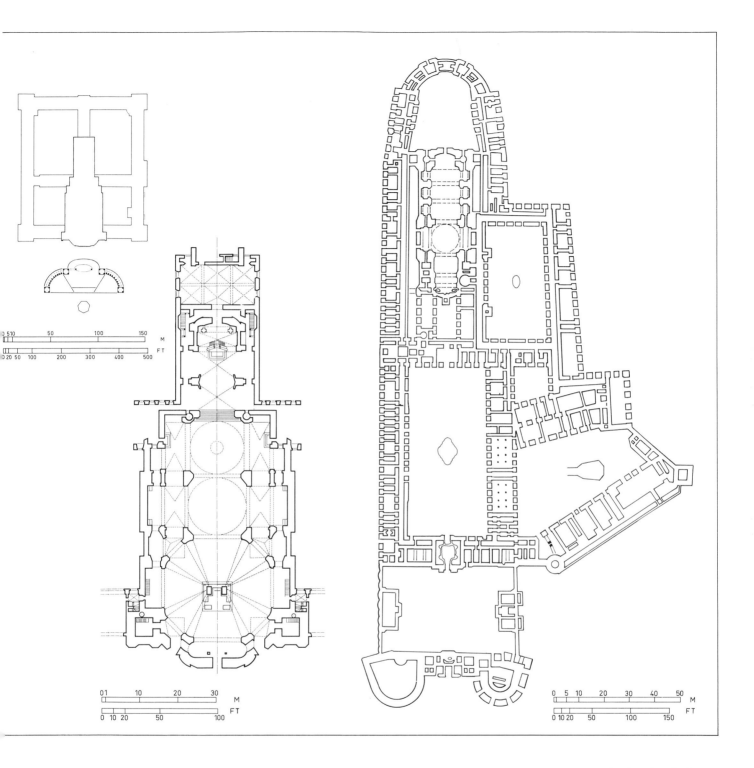

Abbaye d'Einsiedeln (Suisse), construite dès 1719 par Gaspard Moosbrugger et consacrée après sa mort, en 1735. Plan d'ensemble avec situation de l'église, 1:4000, plan de l'église de pèlerinage 1:1000. **Abbaye de Melk** (Autriche), construite de 1702 à 1740 par Prandtauer, qui meurt en 1726. Plan d'ensemble 1:1500. C'est la plus vaste des abbayes baroques. Elle surplombe le Danube.

Links: **Einsiedeln (Schweiz), Benediktinerabtei,** 1719 Baubeginn der Kirche, Caspar Moosbrugger; 1735 Weihe; Chor Mitte 18.Jh. nach Moosbruggers Tod. Grundrißschema des Klosters 1:4000; Grundriß der Kirche 1:1000. Rechts: **Melk (Österreich), Benediktinerstift,** 1702–1740, Jakob Prandtauer (†1726). Dieser größte barocke Klosterbau liegt hoch über der Donau. Grundriß 1:1500.

Einsiedeln Abbey (Switzerland), begun in 1719 by Caspar Moosbrugger and consecrated in 1735, after his death. Overall plan showing the site of the pilgrimage church 1:4000; plan of the church 1:1000. **Melk Abbey** (Austria), begun in 1702 by Jakob Prandtauer (d. 1726) and completed in 1740. Overall plan 1:1500. Built on a rocky cliff overlooking the Danube, this is the largest of Baroque monasteries.

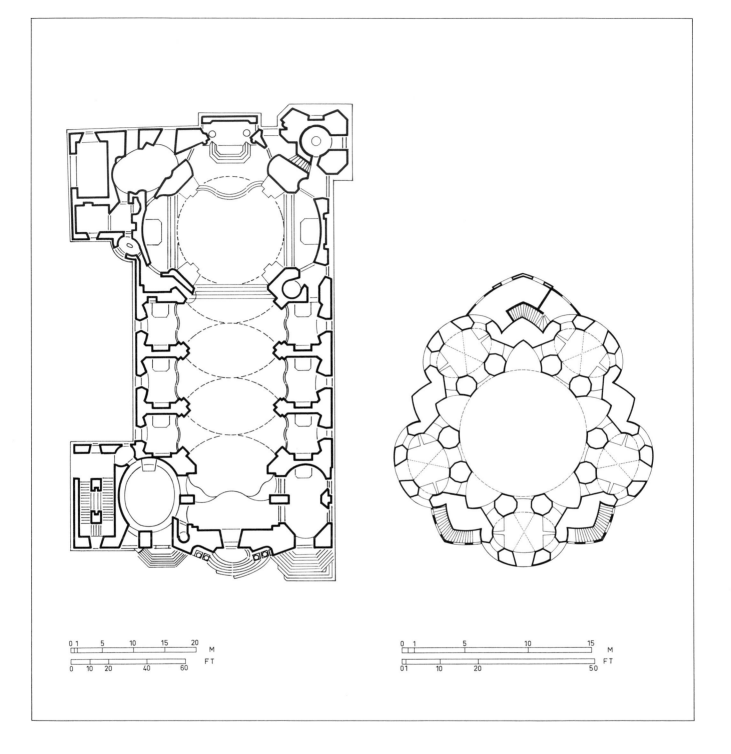

Eglise Saint-Nicolas de Mala Strana, à Prague (Tchécoslovaquie), construite de 1703 à 1711 par Christophe Dientzenhofer, puis de 1739 à 1752 par son fils Kilian-Ignace. Plan 1:600. Eglise Saint-Jean-Népomucène «auf dem Grünen Berg», à Saar (Tchécoslovaquie), bâtie par Johann Santin, dit Aichel, de 1719 à 1722. Plan 1:300. Edifice à plan central fondé sur un pentagone, avec cinq chapelles ovales.

Links: Prag, Sankt Nikolaus auf der Kleinseite, 1. Bauabschnitt 1703–1711, Christoph Dientzenhofer, 2. Bauabschnitt 1739–1752, Kilian Ignaz Dientzenhofer. Grundriß 1:600. Rechts: Saar (Tschechoslowakei), Sankt Johann Nepomuk auf dem Grünen Berg, 1719 bis 1722, Johann Santin Aichel (Giovanni Santini). Fünfseitiger Zentralbau mit fünf ovalen Kapellen. Grundriß 1:300.

St. Nikolaus 'auf der Kleinseite', Prague, built 1703–11 by Christoph Dientzenhofer, added to 1739–52 by his son Kilian Ignaz. Plan 1:600. St. Johann Nepomuk 'auf dem Grünen Berg', Saar (Czechoslovakia), built 1719–22 by Giovanni Santini Aichel. Plan 1:300. A centrally planned church based on a pentagon, with five oval chapels.

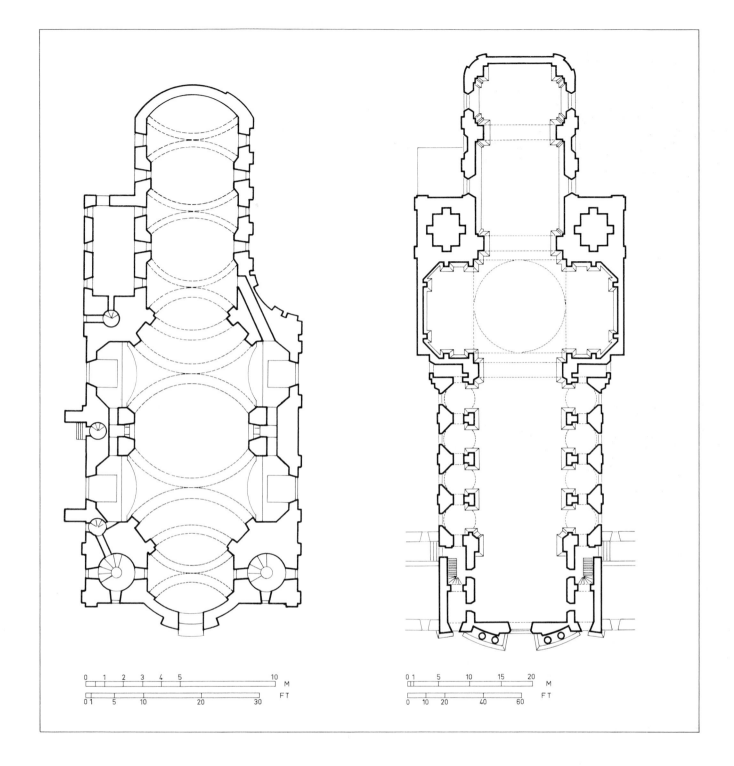

Abbaye de Banz, sur le Main (Allemagne), église de Jean Dientzenhofer, construite de 1710 à 1719. Plan 1:200. Les murs sont presque inexistants. Des tribunes ondulantes répondent aux voûtes ovales. **Eglise abbatiale de Zwiefalten,** en Souabe (Allemagne), édifiée dès 1739 par les frères Schneider, puis dès 1741 par J.M. Fischer. Plan 1:600. Coupole plate de 15 m de diamètre.

Links: **Klosterkirche Banz (Oberfranken),** 1710–1719, Johann Dientzenhofer. Die Kirche hat ein reiches Wölbungssystem, im Schiff Wandpfeiler und geschwungene Emporen. Grundriß 1:200. Rechts: **Zwiefalten (Schwaben), Klosterkirche,** 1739 von Joseph und Martin Schneider begonnen, 1741–1753 von Johann Michael Fischer nach eigenen Plänen ausgeführt. Die Flachkuppel überspannt 15 m. Grundriß 1:600.

Abbey church, Banz (on the Main, Germany), built 1710–19 by Johann Dientzenhofer. Plan 1:200. The walls are virtually non-existent; undulating galleries match the oval vaults. **Abbey church, Zwiefalten** (in Swabia, Germany), begun 1739 by the Schneider brothers, continued from 1741 by J.M. Fischer. Plan 1:600. The shallow dome measures 15 m. in diameter.

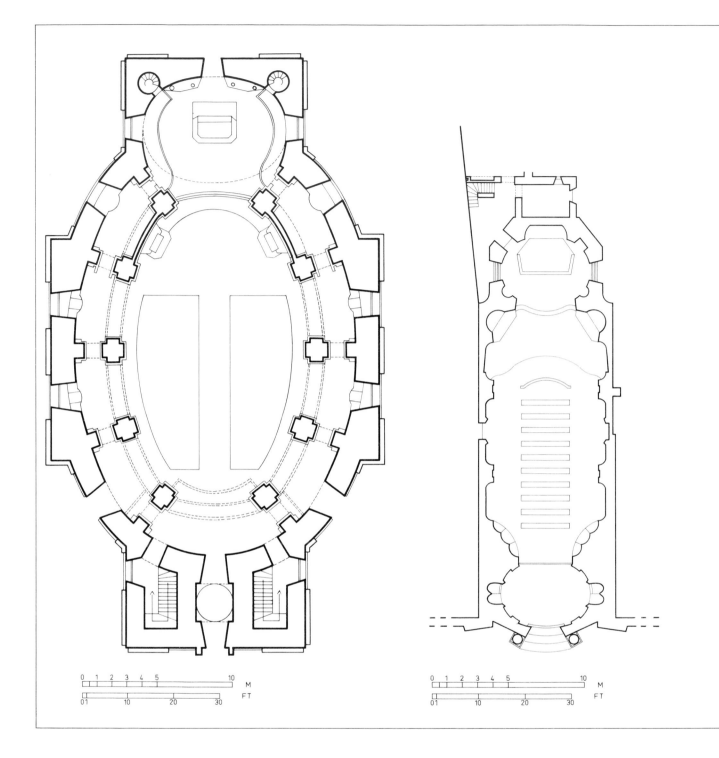

| 0 | 1 | 2 | 3 | 4 | 5 | | | | | 10 | M |
| 01 | | | 10 | | | 20 | | | 30 | | FT |

| 0 | 1 | 2 | 3 | 4 | 5 | | | | | 10 | M |
| 01 | | | 10 | | | 20 | | | 30 | | FT |

Eglise de pèlerinage de Steinhausen, en Souabe (Allemagne) construite par Dominique Zimmermann de 1728 à 1735. Plan 1:250. Nef en ellipse longitudinale et chœur en ellipse transversale. **Eglise Saint-Jean-Népomucène de Munich** (Allemagne), édifiée par Egid Quirin Asam et son frère Cosme-Damien entre 1733 et 1746. Plan 1:250. C'est une fondation privée des architectes.

Links: **Steinhausen (Schwaben), Wallfahrtskirche,** 1728 begonnen, 1733 Weihe, Mitte 18. Jh. vollendet, Dominikus Zimmermann. Das Schiff ist ein längsgerichtetes Oval, der Chor ein Queroval. Grundriß 1:250. Rechts: **München, Sankt Johann Nepomuk (Asamkirche),** 1733–1746, Egid Quirin und Cosmas Damian Asam. Die neben dem Wohnaus der Brüder liegende Kirche ist deren Stiftung. Grundriß 1:250.

Pilgrimage church, Steinhausen (in Swabia, Germany), built 1728–35 by Dominikus Zimmermann. Plan 1:250. The nave forms a longitudinal, the chancel a lateral ellipse. **St. Johann Nepomuk, Munich** (Germany), built 1733–46 by Egid Quirin Asam. Plan 1:250. A private foundation by the architect and his brother Cosmas Damian.

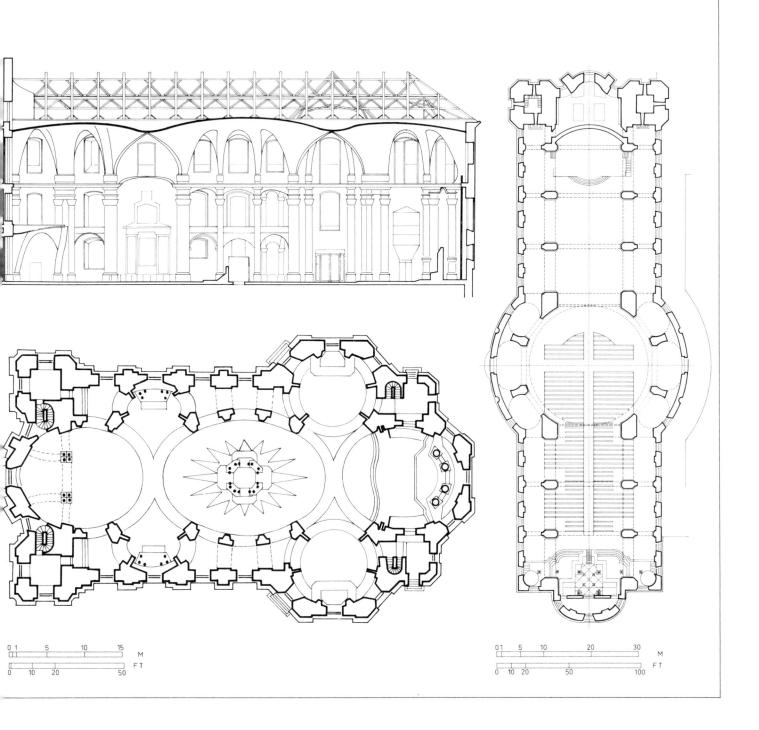

Eglise de pèlerinage de Vierzehnheiligen, sur le Main (Allemagne), construite par Balthasar Neumann dès 1743, achèvement des voûtes en 1763 et consécration en 1772. Coupe longitudinale et plan 1:500. **Abbaye de Saint-Gall** (Suisse), édifiée par Peter Thumb dès 1755, façade à deux tours par Johann Michael Beer von Bildstein. Plan 1:800. Plan basilical avec rotonde centrale en guise de transept.

Links: **Vierzehnheiligen, Wallfahrtskirche,** 1743–1772 (Gewölbe 1763) nach Plänen von Balthasar Neumann. Längsschnitt und Grundriß 1:500. Rechts: **Sankt Gallen, Stiftskirche,** 1755–1760 Langhaus und Rotunde, Peter Thumb, ab 1761 Chor, Johann Michael Beer von Bildstein, Zweiturmfassade von Beer, Loser und Jos. Ant. Feuchtmayer. Zwischen Langhaus und Chor ist die Rotunde eingeschoben. Grundriß 1:800.

Pilgrimage church, Vierzehnheiligen (on the Main opposite Banz, Germany), by Balthasar Neumann; begun 1743, vaults completed in 1763, consecration 1772. Longitudinal section and plan 1:500. **Abbey church, St. Gallen** (Switzerland), begun 1755; church designed by Peter Thumb, two-towered façade by Johann Michael Beer v. Bildstein. Plan 1:800. A basilican plan with a central rotunda/transept.

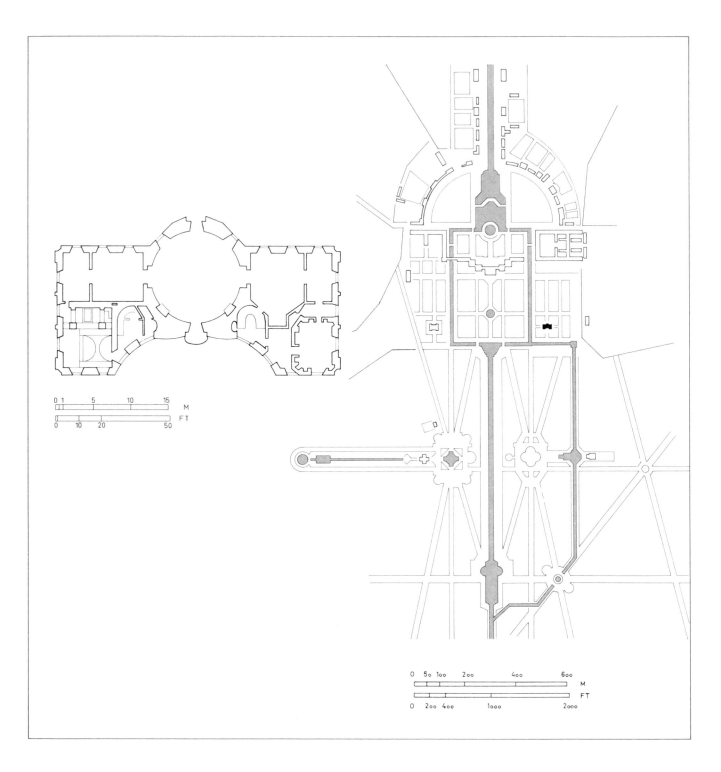

L'Amalienburg, à Munich (Allemagne), pavillon du château de Nymphenburg, édifié par François Cuvilliés de 1734 à 1739. Plan 1:500. Au centre, le salon circulaire des miroirs. Plan général du **Parc de Nymphenburg,** Munich, 1:15000, avec, en noir, la situation de l'Amalienburg.

München, Nymphenburg, Amalienburg, 1734–1739, François Cuvilliés. Die Räume des Jagdschlößchens ordnen sich beidseits des runden Spiegelsaals. Grundriß 1:500. **München, Nymphenburg, Park,** Plan 1:15000, schwarz eingezeichnet die Amalienburg.

Amalienburg, Munich (Germany), a pavilion in the grounds of Schloss Nymphenburg; built 1734–9 by François Cuvilliés. Plan 1:500. In the centre, the circular mirrored salon. Overall plan of **Nymphenburg Park, Munich,** 1:15,000, showing the site of the Amalienburg in black.

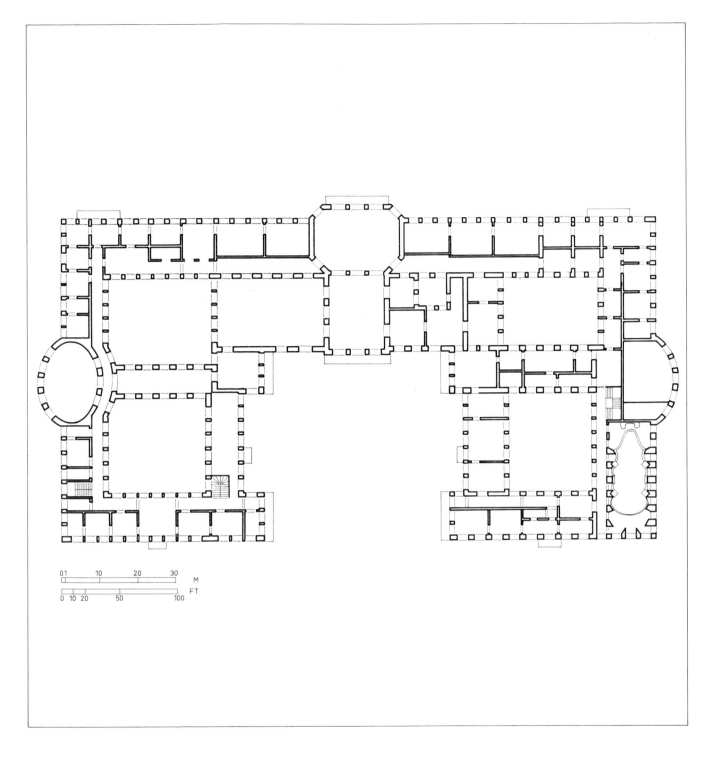

01   10   20   30
                        M
                        FT
0 10 20   50   100

La Résidence de Wurzburg (Allemagne), commencée par Balthasar Neumann en 1723, auquel s'associe Hildebrandt de 1731 à 1736. Plan 1:1000. La construction de l'escalier et des salles centrales a lieu dès 1742. L'immense palais de 170 m de façade a subi l'influence de Versailles, par l'intermédiaire des architectes français Germain Boffrand et Robert de Cotte, consultés.

Würzburg, Residenz, 1723 begonnen, Balthasar Neumann, 1731–1736 Mitarbeit von Lukas von Hildebrandt, Treppenhaus (nur eine Hälfte ausgeführt) und Hauptsäle ab 1742 im Bau, 1744 Rohbau vollendet. Beratung durch M. Welsch, G. Boffrand und Robert de Cotte. Vermutlich ist der Einfluß von Versailles der Vermittlung der beiden französischen Architekten zuzuschreiben. Grundriß 1:1000.

Residenz, Würzburg (Germany), begun 1723 by Balthasar Neumann (1731–6 in association with Hildebrandt). Plan 1:1000. The staircase and the central rooms date from 1742. This enormous palace—the façade measures 170 m.— was influenced by Versailles through the medium of the French architects Germain Boffrand and Robert de Cotte, whom Neumann also consulted.

217

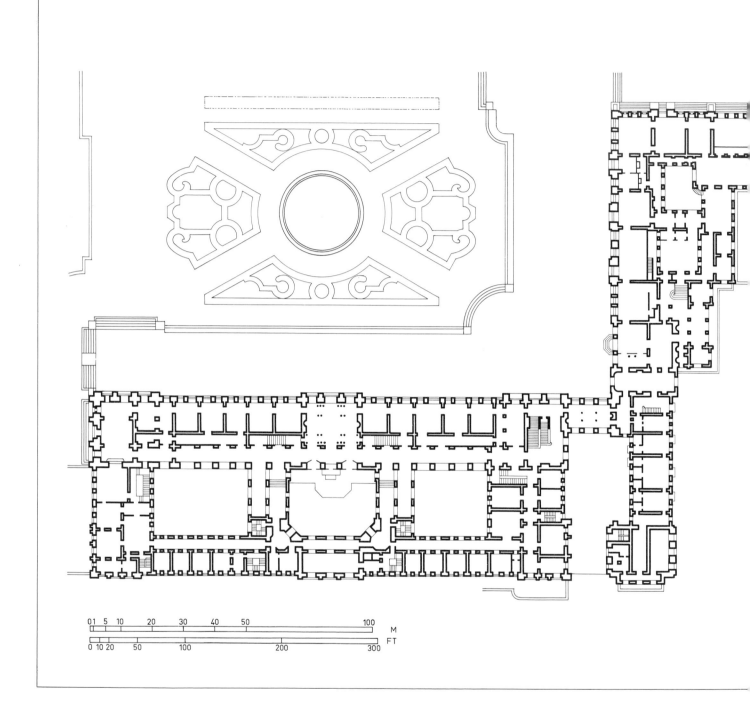

0 1 5 10 20 30 40 50 100 M
0 10 20 50 100 200 300 FT

Château de Versailles, près de Paris (France), construit dès 1664 par Le Vau pour Louis XIV. Plan général de l'état au XIXe s. 1:1250. Seule la partie centrale est édifiée en 1664, dans l'immense parc tracé par Le Nôtre. En 1682, Hardouin-Mansart crée les ailes qui donnent à ce palais son ampleur exceptionnelle.

Versailles, Schloß, 1664 für Ludwig XIV. begonnen, Le Vau. Nur der Mittelbau des Schlosses stammt von 1664, 1682 fügte J. Hardouin-Mansart die Seitenflügel an, durch die der Palast seine ungewöhnliche Ausdehnung erhielt. Der riesige Park wurde von Le Nôtre angelegt. Grundriß (Zustand im 19. Jh.) 1:1250.

Château of Versailles (near Paris, France), begun 1664 by Le Vau for Louis XIV. Overall plan as it was in the nineteenth century 1:1250. Only the central portion was built in 1664, set in the vast park laid out by Le Nôtre. In 1682 Jules Hardouin-Mansart added the wings that give the palace its exceptional breadth.

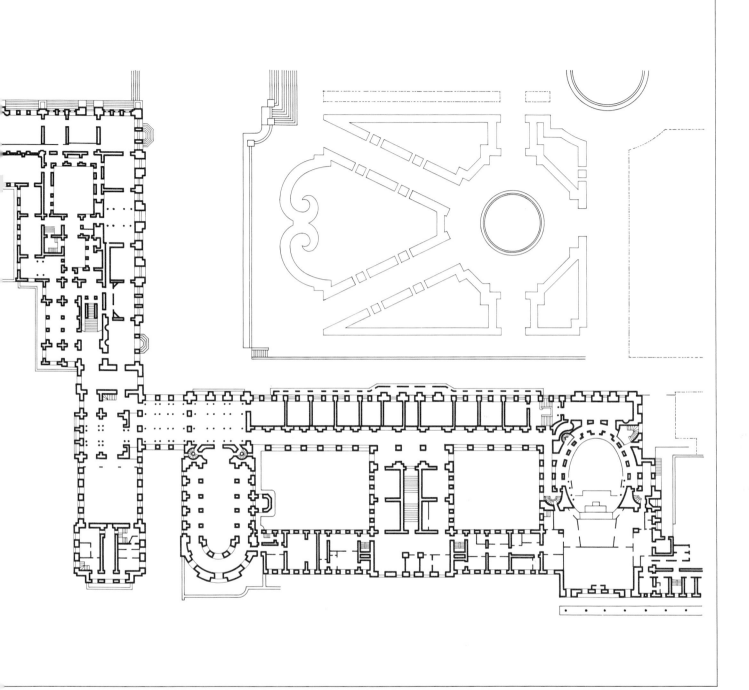

Mansart réalise à **Versailles** la Grande Galerie, puis les communs et met en chantier la chapelle en 1688, pour la reprendre en 1699. Son beau-frère, Robert de Cotte la terminera. Il faut attendre Napoléon pour que soient achevés les travaux au château de Versailles. De 1757 à 1770, construction de l'Opéra de Versailles, par Jacques-Ange Gabriel.

Hardouin-Mansart schuf in **Versailles** die Spiegelgalerie, dann die Wirtschafts- und Nebengebäude, 1688 begann er den Bau der Kapelle, den er 1699 wieder- aufnahm und den sein Schwager Robert de Cotte vollendete. Die Arbeiten am Schloß von Versailles wurden erst unter Napoleon beendet. 1757–1770 baute Jacques-Ange Gabriel die Versailler Oper.

At **Versailles** Mansart built the Grande Galerie, the outbuildings and the chapel, starting the latter in 1688 and taking it up again in 1699; it was com- pleted by his brother-in-law Robert de Cotte. Work on Versailles went on until Napoleon's time. The opera-house was built 1757–70 by Jacques-Ange Gabriel.

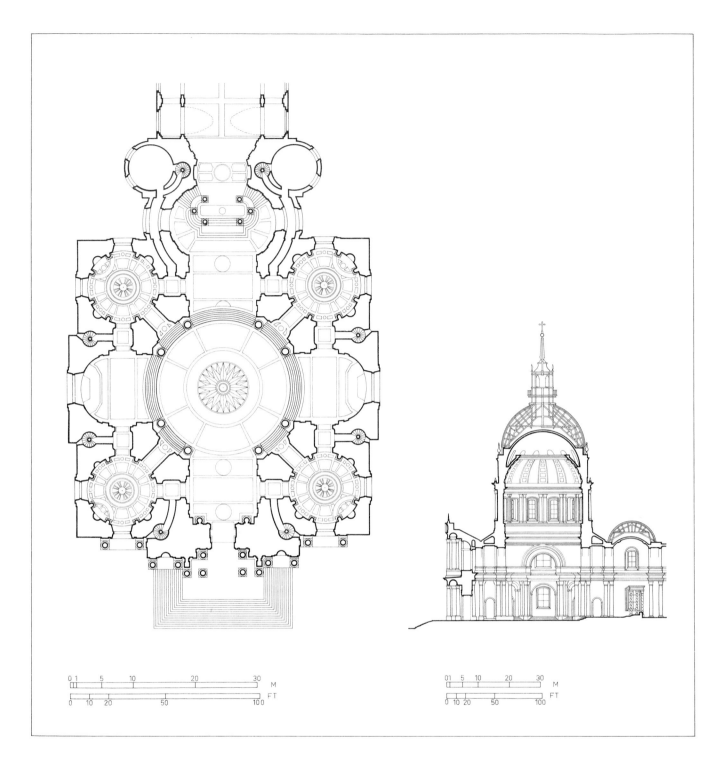

| 0 1 | 5 | 10 | 20 | 30 | M |
| 0 | 10 | 20 | | 50 | | 100 | FT |

| 0 1 | 5 | 10 | 20 | 30 | M |
| 0 | 10 | 20 | | 50 | | 100 | FT |

Eglise Saint-Louis-des-Invalides, Paris, édifiée par Jules Hardouin-Mansart, dont les premiers projets datent de 1676. Plan 1:600 et coupe longitudinale 1:1200. Disposition en croix grecque inscrite, avec coupole centrale dont le dôme interne culmine à 60 m. L'un des chefs-d'œuvre de l'architecture classique française.

Paris, Saint-Louis-des-Invalides (Invalidendom), erste Entwürfe 1676 von Jules Hardouin-Mansart. Ein griechisches Kreuz mit zentraler Kuppel bildet den Innenraum. Eines der Meisterwerke der klassischen französischen Architektur. Grundriß 1:600; Längsschnitt 1:1200.

St. Louis des Invalides, Paris, by Jules Hardouin-Mansart; the first plans date from 1676. Plan 1:600; longitudinal section 1:1200. Built on a Greek cross plan with a central dome rising to an interior height of 60 m., this is one of the masterpieces of the classical period of French architecture.

Baroque ibérique et colonial

Barock (Die Iberische Halbinsel und Lateinamerika)

Iberian and Colonial Baroque

De même que le Baroque italien diffère de celui de l'Allemagne du Sud et de l'Europe centrale, les divers mouvements baroques ibériques (Espagne, Portugal et leurs colonies) revêtent chacun leur personnalité propre. Certes, des liens unissent les provinces d'outremer à la métropole; et pourtant le Baroque du Mexique n'est pas identique à celui de l'Espagne, pas plus qu'il ne peut être confondu avec celui de l'Equateur ou du Pérou; les créations brésiliennes ne sont souvent que lointainement apparentées à celles du Portugal, qui, lui-même, présente moins encore de relations avec l'Italie que le Baroque espagnol.

Ce Baroque ibérique et américain comporte pourtant une relative unité en ce sens qu'il se fonde beaucoup plus sur les éléments décoratifs que structuraux: catafalques, retables-baldaquins, «transparente», «camarín» ou «triunfo» caractérisent cet art qui compartimente l'espace par une ornementation dynamique et surchargée. Or le Baroque consistant généralement à effacer les limites du mur, à masquer les parois en les faisant se fondre dans une zone indéfinie, les moyens pour obtenir ce flou indistinct peuvent être divers. L'Italie et l'Allemagne l'ont réalisé par la respiration du plan curviligne et des espaces torturés, par le refus des lignes droites, dures, claires. L'Amérique coloniale y parvient à l'intérieur de structures généralement orthogonales, par la prolixité d'un décor foisonnant qui envahit toutes les surfaces, par les retables avec leurs sculptures en bois doré, par les stucs, les ornements de plâtre, les marbres et les pierres polychromes, et par les peintures. Ce décor finira même par devenir un simple trompe-l'œil appli-

Die Barockarchitektur hat nicht nur in Italien und den Ländern nördlich der Alpen jeweils eine eigene Ausprägung gefunden, sondern ebenso in Spanien, in Portugal und in deren Kolonien. Zwar gibt es Gemeinsamkeiten zwischen den überseeischen Gebieten und ihren Mutterländern, doch ist der mexikanische Barock dem spanischen durchaus nicht gleich, ebensowenig aber dem ekuadorianischen oder dem peruanischen. Brasilianische Barockbauten sind oft nur ganz entfernt portugiesischen verwandt, die ihrerseits noch weniger enge Beziehungen zum italienischen Barock zeigen als die spanischen.

Dennoch kann man bei den iberischen und lateinamerikanischen Ausprägungen des Barock eine gewisse Einheitlichkeit feststellen: Die Ausstattung und Dekoration spielt hier eine weit größere Rolle als die Struktur. Katafalke, Baldachinaltäre, «transparente», «camarín» oder «triunfo» sind charakteristisch für diese Räume und unterteilen sie durch bewegte, überaus üppige Schmuckformen. Wenn der Barock ganz allgemein dazu neigt, Raumgrenzen zu verschleifen und unbestimmte Übergänge zu schaffen, so kann das doch auf sehr verschiedene Art und Weise geschehen. Italien und Deutschland wählten Grundrisse mit schwingenden Linien und – durch den Verzicht auf die Gerade – vielfach verformten Räumen. In den lateinamerikanischen Kolonien behielt man gradlinige Strukturen bei und erreichte das Ziel durch eine alle Wände überziehende Ornamentik, durch Altäre mit vergoldeten Skulpturen und goldglänzendem Schnitzwerk, durch Stukkaturen, Marmor, vielfarbigen Stein und durch Malerei. All diese Pracht erzielte in der

Just as Italian Baroque differs from that of southern Germany and central Europe, so each of the various Iberian Baroque movements (Spain, Portugal, and their colonies) has a character of its own. There are links of course between the overseas provinces and the metropolis. Yet Mexican Baroque is not the same as Spanish, nor is there any confusing it with the Ecuadorian or Peruvian variants of the style; the architecture of Brazil in this period is often only remotely connected with that of Portugal, which itself has more in common with Italian than with Spanish Baroque.

What homogeneity Iberian and American Baroque does possess is due to the fact that it is based much more on decorative than on structural elements. Catafalque, *baldacchino*, *transparente*, *camarin*, and *triunfo* are the typical features of an art that divides up space by means of dynamic and elaborate ornamentation. If the general trend in Baroque was to disguise the wall as spatial boundary by dissolving it into an ill-defined zone, the ways in which this was achieved were of various kinds. Italy and Germany did it by the 'breathing' effect of the curvilinear plan and convoluted spaces and by avoiding the hard clarity of the straight line. Spanish America obtained a similar result in the context of a basically rectangular building by covering every available surface with a profusion of decoration including altar-pieces with gilded wood-carvings, stucco and plaster ornaments, marbles, polychrome stone statues and paintings. Eventually the decor became one vast illusionist apparatus stuck on to what was in fact a very sober building.

qué sur des structures d'une grande sobriété.

Le Baroque portugais adopte d'abord des églises compactes, de plan rectangulaire, cloisonnées et simples, presque romanes par leur espace et leur volumétrie; on y trouve, dans un second temps, des nefs ovales à enveloppe cellulaire, qui dérivent peut-être de Guarino Guarini et des églises qu'il édifie à Lisbonne. Cette tradition aura un grand retentissement au Brésil, dans le Minas Gerais, au cours de la 2e moitié du XVIIIe siècle. Les géniales créations rococo de l'Aleijadinho (Antonio Francisco Lisboa) à Ouro Preto marquent le stade extrême de ce Baroque colonial qui combine des traditions européennes au goût du faste et de la magnificence propre aux populations indiennes du Nouveau Monde.

nüchtern-klaren Architektur einen eigentlichen Trompe-l'œil-Effekt.

Die portugiesischen Barockkirchen waren zunächst einfache, kompakte Bauten mit rechteckigem, gegliedertem Grundriß, sowohl als Baukörper wie als Raum romanischen Kirchen ähnlich. In einer nächsten Stufe folgen – vielleicht unter dem Eindruck von Guarino Guarinis Lissabonner Kirche – ovale, von einem Gang umschlossene Kirchenschiffe. Diese Lösung fand in Brasilien, in Minas Gerais, starken Widerhall. Die genialen, rokokoartigen Schöpfungen des Antonio Francisco Lisboa, genannt Aleijadinho, in Ouro Preto bilden den Höhepunkt dieser kolonial-barocken Architektur, die europäische Tradition mit indianischer Prachtliebe verbindet.

Portuguese Baroque initially adopted compact churches that were rectangular in plan and simply divided, indeed almost Romanesque in terms of space and volume. A second period was characterised by the oval nave with a cellular envelope, possibly derived from the churches Guarino Guarini had built in Lisbon. This tradition found a considerable echo in the state of Minas Gerais, Brazil, in the second half of the eighteenth century. The brilliant Rococo creations of O Aleijadinho (real name Antonio Francisco Lisboa) at Ouro Preto represent the final phase of this colonial Baroque, an architecture that combined European traditions with the New World Indian's taste for sumptuous display.

1 Escaliers du Bom Jesus do Monte, près de Braga (Portugal), datant du XVIIIe siècle.
2 La façade donnant dans le patio de la Clericía de Salamanque, élevée entre 1750 et 1755 par Andrés García de Quiñones.
3 Façade de l'église d'Acatepec (Mexique), avec son décor polychrome (XVIIIe siècle).
4 Façade de l'église San Francisco de La Paz (Bolivie), datant de 1772.

1 Bom Jésus do Monte bei Braga (Portugal), Treppe (18.Jh.)
2 Salamanca, Fassade der Clericía (Andrés García de Quiñones, 1750–1755)
3 Acatepec (Mexiko), Kirchenfassade mit polychromem Schmuck (18.Jh.)
4 La Paz (Bolivien), San Francisco, Fassade (1772)

1 Staircases of Bom Jesus do Monte, near Braga (Portugal; eighteenth century).
2 Patio façade of La Clerecía, Salamanca, by Andrés García de Quiñones (1750–5).
3 Façade of Acatepec church, Mexico, with its polychrome decor (eighteenth century).
4 Façade of S. Francisco, La Paz (Bolivia; 1772).

1

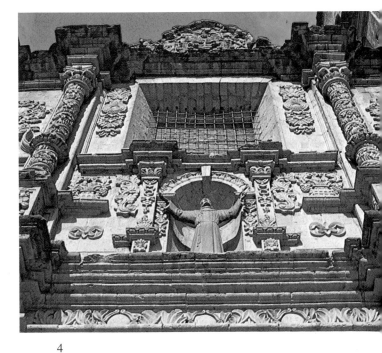

2

3

4

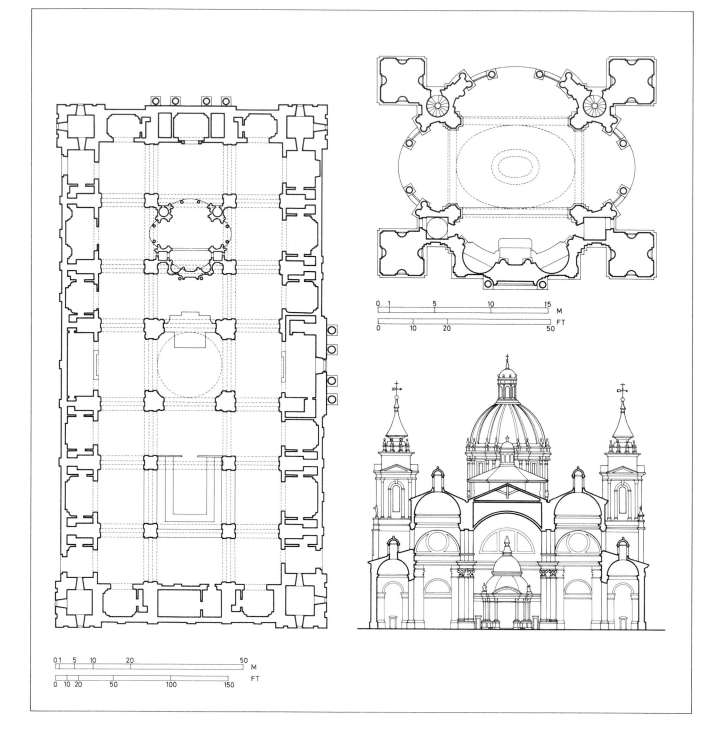

Cathédrale du Pilar à Saragosse (Espagne), construite sur un projet de Herrera le Jeune dès 1680. Plan 1:1000, détail de la chapelle Notre-Dame du Pilar 1:333 et coupe transversale dans la nef 1:1000. L'édifice, couvert d'une série de coupoles, présente quatre tours aux angles et une façade sur l'Ebre, répondant à celle située sur la place.

Saragossa (Spanien), Kathedrale Virgen del Pilar, Baubeginn 1680 nach Entwurf von Herrera d. J. Die von Kuppeln überwölbte Kirche hat vier Ecktürme und je eine Fassade zum Ebro und zum Platz. Grundriß der Kirche 1:1000; Grundriß der Kapelle der Virgen del Pilar 1:333; Querschnitt durch das Langhaus der Kirche 1:1000.

Cathedral of Nuestra Señora del Pilar, Saragossa (Spain), begun 1680 to a design by Herrera the Younger. Plan 1:1000; detail of the chapel of Nuestra Señora del Pilar 1:333; cross section of the nave 1:1000. The building is roofed with a series of domes and has four towers at the corners. A façade overlooking the Ebro matches that on the square.

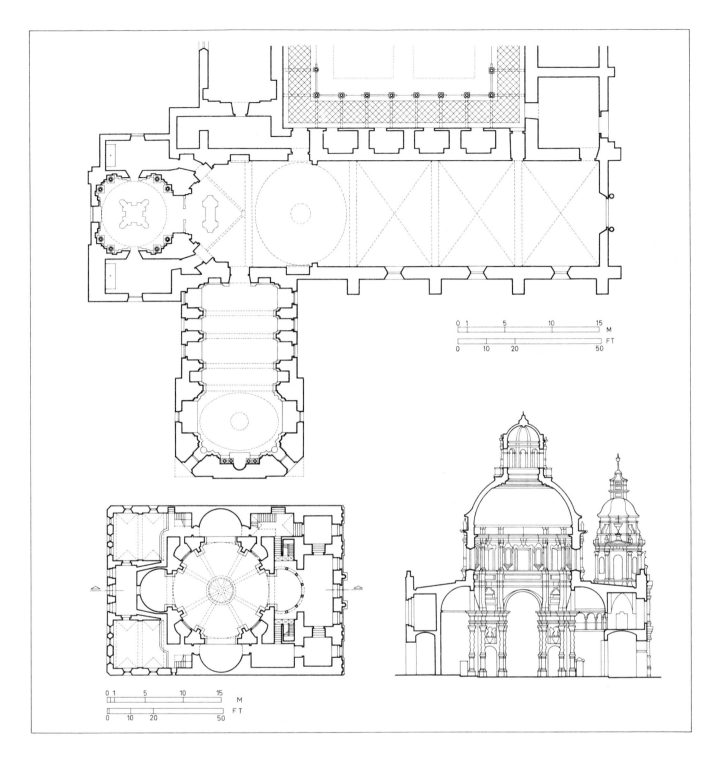

Chartreuse de Grenade (Espagne), construction du milieu du XVIe s. à 1630,
avec décor de l'église en 1662, puis du
Sagrario à «transparente» en 1720 et
enfin sacristie en 1750. Plan 1:400. En
bas, **Eglise San Luis de Séville** (Espagne),
édifiée par Leonardo de Figueroa de
1699 à 1731. Plan au niveau de l'étage
et coupe longitudinale 1:500. Richesse
du Baroque du XVIIIe s.

Oben: **Granada (Spanien), Kartause**
Mitte des 16. Jh. bis 1630, dann 1662
Dekoration der Kirche, 1720 Sagrario
(Sakramentskapelle) mit Transparente
(Tabernakel), 1750 Sakristei. Grundriß
1:400. Unten: **Sevilla, San Luis,** 1699
bis 1731, Luis de Figueroa. Ein Beispiel
der Üppigkeit des spanischen Barock
im 18. Jh. Grundriß in Höhe der Gesimse, Längsschnitt 1:500.

Cartuja (Charterhouse), Granada
(Spain), built between the mid-sixteenth
century and 1630; the church was decorated in 1662, the *sagrario* with its
transparente in 1720, and finally the
sacristy in 1750. Plan 1:400. Below,
S. Luis, Seville (Spain), built 1699–1731
by Leonardo de Figueroa. Plan at the
upper storey level and longitudinal
section 1:500. A gem of eighteenth-
century Baroque.

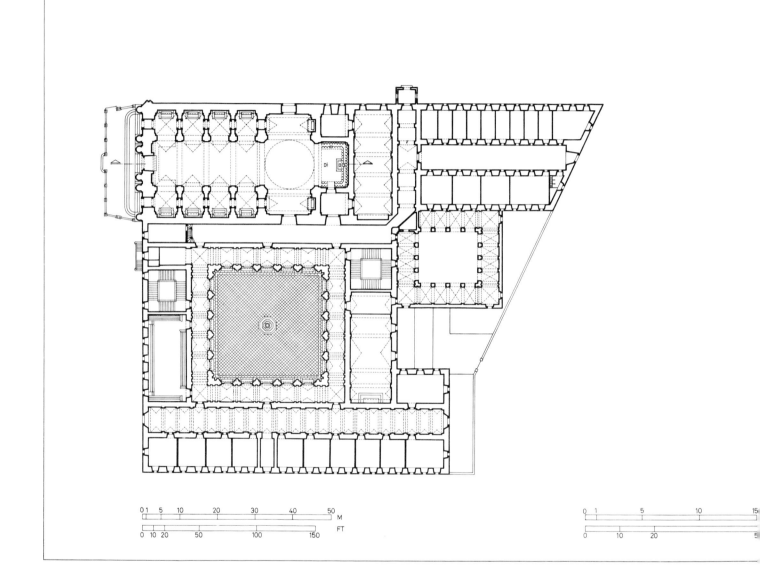

0 1 5   10   20   30   40   50
                                    M
0 10 20   50   100   150   FT

0 1   5   10   15
0   10   20   5

Eglise et Collège des Jésuites de la Clericía de Salamanque (Espagne), dont les plans sont de Juan Gómez de Mora, fondée en 1614. Plan 1:1000. Si le collège reflète encore un esprit proche de la Renaissance, de même que l'intérieur de l'église, en revanche le grandiose patio, le clocher et la façade de l'église datant de 1750–1755, de Andrés García de Quiñones, sont très baroques.

Salamanca, Clericía (Jesuitenkirche und -kolleg), 1614 gegründet; Pläne von Juan Gomez de Mora; Innenhof, Turm und Kirchenfassade 1750–1755, Andrés García de Quiñones. Das Kolleg und das Innere der Kirche stehen der Renaissance nahe, Fassade und Turm der Kirche, ebenso der großartige Innenhof sind dagegen barock. Grundriß 1:1000.

Jesuit church and college of La Clerecía, Salamanca (Spain), planned by Juan Gómez de Mora and founded in 1614. Plan 1:1000. The college and the church interior are still Renaissance in spirit— very different from the splendid patio, belfry, and façade of the church, built 1750–55 by Andrés García de Quiñones, which are very Baroque.

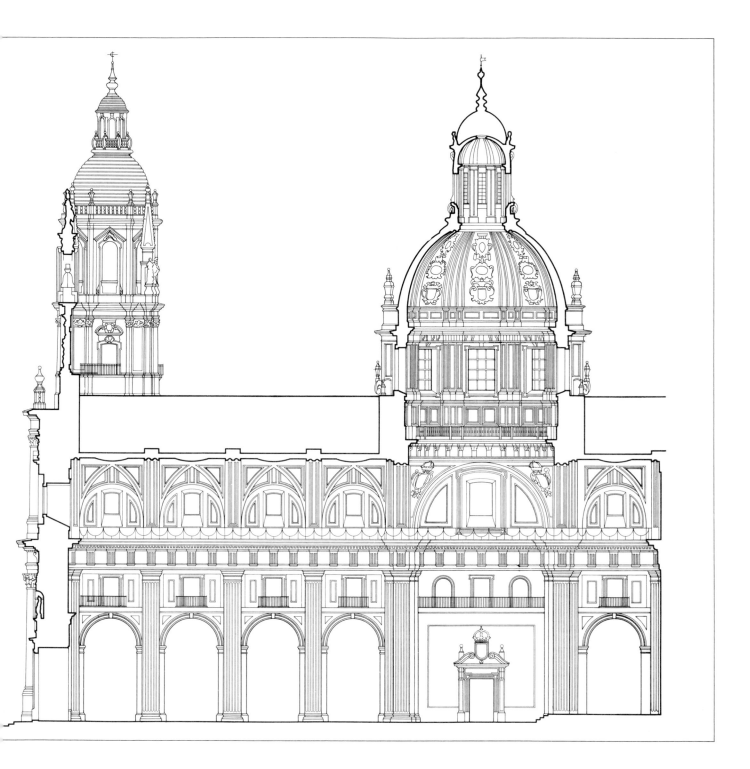

Clericía de Salamanque. Coupe longitudinale de l'église 1:333. Les structures nettes de la nef, la coupole somptueuse et le parti de rigueur sont typiques du style de Juan Gómez de Mora. La tour d'Andrés García de Quiñones relève du Baroque fleuri.

Salamanca, Clericía. Die klare Gliederung des Schiffes, die prächtige Kuppel und die sorgfältige Ausführung sind für den Stil von Juan Gomez de Mora bezeichnend. Der Turm von Andrés García de Quiñones gehört dem churrigeresken Stil an. Längsschnitt 1:333.

La Clerecía church, Salamanca (Spain). Longitudinal section 1:333. The lucid nave structures, magnificent dome and rigorous approach are typical of the work of Juan Gómez de Mora. The tower is in the florid Baroque style of Andrés García de Quiñones.

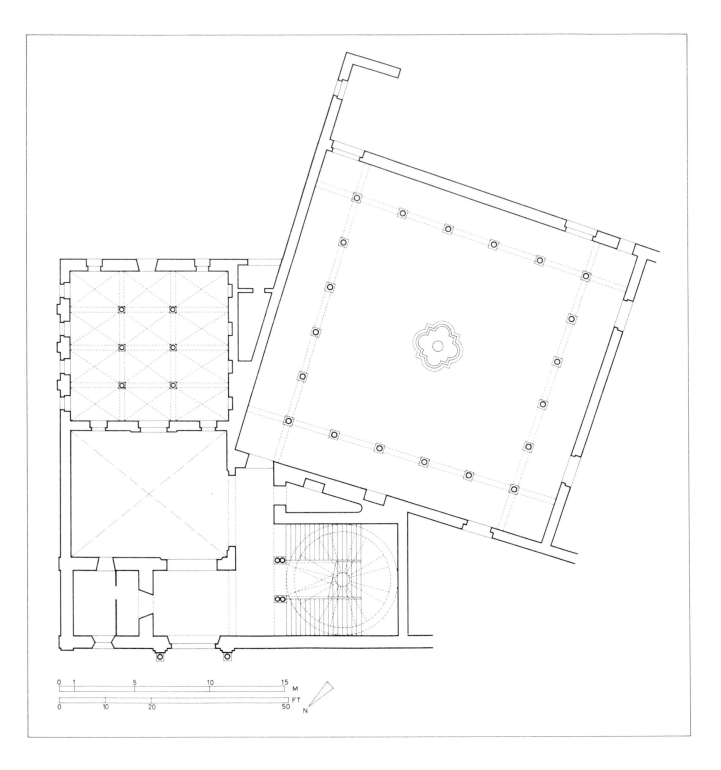

0 1 5 10 15 M

0 10 20 50 FT

N

Palais du marquis de Peñaflor, à Ecija, Andalousie (Espagne), construit en 1726. Plan 1:250. Un patio à arcades s'articule sur un corps de logis, dont l'escalier est richement orné de «yeserías».

Ecija (Andalusien, Spanien), Palast des Marqués de Peñaflor, 1726 begonnen. Ein Patio mit umlaufenden Arkaden im Erdgeschoß und Fenstern unter Rundbogen im Obergeschoß ist im Winkel mit dem Wohntrakt verbunden, dessen Treppenhaus reich mit «yeserias» geschmückt ist. Grundriß 1:250.

Palace of the Marques de Peñaflor, Ecija (Andalusia, Spain), built 1726. Plan 1:250. An arcaded patio adjoins the main building, which has a staircase richly decorated with *yeserias* (plasters).

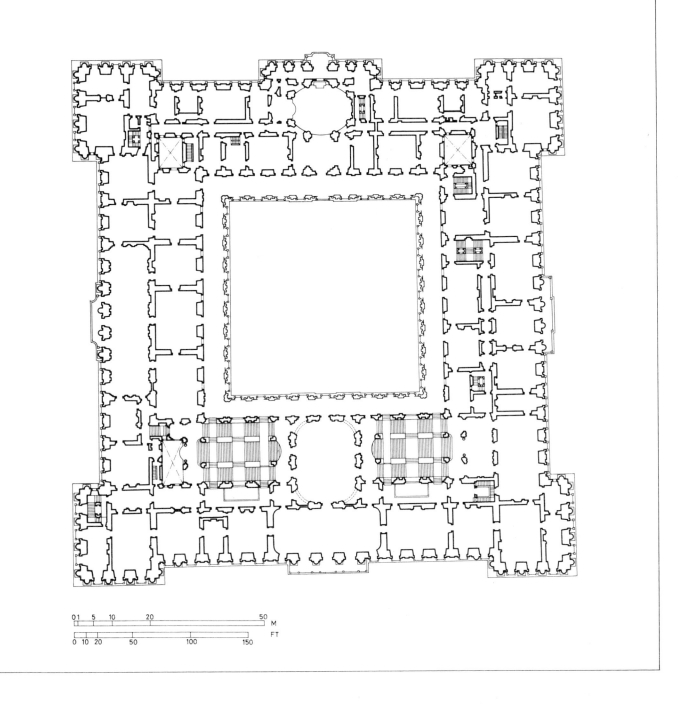

0 1 5 10 20 50 M

0 10 20 50 100 150 FT

Palais royal de Madrid, projeté entre 1735 et 1736 par Juvara, architecte sicilien auquel succède son élève Saqueti de 1738 à 1764. Plan 1:1000. Le premier projet s'étalait en largeur à la manière de Versailles. Saqueti concentre la formule en un carré plus élevé. La distribution se fait autour d'une vaste cour. Escaliers par le Napolitain Sabatini (deuxième moitié du XVIIIᵉ s.).

Madrid, Königlicher Palast, Entwurf 1735–1736 von Filippo Juvarra, Ausführung 1738–1764 durch dessen Schüler Sacchetti. Der erste Entwurf eines breitgelagerten Palastes in der Art von Versailles wurde von Sacchetti in einen quadratischen, höheren Bau geändert, dessen vier Flügel den Innenhof umschließen. Das Treppenhaus baute der Napolitaner Sabatini in der zweiten Hälfte des 18. Jh. Grundriß 1:1000.

Royal Palace, Madrid, planned by the Sicilian architect Juvarra 1735–6 and executed by his pupil Sacchetti 1738–64. Plan 1:1000. The original project was for lateral extension in the manner of Versailles. Sacchetti concentrated it into a higher square arranged round a vast courtyard. The staircases were built in the second half of the eighteenth century by the Neapolitan Sabatini.

229

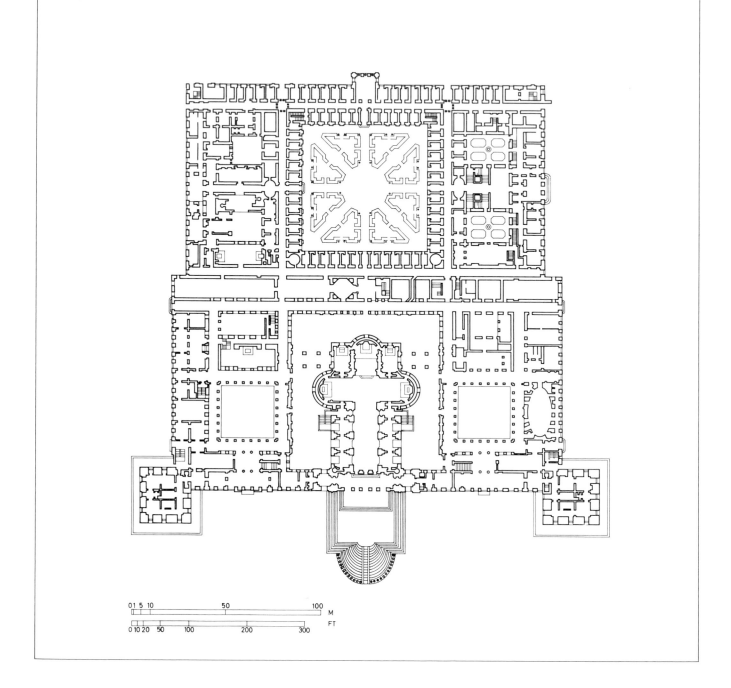

01 5 10   50   100 M
                            FT
0 10 20 50   100   200   300

Palais-monastère de Mafra (Portugal), commencé en 1717, église consacrée en 1733 et achèvement en 1770, conçu par l'architecte Ludovice (Johann-Friedrich Ludwig), d'origine allemande. Plan 1:2000. L'église s'intègre dans une façade aux proportions impressionnantes. Le couvent est rejeté en arrière et le cloître s'ouvre dans l'axe de l'église.

Mafra (Portugal), Kloster und Palast, 1717–1770, Kirche 1733 geweiht; Entwurf des deutschen Baumeisters Johann Friedrich Ludwig (Ludovice). Die Kirche ist in die Mitte der Palastfassade eingebunden. Die nahezu symmetrische Klosteranlage nimmt den rückwärtigen Teil des Komplexes ein, die Achse des Kreuzgangs liegt in der Verlängerung der Kirchenachse. Grundriß 1:2000.

Palace-monastery of Mafra (Portugal), designed by the German-born architect Ludovice (Johann Friedrich Ludwig) and begun in 1717; the church was consecrated in 1733 and completed in 1770. Plan 1:2000. The church forms part of a façade of impressive proportions. The monastery lies behind, and the cloister opens into the axis of the church.

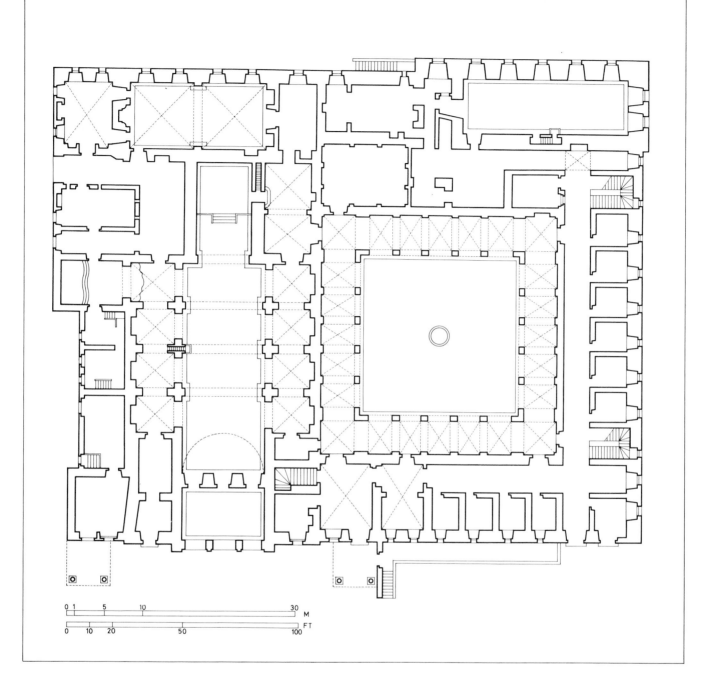

0 1   5   10   30
                                  M
                                  FT
0   10 20   50   100

Monastère de São Bento à Rio de Janeiro (Brésil), dont le plan de Francisco de Frias da Mequita date de 1617; en 1669, la nef est sous toit; nouveau plan en 1670 par Frei Bernardo de São Bento Correa de Sousa qui achève l'église et construit la sacristie (1693); le monastère fut achevé en 1755. Plan 1:500. La sculpture sur bois de l'église, de l'autel de la sacristie et des chapelles, prolixe et riche, date de 1714 à 1800.

Rio de Janeiro, Kloster São Bento, erste Pläne 1617, Francisco de Frias da Mequita; 1669 Dach des Kirchenschiffes; 1670 neuer Plan von Frei Bernardo de São Bento Correa de Sousa, der bis 1693 die Kirche vollendete, ab 1693 die Sakristei baute; Vollendung des Klosters 1755 nach Plan von 1681. Die alles überziehenden Schnitzereien in der Kirche, den Kapellen, am Sakristei-Altar entstanden 1714–1800. Grundriß 1:500.

São Bento Monastery, Rio de Janeiro (Brazil), originally planned by Francisco de Frias da Mequita in 1617; the nave was roofed by 1669, then in 1670 a new plan was drawn up by Frei Bernardo de São Bento Correa de Sousa, who completed the church and built the sacristy (1693); the monastery was completed in 1755. Plan 1:500. The rich and luxuriant wood carving in the church, on the sacristy altar and in the chapels dates from 1714–1800.

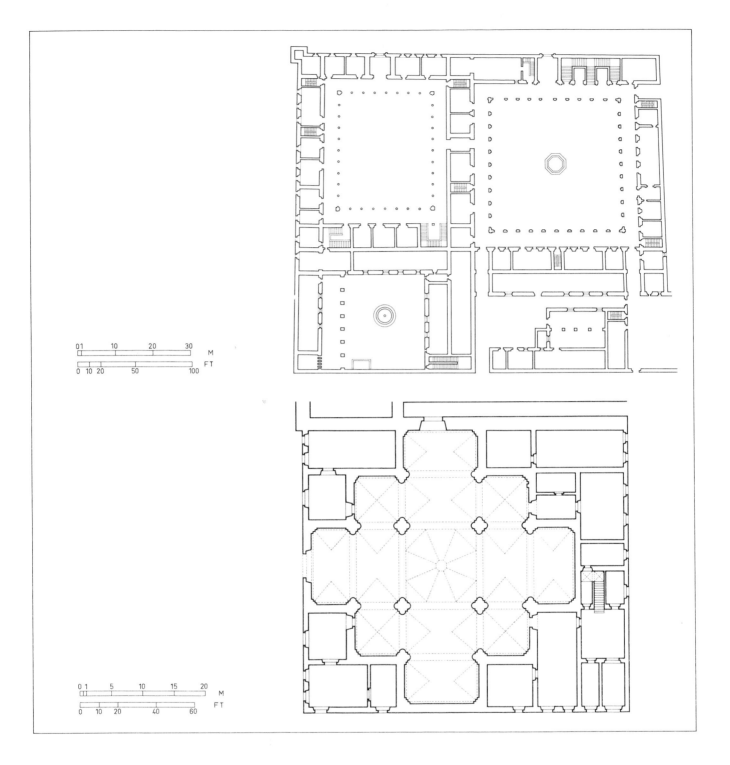

Palais des Vice-Rois à Mexico (Mexique), datant de 1709 et construit par Frey de Valverde, sur les ruines du Palais de Cortès. Plan 1:1000. L'édifice connaît plusieurs agrandissements et groupe trois patios à arcades. **Sagrario de la Cathédrale de Mexico,** construit entre 1749 et 1768 par Lorenzo Rodríguez. Plan 1:600. Structure conçue sur un double axe de symétrie.

Oben: **Mexico City, Palast der Vizekönige,** 1709, Fray de Valverde. Der später mehrfach erweiterte Bau wurde auf den Ruinen jenes Palastes errichtet, in dem Cortéz residierte. Er umschließt drei Innenhöfe mit Arkaden. Grundriß 1:1000. **Mexico City, Kathedrale, Sagrario,** 1749–1768, Lorenzo Rodriguez. Der Grundriß des Innenraums ist ein gleicharmiges Kreuz. Grundriß 1:600.

Viceregal Palace, Mexico, built in 1709 by Fray de Valverde on the ruins of Cortés's palace. Plan 1:1000. The building was enlarged several times and comprises three arcaded patios. **Sagrario of Mexico Cathedral,** built 1749–68 by Lorenzo Rodríguez. Plan 1:600. Designed in double axial symmetry.

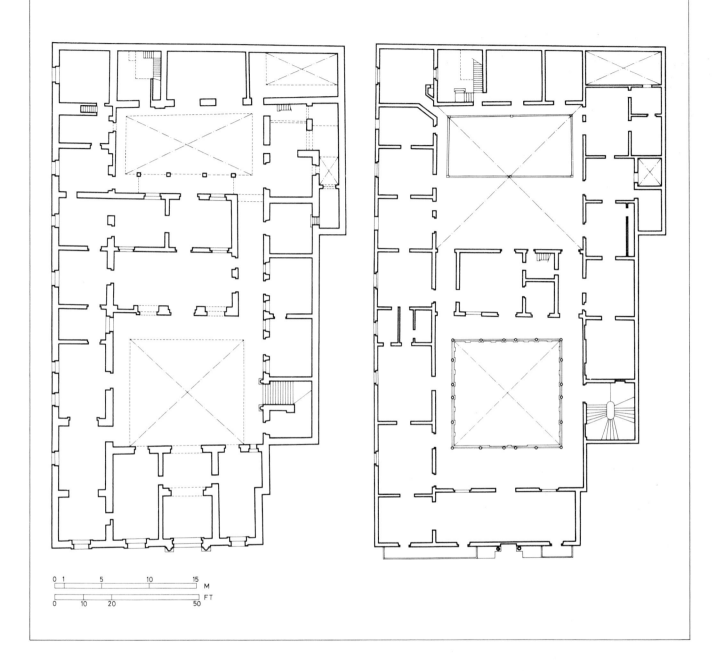

```
0  1       5          10          15
                                    M
                                    FT
0      10     20              50
```

Palais de Torre-Tagle, à Lima (Pérou), achevé en 1735. Plans du rez-de-chaussée et du premier étage 1:400. Ce palais, avec son patio bordé d'une galerie à arcades à rythme alterné, reproduit une demeure noble andalouse. Il est revêtu d'«azulejos» et présente des balcons à grillage de bois influencés par l'architecture musulmane.

Lima (Peru), Palast Torre-Tagle, 1735 vollendet. Der Palast ist nach dem Vorbild eines andalusischen Adelssitzes angelegt. Die Galerie des großen Patio ist durch die wechselnde Spannweite der Arkaden rhythmisch gegliedert. Die Wände sind teilweise mit «azulejos» (Fayencefliesen) verkleidet; die Holzgitter der Balkone gehen auf muselmanischen Einfluß zurück. Grundrisse des Erd- und des Obergeschosses 1:400.

Torre-Tagle Palace, Lima (Peru), completed 1735. Plans of the ground and first floors 1:400. With its patios bordered with an arcaded gallery using an alternating rhythm, this palace constitutes a reproduction of the Andalusian nobleman's house. It is clad with *azulejos* (glazed tiles) and has wooden-grilled balconies that show the influence of Moslem architecture.

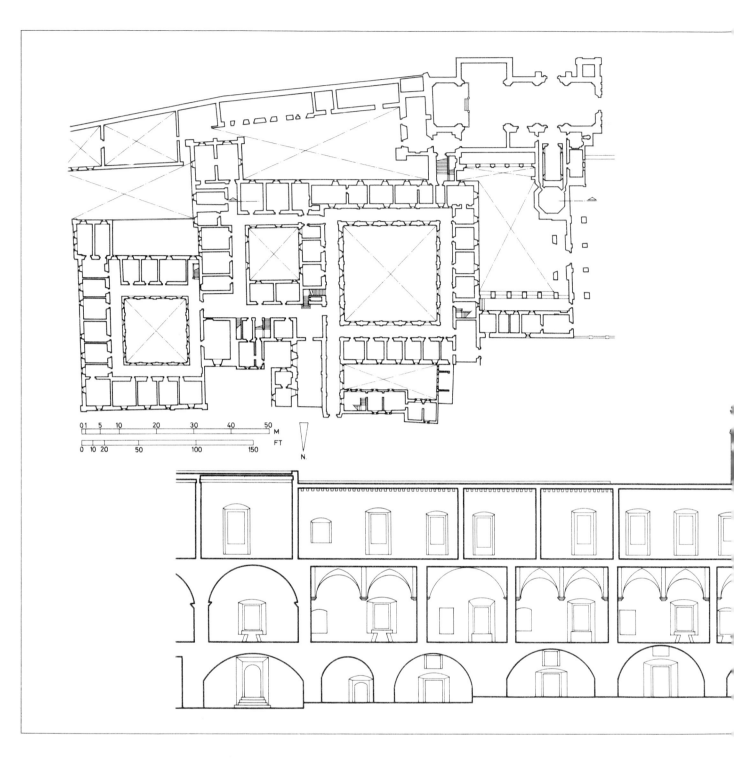

Eglise et Collège des Jésuites à Tepot-zotlán (Mexique). L'église fut construite de 1670 à 1682, mais les travaux de l'ensemble se poursuivent jusqu'en 1762. Plan d'ensemble 1:1000, coupe du cloître et élévation latérale de l'église 1:250. On distingue à droite la coupe de la coupole du «camarín» de la Santa Casa de Loreto.

Tepotzotlán (Mexiko), Jesuitenkirche und -kolleg, Kirche 1670–1682, Vollendung der Gesamtanlage 1762. Grundriß 1:1000; Schnitt durch den Kreuzgang mit Aufriß einer Kirchenseite und Schnitt durch die Kuppel des Camarín der Santa Casa de Loreto (rechts)1:250.

Jesuit church and college, Tepotzotlán (Mexico). The church was built 1670 to 1682, but work on the rest of the complex went on until 1762. Overall plan 1:1000; section of the cloister and side elevation of the church 1:250. On the right, section of the dome of the *camarin* of the Santa Casa de Loreto.

A l'église de **Tepotzotlán,** la Maison de Lorette et son «camarín» ont été inaugurés en 1733. On remarque, sur la coupe, la haute lanterne à trois niveaux superposés.

Die Loreto-Kapelle der Kirche von **Tepotzotlán** und ihr Camarín wurden 1733 geweiht. Im Schnitt ist die dreistufige hohe Laterne der Kapelle deutlich zu erkennen.

Part of **Tepotzotlán church,** the 'House of Loreto' and its *camarin* were dedicated in 1733. Note on the section the tall lantern with its three superposed levels.

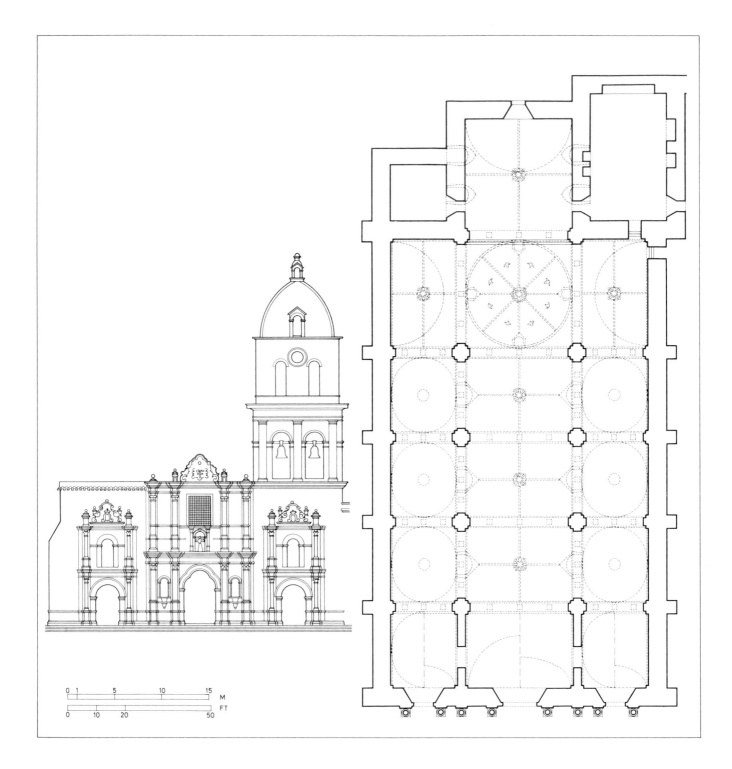

Eglise du couvent de San Francisco, à La Paz (Bolivie), église bâtie au cours du XVIIe s. et façade principale décorée de 1772 à 1784. Elévation et plan 1:400. Edifice à trois nefs avec transept à coupole, derrière laquelle se trouve la «Capilla Mayor».

La Paz (Bolivien), San Francisco, 17. Jh., Fassadenschmuck 1772–1784. Dreischiffiger Bau mit einem nicht über die Seitenwände vorspringenden Querhaus und Kuppel, dahinter die Capilla Mayor. Aufriß und Grundriß 1:400.

S. Francisco monastery church, La Paz (Bolivia), built in the seventeenth century; the main façade was decorated 1772–84. Elevation and plan 1:400. A three-aisled building with a domed transept beyond which is the *capilla maior*.

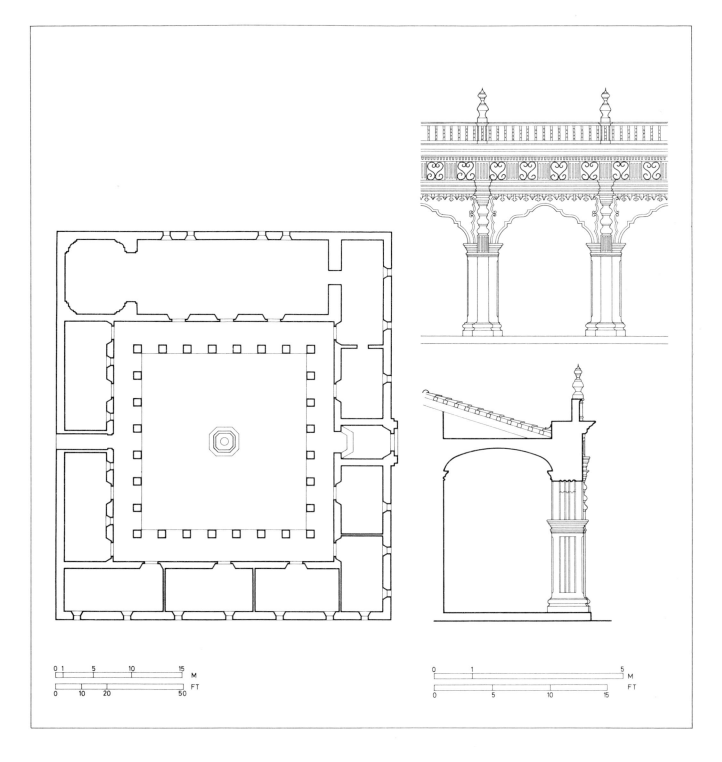

Université San Carlos, à Antigua (Guatémala), construite en 1753. Plan 1:500 élévation et coupe d'un portique 1:100. L'auteur de ce bâtiment sis dans l'ancienne capitale guatémaltèque n'est pas connu avec certitude. On mentionne José Manuel Ramirez et Luis Díez Navarro. Les salles sont réparties autour d'un vaste patio à portiques.

Antigua (Guatemala), Universität San Carlos, 1753. Als Baumeister der in der ehemaligen Hauptstadt von Guatemala gelegenen Universität wird sowohl José Manuel Ramirez als auch Luis Diaz Navarro genannt. Die Anlage umschließt einen Innenhof mit Arkaden. Grundriß 1:500; Aufriß und Schnitt eines Portikus 1:100.

San Carlos University, Antigua (Guatemala), built 1753. Plan 1:500; elevation and section of a portico 1:100. The architect of this building in the former Guatemalan capital is not known for certain; it may have been José Manuel Ramirez or Luis Díez Navarro. The rooms are distributed round an enormous porticoed patio.

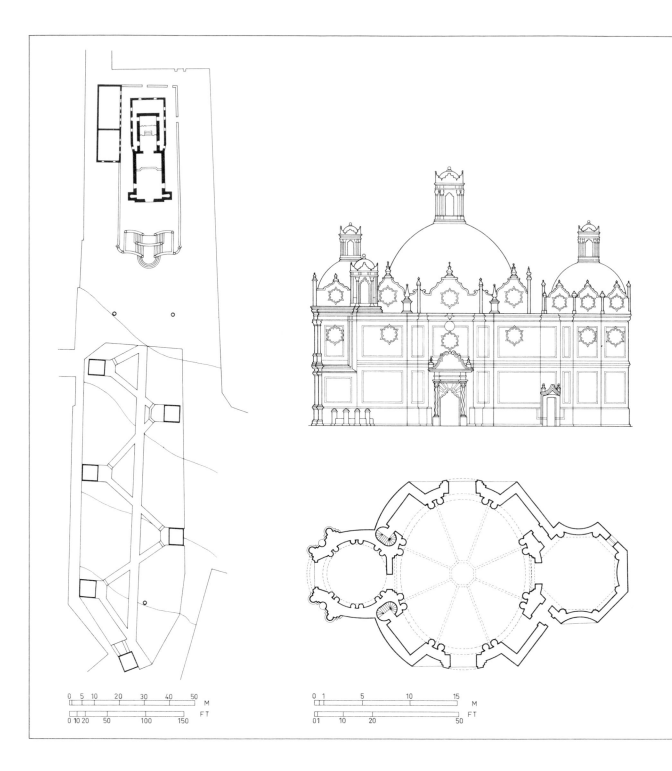

Montagne du Calvaire à Congonhas do Campo (Brésil). Plan général du «Sacro Monte» 1:1500, qui reconstitue la montée au Golgotha, à la manière du Bom Jesus do Monte de Braga (Portugal). La **Capilla del Pocito de Guadalupe, Mexico,** construite entre 1771 et 1791 par Guerrero y Torres. Elévation latérale et plan 1:400. C'est le recours aux courbes et contre-courbes dans l'art mexicain.

Links: **Congonhas do Campo (Brasilien), Kalvarienberg.** Der nach dem Vorbild des Bom Jésus do Monte bei Braga (Portugal) angelegte «Sacro Monte» stellt den Weg nach Golgatha dar. Lageplan 1:1500. Rechts: **Guadelupe (Mexiko), Capilla del Pocito,** 1771–1791, Guerrero y Torres. Ein Beispiel der Verwendung von Kurve und Gegenkurve in der mexikanischen Architektur. Aufriß einer Seite und Grundriß 1:400.

Hill of Calvary, Congonhas do Campo (Brazil). Overall plan of the *sacro monte:* 1:1500, a reconstruction of Golgotha in the manner of the Bom Jesus do Monte de Braga (Portugal). The **Capilla del Pocito Guadalupe, Mexico,** built 1771 to 1791 by Guerrero y Torres. Side elevation and plan 1:400. An illustration of the use of curves and counter-curves in Mexican architecture.

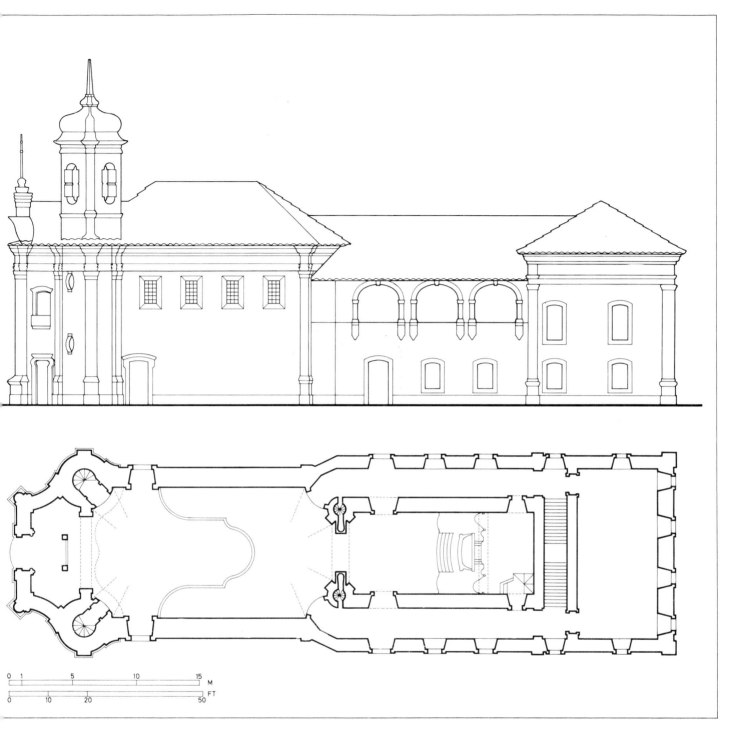

Eglise São Francisco de Assis, à Ouro Preto (Brésil), construite de 1766 à 1794. Elévation latérale et plan 1:300. La façade et l'autel principal sont l'œuvre de l'Aleijadinho en 1774 et 1778. Le mouvement sinueux des murs de la façade, surmontée de deux tours rondes, est caractéristique du Baroque brésilien.

Ouro Preto (Brasilien), Sao Francisco de Assis, 1766–1794; Fassade und Hauptaltar 1774–1778, Aleijadinho (Antonio Francisco Lisboa). Die Schwingung der von zwei runden Türmen überragten Fassade ist für den brasilianischen Barock kennzeichnend. Aufriß einer Seite und Grundriß 1:300.

S. Francisco d'Asis, Ouro Preto (Brazil), built 1766–94. Side elevation and plan 1:300. The façade and the main altar are the work of Aleijadinho and date from 1774 and 1778. The sinuous movement of the façade walls beneath the two round towers is typical of Brazilian Baroque.

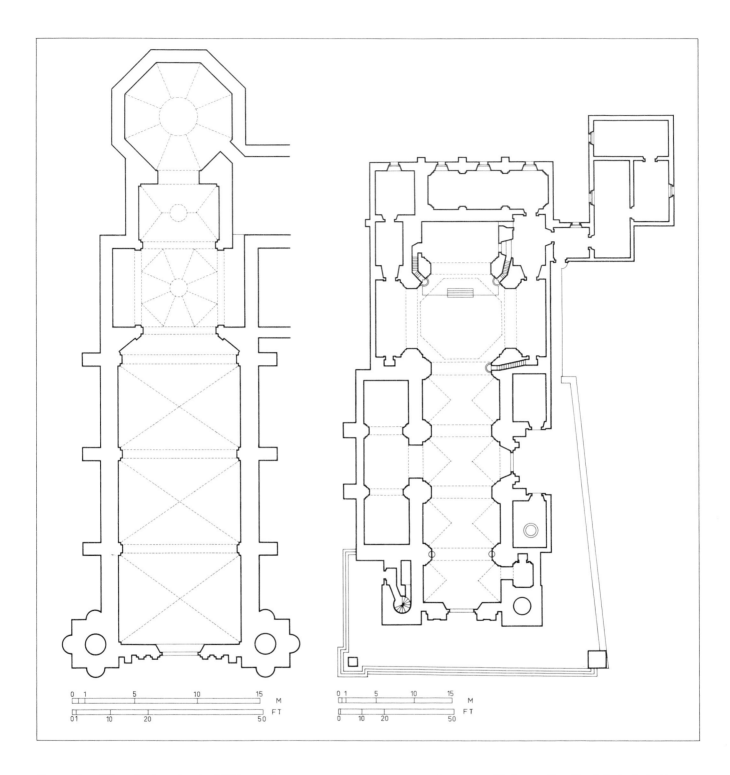

Sanctuaire d'Ocotlán (Mexique), édifié en 1691 par Juan de Escobar, avec adjonction du «camarín» en arrière du maître-autel par le Père Manuel Loaizaga, en 1716, et décoration qui se poursuit jusqu'à la fin du XVIIIᵉ s. Plan 1:300. Eglise Santa Prisca de Taxco (Mexique), construite et décorée de 1751 à 1759 par l'architecte Diego Durán. Plan 1:500. Œuvre unitaire et cohérente, brièvement achevée.

Links: Ocotlán (Mexiko), Wallfahrtskirche, 1691, Juan de Escobar; Camarín hinter dem Hauptaltar 1716, Pater Manuel Loaizaga; Ausstattung bis Ende 18. Jh. Grundriß 1:300. Rechts: Taxco (Mexiko), Santa Prisca, 1751 bis 1759, Diego Durán. Architektur und Dekoration des in sich geschlossenen und einheitlichen Baus stammen vom gleichen Meister. Grundriß 1:500.

Shrine at Ocotlán (Mexico), built 1691 by Juan de Escobar; camarin added behind the high altar by Father Manuel Loaizaga in 1716; decoration continued up until the end of the eighteenth century. Plan 1:300. S. Prisca, Taxco (Mexico), built and decorated 1751–9 by the architect Diego Durán. Plan 1:500. A coherent, unified achievement built in a relatively short space of time.

L'annonce du monde moderne

Beginn der Moderne

The dawn of modern times

Après la frénésie baroque et l'emphase classique, l'architecture se nourrit de réminiscences et puise dans le passé pour alimenter le présent. Dès 1775 et jusqu'à 1880 environ sévit l'éclectisme. Essentiellement néo-classique et néo-grecque, mais aussi néo-gothique, néo-romane, néo-byzantine, néo-florentine, voire néo-égyptienne et néo-angkorienne (!), l'architecture d'inspiration antique submerge l'Europe. Elle culmine avec les canons sévères des Ledoux, Schinkel, Nash, Rossi ou Klenze.

Alors seulement le courant qui inaugure l'époque moderne naît avec le rationalisme. Désormais les bâtisseurs recourent à un matériau nouveau: le fer ou la fonte. Certes, des chaînages et des renforcements de fer existaient déjà auparavant. Mais l'utilisation du fer pour l'ensemble des structures apparaît avec les constructeurs de ponts. Leur technique sera transposée dans les réalisations industrielles ou utilitaires, telles que halles, bibliothèques, grands magasins, fabriques, etc.

En 1843, le français Labrouste édifie la Bibliothèque Sainte-Geneviève, à Paris, où toute la couverture est en fer, supportée par des colonnes de fonte. Il développe encore son art avec la salle de lecture de la Bibliothèque nationale. Les grandes expositions donnent aux ingénieurs-architectes l'occasion de démontrer les possibilités des formules nouvelles dans d'audacieuses salles aux proportions énormes. S'inspirant probablement du Jardin de Verre de Paris (1848), Sir Joseph Paxton construit en 1851 la grande halle de verre et de fer baptisée Crystal Palace, pour l'exposition de Londres: près de 500 m de long sur 125 m de large. La réalisation, entièrement préfabriquée, est montée

Dem barocken Überschwang und dem Pathos folgte in der Architektur eine Zeit der Rückgriffe auf Werke und Formen der Vergangenheit. Vom Ende des 18. bis zum Ende des 19. Jahrhunderts herrschte weitgehend ein ausgesprochener Eklektizismus. Vor allem von der Antike inspirierte Bauten prägten die europäische Architektur – die Schöpfungen von Ledoux, Schinkel, Nash, Rossi und Klenze sind die eigentlichen Höhepunkte. Neben der antikisierenden gab es aber bald eine neugotische und eine neuromanische Architektur, und ebenso baute man in byzantinischem und in florentinischem Stil, sogar ägyptisch und angkorianisch.

Mit dem Funktionalismus und einer rationalistischeren Einstellung wird dann die Moderne eingeleitet. Die Architekten entdecken ein neues Material: das Eisen. Wenn auch Eisen schon früher verwendet wurde, so haben doch erst Ingenieure und Brückenbauer die reine Eisenkonstruktion eingeführt, deren Technik dann für Industrie- und Zweckbauten – Ausstellungs- und Markthallen, Bibliotheken, Kaufhäuser, Fabriken und ähnliche Anlagen – übernommen wurde.

1843 erbaute der Franzose Labrouste die Bibliothek Sainte-Geneviève in Paris, deren eiserne Dachkonstruktion auf gußeisernen Säulen ruht; mit dem Lesesaal der Bibliothèque Nationale entwickelte er sein System weiter. Die riesigen Hallen der großen Ausstellungen boten den Ingenieur-Architekten Gelegenheit, die Möglichkeiten der neuen Techniken zu zeigen. 1851 baute Sir Joseph Paxton, vermutlich durch den Pariser Jardin de Verre von 1848 angeregt, den Kristallpalast der Londoner Weltausstellung, eine Eisen-Glas-

The frenzy of Baroque was followed by a period of reminiscence in which architecture turned for inspiration to a variety of historical sources. From about 1775 to 1880 eclecticism was the rule. Essentially neo-classical and particularly neo-Greek, the historicist architecture that covered Europe during this period was also neo-Gothic, neo-Roman, neo-Byzantine, neo-Florentine, and even neo-Egyptian and neo-Angkorian. It culminated in the strict canons of Ledoux, Schinkel, Nash, Rossi and Klenze.

Only then did a new rationalism mark the beginning of the modern period; moreover, builders now had a new material—cast iron. Tie-irons and other types of iron reinforcement had of course been used before, but the use of iron for whole structures came into architecture via civil engineering, as the technology of bridge-building was translated into industrial or utilitarian terms to erect covered markets, libraries, large shops, factories, and so on.

In 1843 the French architect Labrouste built the Bibliothèque Ste. Geneviève, Paris, in which the entire roof is of iron, supported on cast-iron columns. He went a stage further with the reading room of the Bibliothèque Nationale. The great exhibitions gave engineer-architects a chance to demonstrate the potential of these new formulae in daring halls of enormous proportions. Probably drawing his inspiration from the Paris Jardin de Verre (1848), Sir Joseph Paxton constructed in 1851 the great hall of glass and iron known as the Crystal Palace for the London Exhibition. Nearly 500 m. long by 125 m. wide, it was built entirely of prefabricated elements assembled on

sur place. Puis viendront les halles de Dutert et Contamine, ainsi que la tour de l'ingénieur Eiffel, pour l'exposition de Paris en 1889.

L'édification du Grand Opéra de Paris (1862), par Charles Garnier, allie un luxe inouï à une science brillante pour donner naissance à une véritable «cathédrale laïque» de la société bourgeoise. La coupole qui domine la salle de spectacle est réalisée en poutrelles de fer.

Aux Etats-Unis, Chicago connaît à la fin du siècle, grâce à William Le Baron Jenney et Louis Sullivan, un style qui va caractériser les immeubles d'affaires américains, avec leurs fenêtres en largeur, leurs façades modulées, annonçant les gratte-ciel de l'entre-deux-guerres.

Konstruktion von 500×125 m, die vollständig vorfabriziert und am Ort nur montiert wurde. Es folgten die Pariser Markthallen von Dutert und Contamine und der Eiffelturm, den Eiffel für die Weltausstellung von 1889 konstruierte. Mit der Grand Opéra von Paris (1862), in der Charles Garnier unerhörten Luxus mit brillantem technischem Können verband, schuf er eine «profane Kathedrale» der bürgerlichen Gesellschaft.

In den Vereinigten Staaten bildeten am Ende des 19. Jahrhunderts William Le Baron Jenney und Louis Sullivan einen Stil aus, der mit seinen breiten Fenstern und der gleichmäßigen Gliederung der Fassaden die Architektur der amerikanischen Geschäftshäuser und – zwischen den beiden Weltkriegen – der Wolkenkratzer formte und bestimmte.

site. It was followed by the creations of Dutert and Contamine and by the tower that the engineer Gustave Eiffel built for the Paris Exhibition of 1889.

Paris's Grand Opéra (1862) by Charles Garnier, a marriage of unprecedented luxury and brilliant technology, constituted a veritable 'secular cathedral' for the bourgeois society of the capital. The dome over the auditorium uses an iron-girder construction.

Chicago at the end of the century, thanks to William Le Baron Jenney and Louis Sullivan, saw the emergence of a style that was to define the American office building, its wide windows and modular façades heralding the skyscrapers of the interwar period.

---

1 Façade d'un bâtiment industriel des Salines royales de Chaux, à Arc-et-Senans, par Claude-Nicolas Ledoux (1772 à 1775).
2 Le Grand Escalier de l'Opéra de Paris, bâti de 1862 à 1875 sur l'ordre de Napoléon III par Charles Garnier.
3 Façade des grands magasins Carson, Pirie and Scott à Chicago, édifiés en 1899 par Louis H. Sullivan.

1 Arc-et-Senans, Königliche Saline, Fassade eines Industriebaues (Claude-Nicolas Ledoux, 1772–1775)
2 Paris, Oper, die große Treppe; im Auftrag Napoleons III. erbaut (Charles Garnier, 1862–1875)
3 Chicago, Fassade des Warenhauses Carson, Pirie and Scott (Louis H. Sullivan, 1899)

1 Façade of an industrial building at the Salines royales de Chaux, Arc-en-Senans, by Claude-Nicolas Ledoux (1772–5).
2 The main staircase of the Paris Opéra, built 1862–75 by Charles Garnier by order of Napoleon III.
3 Façades of the Carson, Pirie and Scott stores, Chicago, by Louis H. Sullivan (1899).

1

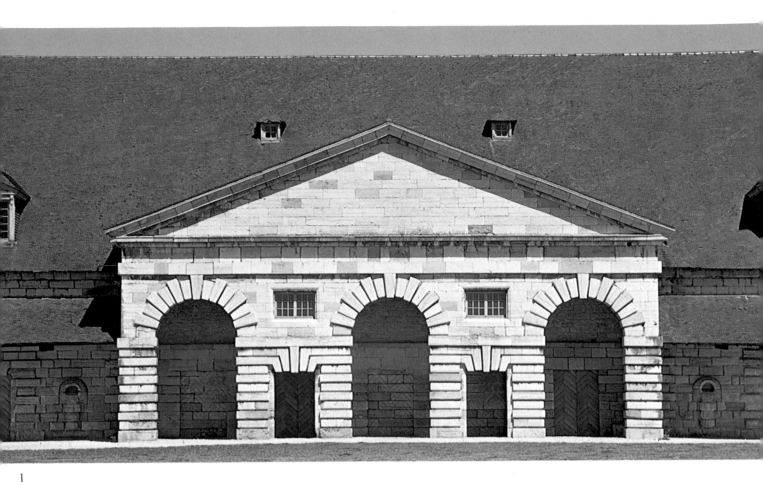

2

3

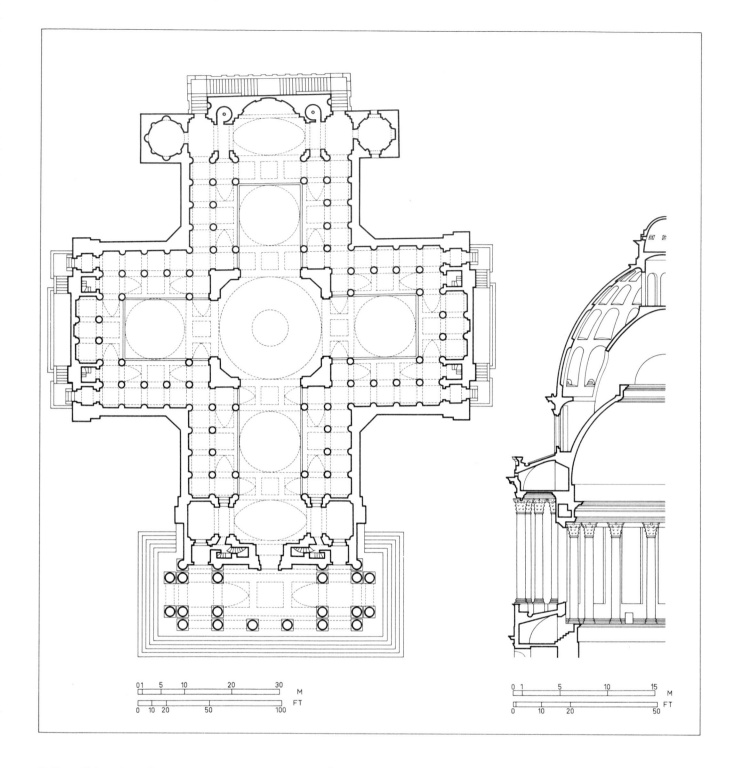

| 0 1 | 5 | 10 | 20 | 30 | | M |
| 0 10 20 | | 50 | | 100 | | FT |

| 0 1 | 5 | 10 | 15 | M |
| 0 | 10 | 20 | 50 | FT |

Eglise Sainte-Geneviève, aujourd'hui **Panthéon, à Paris** (France), par Jacques-Germain Soufflot qui l'édifie de 1756 à 1780. Plan 1:800 et coupe de la coupole 1:400. Chef-d'œuvre de l'art composite qui ne sera achevé qu'après la mort de son auteur, par Rondelet, en 1797. Façade romaine, temple de Vesta à Tivoli et Tempietto de Bramante s'y conjuguent.

Paris, Sainte-Geneviève (Pantheon), 1756 bis 1780, Jacques-Germain Soufflot. Vollendung nach dessen Tod bis 1797 durch Rondelet. Soufflot hat in diesem Hauptwerk die Verbindung antikisierender und gotischer Formen zu einem einheitlichen Stil angestrebt. In der Fassade sind sowohl Anregungen durch den Vesta-Tempel in Tivoli als auch durch Bramantes Tempietto verarbeitet. Grundriß 1:800; Schnitt der Kuppel 1:400.

Ste. Geneviève, now known as the Panthéon, Paris, begun in 1756 by Jacques-Germain Soufflot, who worked on it until his death in 1780; completed by Rondelet in 1797. Plan 1:800; section of the dome 1:400. This masterpiece of composite architecture combines a Roman façade with echoes of the temple of Vesta, Tivoli, and Bramante's Tempietto, Rome.

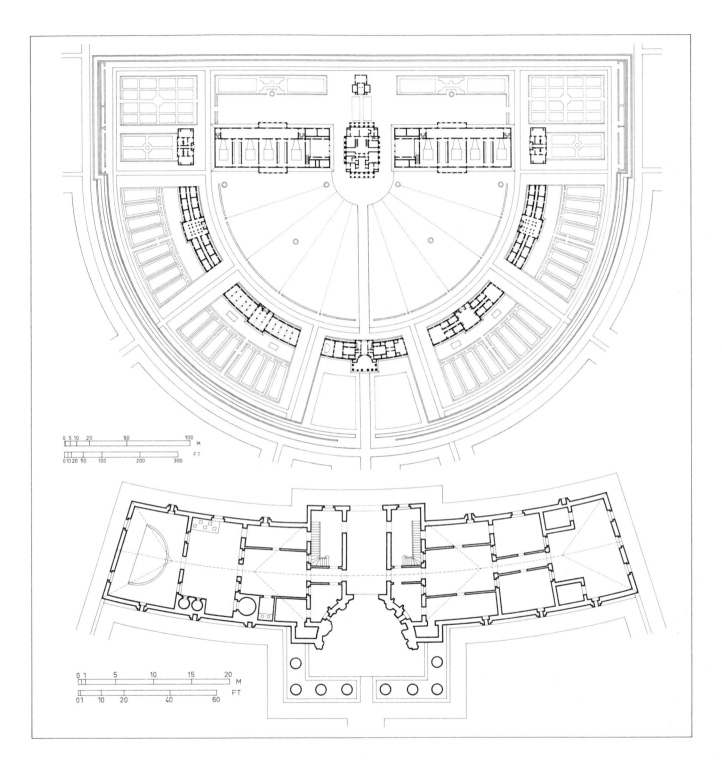

Salines royales de Chaux, à Arc-et-Senans (France), aménagées par Claude-Nicolas Ledoux de 1772 à 1775. Plan d'ensemble réalisé 1:3000 et plan des **Propylées** 1:500. Projet prophétique pour une cité industrielle, qui annonce les préoccupations sociales du XIXe s. De style néo-classique, Ledoux crée une forme d'expression puissante, inspirée de Sansovino et de Sanmicheli.

Arc-et-Senans (Frankreich), Königliche Saline, 1772–1775, Claude-Nicolas Ledoux. In diesem frühen Projekt einer Industriestadt kündigen sich bereits soziale Tendenzen des 19. Jh. an. Der ausdrucksstarke Klassizismus geht auf Sansovino und Sanmicheli zurück. Grundriß des ausgeführten Teils 1:3000; Grundriß des Torbaus 1:500.

Salines royales de Chaux, Arc-et-Senans (France), 1772–5, by Claude-Nicolas Ledoux. Overall plan 1:3000; plan of the **Propylaea** 1:500. This prophetic project for an industrial estate anticipated the social concern of the nineteenth century. Inspired by Sansovino and Sanmicheli, Ledoux moulded his Neo-classical style into a powerful instrument of expression.

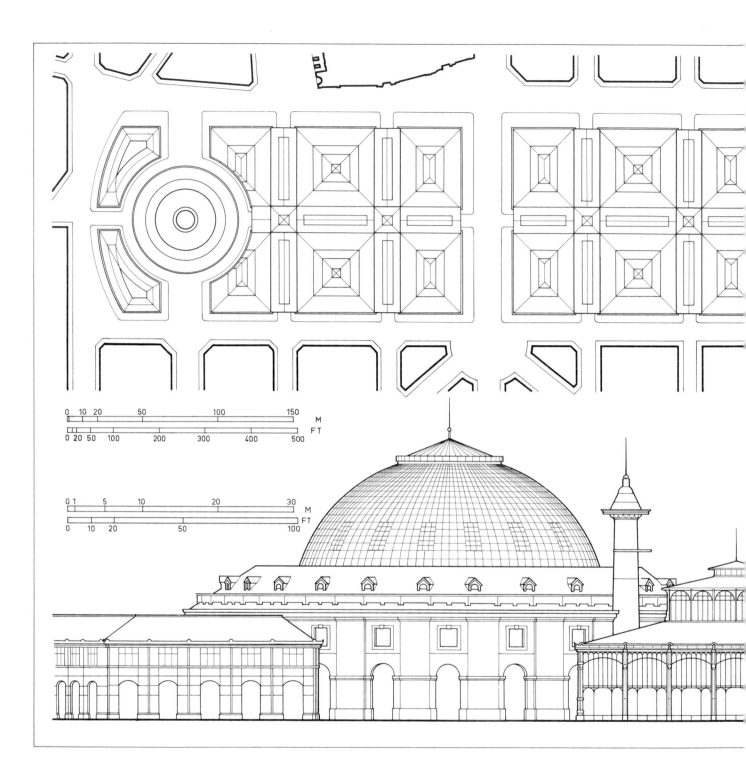

0 10 20   50   100   150   M
0 20 50 100   200   300   400   500   FT

0 1   5   10   20   30   M
0 10 20   50   100   FT

Halles Centrales, à Paris (France), construites par Victor Baltard de 1851 à 1859. Plan d'ensemble 1:2500, élévation de la **Halle aux Blés,** par Ballangé, 1811, et liaison avec les Halles 1:500; élévation des structures de fer des Halles Centrales 1:200. Autour de la Halle aux Blés, construite un demi-siècle plus tôt en forme de rotonde, et qui deviendra la Bourse de Commerce, s'élèvent les Halles de Paris.

Paris, Halles Centrales, 1851–1859, Victor Baltard. Die Pariser Markthallen schließen den um fast ein halbes Jahrhundert älteren Rundbau der **Kornhalle** ein, die später zur Börse wurde. Gesamtplan 1:2500; Aufriß der Kornhalle (1811, Ballangé) und der vorgelagerten Bauten der Halles 1:500; Aufriß der Eisenkonstruktion der Halles Centrales 1:200.

Halles Centrales ('Les Halles'), Paris, built 1851–9 by Victor Baltard. Overall plan 1:2500; elevation of the **Halle aux Blés** (Corn Hall) by Ballangé, 1811, and its link with the other halls 1:500; elevation of the iron construction of the Halles Centrales 1:200. Paris's 'Les Halles' were built round the circular Halle aux Blés, which had been erected nearly half a century earlier and became the Bourse de Commerce.

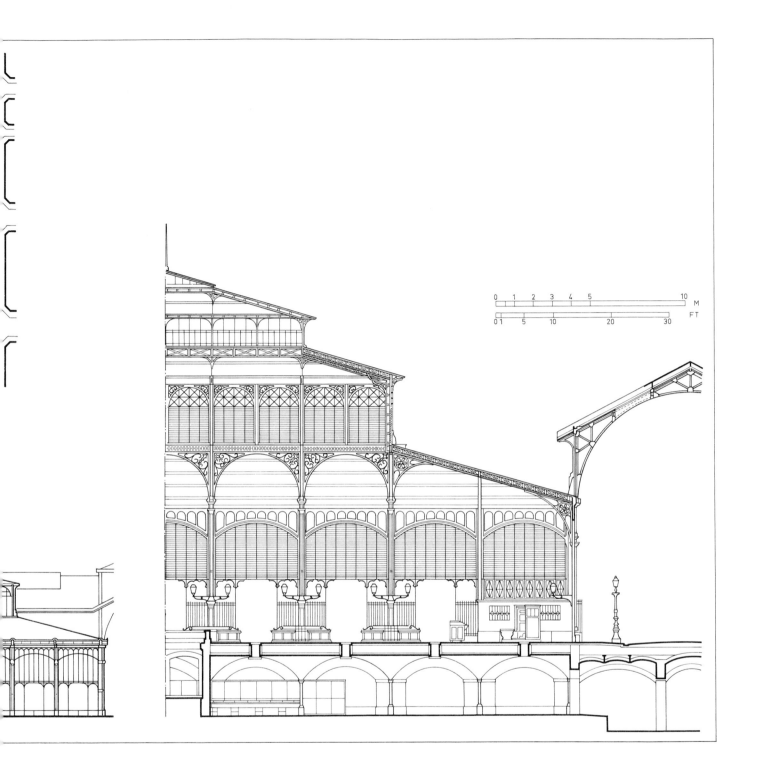

La réalisation des **Halles** constitue une démonstration des possibilités offertes par les structures de fer et de fonte dans l'architecture industrielle du XIXe s. Leur récente démolition est regrettable à plus d'un titre, car les réalisations architecturales de cette époque sont de plus en plus rares.

Die **Halles de Paris** zeigten deutlich, welche Möglichkeiten sich aus der Verwendung von Eisen und Stahl für den Industriebau des 19.Jh. ergaben. Der Abbruch der Hallen ist aus mancherlei Gründen zu bedauern; Bauten jener Zeit werden immer seltener.

Les Halles showed what iron and cast-iron construction techniques had to offer the industrial architecture of the nineteenth century. Their recent demolition is to be deplored on more counts than one: examples of the architecture of this period are becoming increasingly scarce.

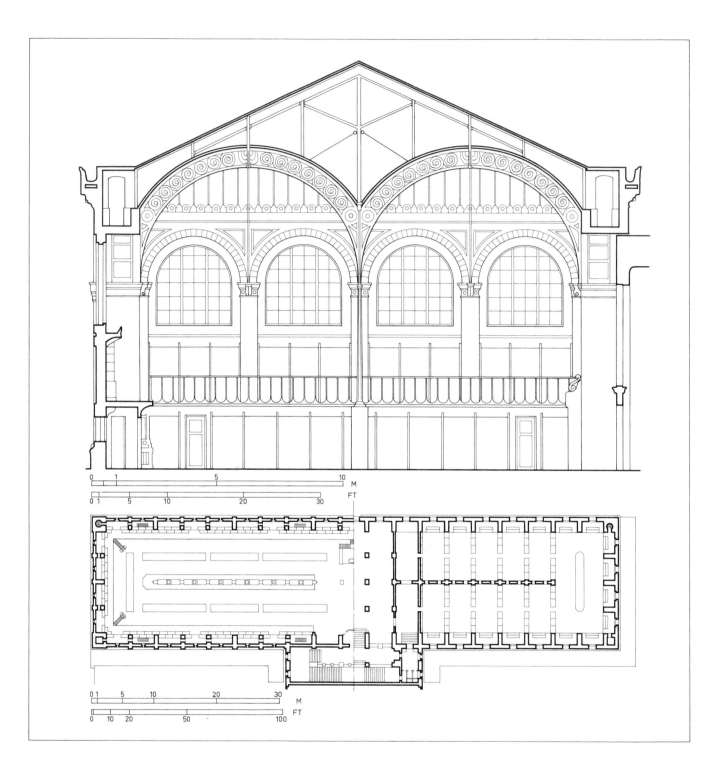

| 0 | 1 | | | | 5 | | | | | 10 | M |
| 0 | 1 | 5 | | 10 | | | 20 | | | 30 | FT |

| 0 | 1 | 5 | | 10 | | 20 | | | 30 | M |
| 0 | 10 | 20 | | 50 | | - | | 100 | | FT |

Bibliothèque Sainte-Geneviève, à Paris, par Henri Labrouste, entre 1843 et 1850. Coupe transversale 1:150 et plan à deux niveaux différents 1:600. Labrouste fut l'un des premiers architectes à marier des structures entièrement en fer à une architecture traditionnelle. Son apport culminera à la salle de lecture de la Bibliothèque nationale, à Paris, édifiée en 1854.

Paris, Bibliothek Sainte-Geneviève, 1843 bis 1850, Henri Labrouste. Labrouste hat als einer der ersten reine Eisenkonstruktionen für traditionelle Bauten verwendet. Seine größte Leistung war der 1854 erbaute Lesesaal der Bibliothèque nationale in Paris. Querschnitt 1:150; Grundriß zweier Stockwerke 1:600.

Ste. Geneviève Library, Paris, built 1843 to 1850 by Henri Labrouste. Cross section 1:150; plan on two different levels 1:600. Labrouste was one of the first architects to combine all-iron construction with traditional architecture. His finest contribution was to be the reading room of the Bibliothèque nationale, Paris, which he built in 1854.

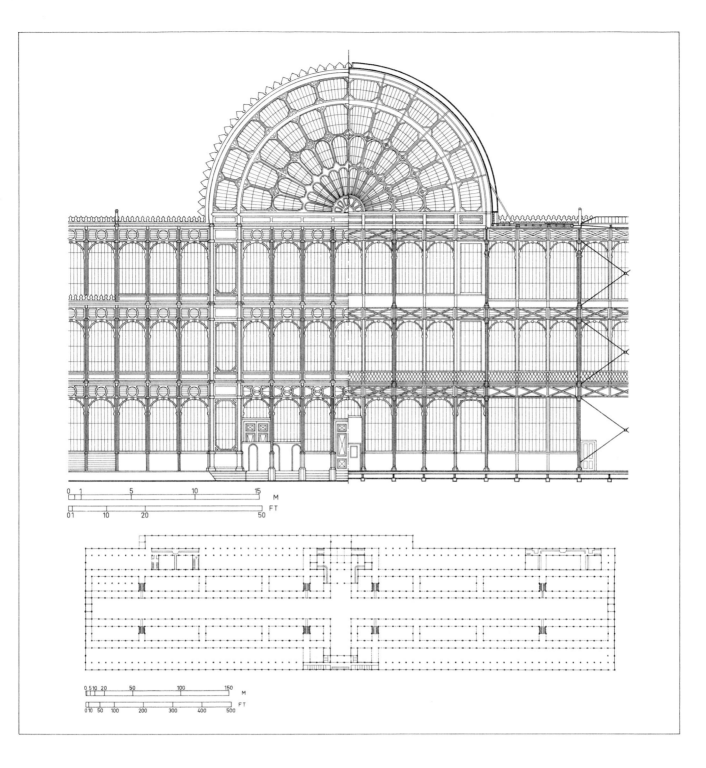

Crystal Palace, Londres (Grande-Bretagne), construit par Sir Joseph Paxton pour l'Exposition universelle de Londres en 1851. Elévation de la partie centrale 1:300 et plan général 1:4000. Halle de fer et de verre, édifiée en neuf mois, le Crystal Palace ne mesure pas moins de 550 m de long pour 140 m de large. Cette œuvre fut le clou de l'exposition, comme plus tard le sera la Tour Eiffel à Paris (1889).

London, Kristallpalast, von Sir Joseph Paxton für die Londoner Weltausstellung von 1851 erbaut. Die in neun Monaten errichtete Halle, eine Eisen-Glas-Konstruktion, war nicht weniger als 550 m lang und 140 m breit. Der Kristallpalast war, wie später – 1889 – der Eiffelturm in Paris, das Prunkstück der Weltausstellung. Aufriß des mittleren Teils 1:300; Grundriß 1:4000.

Crystal Palace, London, designed by Sir Joseph Paxton for the 1851 World Exhibition in London. Elevation of central part 1:300; overall plan 1:4000. The vast hall of iron and glass that London christened the 'Crystal Palace' measured no less that 550 m. in length and 140 m. in width and took only nine months to erect. It was the star of the exhibition, as the Eiffel Tower was to be the star of the 1889 Paris Exhibition.

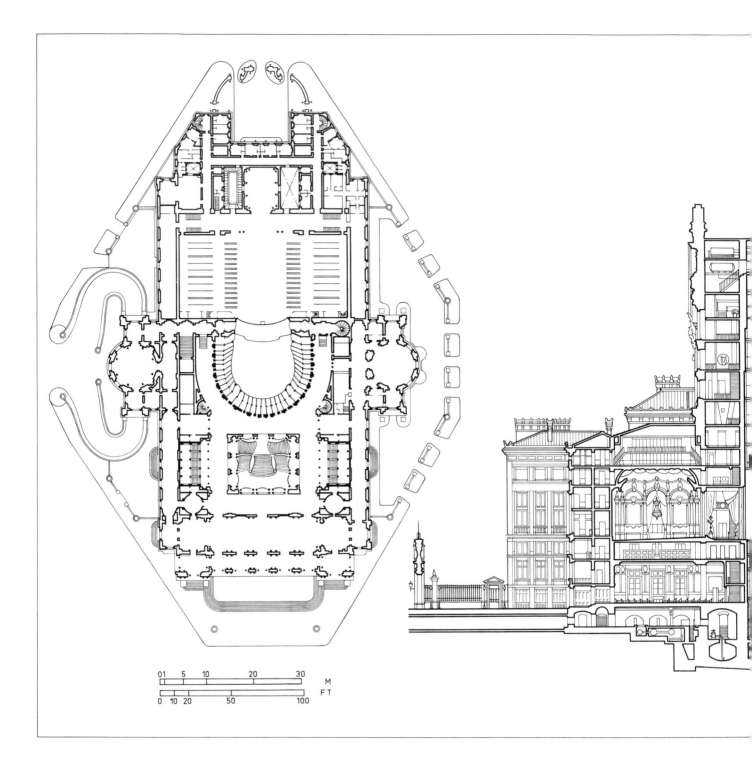

Opéra de Paris, édifié par Charles Garnier de 1862 à 1875. Plan 1:800 et coupe longitudinale 1:400. Ce théâtre immense – le plus grand du monde – est marqué au coin de l'éclectisme le plus exacerbé, tant pour ce qui est du plan que de la décoration. Mais l'édifice ne cesse de conserver au premier plan les impératifs de fonctionnement.

Paris, Oper, 1862–1875, Charles Garnier. Dieses größte Theater der Welt ist in Grundriß und Dekoration im höchsten Grade eklektizistisch, bei seinem Bau standen funktionelle Erwägungen im Vordergrund. Grundriß 1:800; Längsschnitt 1:400.

Opéra, Paris, built 1862–75 by Charles Garnier. Plan 1:800; longitudinal section 1:400. This enormous theatre—the largest in the world—is characterised by the most extreme eclecticism as regards both plan and decoration. Yet at no point does it abandon its primary allegiance to functional imperatives.

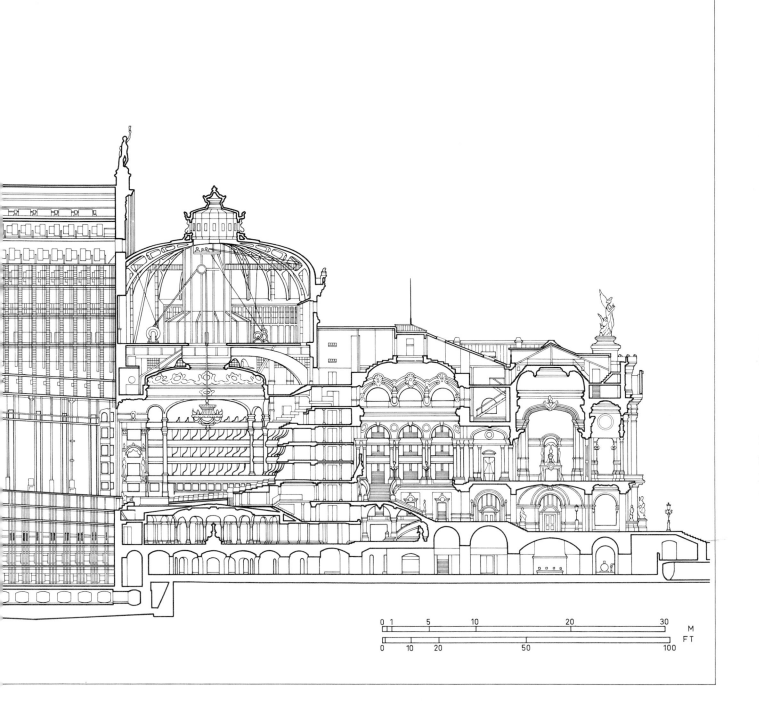

0	1		5		10			20			30		M

0	10	20		50		100		FT

Réalisé sur l'ordre de l'empereur Napoléon III, l'**Opéra de Paris** incarne un style qui fera école dans le monde entier. Les techniques modernes y tiennent une place importante: ainsi, toute la coupole couvrant la salle est réalisée en charpente de fer. Le grand escalier y atteint un faste baroque et pompeux.

Der Stil der auf Anordnung Napoleons III. erbauten **Pariser Oper** machte in der ganzen Welt Schule. Moderne Techniken spielten dabei eine wichtige Rolle: Die große Kuppel über dem Zuschauerraum ist eine reine Eisenkonstruktion. Das Treppenhaus ist von «barocker» Großartigkeit.

Commissioned by Emperor Napoleon III, the **Paris Opéra** embodied a style that was to set a fashion throughout the world. Modern techniques have an important place in it, the dome over the auditorium, for example, consisting solely of iron girders. The great staircase is a particularly fine piece of Baroque ostentation.

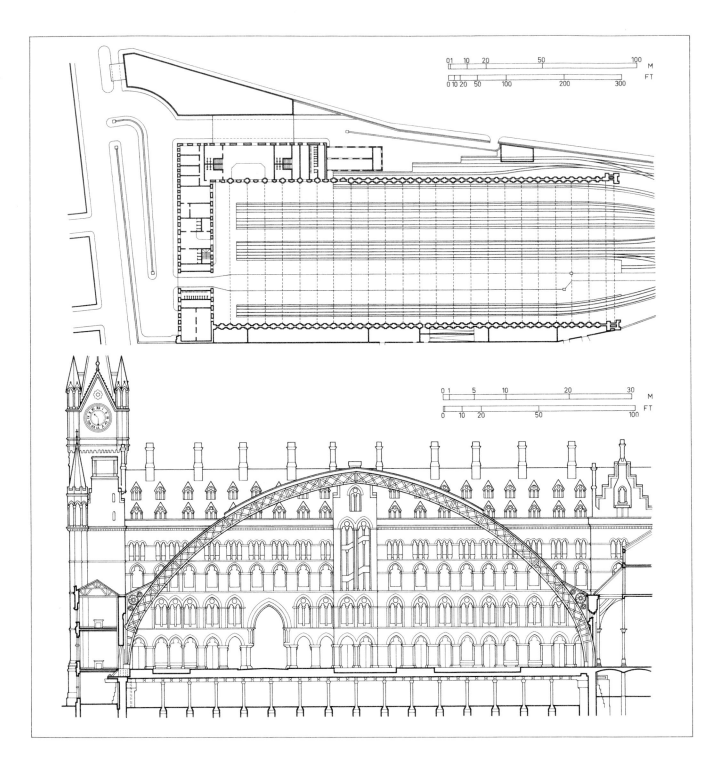

Gare ferroviaire de Saint-Pancrace, à Londres (Grande-Bretagne), construite par W. H. Barlow en 1868. Plan d'ensemble 1:2000 et coupe de la couverture des quais devant l'Hôtel St. Pancrace, édifié en style néo-gothique par G. Gilbert Scott en 1865, 1:600. La portée de 80 m de la structure métallique prépare, avec vingt ans d'avance, la Galerie des Machines de Dutert et Contamine, à Paris, 1889.

Oben: London, St. Pancras Station, 1868, W. H. Barlow. Grundriß 1:2000. Unten: Der Schnitt durch die überdachten Bahnsteige vor dem neogotischen Hotel St. Pancras (1865, G. Gilbert Scott) zeigt die 80 m überspannende Eisenkonstruktion, einen Vorläufer der zwanzig Jahre später von Dutert für die Pariser Weltausstellung von 1889 erbauten Maschinenhalle. Schnitt 1:600.

St. Pancras Railway Station, London, built 1868 by W. H. Barlow. Overall plan 1:2000; section of the canopy over the platforms in front of the St. Pancras Hotel (built in the Neo-Gothic style by George Gilbert Scott in 1865) 1:600. The 80 m. span of this metal structure anticipates Dutert's and Contamine's 1889 Galerie des Machines, Paris, by twenty years.

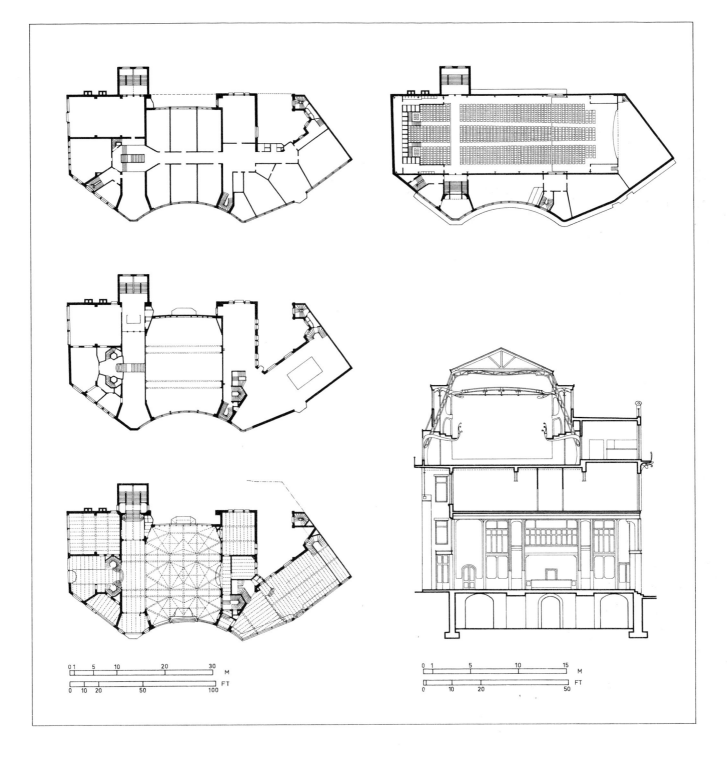

Maison du Peuple, à Bruxelles (Belgique), construite par Victor Horta entre 1896 et 1899. A gauche, plans du 2ᵉ étage, du 1ᵉʳ étage et du rez-de-chaussée, et, à droite, plan de la salle au 3ᵉ étage 1:800 et coupe transversale 1:400. Par la liberté du plan, Horta annonce les architectes du XXᵉ s., mais il recourt aux techniques du fer, désormais traditionnelles, pour la salle.

Brüssel, Maison du Peuple, 1896–1899, Victor Horta. Mit der freien Grundrißgestaltung nimmt Horta bereits Eigenheiten der Architektur des 20.Jh. voraus; für den Saal benutzte er die inzwischen gebräuchliche Eisenkonstruktion. Links von oben nach unten: Grundriß des 2.Geschosses, des 1.Geschosses und des Erdgeschosses 1:800; rechts: Grundriß des Saals im 3.Geschoß 1:800; Querschnitt 1:400.

Maison du Peuple, Brussels, built 1896–9 by Victor Horta. Left, plans of the second, first and ground floors; right, plan of the third-floor hall 1:800; cross section 1:400. Horta's freedom of plan is almost twentieth-century, but he used the by now traditional iron construction techniques for the hall.

Le lecteur trouvera à la fin du volume 2, aux pages 479–500, un index des monuments, sites et personnes et une table des matières détaillée.

Ein Index der Orte, Bauten und Personen und ein ausführliches Inhaltsverzeichnis beider Bände befinden sich am Schluß von Band 2, auf den Seiten 479–500.

In volume II, pp. 479–500, the reader will find an index of monuments, places and proper names, and a table of contents.

Printed in Switzerland